THE LONG ARM OF EMPIRE

By the same author

Fred T. Jane: An Eccentric Visionary

THE LONG ARM OF EMPIRE

Naval Brigades from the Crimea to the Boxer Rebellion

Richard Brooks

CONSTABLE · LONDON

First published in Great Britain 1999
by Constable and Company Ltd
3 The Lanchesters, 162 Fulham Palace Road
London W6 9ER
Copyright © Richard Brooks 1999
The right of Richard Brooks to be identified
as the author of this work has been asserted by him in accordance
with the Copyright, Designs and Patents Act 1988

ISBN 0 09 478840 5

Set in Monotype Janson 11pt by
Servis Filmsetting Ltd, Manchester
Printed in Great Britain by
St Edmundsbury Press Ltd
Bury St Edmunds, Suffolk

A CIP catalogue record for this book
is available from the British Library

Contents

List of Illustrations

Copyright holders are indicated in brackets

Introduction

The disasters of the Crimean War have lost none of their power to shock. Among those whose heroism brightened the gloom were a small force of sailors and marines known as the 'Naval Brigade', landed to help the British Army in its hour of need. They not only provided fire power for the siege, and defended the base at Balaklava, they brought a refreshing air of professional competence into a war not widely remembered for that quality. Such was the sailors' skill at foraging they provoked threats of retaliation from the professional burglars enlisted in a neighbouring French infantry regiment.

The Royal Navy displayed similar professional and personal qualities during the next great Victorian military crisis: the Indian Mutiny of 1857. HMS *Shannon* and *Pearl* intervened in a variety of ways that illustrate the breadth of the navy's contribution to Imperial defence. They brought infantry reinforcements from Hong Kong, overawed the population of Calcutta with their guns, then despatched most of their crews into the heart of the sub-continent. The sailors had difficulty marching in step, but they manhandled their 8-inch guns out of situations where draught oxen were helpless. As in the Crimea, Naval Brigades proved well able to look after themselves, with their own riflemen, gunners, and tradesmen. The fighting often resembled later counter-insurgency operations, pursuing an elusive enemy through blistering heat or pouring rain. Despite this, campaigning in India sometimes suggests a grand picnic. Sailors went into action with a parrot upon one shoulder, junior officers kept half a dozen servants, while naval camps were distinguished by a menagerie of goats, monkeys, and even a pig that smoked a pipe.

Such naval interventions in purely land campaigns became commonplace in the later nineteenth century. If one excludes technological developments, they provide the meat of Victorian naval history, properly so-called. The navy did not fight a single major ship-to-ship action during this period. Most Victorian sailors who saw action did so as part of a Naval Brigade. Such formations were not hastily improvised to meet unexpected emergencies. They were organised on well understood principles, and generally accepted as one of the navy's routine functions. Officers and men received regular training in the techniques of land warfare, the Gunnery School at HMS *Excellent* providing a central forum for tactical doctrine, including landing drills. The first printed field exercise for use in HM Ships appeared in 1859, shortly after the Crimea and Mutiny, with sections on skirmishing, field fortification, demolitions, and a field-gun drill not unlike that still used for the Royal Tournament's Field Gun event.

Strictly the term Naval Brigade meant a number of detachments landed from different ships, consisting of both bluejackets and Royal Marines, that is, soldiers raised for service at sea. This narrow definition obscures the wide variety of naval operations ashore. The term Naval Brigade often described a detachment from a single ship, and on one occasion a single lieutenant with an RMA sergeant. Landings in force came at the more violent end of a range of options which ran from peaceful demonstrations by a single gunboat to full-scale military campaigns, like that of the *Shannon*. Between these extremes lay the drudgery of blockades, symbolic detachments landed to protect consulates, and spectacular shore bombardments, as well as punitive expeditions to blow up the stockade of some recalcitrant potentate.

Contemporary critics debated the 'misuse' of naval assets by Naval Brigades, but generally agreed that the navy's ability to react quickly to emergencies represented an economy of force that justified such operations. The British Empire was large, communications poor, and causes of conflict widespread. The absence of any credible naval threat to the home base left ambitious officers, not to mention bored sailors, with no other professional outlet for their energies. They greeted the prospect of action ashore with enthusiasm, despite the risks of fever, while the navy took pride in its ability to outmarch regular infantry, even in bare feet.

Although Naval Brigades were the only significant source of combat experience in the Royal Navy between 1850 and 1914, they have been sadly neglected by historians. Campaign narratives ignore the naval contribution, or treat it as light relief, presenting a sentimentalised image of the navy's Handy Man. Accounts based on individual diaries or letters, on the other hand, appear in isolation, lacking context. I have tried to place Naval Brigades in their strategic setting, with sufficient narrative to provide the chronological framework that is currently lacking. I have also sought to address the human issues: how naval personnel were trained, organised, and equipped for their role ashore, how they fought and lived in the field, and what they thought about it.

The source material for the study of Naval Brigades is extraordinarily rich. Almost every nineteenth-century naval officer who published his memoirs had some tale of adventure ashore, often based on journals they kept as midshipmen. The voice from the lower deck is more muffled. Fewer diaries and letters of ratings have survived, but their freshness and lack of inhibition often steal the show, addressing issues that appeared commonplace to the gunroom or wardroom. Royal Marines, an essential part of every Naval Brigade, were particularly vocal, often providing eyewitness accounts where no others are available.

I have generally adopted modern transcriptions of place names, without altering contemporary spellings in quotations. Occasionally I have not used modern names, where the traditional English versions have strong historical resonances, for example Peking and Canton.

Acknowledgements

I would like to thank all those who have helped me with this book, both materially and with encouragement or advice, even if I have not always taken it.

The Trustees of the following institutions have kindly given permission to refer to their original archive material: The National Maritime Museum, Greenwich, London, The Royal Marines Museum, Eastney, Portsmouth, The Royal Naval Museum, HM Naval Base, Portsmouth.

The Council of the Navy Records Society has granted permission to reproduce passages from their invaluable published collections of documents. Lieutenant-Commander Brian Witts most generously allowed me access to the collection of Gunnery Manuals in his care at HMS *Excellent*. Full references may be found in the bibliography and footnotes.

Illustrations are Author's Collection, except where shown:

RMM: courtesy of the Royal Marines Museum, Eastney.
RNC: courtesy of the Royal Naval Club, Old Portsmouth.

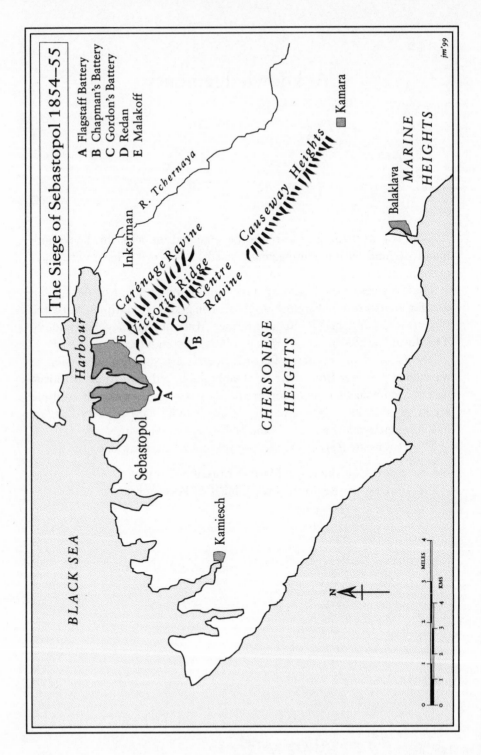

The Siege of Sebastopol 1854–55

A Flagstaff Battery
B Chapman's Battery
C Gordon's Battery
D Redan
E Malakoff

jm'99

BLACK SEA

Kamiesch

Sebastopol

Harbour

Inkerman

R. Tchernaya

Carénage Ravine

Victoria Ridge

Centre Ravine

Causeway Heights

Kamara

Balaklava

MARINE
HEIGHTS

CHERSONESE
HEIGHTS

N

MILES
KMS

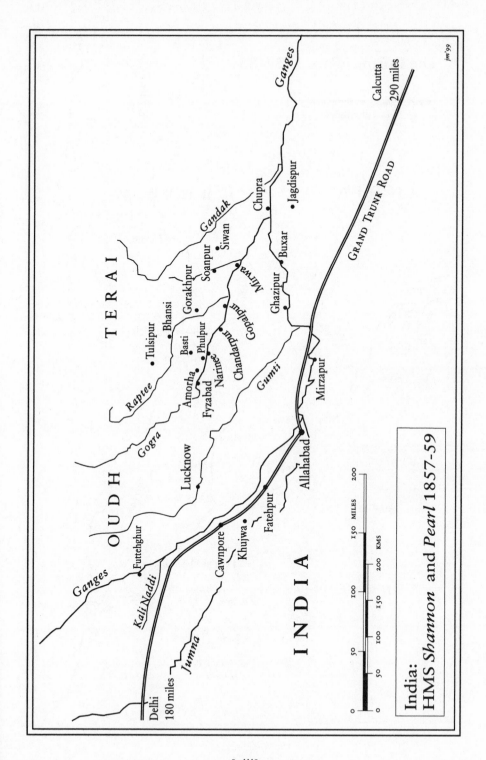

India:
HMS *Shannon* and *Pearl* 1857-59

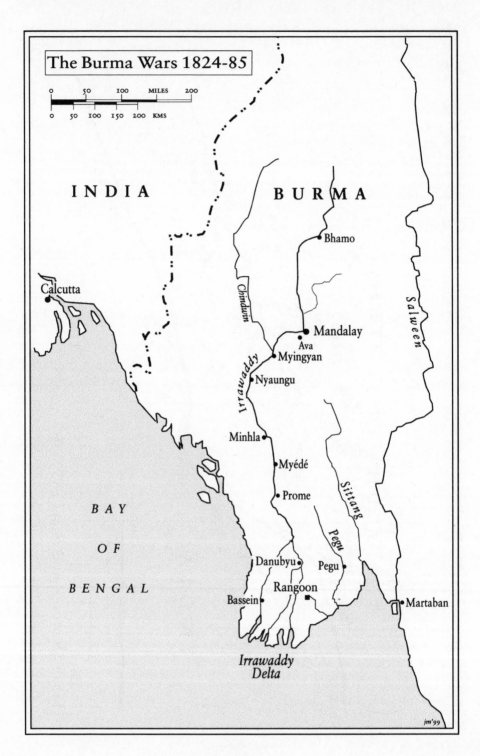

The Burma Wars 1824-85

INDIA

BURMA

Calcutta

Bhamo

Chindwin

Irrawaddy

Mandalay

Ava

Myingyan

Nyaungu

Salween

Minhla

Myédé

Prome

Sittang

Pegu

Danubyu

Pegu

B A Y

O F

B E N G A L

Bassein

Rangoon

Martaban

*Irrawaddy
Delta*

jm'99

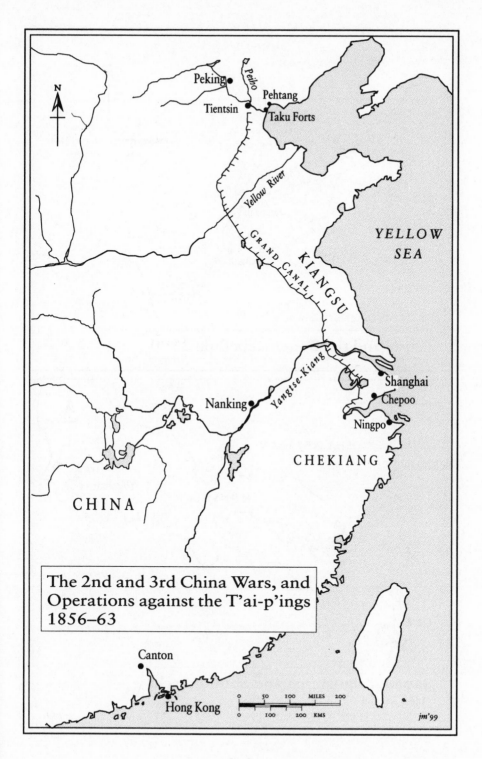

The 2nd and 3rd China Wars, and Operations against the T'ai-p'ings 1856–63

N

Peking
Peiho
Pehtang
Tientsin
Taku Forts

Yellow River

GRAND CANAL

KIANGSU

YELLOW SEA

Yangtse-Kiang

Nanking

Shanghai
Chepoo
Ningpo

CHEKIANG

CHINA

Canton

Hong Kong

0   50   100   MILES   200
0   100   200   KMS

jm'99

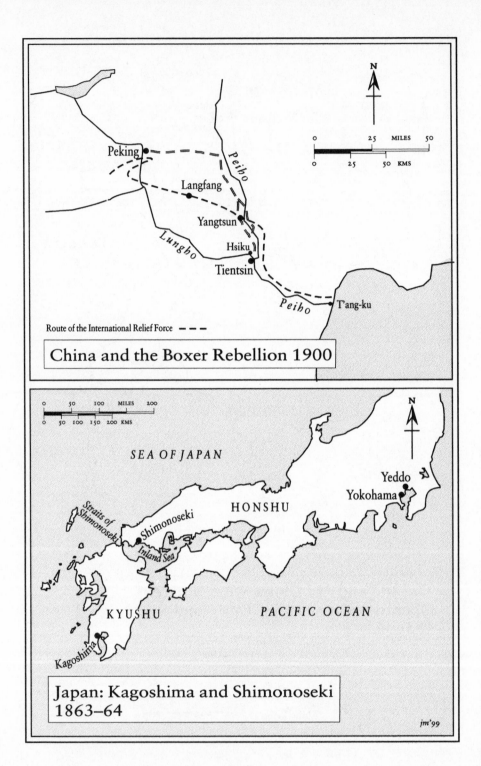

Route of the International Relief Force – – –

China and the Boxer Rebellion 1900

Japan: Kagoshima and Shimonoseki 1863–64

jm'99

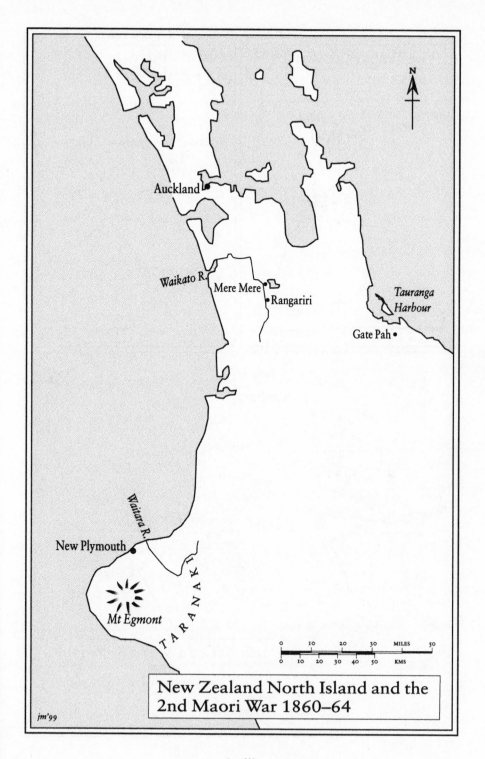

Auckland

Waikato R.   Mere Mere
  Rangariri

Tauranga
Harbour

Gate Pah •

Waitara R.

New Plymouth

T A R A N A K I

Mt Egmont

| 0 | 10 | 20 | 30 | MILES | | 50 |
| 0 | 10 | 20 | 30 | 40 | 50 | KMS |

New Zealand North Island and the 2nd Maori War 1860–64

jm'99

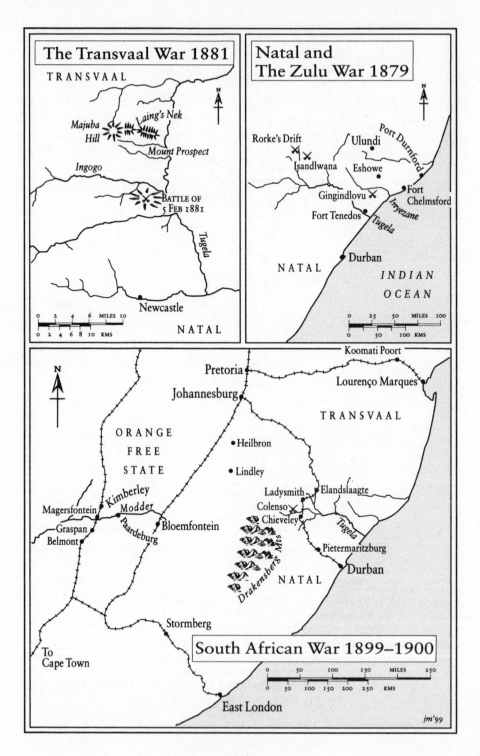

The Transvaal War 1881

TRANSVAAL

Majuba Hill
Laing's Nek
Mount Prospect
Ingogo
BATTLE OF 5 FEB 1881
Tugela
Newcastle
NATAL

MILES

KMS

Natal and The Zulu War 1879

Rorke's Drift
Ulundi
Port Durnford
Isandlwana
Eshowe
Gingindlovu
Fort Chelmsford
Fort Tenedos
Inyezane
Tugela
Durban
NATAL
INDIAN OCEAN

MILES

KMS

South African War 1899–1900

Koomati Poort
Pretoria
Lourenço Marques
Johannesburg
TRANSVAAL
ORANGE FREE STATE
Heilbron
Lindley
Ladysmith
Elandslaagte
Kimberley
Modder
Colenso
Chieveley
Magersfontein
Paardeburg
Bloemfontein
Tugela
Graspan
Belmont
Pietermaritzburg
Drakensberg Mts
Durban
NATAL
Stormberg
To Cape Town
East London

MILES

KMS

jm'99

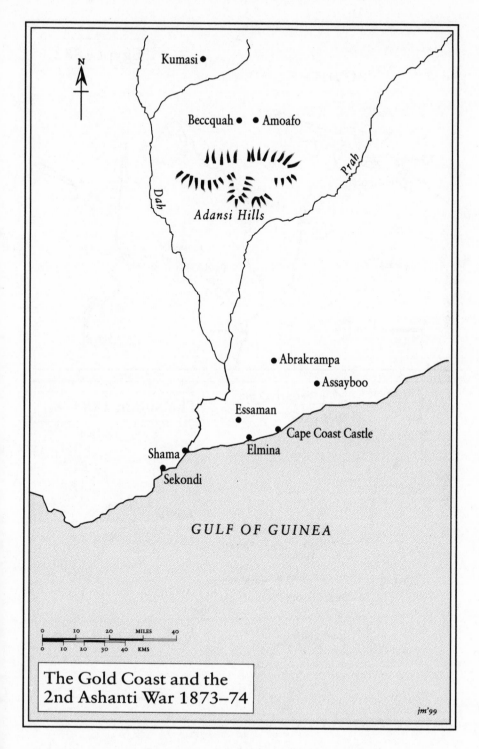

Kumasi ●

Beccquah ● ● Amoafo

Dah

Prah

Adansi Hills

● Abrakrampa

● Assayboo

Essaman
●

● Cape Coast Castle

Shama ● Elmina

● Sekondi

GULF OF GUINEA

0   10   20   MILES   40

0   10   20   30   40   KMS

The Gold Coast and the 2nd Ashanti War 1873–74

jm'99

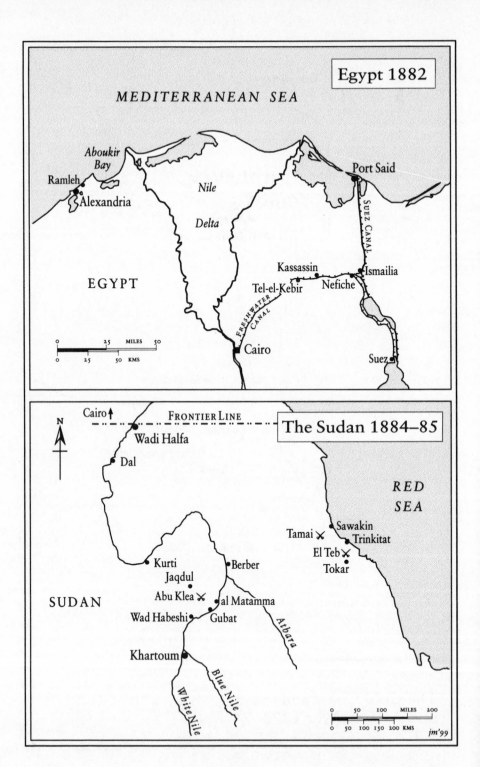

Egypt 1882

MEDITERRANEAN SEA

Aboukir
Bay

Ramleh
Alexandria

Port Said

Nile

Delta

SUEZ CANAL

EGYPT

Kassassin
Ismailia
Tel-el-Kebir   Nefiche

FRESHWATER CANAL

Cairo

Suez

0   25   MILES   50
0   25   50 KMS

Cairo ↑   FRONTIER LINE   The Sudan 1884–85

N

Wadi Halfa

Dal

RED
SEA

Tamai ✕   Sawakin
Trinkitat
El Teb ✕
Tokar

Kurti   Berber
Jaqdul
Abu Klea ✕   al Matamma

SUDAN

Wad Habeshi   Gubat

Atbara

Khartoum

Blue Nile

White Nile

0   50   100   MILES   200
0   50   100   150   200 KMS   jm'99

[xx]

Naval Interventions 1824–1920

1894	West Africa: Brohemie, Gambia
1895	West Africa: Brass River
1895	East Africa: Mwele
1896	East Africa: Zanzibar
1897	Turkish Empire: Crete
1897	West Africa: Benin
1899	Samoa
1899	Central America: Blewfields Nicaragua
1899–1900	South Africa: Boer War
1900	China: Boxer Uprising
1904	Somaliland
1907–10	Persian Gulf: Gun Runners
1913	Central America: Belize
1914	Antwerp: RND
1914	Turkish Empire: Akaba
1914–15	Serbia
1914–16	West Africa: Cameroons
1914–17	Turkish Empire: Mesopotamia
1915	Turkish Empire: Gallipoli
1915	Persian Gulf: Tangistan
1916–17	German East Africa
1920	Somaliland

The list is not exhaustive. It serves to locate Naval Brigades and other operations discussed in the text.

CHAPTER ONE

The Raid that Failed – Sebastopol (1854–55)

ONE Saturday afternoon in February 1996, a Royal Marine bugler sounded the Last Post in Woolwich cemetery, over a new memorial to one of the first recipients of the *Victoria Cross*. John Taylor, Captain of the Forecastle in HMS *London*, was one of three members of the Royal Navy decorated for rescuing a wounded comrade under fire, on 18 June 1855.[1] However, like many early naval recipients of the medal, John Taylor did not win it in a ship-to-ship action at sea. He had been fighting on land. With Commander John Raby and Boatswain's Mate Henry Curtis, Taylor ran seventy yards under a hail of fire to bring in an infantry soldier wounded at the Redan, one of several redoubts defending the Russian naval base of Sebastopol. Already besieged, for eight months, the fortress would hold out until September 1855, making the Crimean War one of the longest and bloodiest wars fought in Europe between the downfall of Napoleon and the outbreak of the First World War.

The Crimean War is remembered, if at all, for the incompetence that characterised its conduct, or perhaps for the subsequent reforms in military medicine associated with Miss Florence Nightingale. The everyday heroism of the ordinary soldiers and sailors taking part is generally forgotten. Few of them, other than officers, left written accounts of their experiences. John Taylor himself died in poverty without ever receiving his medal. Its location, and that of his pauper's grave, is unknown. His story forms part of a forgotten epic that deserves to be rescued from obscurity. Why were a Commander RN and two sailors taking part in so forlorn a hope as the assault on the Redan? What was their role in a struggle that in many ways foreshadowed the stalemate of 1914–18, with its trenches, snipers, and bombardments? How were sailors organised and trained for this role? What did the navy itself, from the Admiralty down to the lower deck, think about such terrestrial excursions?

These questions have a wider significance than the narrow context of the trenches before Sebastopol. They shed light on important issues of late nineteenth-century British naval and imperial history: the professionalisation of the Royal Navy, its role *vis-à-vis* the army, and the navy's contribution to the imperial order that made Britain the first world power. Throughout the later nineteenth century the majority of the Royal Navy's experience of active service would be ashore, as it was in the Crimea. Such expeditions, popularly labelled Naval Brigades, were not distractions, or amateurish playing at soldiers. They were central to the use of naval power in a period when the British faced no serious competitor at sea. Together they demonstrate the growing professionalism of a navy that had undisputed command of the sea, and was turning its attention to the exercise of that command.

THE CRIMEA IN CONTEXT (NOVEMBER 1853–AUGUST 1854)

The decline of the Turkish Empire destabilised the Eastern Mediterranean throughout the later nineteenth century. Fears that Tsar Nicholas I of Russia meant to redistribute the property of the Sick Man of Europe, before the invalid was decently out of the way, drew Anglo-French naval forces into the Black Sea during 1853. A devastating Russian attack on a Turkish squadron at Sinope on 27 November precipitated more serious allied action. British and French military forces concentrated in the Eastern Mediterranean early in 1854, and moved forward to Varna on the Bulgarian coast where they could counter a Russian advance on Constantinople. Inconveniently the Russians abandoned their Rumanian bridgehead, occupation of which had inspired the British commitment to support Turkey. The Allies had gained their strategic aim without striking a blow, or inflicting sufficient damage on the Russians to prevent a resumption of hostilities as soon as Franco-British forces withdrew. Public opinion and strategic necessity ruled out the sensible military step of withdrawing the cholera-ridden armies to Corfu or Malta for the winter. Instead the Allied commanders received orders to destroy the Russian naval base at Sebastopol in order to reduce their capacity for future mischief. Such a strategy was not necessarily misguided. In August 1854 a scratch force of French soldiers, British sailors and marines had easily taken the Russian base at Bomarsund, in the Baltic.

Sebastopol was heavily fortified, so naval forces alone would be insufficient for the job. However, the Allies could exploit seapower to launch a large-scale raid, moving their armies directly across the Black Sea, while the Russian Army took the longer route home by land. Lack of intelligence about enemy forces in the Crimea marred this amphibious strategy, as did the lack of landing craft and disagreements over landing sites. Lord Raglan, Commander-in-Chief of the British Army in the East, was sent his orders on 28 June 1854, but the first landings in the prophetically named Kalamita Bay in the Crimea did not take place until mid-September. More than one observer doubted whether it was not already too late to achieve the aim of the expedition before winter set in. Among them was the chaplain of HMS *Queen*, who wrote home for a supply of potted anchovies and the best Scotch marmalade, little realising that he would eat those delicacies ashore.[2]

INITIAL LANDINGS (SEPTEMBER–OCTOBER 1854)

Allied landings began at Old Fort in Kalamita Bay on 14 September 1854, using a mixture of improvised craft: pontoons made from Turkish boats planked over in pairs, flat-bottomed paddle-box boats, and ships' cutters and gigs. While the navy's heavy units cruised offshore as a covering force, sailors worked round the clock, in the surf, to ensure their military colleagues got ashore dryshod. However, the sailors' role was still essentially naval.

A new departure came on 18 September, with the first Royal Naval detachment landed for combat duties ashore. North of the landing beaches lay the little harbour of Eupatoria which, in the absence of anywhere better, might provide a more reliable means of communication than the open beach. Captain T.S. Brock RN, from HMS *Britannia*, took 430 Royal Marines 'to act in conjunction with the French, afloat and ashore, in securing and protecting the town of Eupatoria from incursions or attacks by the enemy'.[3] The marines came from different ships, including a proportion armed with the still scarce Minié rifles. They took their bags and bedding, a plentiful 200 rounds per man, and the Assistant-Surgeon of HMS *Fury* in case of casualties. They loopholed and sandbagged strongpoints around the bay, and drove off a number of Russian probing attacks. Small parties of 'Horse Marines' borrowed Tartar ponies to skirmish with whole sotnias of Cossacks.

Such a garrison role was nothing new for Royal Marines, who had carried out many such operations during the Napoleonic Wars. However, the day after the Eupatoria landing, 20 September 1854, provided less conventional employment ashore for the navy; work that demonstrated how the British Government was gambling with the lives of its soldiers and sailors. While the marines dug in at Eupatoria, the Allied armies set off southwards from Old Fort. The British military transport service had fallen victim to defence cuts after the Napoleonic Wars, so the fleet followed along the coast with the army's impedimenta. Field ambulances had not arrived at all.

The aftermath of the successful Allied attack on the Heights of Alma, on 20 September, was therefore unusually appalling. Almost 2,000 British and 1,000 Russian wounded lay on the field, with no means of removing them. Luckily the fleet was on hand. For two days 'all the boats of the fleet, 1,000 men, and all the Medical Officers, were employed in bringing the wounded and sick men from the field of battle (four miles off) to the beach, and embarking them'.[4] HMS *Queen* contributed a lieutenant and fifty bluejackets, accompanied by their chaplain, the Revd Kelson Stothert:

> We took cots and hammocks slung on oars, on which to convey them away to hospital ... only stopping now and then to 'shake a dead Russian out of his boots' for these are of 'Russian leather' and greatly prized by Jack.[5]

They cared for Russian and British wounded impartially, although sometimes the Russians fired on their would-be helpers, with disastrous results for themselves. The improvised ambulance service may have been less satisfactory than secondary accounts suggest. The sailors were rough and unskilled ambulance men, their baggy hammocks providing little support for amputated limbs. Many Russians still lay out when the army and its attendant ships moved on. Captain Stephen Lushington of HMS *Albion* picked up the last survivors on 26 September. Skilfully deploying covering parties of marines and small-arms men, Lushington set his seamen to work. They brought off 300 wounded Russians before the Cossacks arrived, forcing the *Albions* to make an orderly retreat.

THE NAVY GOES ASHORE (OCTOBER 1854)

Meanwhile, two critical events had taken place that would decisively shape the course of the campaign. On the night of 21/22 September the Russians sank five battleships and two frigates to block the mouth of Sebastopol harbour.[6] Five days later the Allied armies, after marching inland around Sebastopol, regained touch with their supporting fleets by occupying Balaklava and Kamiesch Bay, south-west of the Russian fortress. The subsequent decision not to assault the still incomplete defences of Sebastopol marked the definitive failure of the invasion as a raid. The disembarkation of the army's siege train between 28 September and 2 October underlined the strategic shift. The task was a difficult one: ships were not loaded tactically, and there was no transport for the guns and mortars once ashore.

The neutralisation of the Russian fleet freed Allied naval resources for direct support of an army that was now seriously overstretched. On 29 September Lord Raglan requested the landing of 1,000 marines to replace the Guards Brigade on the heights above Balaklava. Another 200 followed three days later.[7] As his steam vessels were constantly in action, Rear-Admiral Sir James Dundas, Naval Commander-in-Chief in the Black Sea, left their detachments intact, but his sailing ships were now denuded of Royal Marines. Dundas took still more serious steps on 1 October 1854, ordering each of the five battleships present to land 200 sailors per ship, with officers in proportion, for service with the army.[8] The navy was no longer restricted to an *ad hoc* supporting role, but had become an integral part of the land campaign.

The Captain of HMS *Albion* had overall command of the Naval Brigade's 1,040 ratings and fifty officers, perhaps in recognition of the tactical skill he had shown at the Alma. Lushington's second was Captain of HMS *Diamond*, the dashing William Peel who would do more than any other individual to set the standards for future Naval Brigades. Unable to resist the prospect of action at the Alma, Peel had anchored half a mile from the shore, in water so shallow his ship touched bottom. He then manned and armed boats, and went ashore to help the French and Turks across the Alma River, accompanying their further advance with the crew of his gig.[9] Peel and his men had landed without authority, so were denied an Alma clasp for their Crimea medals. However, Peel did win the second naval VC a month later, when he threw a live 42pr shell, its fuse still burning, out of his battery.

Volunteers for land service were called for, but the real problem was deciding who should stay behind. Officers and men, with few chances for action afloat, were mad to go ashore, raising the prospect of ships being left in the same state as those in Sydney harbour when gold was discovered in Australia. No one anticipated a prolonged stay ashore. Sebastopol was expected to fall within a week or a fortnight:

> So we took with us just what we could carry and very little else . . . a haversack with two day's provisions, a spare pair of socks and a spoon(!), sword, revolver, waterbottle, small spy-glass, and a blanket tightly rolled up in an oilskin cape across my shoulder . . . I need hardly add that we were not in full dress and epaulettes like the gallant sister service at the Alma, but much *au contraire*.[10]

Ratings took their pilot coats and two blankets, with a cutlass apiece, and one singleshot pistol between three.

The navy set up their sheerlegs on the Balaklava quayside to unload the army's own siege train, but they soon began landing naval guns too. Six 32pr guns came from the upper decks of each battleship, and another twenty from HMS *Diamond*, an ill-sailing frigate, moored in Balaklava harbour as a hospital ship. Each gun had 150 shot and thirty shell, with firing platforms and an appropriate quantity of cartridges.[11] As the army had insufficient transport for its own needs, the navy adopted their own technique for moving heavy guns. They fixed two ropes to each of the two-ton 32prs, and dragged them along on their wooden trucks:

> to each rope fifteen men stripped to their flannels; cross-legged on the breech sat a fiddler, with a boat's ensign flying by his side. In the muzzle which pointed to the rear was a long hand spike, or wooden bar to steer with worked by two or three men.[12]

Men worked in shifts, from 4.30 in the morning to 7.30 in the evening, with an hour-and-a-half for meals. Then the night shift took over, working until dawn. Discipline was relaxed by military standards. The different teams raced their guns against those of other ships, to the peril of passers by, and then sauntered back to Balaklava, 'without being marched, for Jack couldn't bear being *sodgered* about'. The main problem was drink, for there were numerous sheds of fermenting grape juice, which the men drank like horses, straight from the troughs. There was little hint of the bleak conditions usually associated with the Crimea and the weather remained good throughout October. Dosed with quinine and lime juice, the Naval Brigade remained healthy, although Field Marshal Sir Evelyn Wood, once a Midshipman in HMS *Queen*, still remembered the horrors of washing in a ditch. Sailors:

> regarded the campaign as little more than picnicking on a large scale for though there was plenty of work, there was not much hardship – except the want of a change of clothes . . . We were young, healthy, and full of spirits; and amid the surroundings of a life that was new to us, it was really most interesting and exciting to find ourselves taking a soldier's part in a real siege on foreign soil.[13]

Once the guns were on their way, the 1,400-strong Naval Brigade pitched camp nearer the frontline, on the Victoria Ridge, left of the Woronzov Road.

Two-and-a-half miles from the head of Sebastopol harbour, they could see some of its white buildings, tantalisingly close, between the hills.

THE FIRST BOMBARDMENT (17 OCTOBER 1854)

The engineers were now ready to break ground for the First Parallel, pressing 300 sailors into service as sappers. More sailors formed carrying parties, taking up planks for the ships' carpenters to make into firing platforms for the heavy guns:

> The way at first lay along the Woronzoff Road, till we reached that bend in it, afterwards (too well) known as the Valley of the Shadow of Death; then we turned sharp to the right up the hill, on the top of which we had to run exposed fifty or sixty yards before we got the shelter of the newly constructed covert way which led to the *Diamond* battery ... The Russians knew their opportunity and took prompt advantage of it, for keeping their spy-glasses to bear, as soon as they saw a man or two make a rush, bang! bang! came a shot so we could not cross in file – only two or three occasionally. Then I first saw a man killed by a round shot, but we hadn't much time to think about it.[14]

The batteries were armed during the night of 14/15 October. On the right the navy manned seven out of the twenty-six guns deployed in Gordon's Battery, at ranges up to a mile. On the left, in Chapman's Battery, they crewed seventeen out of forty-one guns. Two 'Lancaster' batteries on Victoria Ridge held six naval guns of heavier calibre. Lancaster guns had a twisted oval bore, intended to achieve greater range and accuracy by imparting a spin to their projectiles. In practice they were hated for shooting 'like an Irish gun, round a corner',[15] and were later condemned as unsafe. One 68pr Lancaster from HMS *Beagle* engaged the remaining Russian battleships in Dockyard creek from the Left battery. Another was emplaced in the Right battery with five conventional smooth-bore 68prs to fire on the Malakoff Tower, named after an old Russian purser who once kept a vodka shop there. In all, the Royal Navy provided detachments for thirty out of the seventy-three guns in the British batteries, a similar proportion to their French allies, who fielded twenty-one naval guns out of their total of forty-nine.[16]

No reply was made to Russian harassing fire, as Lord Raglan wished to husband his limited assets for a single crushing blow. Optimism prevailed. The Naval Brigade laid bets that Sebastopol would fall within twenty-four hours, and Evelyn Wood refused to buy a Russian gold watch for a pound, as such items were soon expected to be much cheaper. The Naval Brigade's first relief of some 200 men marched off for the trenches before dawn on the morning of 17 October 1854. Officers checked the men's haversacks and waterbottles to ensure they contained their rations of salt pork, biscuit, and water with a dash of rum. Those left out of battle complained bitterly, and many found their own way into the trenches regardless of orders.

The sailors in Chapman's battery went eagerly to work, stripping to their flannels, and sitting quietly under the parapet ready for the signal at 6.30 a.m. At last this went up: 'instantly a flash ran along the whole length of the Allied lines from left to right – six or seven miles, as if a train of gunpowder had been fired'. For the first two hours Acting Mate F.M. Norman had no clear recollection of anything:

> beyond the general roar and din, flashes, columns of smoke, clouds of dust, whistling and roaring of a continual storm of shot and bursting shell, cries of the wounded, and calls for the Doctor.[17]

The Russians' Flagstaff Battery enfiladed Chapman's Battery from the left. It sent 42pr shot screeching overhead, or whizzing through an embrasure, knocking splinters off carriages, dismounting guns, and injuring the detachments. Norman's loader lost his arm to a shell fragment, so he found himself applying part of his own shirt as a tourniquet: 'the man meantime coolly observing that I didn't handle it as if I were used to the business'. Norman himself had a narrow escape when his lieutenant took a turn aiming through the smoke at the Russian muzzle flashes, to be killed instantly. As the morning wore on the rate of fire was reduced to save ammunition. Norman sat down beneath the parapet with his rations, but found he could not eat.

In the Right Attack, under Peel's direction, matters went better, although losses were still heavy. The detachments from *Queen* and *Diamond* insisted on firing broadsides, as if they were at sea. Despite a three-to-one Russian superiority in guns, the Five Gun Lancaster battery established its superiority over the Malakoff by 8.30 a.m., and later in the day the other key Russian position, the Redan, fell silent when its magazine blew up. The Royal Artillery's official analysis of the operations commented: 'For some minutes at this period of the day we appeared to have got the Russian fire under.' However: 'Opposite the French, the enemy remained unsubdued.'[18] Disaster had struck when a Russian shell penetrated the principal French magazine. The explosion caused over 100 casualties, and wrecked their 4th battery.

Greatly encouraged, the Russians silenced the French by 1.30 p.m., when a second magazine blew up.

Further disappointment arose from the other major event of the day. The French military Commander-in-Chief, General Canrobert, had insisted on naval cooperation with the land bombardment, regardless of the strategic risk to allied lines of communications if the ships' attenuated crews should suffer heavy losses. The Russians fired high, cutting up the rigging or sweeping decks vacated by the men and guns ashore with the Naval Brigade, but there were some tense moments. HMS *Rodney* went aground, set on fire with red hot shot, and was towed off with her last intact hawser. HMS *Queen*'s chaplain acquired a souvenir: a Russian shell which missed his head and stuck in the ship's side, like a giant pea, without exploding. The fleets got away with light damage, but their efforts did little to affect the issue of the day.

This had been decided by the explosion of the French magazine, which disrupted the Allied plan for a quick bombardment followed by an immediate assault. The troops formed up, with their field guns hooked in ready to move, but were never committed. Only the combative Peel thought it possible to launch an assault, offering to storm the shattered Redan with his bluejackets. Norman's men had mocked an Order of the Day predicting that a two-hour bombardment would do the business, but they were still discouraged by their failure to beat down the Russian fire:

> black with powder and stained with blood, I regained my tent on the ground of which I sank just as I was, faint for want of food, with all my accoutrements still girt about me, and fell into a deep sleep, from which I did not awake until the shrill pipes of the bosuns summoned us at daylight.[19]

The ensuing days confirmed the failure of the Allied bombardment. Drawing on the arsenal at their backs, the Russians could repair their losses much faster than could the Allies. The exchange of fire continued at a reduced level, but the Allies were quite unable to silence the enemy. The guns in the Redan and other batteries were more numerous than at the start of the siege, and of heavier calibre. A naval officer in the defences at Balaklava wrote with some prescience:

> To all appearances matters may go on as at present for a long time; the Russian earthworks are certainly a good deal knocked about, but they are still embrasured, and I am told that if a gun is dismounted today it will be

replaced in the night. We have but one advantage over the besieged, which is that all our shot which miss the earthworks go into the town, whereas theirs bound harmlessly away.[20]

The unfavourable result of Lord Raglan's throw of the dice called for an increased naval contribution. Sailors manned thirty-seven out of the eighty guns in action by late October, while naval 32prs replaced twenty-two guns disabled in the batteries. Almost 4,000 sailors and marines were ashore, of whom 133 became casualties during the bombardment, compared with 115 lost by the Royal Artillery.[21] There was little hope of a quick end to the siege, however. Operations were about to enter a new phase that would threaten the expedition with complete disaster. The Naval Brigade would show that not only were they almost as good at soldiering as the soldiers themselves, but they made far better campaigners.

MARINE HEIGHTS

While the seamen gunners of the Naval Brigade were in the thick of the action at Sebastopol, the Royal Marines had quietly secured the expedition's base at Balaklava. So important was this task that Raglan entrusted it to his most reliable subordinate, Sir Colin Campbell of the Highland Brigade. Two of Campbell's original three battalions were committed to siege operations, leaving him with one of Highlanders, supplemented by two of Royal Marines. This inclusion in a somewhat nominal Highland Brigade may have contributed to the historical neglect of the Royal Marines in the Crimea. However, among them was a Red Marine whose reminiscences in the *Globe and Laurel* provide us with our only lower deck witness of the siege of Sebastopol. 'Young Turner of the Old Brigade', as he was known even as an octogenarian, went ashore with Peel at the Alma. Years later he could still remember the raw patches the stretcher poles had left on his shoulders.

Turner landed at Balaklava on 30 September. After a night in the open rolled up in their blankets, the marines began to cut roads up to gun positions on the surrounding hills that became famous as Marine Heights. Captain Simon Fraser took over No. 3 Battery, on a knoll in the centre of the line. There was a piece of wall with six short brass guns and one mortar looking over it, but no cover from fire, and no obstacles against horse or foot. The marines suffered the same neglect as the rest of the army:

A quantity of old dilapidated tents were served out to our Battalion, which it sorely tried us to make fast at the outset. No lines were formed, each party choosing his own ground. There were plenty of holes in the tents through which to peep out at one another, and which let in a constant current of fresh air to keep us cool.[22]

Commissariat officials suggested that as marines belonged to the fleet they should apply to the Admiral for their rations, or simply gave short weight. More than one witness remembered the green coffee beans that men had to roast over scarce scraps of firing, before eating their pork raw, which helped many a good soldier out of the world. There was water of a sort, but Turkish soldiers washed in it, leading to a fresh outbreak of the cholera that had plagued the expedition since Varna. There were no medicines, except some arrowroot the boatswain of HMS *Diamond* happened to have. The one redeeming feature was the care that officers and men took of one another, regardless of rank. When Turner's Lieutenant of Marines fell sick, he washed the officer's clothing, and sat up at night to give him boiled rice and toast water, made in his canteen from burnt biscuit. Later Turner admitted:

We Joeys made many mistakes when we first landed. We made bonfires of all the available wood we could lay our hands on. Oh how we regretted it afterwards when we had to grub about for roots to roast our green coffee. We did not husband our boots as we should have done. The legs of our trousers were torn and tattered by the short scrub about the hills, and we presented a pitiful sight until our knapsacks were converted into leggings, or our legs bandaged up with biscuit bags.[23]

Despite their problems, the marines busily armed their batteries with a variety of guns landed from the fleet, from 12pr field guns to 32prs on naval carriages. By 25 October they were ready to play a crucial though neglected role in one of the most celebrated of British battles. The Battle of Balaklava began with heavy Russian columns storming some Turkish redoubts, a mile in front of the main line of resistance on the heights. Marines who saw the action thought the Turks fought well against overwhelming odds, contrary to second-hand reports. Pursuing Russian cavalry approached Balaklava, to meet accurate Royal Marine shellfire, the fuses previously cut to measured ranges, and a counter-charge by the Heavy Cavalry Brigade. 'See that ridiculous print called the "Red Line",' wrote Sergeant Turner in 1901; 'never was such a thing, the Marines fired the first and last shot in the Battle of Balaklava.'[24]

In No. 3 Battery Captain Fraser had to threaten his impassioned gunners, lest they fired into the confused mass of British and Russian horsemen. As the Russians reformed and showed signs of renewing the action, Fraser saw his chance:

> 'Now is our time, my lads! Do you cover?', I cried. 'Yes, sir!' was the quick hearty reply from my stalwart Marines. 'Then fire from No. 1 gun, and so on' was my next order. Every shot went right into the midst of the enemy. As men and horses rolled over there was evidently great consternation among the Russian cavalry, and with a parting salute from our No. 1 gun they went to the right about, and with men's breasts to horses' manes they galloped out of sight round the sand hills.[25]

The marines had little to do with the subsequent disastrous charge of the Light Cavalry, which took place out of sight, beyond the line of Turkish redoubts. However, its failure to clear the Russians off the Causeway Heights began seven restless weeks of constant alarms for the defenders of Balaklava. Lord Raglan was so shaken by the Russian threat to his communications that he sent HMS *Sanspareil*, 'rather a seedy specimen of a screw line of battleship', and some steam gun vessels to remove the British installations to the French base at Kamiesch Bay. Calmer counsels prevailed, however, and the steamships' crews landed to defend the harbour instead. Captain Heath RN took a further 200 Royal Marines from HMS *Algiers*, and went up to No. 4 Battery covering the centre valley:

> Our position is by no means pleasant. We see the Russian army two miles from us, its advance guard is only 2,600 yards off, it is estimated at from twenty to thirty thousand men, whereas we have but 3,000 Englishmen, and 2,000 Turks; with however 4,000 French a mile in rear ... We have entrenched ourselves and are safe if the Turks stand like good men and true, and the Russians do not attack at night.[26]

Night attacks also exercised the commander of No.3 Battery, as did the defenceless state of his position, with nothing but a few old wheelbarrows to block the entrance. However, the attack on Balaklava was only the first of two tremendous blows which the Russians hoped would drive the Allies into the sea. Their nocturnal demonstrations were a diversion from their second major effort, this time against the Allies' exposed right flank on the heights of Inkerman.

INKERMAN – THE SAILOR'S BATTLE

The Russians worked themselves up gradually. On 26 October a reconnaissance threatened the flank of the Right Lancaster Battery, providing the opportunity for another Naval *VC*. Ordered to spike his guns and retreat, Acting Mate William Hewett of the *Beagle* stuck to his post, slewing his gun around to blow away part of the parapet and open fire on the Russians. So began the career of Admiral Sir William Hewett *VC*, perhaps the Victorian navy's foremost exponent of combined operations, commanding Naval Brigades in West Africa, Egypt, and the Sudan.

Ten days later, F.M. Norman had spent a night in the batteries, sitting in the rain on an up-ended shot box. He was eating his breakfast, on the morning of 5 November 1854, when the alarm sounded. Cramming his sardines and biscuit into his pocket, he ran off to spend an unnerving day dodging cannonballs, and watching hungry but undaunted infantry moving up into the smoke of the firing line. The Naval Brigade had just received 300 new Minié rifles, but stayed in reserve 600 yards from the hotly contested Sandbag Battery, 'with the understanding that if the enemy succeeded in forcing his way, we were to fall upon him with our six hundred cutlasses'. Luckily for Norman this was not necessary. His most dangerous moment came when he was sent with a message for Hewett at the Lancaster Battery:

> a perilous journey ... for I had to traverse a space of 400 yards or so, across which from several directions, and several sources were flying shot and shell of all sorts, sometimes in rushes of several together, at others in succession so slowly that it was almost a pain to listen when the next would be.[27]

Hewett's battery was again in the path of the Russian advance. Five bluejackets picked up the rifles of wounded soldiers, mounted the banquette, and under a hail of bullets kept up a rapid fire, whilst others below reloaded and handed up fresh weapons. Two of the five were killed, but the three survivors all won *VCs*.

Unnoticed by historians, Royal Marines also fought at Inkerman. Four companies had replaced 2nd Rifle Brigade, in the Light Division. Like the Naval Brigade, they were roused on 5 November by the musketry of picquets driven in by the Russian advance. Posted near the Right Lancaster Battery on Victoria Ridge, the marines were on the flank of General Semenov's advance along the Carénage Ravine:

The roll of musketry was terrific; we were advanced cautiously until bullets began to fall in amongst us, the sergeant-major was the first man killed; order given to lay (*sic*) down; it was as well we did so; a rush of bullets passed over us; then we gave them three rounds kneeling into their close columns. At the same time some seamen opened fire from some heavy guns into their left flank, and this drove them back into the fog and smoke.[28]

The firing was intense: a drummer had his drum shot away, and a piece of his trousers, all without getting a scratch himself. Many marines still carried old smooth-bore muskets, which clogged with half-burnt powder, forcing their owners to hammer down the ramrods with stones. The choked muskets kicked dreadfully, their barrels so hot they could not be touched. Twenty-one Royal Marines were killed or wounded, including Captain March who was shot through the head, and sent back on board HMS *Queen*.

Our Captain of Marines (March) has been sent here badly wounded . . . in the engagement [he] received a ball under the right ear which came out of his mouth, scoring the inside of his cheek in its passage. The jaw is slightly fractured, and some of the auricular nerves cut so that his mouth is twisted on one side, and his beauty gone for ever . . . he was picked up for dead, but may after all be not much worse.[29]

Despite the appalling losses of both sides at Inkerman, the Russians failed to stop the Allied bombardment. However, the battle began a period of complete stalemate. For almost six months the British Army was paralysed, partly through the efforts of the Russian Army, but overwhelmingly by more impersonal forces.

GENERAL WINTER (NOVEMBER 1854–MARCH 1855)

In November the weather became piercingly cold, a north-easterly gale preventing communication between ship and shore. This was followed on the 14th by the Great Storm. Twenty-one transport ships were wrecked, perhaps the most disastrous loss being the *Prince*, which carried enough greatcoats to equip the British Army of the East twice over. On Marine Heights, men clung face down to the sodden ground, while empty shot boxes blew about like feathers.

The Marine Brigade lost both their supplies and their commander: the

Quarter-Master's magazine hut collapsed, while Colonel Hordle was blown into a ravine, complete with his tent and bedding. Matters were no better in the Naval Brigade camp. Evelyn Wood was in bed suffering the ill-effects of raw salt pork when his tent blew away, leaving him lying in the rain. F.M. Norman returned from the batteries to find all the tents down, in particular the hospital marquee, its sodden struggling canvas prostrate across the wounded men inside. Norman took shelter in an old cowshed with 100 others, passing the whole day 'marking time', jumping and stamping to keep warm. Unable to find a dry spot anywhere, he fell asleep at last on a pile of empty bottles, leaning back on a tent pole.

The storm completed the collapse of a logistics system that was already overstrained by the siege's never-ending demands for *matériel*. It destroyed a vast quantity of stores, and reduced the route up to the Chersonese Heights to churned up mud. In October heavy guns had been dragged up on their trucks. Now it was impossible to do so on field carriages. The roads were a foot deep in stiff mud: 'the commissariat have given up their wheel carts and turned all their beasts into pack horses'.[30]

Pack animals move smaller loads than draft, so the troops, already on short rations, starved. Even mules broke down and stuck in the mud, their precious loads of tea, bread, and sugar having to be rescued, slung from hand spikes. The naval doctors ran out of the 'acetate-of-lead-cum-opium pills' used to treat diarrhoea, so they issued bread pills instead, making no apparent difference. Soldiers and sailors alike spent their days off from the trenches on 'Araba Guard', carrying their provisions the five miles from Balaklava on their shoulders, as the local carts known as arabas were long consumed as firewood. William Turner reckoned he had walked 5,000 miles in the Crimea on such duty. As siege operations were still going on, a man's load was a 32pr shot or a 64lb piece of salt pork slung between two.

Although the army, or rather the Treasury's commissaries, could not keep transport animals alive, the navy did rather better:

scores of half-starved Russian horses and ponies roamed about the hills, some of which Jack often managed to catch and press into the day's service ... in fact the number of stray animals of all sorts was surprising, and our bluejackets used to look after them with the utmost solicitude, especially sheep ... horses and ponies without any very definite owners were constantly to be seen tethered about various parts of our camp; so much so that there was an idea prevalent throughout the divisions that missing horses were sure to be found in the sailors' camp.[31]

In December the only units where food was not scarce were the Guards and the Marines, some of the credit for which must go to Young Turner, pressed into service as Quarter-Master. When the transport collapsed, he seduced six stray camels with ship's biscuit. They could carry a week's supply of biscuit between them, or drag up a 74-gallon rum puncheon on a makeshift cart. King Grog presented Turner with more problems than either the slippery roads or unhelpful commissariat officials. He kept the rum half buried in the ground, under a fourteen-day reserve supply of biscuit, to preserve the barrel from gimlet holes. Nevertheless, several men were reported drunk, which prompted an inspection:

> when they tried to turn the puncheon up it would not move so they began to dig it out. As they did so they came across what appeared to be an iron bar run into the puncheon, and leading outside for over ten yards into a dug-out. This turned out to be an iron pipe. The hole had been covered over with boards and the pipe earthed over and fitted with a plug. When the pipe was withdrawn from the puncheon there was not four gallons of rum in it![32]

Somehow, when their military neighbours had not a scrap of meat in the whole division, the Naval Brigade got their Christmas dinners, even in the trenches. F.M. Norman laid out a pound on the makings of a 'war-pudding':

> Pearce the captain of the gun made the pudding, and got a clean sandbag to boil it in, which was satisfactorily effected in an empty powder case, old shell boxes being used as fuel, close under the parapet, twenty or thirty shot having passed over the spot – so our duff, which was really very good, was not only over but under fire![33]

Conditions remained bleak throughout January. Carrying parties plodded down to Balaklava with ice in their beards, sometimes through snow three feet deep, sometimes through mud that sucked the boots off their feet. Overnight temperatures fell to fifteen degrees Fahrenheit, so breakfast had to thaw out in men's pockets:

> During winter our tents were often just stiff glassy sheets of ice; and icicles formed everywhere, inside and out, for we had no fires nor fuel to make them, except the cook for each line of tents.[34]

The writer kept four pairs of socks and wore two at a time, rubbing the ice out of the day pairs before he could put them on, and tie up the loose sole of his boot. With sailors parading barefoot in the snow, every fight was followed by the cry: 'Boots, lads, Boots!', when you could see men sitting down, measuring their feet against those of dead Russians.

The main problem continued to be transport. The Naval Brigade moved camp to a more sheltered spot near the Centre Ravine, but everything had to be carried by the men. Planks appeared at Balaklava in November, but huts did not go up until January and February. The first at the Naval Brigade camp became a hospital and a drying shed. Another became a wardroom, dug into the hill, with a solid chalk floor, a chimney made from iron water-pipes, and a unique luxury for the Crimea – a window affording views of the legs of passers by:

> the original proprietors despaired of ever getting wood enough to make the pole and rafters, but at last the difficulty was overcome by a party of bluejackets, who entirely of their own accord, and of course without leave, went by dark right away down among a lot of old houses in the sur-burbs of Sebastopol close under the batteries, passing I should think some Russian sentries by the way, and returned laden with joists, rafters, planks, and window frames.[35]

With the protagonists' energies absorbed by the struggle for survival, the siege languished. In December insufficient ammunition reached the front to maintain even a pretence at bombardment. A good rate of supply was 100 rounds a day, only enough for one gun. Russian roundshot carpeted the ground near British batteries, making it difficult to walk about. The sailors collected cannonballs that fitted British guns, and fired them back with chalk caricatures of Prince Makemskoff, as they dubbed the Russian commander. Some light relief was needed, as every round fired from the British batteries brought ten and sometimes twenty in reply. The most feared projectiles were mortar shells, or 'Whistling Dicks', fired at high elevation. Unlike cannon shot, these could not be avoided by lying close to the parapet. Overmatched by the weight of Russian fire, the navy relied on superior gunnery:

> we used to make such good practise with the 68pr that sometimes I had the satisfaction of seeing one of their guns cock right up in the air, as our solid shot entering the embrasure, knocked away its carriage, and sent the splinters flying.[36]

[17]

At other times a live and let live attitude prevailed:

> The whole line of the Russian sentries from the Malakoff Tower towards
> Inkerman walked up and down in the open in the most cheeky manner,
> but it is not our policy to interfere with any of their doings just now, as
> we have enough to do to keep ourselves alive, and to prepare for the
> second bombardment, when great things are expected.[37]

On warmer days officers sat in the batteries and read Charles Dickens'
Household Words. At night the men smoked, made coffee and soup, and read
books. Such was the demand for reading matter that the chaplain sent home
for 1,500 Bibles. He thought the sailors might even read them; there were no
other books, and nowhere the men could sell them!

RECRIMINATIONS AT HOME

If the Admiralty had had their way, the Royal Navy would have taken no
part in future bombardments. Even as the British Army was struggling to
avoid a worse catastrophe than the retreat from Kabul, their Lordships were
putting pressure on Dundas to withdraw the Naval and Marine Brigades; a
tenth of the Army's strength, including a third of the siege gunners.[38]

From first receiving the news of the landings at Eupatoria, the Admiralty
gave Dundas' actions grudging approval, although admitting that he could
not have done otherwise. As time passed they hardened their line. They
began with criticism of the detail of Dundas' actions, objecting to the dis-
armament of gunboats, such as the *Beagle*, and the simultaneous weakening
of all Dundas' ships by landing men from each. They argued that it would
have been better to disarm a few entirely, as had been done with HMS
Diamond, keeping the rest at full efficiency. In early December their
Lordships showed their misreading of the desperate state of affairs in the
Black Sea with a stinging critique of Dundas' response to Lord Raglan's
courteous but importunate pleas for help. Remarking on the need for a
sufficient number of ships of the line to meet the enemy at sea, the
Admiralty insisted that none of the screw battleships should furnish seamen
or marines for land service. They further expressed the hope that drafts of
Royal Artillerymen would allow the withdrawal of seamen from the batteries.[39] Where the Russians would find ships to oppose the Royal Navy at sea
is not clear, as by this time the Russian battleships were on the bottom of
Sebastopol harbour, their crews fighting ashore. As for the Royal Artillery,

there were never enough of them in the Crimea, gunners spending sixteen hours in the trenches for days at a stretch. Only the Naval Brigade succeeded in forming the three reliefs conventionally required to man siege guns round the clock.

To some extent the Board's position was understandable. There was no adequate system for recruiting sailors in wartime, and men were needed for ships in the Baltic, as well as the Black Sea. Naval Brigade officers themselves were conscious of the lack of drafts to replace casualties, and complained of the poor quality of the 'Tower Hill mob' drawn from recently arrived ships. It took a new Commander-in-Chief to convince the Admiralty of the necessity for the Naval Brigade. Dundas went home at the end of 1854, to be replaced by his second-in-command, the dynamic, or at least more visible, Rear-Admiral Sir Edmund Lyons. Unlike Dundas, who remained at sea in HMS *Britannia*, Lyons was often ashore. In November the Marine Brigade had cheered him for preventing the precipitate evacuation of Balaklava. Lyons accepted the loss of some men from the Naval Brigade in January 1855, and their return to Devonport, but he argued vehemently for keeping the others:

> the breaking up of the naval brigade ... would considerably increase Lord Raglan's difficulties and dishearten the troops – French as well as British – by leading them to apprehend an indefinite postponement of the assault ... and consequently a prolongation of their exposure and privations on the heights.[40]

Withdrawal might also cause diplomatic difficulties with our French allies at a time when Lord Raglan was asking them to hold a larger share of the front line, perhaps a decisive argument for a politically dominated Board. A new Ministry committed to more forceful prosecution of the war may have seen the impossibility of abandoning the army. Either way, Lyons suspended embarkation of seamen from ships remaining in the Black Sea. He even landed 400 more in April 1855, drawing only a feeble protest.

THE SECOND BOMBARDMENT (APRIL 1855)

January and February were quiet months in the trenches. The chaplain had 300 sick on his hands every week, but the Naval Brigade suffered not a single casualty from enemy action. Fresh siege *matériel* awaited the return of better weather at Balaklava, and by March 1855 the horrors of the winter were a

fading memory. The Naval Brigade's sicklist fell to nineteen out of a victualling strength of 1,000, and a reserve of fourteen days' rations was accumulated. HMS *Sanspareil*'s engineers even resolved the intractable problem
of green coffee. They took time off from rebouching the vents of overworked
siege guns to make coffee-roasting machines out of empty oil drums. The
fine weather allowed Captain Lushington's men to make rapid preparations
for re-opening fire. The navy had agreed, with the assistance of 200 more
men from *HMS Leander* (landed 2 April), to man thirty-seven guns.
Transport was still short, so 200 sailors set to work on the railway from
Balaklava, the only reliable way of nourishing lengthy bombardments. The
first load of ammunition moved on 28 March, and from then on the railway
supplied forty to fifty tons a day. The sailors' arms and legs were still in
demand; to drag up two 68prs on 2 April, and to carry up enough ammunition for a reserve of 400–500 rounds per gun. This did not always go down
well, as a Staff Officer found when he reproached a member of the Naval
Brigade for grumbling:

'I thought you Bluejackets were always cheery and contented?'

'Oh, that's where you are wrong. I ain't a Bluejacket now – nothing but a
broken down *blessed* commissariat mule.'[41]

The Second Bombardment began on Easter Monday 9 April 1855, despite
drizzling mist that obscured the enemy batteries. Heavy watery clouds
drenched the Allied gunners, and flooded the trenches: the tackles used to
work the heavy guns would not run, ropes would not bite, and handspikes
failed to grip the slippery mortar platforms. Men's feet were so swollen from
standing in water that they were afraid to remove their boots, lest they could
not get them on again. The bombardment surprised the Russians who
returned only one shot to three. However, their works were much stronger
than in the previous October, and defended by a far more powerful artillery.
Despite the optimism of Lushington's reports to Lyons, he had to admit after
a week of heavy firing that the Russians were still giving as good as they got.
Evelyn Wood found this out the hard way. In the first hour of the bombardment the embrasure of his 8-inch gun was demolished three times by
Russian fire, and rebuilt. While he was observing the effect of the battery's
fire, a shot from the Redan took off the head of the man on whose shoulder
Wood was resting his telescope, spraying the No. 1 of a neighbouring 32pr
with blood and brains. Fortunately for the rest of his crew, the No. 1 did not
flinch, as he was serving the vent of his gun. Calmly he wiped his face with

the spare left hand, checked with his No. 3 that the fresh charge was rammed home, and laconically gave the word to run out the gun.[42]

HMS *Rodney* landed 200 more sailors on 11 April, after another request from Lord Raglan. They took over ten guns in the Right Attack, bringing the naval contribution up to forty-nine, over a third of the guns in action. Midshipman William Kennedy was among the new arrivals:

> The next day [13 April] I had my first taste of the trenches: my turn for duty came on at 6 P.M., and I remained there till 9 P.M. on the following day – twenty-seven hours of the most miserable time I ever experienced. Sleep was out of the question, for I was running messages all through the night, and the shot, shell, and rifle-bullets flying about kept things lively. At day break the firing increased, and continued till sundown. One soon got used to it, but at first it was rather trying, and I expected to be killed any moment.[43]

Despite the reinforcements, it was evident after eight days that the Allies had again failed to establish sufficient advantage to justify an assault. Every day they achieved fire superiority, but the Russians replaced their damaged guns overnight. Allied *matériel* was giving problems:

> the supply of shot and shell for the heavy guns is so defective that most of them are left entirely without either. Our platforms are wearing away very fast, and most of the guns are beginning to run at the vents. I change such guns as I can obtain, and we do as well as we can.[44]

The brigade worked with their usual cheerfulness, but naval losses were disproportionately heavy: eighty-nine compared with 104 Royal Artillery.[45] Some observers put this down to 'skylarking' under fire, sailors jumping on the parapet to watch the effect of their shooting. Evelyn Wood denied that such behaviour was allowed. In his opinion the Right Attack had been too dangerous for civilian visitors, who based their stories on exaggerated second-hand reports. Wood attributed the navy's losses to its larger detachments, and the difficulties of hauling naval guns into firing position on their small-diameter trucks, compared with the army's more manageable field carriages.

On 17 April the attack was abandoned, while resources were collected for a renewed effort. Officers and midshipmen went off for a picnic and to play cricket at St George's Monastery, 'the one quiet spot accessible to fighting men where they could momentarily forget the painful scenes of their daily lives'.[46]

SUPERIORITY OF FIRE (JUNE–AUGUST 1855)

It was almost two months before operations resumed a level of violence comparable with the Second Bombardment. The British alone deployed 154 guns and mortars for the successful attacks on the Quarries and the Mamelon on 7 June, firing 32,883 rounds over five days. The Naval Brigade reached a peak strength of fifty-six guns, their fire achieving an intense fury that won horrified admiration: 'The sailors and gunners, rivalling each other in their exertions, worked the guns with almost incredible rapidity.'[47] The effect on the Russian infantry packed into the Redan was frightful, the setting sun lighting up the massed ranks through which the shells plunged, blowing the bodies of their victims high into the air.

On the 17th a Fourth Bombardment followed, this time to prepare what was expected to be the final blow against the Redan and Malakoff, leading to the fall of the city itself. Over two days 23,946 rounds were fired, twice the intensity of any previous bombardment, but both attacks failed. Among the casualties were Peel and Evelyn Wood, shot down leading a ladder party of sixty seamen. Bets had been laid at five-to-one against Wood's survival, but he escaped with his elbow smashed by case shot. Fifty-eight sailors were hit, and almost none of the attackers got further than the abattis along the near edge of the ditch.[48] The one exception was an Irish sailor, Michael Hardy, whose *sang-froid* while serving the vent of his 32pr had so impressed Wood. His body was found in an embrasure of the Redan next day during a truce for casualty evacuation. The most distinguished casualty of the assault was Lord Raglan who died ten days later worn out by disappointment and criticism. The Royal Navy that contributed so much to his last campaign provided a Royal Marine guard of honour for the cortège, the only infantry present. Picked sailors from the fleet lined the pier at Balaklava, unhitching the horses from the gun-carriage to wheel the coffin onto the pier.

The stress of the long siege told on the nerves of other combatants. The Revd Kelson Stothert returned to the Naval Brigade after a bout of cholera, and found it hard to adjust to trench life. He took comfort from the admission of even the most gallant officers that anxiety and suspense were never far from their minds. He himself was tired of the endless scene:

> of ruined walls and towers; shaken and scattered batteries; broken guns and shot; trenches hot and miserable, reticulating the face of the country; camps foul and filthy; swearing soldiers, drunken sailors, thieving merchant captains, lying newspaper reporters, putrid bullocks, dying horses, and burning heat;

He longed 'to look once more upon a man without a musket, a woman not drunk, a tree with leaves on it, [or] a church without shot holes in its roof'.[49] The sailors indulged in grim practical jokes, failing to warn newcomers of dangerous corners in the saps, and then picking the flattened Minié balls out of the parados, still hot. Bored with making gabions, they amused themselves by putting the empty ones over their heads, and running full tilt at one another. Sometimes the humour was very black. Captain Henry Keppel found a man in hospital carving a heart on a ring for his sweetheart, allegedly made from a section of his own thigh bone. Some found less macabre outlets for their skills, decorating their tents with strangely devised weathercocks and boards showing their ships' names. Off-duty sailors wandered about the soldiers' camps doing odd jobs, in return for grog, which they shared with the first 'soger' they met.

Casualties among the ratings were no longer replaced, although the Royal Marine Artillery from Marine Heights joined the Naval Brigade in time for the bombardment of 18 June, manning 13-inch sea-service mortars and 68pr guns. The Russians had despaired of taking Marine Heights by surprise, falling back across the Tchernaya River where they were watched by the Sardinian contingent. The Royal Marine battalion pushed forward on the extreme right to the village of Kamara, where headquarters reserved a flat stone for Sir Colin Campbell to sit and smoke his pipe. Naval Officers continued to volunteer for land service until the very end of the siege. Keppel himself transferred to *Rodney*, whose men were still ashore, as he saw little chance of action at sea. Lushington was promoted Rear-Admiral in July, prompting Lord Raglan's successor, General Sir James Simpson, to write to the Secretary of State for War, paying generous tribute to Lushington's personal ability, and to the services of the Brigade as a whole.[50]

THE FALL OF SEBASTOPOL (SEPTEMBER 1855)

By August the Allied trenches were so close to the Russian positions that sapping proceeded with the greatest difficulty. One sailor was hit, although not killed, by a Russian shot that penetrated the battery parapet, while the nights were too bright to allow much work. The French were so close that their sap appeared to touch the Malakoff. A Fifth Bombardment came and went with the expenditure of another 26,270 rounds. Although no immediate assault followed, Allied intelligence reported enormous casualties inside Sebastopol, often reaching a thousand a day, and great discontent among the defenders. Even the Russian high command admitted the city was untenable under the '*feu d'enfer*', which searched every street. By contrast the Royal Navy sustained sixty casualties during August 1855, half the level suffered during previous peaks of activity in April and June.[51]

Captain Keppel, now commander of the Naval Brigade, received a memorandum on 5 September, from the senior Allied engineer and artillery officers, detailing how the siege should be brought to an end. The French would launch the main attack against the Malakoff, with a subsequent British attack to fix the Russian reserves at the Redan. The moderate artillery fire that had succeeded the Fifth bombardment was proving ineffectual, so fire was to be resumed 'with warmth' for three days. The final assault would be on 8 September, the expenditure of ammunition being so regulated that only enough remained in the batteries for a heavy bombardment that morning. The Allies were short of guns and ammunition to the very end, the fleet landing 2,000 rounds of 8-inch ammunition for the final bombardment. Some 8-inch pieces were withdrawn altogether for want of ammunition, to be replaced by 32prs condemned in July as unsafe. Only three guns burst, despite their heavy use, one a grossly overworked 68pr 95cwt fired at extreme elevation, with disastrous results for its detachment. Of 140 32pr 46cwt guns used during the siege thirty-two were destroyed, and seventy-three condemned: an indication of the high attrition rate of *matériel* during the siege.[52]

The bombardment proceeded according to plan, as did the French assault on the Malakoff, which they attacked during the Russian rest hour at 11.30 a.m. When the rush for the Redan started, Keppel's seamen gunners wanted to take stakes from the gabions and join the infantry, as their own small arms had been left behind to deter such an attempt. Luckily they did not, as the Russians kept up a hail of grape shot, preventing supports reaching the handful of British infantry who entered the Redan. In the confusion the guns of the Right Attack ceased fire, but Keppel took the responsibility of directing his own guns to re-open, persuading a neighbouring battery of Royal Artillerymen to do likewise. Despite these efforts, superior masses of Russians drove out the surviving British infantry, and threw them back in hopeless confusion.

The French capture of the Malakoff, however, was decisive. That night, 8/9 September, the Russians withdrew across the harbour, blowing up their fortifications behind them. Even before the Russians were gone, Zouaves and bluejackets entered the city, staggering back with vast accumulations of worthless plunder. Lieutenant George Tryon, who drowned in the collision of HMS *Victoria* and *Camperdown* in 1893, met a group who had eluded the sentries:

decorated in the most extraordinary manner; one with a Russian helmet on, a woman's yellow petticoat with a coloured body, and cross belted all over, with high boots and spurs and swords and bayonets stuck in the gown to such an extent that made you fancy you had met a female war hedge-hog.[53]

Tryon himself got a Russian camp bed and a flag, but had to hand them over to Sir Edmund Lyons as souvenirs. Keppel went down to see the devastation for which he was partly responsible:

inspection of the evacuated forts showed how destructive had been the fire of our batteries, and how great a share the Naval Brigade had in the fall of Sebastopol. It is an immense place, but there was not a spot where our shot had not penetrated.[54]

The sudden end of the siege took most observers by surprise. In August the Admiralty had written to Lyons, urging timely preparation for a second winter in the Crimea. Their helpful suggestions about drainage, refuse disposal, and ventilation of huts contrast strangely with the Board's criticism of Dundas the previous autumn. Now they implicitly recognised the Naval Brigade's contribution to the campaign, admitting the indispensable necessity for General Simpson's complete concurrence in any measures adopted. A telegram to Lyons from the First Sea Lord dated 12 September reveals the same change in attitude, suggesting that, 'If the Generals have no objection you may re-embark the Naval Brigade.'[55]

That same day the Naval Brigade fired some of the last shots of the siege, from a captured 8-inch gun, against one of the few Russian warships still afloat in the harbour. The Brigade was broken up on 16 September, handing over their surviving guns to the Royal Artillery. Two regiments, the 14th and the 18th *Royal Irish*, sent their bands to play off the Naval Brigade, with no end of cheering, and, 'One more for Captain Kaple':

They then marched off with about twenty different colours flying – an English Jack almost too big to carry, white ensign, blue ensign over Russian pendants, and a Russian standard . . . of green silk, with a huge double-headed eagle on it.

Many of the men had Russian helmets and boots on, and some rejoiced in towering shakos, and nearly everyone had a bundle of Russian arms under his arm.[56]

The *Times* correspondent wrote, with his usual sourness, of the Naval Brigade's 'long, brilliant, and ill-requited services', but a flurry of congratulatory General Orders and Memoranda marked their departure. The first came from Sir Edmund Lyons, read out to the men by Keppel, and 'received by them in the most enthusiastic manner'. Most striking was the Admiralty's approval of the conduct of all ranks of the Royal Marine battalion, and especially of the Naval Brigade:

> That Brigade has shown the most cheerful endurance of the hardships and fatigues of the trenches, as well as the greatest skill and gallantry in working the guns, and bearing their part in the dangers of the advanced works in the assault on the enemy's lines.[57]

Such eulogies should not, for once, be dismissed as mere formalities. When the Naval Brigade regained their ships on 19 September 1855 they had defined a new role for the Royal Navy. The Royal Navy and Marines landed 4,469 officers and men, suffering 100 dead and 475 wounded, and winning thirteen *VC*s:

> Seldom before had the Navy had so much to do on land; and it seized the opportunity of making a new reputation for itself.[58]

Not only did the navy provide additional firepower for the siege and marines to defend the base at Balaklava, it brought a refreshing air of professional competence into a war not generally remembered for that quality. While over-worked soldiers died of hunger and exposure, the navy, used to working round the clock in severe conditions, fed its men hot cocoa, and dried their clothes. As a result of such commonsense measures, their overall mortality rate was a quarter of that among infantry units.[59] Young Turner contrasted the marines in their underground huts, always ready with the makings of a fire, with the hapless groups of soldiers, huddled under a few rocks trying to comfort each other, and collecting bits of sticks to boil some water. In the trenches the 'Naval Brigands' aroused the jealousy of the army's technical troops, as the 'only persons capable of "knocking about" the big guns', while Sir John Fortescue thought that if anyone could have reached the ditch of the Redan it was Peel's tiny group of ladder men.[60] Such remarkable skills on the battlefield and elsewhere would not be overlooked in any future imperial emergency.

CHAPTER TWO

India's Sunny Clime (1857–59)

THE 1850s were a period of crisis for the British Empire. Ill-sustained offensives in Burma, China, Russia, and Persia betrayed the imbalance between an aggressive foreign policy and inadequate military means. However, the most serious threat to British power came not from outside, but from within the Empire itself. Warning signs had not been wanting, but the sudden outbreak of the great sepoy revolt in India in 1857, with its massacres and attacks on cantonments, took everyone by surprise. Despite the notorious unreliability of the Bengal Native regiments, British troops had been withdrawn for campaigns elsewhere and never replaced, providing the rebels with their strategic opportunity. Fortunately, political and naval preparations for hostilities with China provided a sound basis for a prompt response to the emergency in Bengal. A senior political figure in the shape of Lord Elgin had gone out to Hong Kong to ensure a positive outcome to the Second China War after earlier British adventures in China. Among the forces sent to back him up were the brand-new fifty-one-gun steam frigate HMS *Shannon* and the twenty-one-gun steam corvette HMS *Pearl*. These ships would play a remarkable role in the suppression of the Mutiny, becoming household names in the process.

THE DELHI MARCH (JULY–AUGUST 1857)

The parts the two ships would play in the Mutiny were quite different: *Shannon* took the traditional role of augmenting the army's heavy artillery, while *Pearl* provided a complete army in miniature. The activities of the latter look forward to the subsequent use of Naval Brigades in Africa, and for a twentieth-century reader to more recent counter-insurgency campaigns. Captain Edward Sotheby of the *Pearl* was enjoying his first commission after four years on the beach. *Shannon*'s Commanding Officer was

Captain William Peel *VC*, his laurels fresh from the Crimea. Perhaps for this reason, the Shannons' exploits have overshadowed those of the *Pearl*'s Brigade.

Shannon and *Pearl* carried a remarkable group of memoirists, diarists, and letter writers, ranging from Sotheby himself to some of the best lower-deck witnesses of any Naval Brigade. This is fortunate as there are no official records for much of the *Shannon*'s period ashore.[1] No one, however, was expecting the orders that, on the evening of 16 July 1857, had both ships racing for Calcutta, more like Lord Elgin's private yachts than major units of the Royal Navy. Such was the urgency that both acted as troopers: *Shannon* took on board 300 Royal Marines at Hong Kong, while *Pearl* picked up three companies of the 90th Light Infantry at Singapore. Peel won the race, arriving at Calcutta on 8 August, having passed the word for every man to sharpen his cutlass.

The anxious European population of Calcutta cheered the arrival of the big ships in the Hooghly River. The original underestimate of the mutinous sepoys' capabilities had given way to panic as murder and arson swept across Oudh in June and July. Four hundred European women and children were massacred at Cawnpore the day before Elgin left Hong Kong in the *Shannon*, while the imminence of the great festival of Mohurrum fuelled fears of a rising in Calcutta itself. Even the level-headed Sir Colin Campbell, who took over as Commander-in-Chief in mid-August, thought that *Shannon* and *Pearl* had been 'as good as the right wing of an army', over-awing the city with their heavy guns.[2] Once the immediate panic had eased, plans matured for the Navy to take a more active part in suppressing the revolt. Sotheby remembered a conversation at dinner with Lord Canning, the head of the Indian Government:

> 'I hear, Captain Peel, that your band aboard the *Shannon* plays the *Sebastopol March.*' Peel answered, 'No, my lord, it now plays the *Delhi March.*' Upon which the Viceroy said to Peel, 'Will you come into my private room after dinner.' And in that room they planned to form a Naval Brigade to march to Delhi.[3]

For two months a small British force had been clinging to the ridge overlooking the ancient capital of India, but lacked guns heavy enough to breach the city's massive walls. The Commander-in-Chief of the Bengal Army had already recognised the potential value of a Naval Brigade equipped with the *Shannon*'s 68pr guns,[4] but it seems unlikely that a man of Peel's energy and expertise would have waited to be asked. Lieutenant Nowell Salmon wrote home before *Shannon* had moored off the Calcutta Esplanade that Lord Elgin had given Peel permission to form a Naval Brigade.

No time was lost. *Shannon's* hands were fell in on 11 August 1857, and the names called over of the men chosen to form the initial detachment. They went in their usual clothing, except for white cotton covers added to the sennet hats, with curtains over the back of the neck against the sun. Field equipment, such as waterbottles and haversacks, they acquired later, as the first stage of the Brigade's advance upcountry would be by river steamer. *Pearl's* Brigade set off some weeks after the *Shannon's*. They moved in a similar manner, forming two echelons. The captains commanded the first echelons, which included most of the marines and artillery, the first lieutenants taking the second. These were reinforced by merchant seamen enlisted in Calcutta, who turned out well, despite their lack of training. Lieutenant Vaughan of the *Shannon* displayed a particular knack for turning sailors of all sorts into well-drilled light infantry.

On 18 August Captain Peel embarked with nineteen officers, 380 sailors, and fifty marines in a river steamer and her tow, a flat-bottomed iron barge with a thatched roof, to the tune of 'Cheer, Boys, Cheer!'[5] The sailors formed three companies, among them Joseph Hoskins, an Ordinary Seaman 2nd Class, whose journal, for all its idiosyncratic spelling, records details neglected by more august witnesses:

the first company are men out of different tops in the ship. the second company his all the boats crews. the first and second have the short Minié rifle, the third company his all cutlass men as there was no more rifles in the ship (*sic*).[6]

The heavy ordnance included: ten 65cwt 8-inch shell guns with 400 rounds per gun; eight rocket tubes (four 24pr and four 12pr); and the ship's field guns, a 6pr gun and a 24pr howitzer. Lord Elgin gave an emotional farewell speech, saying that Captain Peel would lead them to honour and glory if anyone could, receiving 'three hearty British Seamanlike cheers' in return. Sotheby's first division left on 12 September with twelve officers, 106 seamen, and thirty-nine marines.[7] The marines had Minié rifles, for lack of modern Enfields, while the seamen made do with obsolete Brown Bess muskets or cutlasses. Their artillery was limited to a 12pr and 24pr howitzer, and a supply of rockets. A further 120 men set out from the *Shannon* on the 18th, and the final party of 100 Pearls on 12 October, after raiding the jails for time-expired convicts.

JOGGING ALONG UP-RIVER (SEPTEMBER–OCTOBER 1857)

The steamers' slow progress up the swollen Ganges was an anticlimax after the dash from Hong Kong, although there were plenty of signs of the war with bazaar rumours of planned risings, bungalows loopholed and barricaded, and broken telegraph wires. Sotheby arrested a Brahmin who sought to undermine the loyalty of his pilots by declaring the Company's Raj at an end. More serious problems came from steamers so under-powered they were lucky to make twenty miles a day against the 12-knot current. Often they ran aground, or blew out their boilers, the feedpipes choked with sand. Conditions on board varied: the *River Bird* was large, and comfortable, but the *Mirzapore* was 'a perfect floating pandemonium, as full as she could hold of boilers, engines, and mosquitoes'.[8] The men were ordered to keep out of the sun, or lose their grog, but sickness soon took its toll. Nine Shannons died during the two months after their departure, mostly from cholera, typhoid, and dysentery:

> on board of the steamers we have to drink the river water which his as red as mud can make it and worst of hit his all we can see dead bodies floating down every hour of the day only fancy just as you was drinking you cast your eyes on the river and then to see two or three dead bodies passing down with a crowd of crows flying after it why its enough to force one's insides up (*sic*).[9]

Rations were plentiful, despite Hoskins' grumbles about weevilly biscuit and mahogany beef:

> 1lb bread, 1 pint of tea for breakfast, dinner 1lb fresh meat, 1 pint soup, 1lb of vegetables and some boiled rice and 1 quart of Porter, very good. 4PM 1 pint of tea and at 7PM one drahm of rum.[10]

The last item caused trouble. *Shannon*'s Brigade had hardly started before Peel disrated the Captain of the Main Top after a row over a double ration of grog issued by mistake. Sotheby sent a drunken Midshipman back to Calcutta. A seaman was less lucky, receiving thirty lashes after several men had been drunk. In general, however, discipline was good. Peel was at pains to emphasise in his reports that no departure whatever was allowed from the ordinary rules and custom of the service. *Shannon*'s Brigade were not even allowed to grow their beards, making them an exception in a campaign notable for extravagant facial hair. Indian barbers charged four annas a month, about two pence, so a clean chin cannot have been too serious a hard-ship.

Pearl's chaplain, the Revd E.A. Williams, found the flooded banks of the Ganges a depressing sight, but there were palaces straight out of the Arabian Nights, in striking contrast to the poverty around them, and exotic animals: five-foot-long cobras, monkeys as big as four-year-olds, and jackals whose nocturnal howling prevented sleep. Water buffalo swam about near the riverside villages, taking flight when the riverboats blew off steam. Lieutenant Salmon admired the graceful attitudes of the women drawing water at the *ghats*, but was disappointed on closer inspection through his telescope. Further disappointment awaited him at Mirzapur, a town celebrated for its women, but he was too busy coaling ship to judge for himself.

Peel and Sotheby drilled their men on the flats twice daily; once before the sun became too hot, and again in late afternoon. Whenever possible everyone went ashore for light-infantry or field-gun drill. There was mus-ketry training 'with ball cartridge at a mark', and the field guns fired blanks. Bengali peasants proved shy in the face of informal target practice from the boats, taking cover when even a telescope was directed towards the bank.

The Naval Brigades concentrated during October, at a couple of for-tresses on the Ganges; *Shannon*'s at Allahabad, and *Pearl*'s at Buxar. The former was the main arsenal for Northern India, and the strategic base for projected operations in Oudh. On 3 October news came of the British capture of Delhi. Bowman feared this would relegate the Naval Brigade to a garrison role, but preparations for open warfare continued. Field carriages large enough for *Shannon*'s 8-inch guns were not available, so the naval guns went into store, to be replaced by standard army siege equipment: 24pr guns, and 8-inch howitzers. There were no ammunition waggons, the navy making do with country carts, known as hackeries.

Pearl's Brigade equipped themselves as a field battery, picking out the most horsey bluejackets for drivers. They had to learn the various evolutions expected of them, besides improvising harness for their horses which were quite unbroken, and carried away the traces when first hitched to the guns. The calibre of their guns reflected a more mobile role: two 12pr howitzers and two 12pr mountain-train howitzers in place of the ship's 24pr. The rest of the Pearls' transport was on a pack basis. Ordinary Seaman James Chappel described the disadvantages of this in his diary. Usually seamen's notebooks look much like any other exercise book, but Chappel's is clearly that of a sailor, with a roughly sewn oilskin cover and stained pages:

the only mode of conveyance we had was bullocks the baggage being slung across their backs and one native driver to each pair of bullocks and sorry marches we made of it for every twenty yards they would contrive to get the baggage off their backs and scamper across the fields and the driver after them, leaving everything lying about the road and our men would get excited and begin to thrash them which made matters still worse as they got sulky and done everything wrong.[11]

Both Brigades began the last stage of their approach to the combat zone in late October. The Mutiny was so widespread, and the sepoys' forces so fluid, that there never was a clear frontline. There were points where fighting flared, such as Delhi or Cawnpore, with large concentrations of regular troops on both sides. In other areas there was sporadic guerrilla warfare, looting, and a general settling of old scores, sponsored by discontented land-owners or bandits profiting from the general breakdown of law and order. In other areas there was no trouble at all. Indeed, without the help of loyal Indian troops from the Madras and Bombay Presidencies, and new regi-ments from the Punjab, the British could never have mastered the rising in Bengal. Among the loyal native units were Gurkha regiments from the friendly kingdom of Nepal who moved into the provinces north-east of the Gogra River. Except for Sotheby's command, there were no European troops to support them, so *Pearl*'s Brigade moved back down the Ganges to its confluence with the Gogra. Sotheby's 2nd division arrived on 7 November, *Pearl*'s Brigade concentrating, 250 strong, at the town of Siwan. They were the only British troops north of the Gogra.

Shannon's Brigade were to play a key role in dramatic events at Lucknow, the capital city of Oudh. Here, a handful of Europeans had been under siege since July. In September a relieving column had fought its way into the besieged enclave at the Residency, but could not get out again. Sir Colin Campbell's first operational task as Commander-in-Chief was to bring off the beleaguered garrison and the large number of women and children trapped with them. On 27 and 28 October two companies of Peel's men set off along the Grand Trunk Road for Cawnpore, the forming-up point for what would be known as the 2nd Relief of Lucknow.

Marches of twelve to fifteen miles a day left the sailors dreadfully foot-sore. Early-morning starts at 2 a.m. were cold enough for overcoats, but the rising sun soon had everyone bathed in sweat and white dust, marching along like so many millers. Sometimes the Highlanders' bagpipes struck up, or else the sailors' old windlass tunes and forecastle ditties rang out incon-gruously amid the jungles. When the sun became too hot for marching there was an inter-service race to pitch the tents, followed by breakfast of fried beef, and a siesta. The enforced inactivity during the heat of the day may explain the number of diaries kept. Everyone fell in at 5 p.m. after cleaning their arms, for an inspection and the day's grog, turning in at seven. Nowell Salmon enjoyed the rough work and good-fellowship of campaigning, with mounted expeditions into nearby villages for fresh mutton, eggs, and milk. He took his revolver, but had yet to see anything of the enemy. However, the Shannons' three-month approach march was about to reach a dramatic conclusion.

KHUJWA (1 NOVEMBER 1857)

During the afternoon of 31 October, reports came in that 4,000 rebels had crossed the Jumna, threatening the small British garrison at Fatehpur. The column moved off to forestall them, reaching Fatehpur at midnight. Learning that the rebels were twenty-four miles ahead at the village of Khujwa, Colonel Powell of the 53rd Foot pushed on with 500 men, after an uncomfortable night without tents. His force included 103 marines and sailors serving as small-arms men, their heavy guns left behind with the balance of the Naval Brigade, the sick, and 150 soldiers.[12]

Contact was made at 2 p.m., 1 November. The rebels occupied a strong position behind an embankment, their guns sweeping the road along which the British had to come. Exhausted, and outnumbered eight to one, the British attacked at once, lines of skirmishers and supports screening the advance of the main body. Kept in reserve at first, the Naval Brigade edged to the right through the cornfields beyond the road, arriving on the enemy position just as Colonel Powell was shot through the head among the enemy guns. Peel took command, as senior officer surviving. He displayed more tactical sense than his predecessor, leaving Lieutenant Hay RN to consolidate, while turning the end of the embankment with whatever fresh troops came to hand. By 4.30 p.m. they had driven the enemy from the position, killing 300 rebels and taking two guns. The Commander-in-Chief commented on the providential non-arrival of the rebel cavalry: 'Had they done so, not a man of the detachment would have escaped to tell the tale.'[13] Sir Colin felt that Powell, despite his glorious death, had put the siege train at risk.

His further remarks on the misuse of specialist Engineers as skirmishers echo Admiralty criticism of the misuse of irreplaceable seamen in the trenches of Sebastopol. Campbell's comments might have applied with equal force to the Naval Brigade's assault role at Khujwa where they were lucky to escape with fifteen casualties from an action where a fifth of the force were lost.[14] Peel and his men had no business taking part in chance encounters, when escorting guns and ammunition vital for the Relief of Lucknow.

Peel could be pleased with the conduct of his Brigade in its first action, however: 'a soldier's fight if ever there was one'.[15] They arrived back at Fatehpur in high spirits, despite marching seventy-two miles in three days, and fighting a battle in between. The Brigade had boosted their own morale, and established a rapport with the infantrymen of the little force, charging with the 93rd's skirmishers: 'every bluejacket picking out his own acquaintances to fight with'.[16] Even the Admiralty hastened to express their satisfaction that the *Shannon*'s Brigade 'has had opportunity to share in the arduous services which the existing state of affairs in India has called for from all Her Majesty's subjects'.[17]

IN RELIEF OF LUCKNOW (NOVEMBER 1857)

The whole pace of the *Shannon*'s campaign now accelerated. Within days of Khujwa Ordinary Seaman Hoskins and his mates were dragging their 24prs over the bridge of boats at Cawnpore, bound for Lucknow. Campbell had to extricate Lucknow's garrison before powerful rebel forces in his rear could strike at his communications. Leaving 500 men at Cawnpore, Campbell had 4,500 for the relief, a strong force by Mutiny standards, but outnumbered eight to one by an enemy holding strong defensive positions, with plenty of artillery. If Sir Colin were to succeed without disproportionate losses, he would have to make full use of the Naval Brigade's guns to clear the way for his infantry.

On 10 November the Shannons were distributed as follows:
– 240 at Allahabad as garrison, or in hospital.
– 50 at Cawnpore under Lieutenant Hay, as garrison artillery.
– 100 under Lieutenant Vaughan sent ahead with Sir Colin, reinforced by 120 more under Lieutenant Young, with Peel in overall command.[18]

The latter formed part of the siege train with six 24pr guns, two 8-inch howitzers, and some infernal machines made by lashing four rocket tubes onto a hackery. The Marine detachment escorted the guns, acting impartially as gunners and sharpshooters, although contemporary illustrations never showed them at Lucknow. In his retirement Sergeant William Turner RMLI collected oral accounts from other veterans. Among them was seventy-five-year-old Henry Derry, a colourful source of information about the Naval Brigade at Lucknow, although a little confused over details:

You see, chum, I can't separate we Joeys from the Jacks, nor the Jacks from we Joeys, so we get lost in the Naval Brigade . . . There were 140 reds and 15 blues, and every man had to pull his pound. We had to land a siege train and 68prs and it was no joke to move about with rafts, but by Jove they were stubborn customers over soft ground. We had to be our own horses and bullocks and face the fiddle and enemy too, I can tell you in a blazing sun. There was no galloping away with our guns like the soldiers did. We had to stick to them under all conditions.[19]

Before leaving Cawnpore, there was an opportunity to see the Yellow Bungalow, where Nana Sahib held 400 British women and children prisoner, before their massacre on 15 July. Years later Arthur O'Leary of East St Louis, Illinois, once a member of *Shannon*'s 2nd company, still recalled, 'History scratched upon the walls by the wives and daughters of the 32nd', which would never be erased from his memory.[20] Crimean veterans compared the battered Wheeler Barracks unfavourably with Sebastopol:

> every part of the building shows marks of shot and bullets, altogether it presents an awful looking place to look at . . . the rebels must have been devils in human form to hammer away at such a small building as they did but they will pay for it when we march on Lucknow.[21]

They were already paying: sepoy outrages provoked reprisals which would cast a dark shadow over Anglo-Indian relations. Prisoners were rare, and soon polished off:

> there his not much fuss about hanging a few blacks here, they mount the drop and the rope his put over their head and the stanchion under the drop his withdrawn and of they are swung . . . they cannot afford to cut the rope at there his hangings here nearly every day.[22]

Sir Colin spoke to each regiment, before launching his drive on Lucknow. He gave the Naval Brigade 'a first rate speech about Jack's bravery and the name that the Navy had got', receiving four cheers in return.[23] That evening there were orders to make up heavy marching order, with thirty rounds per man, and a shift of clothing rolled in a blanket. Four months after leaving Hong Kong the Naval Brigade were about to close with the enemy. The first objective was the Dilkusha, or Heart's Delight, a walled garden on the outskirts of Lucknow. Here they left the baggage, the rest of the force pushing on towards the Martinière, a palace named after a French officer who had once served the King of Oudh. Hoskins' account of the ensuing assault demonstrates the close cooperation between the gunners and their accompanying infantry, marred on this occasion by an unfortunate accident:

> we unlimbered and soon commenced playing long ball with them [i.e. the rebels]. the 93rd Highlanders and 53rd were drawn up in rear ready for a charge we loaded the eight guns and charged the three rocket tubes the Captain gave the word fire and the troops charged through our guns.

Just as they did so:

> one of the guns went off killing one bluejacket and wounding two others and also wounding one of the 93rd. it appears that the gun hung fire and in the confusion and smoke the men went up to the muzzle and the gun went off killing No. 3 on the spot and wounding No. 4 and also the man that was serving the vent.[24]

None the less the 93rd took their objective, and the Naval Brigade slept by their guns, firing occasional shots to discourage counter-attacks. Next day they buried their dead, drank the three drams of rum issued for each day spent under fire, and went sightseeing, while the army mounted diversions on the west of the city. On 16 November the men rolled up their blankets horse-collar fashion, and with two days food in their haversacks moved off in the other direction to attack the Secunderbagh, a fortified enclosure blocking the indirect route to the Residency. Under sporadic sniper fire, and pausing only to shoot a rocket into some rebel cavalry, the Brigade pressed on, until heavy firing was heard just beyond some trees to the front. The covering party of small-arms men cleared the copse, for the guns to hurry up the lane to the Secunderbagh. Here they unlimbered at eighty yards range with enemy bullets pattering on their iron tyres, and set to work breaching the south-east corner. The first shots passed through the wall as if it were made of cloth, without bringing down any of the brickwork, but after half an hour large blocks of bricks and mortar began to fall out, leaving wide gaps. Behind the guns the Highlanders and Brasyer's Sikhs had been waiting under cover, and now they stormed into the Secunderbagh, killing every one of its two thousand defenders. Hoskins did not stop long when he went to look around the building, for all his wish to make the sepoys pay.

The day's business was not yet concluded. The great Shah Najif Mosque still barred access to the Residency, so the seamen and Highlanders seized the 24prs' drag ropes and hurried them forward in the teeth of a perfect hail of lead and iron:

> a poor sailor lad just in front of me, had his leg carried clean off above the knee by a round shot, he sat bolt upright on the grass with the blood spouting from the stump of his limb like water from the hose of a fire engine and shouted, 'Here goes for a shilling a day, a shilling a day! Pitch into them, boys, pitch into them. Remember Cawnpore, 93rd, remember Cawnpore! Go at them my hearties!'[25]

Sir Colin Campbell thought it was an action almost unexampled in war: 'Captain Peel behaved very much as if he had been laying the Shannon alongside an enemy's frigate.'[26] 'It's no use', Henry Derry recalled him saying, 'unless we are close up, we must bring the whole place about our ears and then get to close quarters.' Marines and Highlanders did their best to keep down the enemy fire with their own rifles, but Hoskins thought the Shah Najif was the worst moment of his active service:

> It was in this place and on this memorable day that I became acquainted with the horrors of war and the dreadful scenes of a battlefield. the wounded and dead on both sides was laying around in all directions, our other four guns was busily engaged in firing on some old mud huts which was full of men. the shot was flying in all directions and as thick as hail, lucky for us that they were not good marksmen or else we should have rued the day that we engaged them so close.[27]

The result of the day was still in doubt after three hours. Warning orders were given to retire, when Peel brought up his infernal machine to send a salvo of rockets through the crowd on the ramparts, allowing the 93rd and Sikhs to force their way in. Next day the last rebel positions before the Residency fell, the 90th Light Infantry linking up with their besieged comrades at 3 p.m.

Campbell was not yet strong enough to clear the entire city, so he employed a well thought out deception plan to cover the evacuation of the garrison to Cawnpore. Naval guns kept up a constant fire as if preparing for a further advance, while the women and children crept away behind canvas screens hung between the buildings. On 23 November the last of the garrison left the Residency, followed by the Naval Brigade:

our first gun was fired off and limbered up and the bullocks shackled in and it moved off down the road to the Dilkusha. the other guns were limbered up and sent off one by one the last keeping up as sharp a fire as possible to make the rebels believe that all the guns were still there.[28]

Three days later they were all back at the Alambagh, south-east of Lucknow, on the road to Cawnpore. A rebel 24pr known as 'Nancy Dawson' kept the camp under harassing fire, but on 26 November the Brigade paraded 'cleaned in whites with our arms', to be praised for their exertions, and to hear the names of four recommended for the *VC*. These included Nowell Salmon, who had shinned up a tree with a rifle to deal with a sepoy throwing hand grenades, before being shot through the thigh himself. Two more went to Lieutenant Young and William Hall, a black sailor, who had manned a gun ten yards from the Shah Najif wall, amidst splinters sent flying by their own fire. Sergeant Forbes Mitchell of the 93rd provides impartial testimony to the navy's contribution, listing the navy and Royal Artillery among the corps he felt had done most of the work. Together they suffered losses second only to his own corps.[29] Two days of forced marches back to Cawnpore followed the parade; a nightmare for the wounded, 'jolted along in a dooley (*sic*) about twenty paces at a time and then grounded with a jerk'.[30] The Brigade encamped within sight of the lights of Cawnpore late on the 28th, so tired they 'stretched the tents out on the ground, had one drahm of rum and then laid on the tents drawing the curtains over us'.[31]

CRISIS AT CAWNPORE (NOVEMBER–DECEMBER 1857)

Fifty seamen had stayed at Cawnpore as garrison artillery, when Peel set off for Lucknow. This included his broken-hearted ADCs, Midshipmen Lascelles and Watson, whom he considered too young to go on so desperate an enterprise. As it turned out they would have quite enough excitement. Tantia Topi, the only effective Indian leader to emerge from the Mutiny, advanced on Cawnpore with 20,000 men as soon as Campbell had departed for Lucknow. General Wyndham, left in command, went out to meet Tantia, but was too weak to follow up an initial success on 26 November. Next day he brought up the Naval battery from Cawnpore with two 24pr siege guns to counter Tantia's long-range guns. The detachments were enjoying breakfast by the roadside, when the general alarm sounded:

you never saw such a race and scramble, soldiers rushing for their arms and belts, sailors running to their guns, cavalry saddling horses, and the deuce's own hubbub. We were the first ready, loaded our guns and limbered up for advancing. Just as we were all ready, the noon gun fired in the entrenched camp in the town, and it was answered all around us in every direction by a volley of artillery from the enemy, not very far off. Never were any fellows more surprised.[32]

The force deployed around a crossroads, surrounded by jungle, the Brigade unharnessing their bullocks to engage a hostile gun 800 to 1,000 yards further down the Kalpi Road:

No sooner had the smoke cleared off than a kind of murmur ran round the men, 'Here's one for us!' and they were not far wrong, for immediately we saw a cloud of white smoke from our adversary's gun . . . The shot knocked up the dust about two hundred yards in front of us, and came tearing along at a tremendous pace right between our two guns. Luckily no one was standing in the way, or they would have been eased of their legs very quickly.[33]

The Naval Brigade silenced their immediate opponents, but were in a trap. Showers of grapeshot poured in from rebel guns hidden in the woods on both flanks, and even to the rear, roundshot 'bounding along at a furious rate, sometimes right over our heads, knocking down trees and cutting off branches'.[34] A shell burst over the guns, stampeding the bullocks and their terrified drivers:

The niggers were perfectly mad with fright. Our men rushed back and tried to stop them, officers came out with their swords, and did all in their power to stop them but it was no good. Some of the bullocks had their ears and horns cut off with the shot and were frantic with pain, and this combined with the beating and yelling of their frightened drivers made them quite dangerous to go near.[35]

The whole British line gave way in confusion. Only the steadiness of three companies of the Rifle Brigade gave the sailors time to catch enough bullocks to extricate their guns. One joined the Rifles to cover the retreat, while the other went ahead, only to capsize in Cawnpore's narrow streets, jammed with guns, riderless horses, bullocks and men, all trying to make their way back to the entrenched camp by the bridge of boats. Piles of kit and stores lay about, including casks of beer and wine, somehow broached by the disbanded soldiery.

The sailors remained sober in this moment of crisis, manning the guns around the camp's perimeter with native Madras gunners who had survived the action at the cross roads and some 'sheikhs', by which Watson seems to mean Sikh infantrymen. A grapeshot wounded Lieutenant Hay in the stomach, so Mr Garvey (Acting Mate) took over. A Commander Rowley Lambert RN, who just happened to be in Cawnpore sightseeing, goodnaturedly lent him a hand. Later that night Garvey was awakened and sent to bring in the lost 24pr: 'an ugly job'. Soldiers escorted the native guide, '"at full cock" ready to blow his brains out', but he led them faithfully to the missing gun. Sentries were posted, and the sailors went silently to work:

> Not a man spoke above his breath, and each stone was laid down quietly. When we thought we had cleared enough, I ordered the men to put their shoulders to the wheels and gun, and when all was ready, and every man had his pound before him, I said 'heave' and up she righted.[36]

Next day Tantia pressed his advantage, bottling up the British, and floating fire rafts down against the bridge of boats, across which help must come. The rebel artillery fired with unusual precision, hitting the field hospital, and nearly knocking Watson's head off with a near miss that sent him sprawling into a pile of bayonets.

The return of Sir Colin Campbell relieved the pressure. The Naval Brigade deployed three 24prs and a howitzer to fire across the Ganges to clear the bridge of boats, aiming by the bonfires of abandoned British baggage. Peel rode across the bridge with his other guns on the afternoon of 29 November, a welcome surprise for the demoralised garrison. Rebel guns were still firing into the camp with uncomfortable accuracy, so the Brigade set about counter-battery work with three guns. Peel took the rest into Cawnpore to mix it with the rebels, as he had done at Lucknow – using the 24prs as lesser gunners might use field pieces. The inhabitants had vanished, leaving the city deserted except for sepoys:

> We saw from the smoke where the enemy were, and fired a rocket right into the middle of them. This seemed to surprise them very much, and their musketry slackened for a minute or so, but not for long as they had seen where our rocket came from, and down came a tremendous shower of bullets, quite like a storm of hail; luckily there was a kind of shed place which was roofed, and we got under it for the time, the bullets whistling

past and spattering down over our heads. Every now and then two or three of us jumped out and fired one of our rockets and then popped into our shed again, however we fired the rockets so fast at last that they did not seem at all to appreciate it and their fire slackened very much.[37]

This gave Peel the chance to deal with an enemy gun firing down the street, in a manner that demonstrates the Brigade's confidence in themselves, and their weapons:

> one gun was unlimbered and loaded and the muzzle pointed down the street. the drag ropes were hooked onto the axle trees and all the men ran the gun down the street to within three hundred yards of the enemy's gun.[38]

They despatched the rebel gun with four rounds, but found they had bitten off more than they could chew: a shell took off the legs of two sailors and wounded another, the marine sharpshooters in their red tunics got a good peppering, while the covering party of 'sheikhs' took a dozen casualties. The rebels even dragged away their own disabled gun with a bit of rope, so, after sharing tiffin with the troops, the Naval Brigade returned frustrated to camp.

The next few days saw a lull, as Campbell awaited reinforcements. The naval gunners organised themselves into regular reliefs, and began to get the upper hand over the rebel gunners, returning fire whenever provoked, and not giving in until their opponents fell silent. Refugees and wounded streamed over the bridge of boats to go downcountry. Only the worst cases travelled in ambulances. The rest went in hackeries, 'the most primitive conveyance in the world ... tied together with grass ropes', and drawn by bullocks so recalcitrant that fires had to be lit under them before they would move. Some even lacked a thatched roof to protect the wounded from the fierce Indian sun on the 120-mile journey to Allahabad.[39]

Sir Colin Campbell lost no time in settling accounts with Tantia, once relieved of his humanitarian concerns. The naval cooks prepared two days meat on 5 December, a sure prelude to action, and next day the army marched out to attack the rebels' right wing south of Cawnpore. The Naval Brigade led with four heavy guns and two rocket tubes, followed by two more heavy guns of the Royal Artillery, and then the rest of the army. The enemy appeared surprised, allowing the British to advance to within 800 yards before opening fire from their positions along the Ganges Canal. The Naval Brigade wheeled their heavy guns alongside the skirmishers, as if they had been light field pieces, the rest of the force in a long line, a few hundred yards to the rear. Soon the enemy fire became very hot indeed, wounding several sailors, who became impatient:

> By the time we had reached the canal, Peel's Bluejackets were calling out 'Damn these cow-horses' – meaning the gun bullocks – 'they're too slow! Come, you 93rd, give us a hand with the drag ropes as you did at Lucknow!'[40]

A company of Highlanders slung their rifles and dashed to the sailors' assistance, while the pipes struck up 'The Battle of the Alma', the closest musical allusion they could make to the cooperation of Highlanders and Royal Navy in the Crimea. The rebels could not stand the combined fire of artillery and Enfield rifles. They fairly ran away, pursued at the double by Highlanders, the Naval Brigade still dragging the guns forward in case the enemy should rally. Garvey's battery inside Cawnpore had contributed a heavy bombardment to fix the centre of the rebel army, firing seventy-five rounds per gun in just over an hour:

> At 10 a.m. an order came from Sir Colin to blaze away from every gun and keep it up. We took our time from the right, and such a crash of artillery you never heard, houses fell, trees disappeared, and the air rang again with the whistling of shot, fizzing of shells, etc. It was noble fun.[41]

The enemy defeat was total, cavalry chasing them thirteen miles down the Kalpi Road. The next day, 7 December, was marked by a return to daily Manual and Platoon Exercise and by a hunt for rebels disguised as civilians. Watson's moustachioed servant of sepoy-like bearing was nearly shot by mistake, although Campbell discouraged indiscriminate reprisals, sentencing the whole camp to muster every half an hour for ill-using Indian civilians. Peel enforced naval discipline firmly. Some of the men left at Allahabad found their own way to the front, believing the Captain would admire their keenness, only to be arrested and sent back again. On 12 December the Naval Brigade received proper reinforcements: ninety men of the 1st company and the band, 'a great acquisition'. They were now concentrated, ready to take part in Campbell's drive through the country between the Ganges and Jumna rivers, to restore communications between Calcutta and Delhi.

ALONG THE GOGRA (NOVEMBER 1857–MARCH 1858)

While *Shannon's* Naval Brigade were in the eye of the storm around Lucknow and Cawnpore, Captain Sotheby's force from HMS *Pearl* had yet to make contact with the enemy. His men despaired of ever seeing a mutineer at all. In their isolated post at Mirwa, beyond the Gogra River, in what is now Uttar Pradesh, they felt they had been brought upcountry for nothing, left in the background with no chance of a crack at the rebels.

Taking no chances, the little force entrenched themselves in a mango tope, with rifle pits and dummy guns to impress the spies that swarmed in the bazaar. Training continued apace, with live musketry practice after morning prayers:

> We set to work, formed our force in fighting order, and drilled like the devil, morning and night; marched out to practise the men, and got them into the ways of battalion drill: in fact turned the British tar into a soldier.[42]

The Brigade formed the nucleus of a miniature army, the Saran Field Force, under overall command of a Colonel Rowcroft. A Gurkha regiment joined the Brigade on 1 December. Their appearance was not 'strikingly Hyde Park', but Sotheby found them 'a fine set of thick strong short men'. Their crooked knives or kukris achieved an instant and enduring popularity as souvenirs. Apart from cold steel, the Gurkhas had matchlock muskets, discharged haphazardly at forty-five degrees elevation. Fifty armed Sikh police completed the force, after a flying column of bluejackets and Gurkhas rescued them from a mob. The reinforcements were timely, for on 18 December 6,000 rebels bore down on Mirwa. The Saran Field Force was only 750 strong,[43] so Rowcroft withdrew across the River Dyerai and dug in: 'having no prospect of a plum pudding, Jack jocularly expressed his disappointment at not having a "sea-pie"' instead.[44] The arrival of another 450 Gurkhas on Christmas Day changed all that, Rowcroft moving out at 8 a.m. on 26 December to meet the rebels seven miles away at Soanpur.

The battle foreshadowed many that the *Pearl's* Brigade would fight over the next year. Time and again, they faced overwhelming numbers of rebels, driving them off by resolute offensive action. At 10 a.m. the Field Force came upon the enemy and formed line, the four 12pr howitzers in the centre, with a Gurkha regiment on each flank. Marines and Sikhs skirmished in advance with their rifles, a couple of companies of Gurkhas in reserve. James Chappel described the action that followed:

The enemy opened the ball by firing two guns which were quickly returned by shell, and then the first field fight that I saw in India commenced. They then under cover of the jungle shifted their guns on our left flank and at the same time made a movement to cut off our baggage in the rear, but their designs in this quarter were frustrated by two companies of Gurkhas and the Sikhs.[45]

The rebels seemed to expect a straightforward frontal attack and were nonplussed when the British failed to cooperate. Still at long range, Rowcroft changed front to put pressure on the rebel flank. His Marine and Sikh skirmishers got well up to them, while the 12prs made splendid practice, knocking one Rajah clean off his elephant at 800 yards:

In the meantime the enemy on our right was not idle for under cover of the jungle they drew up in line and advanced upon our right flank which again made us change our front, but when we got our guns to bear on them they retreated in confusion and we advanced upon their camp where we found plenty of rice and sugar and all sorts of provisions lying on the ground which made a grand haul for our coolies and bullock drivers.[46]

The British had no cavalry, so the rebels escaped lightly: 'If we had been a little quicker', thought Sotheby, 'we might have destroyed the whole party.'[47] The Sikhs took a gun and two tumbrils full of ammunition, promptly pressed into service. Shells and rifles had kept the rebels at a respectful 400 yards, so British losses were slight. Sotheby thought it, 'a perfect miracle how the skirmishers and gunners escaped for the shot flew about in all directions, but much too high'.[48] The little victory was 'not a very worthy engagement', only 1,200 real sepoys being present, but it was politically valuable.[49] The local Rajah, threatened by the rebels, welcomed the troops. Villagers brought water to slake thirsts aroused by ten hours marching and fighting under an Indian sun. They too had suffered at the hands of their countrymen, and were glad to make friends with the winners, who paid for what they took. The rebel defeat restored confidence in British rule across a wide area between the Gogra and Nepal. Disaffected zemindars began to pay their rent, and the fertile district of Saran was spared a good looting.

Not everyone was pleased to see the British, who blew away seven sepoys from fields guns, and hanged eight more, after explaining to the Gurkhas that this was not the usual British way with prisoners of war. A number of villages known to have supported the wrong side at Soanpur were burnt, the inhabitants having an hour to clear out:

It was rather pitiable to see these people wandering out into the open, some carrying a charpoy, others limping along with all the goods and chattels they could collect in that short hour. I felt sorry for them; but it was a regular 'budmash' (rebel) village and its destruction richly deserved.[50]

Early in the New Year gunfire to the north, around Gorakhpur, announced the approach of an allied Gurkha Army, led by the Nepalese Prime Minister Jang Bahadur. They were bound for Sir Colin Campbell's offensive at Lucknow, but had to cross the Gogra River first. The river steamer *Jumna* was at Gopalpur ready to escort boats for a floating bridge fifty miles upriver to the Gurkhas, but rebel bands roamed the banks, which bristled with antique fortresses. The talents of a Naval Brigade might have been designed to resolve such a difficulty. Sotheby manned the flotilla with some Gurkhas, the Sikh police, and 145 of his own men, in the hope that 'the sailors would then be in their element, and in the event of their getting into difficulty, would no doubt be well able to get out of it'.[51] They set off on 13 February, tracking the boats upstream against the wind, cables constantly fouling one another. The bamboo and prickly pear on the river banks provided good cover for an ambush, so the *Jumna* was barricaded, with riflemen ready to open fire. However, much to Sotheby's surprise he made his rendezvous with the Gurkha Army on 19 February 1858.

Local rebels were dealt with in the usual expeditious manner at Phulpur, the British force advancing so quickly that the rebel gunners lost the range, and fired harmlessly overhead. The brunt of the fighting fell upon the Naval Brigade and the Indian troops whom they had grown to trust since Soanpur. The new Gurkhas were less satisfactory. They disappeared when the firing began, returning to claim several guns taken by the marines and Sikhs as their own trophies. Then the Naval Brigade turned to as engineers, bridging the Gogra with the boats brought from Gopalpur. The cool winter weather was over; the temperature in the nineties. Flies became troublesome, and the sick list grew to thirty, Sotheby supposed from exposure to the night air.

The Naval Brigade were first across the new bridge, back to the north side of the river, for they were not to go down to Lucknow. Chappel's journal reflects the disgust of the ordinary seamen at their subordinate role, containing the rebels still at large beyond the Gogra:

Since we left the Chupra we have been in five engagements took fifteen guns with ammunition camps and baggage, two forts at the point of the bayonet and have undergone every sort of privation and fatigue without complaint while our numbers were very inadequate to the work we had to perform. and although we have done our best our services are hardly recognised while the hordes under the command of Jung Bahadur who have done little or nothing have been praised and applauded to the skys (*sic*).[52]

The Pearls were on excellent terms with the Sikhs and Gurkhas of the field force, but the arrival of 200 sabres of the Bengal Yeomanry cavalry relieved an understandable sense of cultural isolation. Even trusted allies looked askance at the beef that formed the Europeans' staple diet. A further accession of strength was the acquisition of Enfield rifles for all the sailors, who practised judging distances to exploit the range of their new weapons.

The renamed Gorakhpur Field Force soon had to fight for their lives again, as several of the swell rebel Rajahs turned out in force. Rowcroft dug in at Amorha, using elephants like bulldozers, to clear the field of fire. When the crisis came on 5 March 1858, however, he took the offensive. To make the most of his small force, Rowcroft formed it in a single shallow line, one rank deep, with no supports at all. As at Soanpur, the Naval Brigade took the centre with their guns, with Gurkhas on either side, but this time there were cavalry squadrons on both flanks, promisng a more decisive outcome to the encounter.[53] Outnumbered ten-to-one, the British advanced steadily, cheering along the line, while some well-directed shells sent the Rajahs' elephants roaring to the rear. The rebel artillery opened fire at 1,500 yards, outranging the short 12pr howitzers used by the British, but doing little damage to the extended line beyond repeated hits on the guns and limbers in the centre. Sotheby thought there were enough rebels to swallow up his little force, while his men were puzzled by the collapse of 'those rascals': '"If they would only come on with sticks they would beat us."'[54] Rowcroft's 1,261 men routed 4,000 well-trained sepoys and swarms of irregulars, killing or wounding 500 of them for the loss of four killed: three Gurkhas and Mr Fowler the Second Master, who had piloted the *Jumna* through the shoals of the Gogra.[55] For all their bravado the rebel force had been ill-led, with no system of fighting, and a record of previous defeats:

> Many of the sepoys had come over from Oudh. There they had been thoroughly thrashed; and they fought us that day with their tails between their legs.[56]

The Field Force were in the highest possible spirits, despite their exertions in a temperature of 89 degrees. The Gurkhas said that Rowcroft's lucky star brought certain victory for few losses. The Europeans also acknowledged divine assistance, with a thanksgiving service next morning. Amorha completed the equipment of the naval field battery. Limbers and ammunition wagons were captured in abundance, and the best ones adapted 'by the incessant industry of Mr Burton, the ship's carpenter'.[57] The victory drew the tiger's teeth, the rebels losing so many guns that they never took the field in such strength again. The Pearls would see much hard service, but their war became one of detachments, as the rebels tried to use the climate and superior numbers to wear down their opponents in a guerrilla war.

UNFINISHED BUSINESS (JANUARY–MARCH 1857)

While *Pearl's* Brigade chased rebels across Uttar Pradesh, accompanied by their mobile gallows, the Shannons were playing a similar rôle in Oudh. On Christmas Eve 1857 Sir Colin Campbell set out to scour the country between Cawnpore and Futtehghur, as a preliminary to his final drive on Lucknow. Futtehghur was the East India Company's main centre for the manufacture of gun-carriages, so it might provide the means for Peel to bring into action the 68pr guns left at Allahabad. The march to Futtehghur provided more immediate excitement. There was a pause at the Kali Naddi River on 1 January 1858, to mend the suspension bridge. Next day the rebels came down to attack an isolated detachment of naval artillery covering the repair work. One rebel gun was particularly annoying, concealed behind the corner of a house. Lieutenant Vaughan laid one of the 24prs under Peel's direction, his first shot striking the roof of the house, his second the angle of the wall, and his third dismounting the rebel piece. Two more rounds blew up the limber, and the 53rd Regiment clinched the affair by charging without orders, which precipitated the usual panic amongst the rebels. So rapid was the pursuit that when the Brigade came to pitch camp that evening:

> no baggage or provisions had arrived, except the spirits, a cask of which is carried on some old limbers and, under charge of two old quartermasters, is always foremost in the field or the march; we were each glad to drink our day's double allowance, and even Captain Peel, who rarely drinks spirits, tossed off with gusto the abominable arrack that is served out in lieu of rum.[58]

The local people at Futtehghur brought out milk and fruit for the victors, who sent off punitive columns accompanied by detachments of naval artillery. At Mhow they hanged 127 'rebels' from one tree. Edmund Verney, recently arrived from Allahabad, objected to reprisals:

> this is a war in which the worst passions are likely to be excited, and without doubt dreadful scenes have been enacted; but I have heard of great cruelties being perpetrated by our people during some of the sieges in Spain and elsewhere, and yet we claim to be the most enlightened nation in the world.[59]

He felt the Mutiny had been provoked by English contempt for the native Indians, especially among those who had done well out of the sub-continent. He thought it was idle to talk of the benefits of British rule when to high caste Hindus a European was worse than a dog, and every supposed blessing a curse.

The rebels had left Futtehghur too precipitately to set light to the East India Company's store of seasoned gun carriages, so the carpenters adapted some of them to take a 68pr, while Peel kept everyone else busy, marching and skirmishing. There was even a hint of future naval tournaments, the Naval Brigade amusing the soldiers by dismounting the 24prs from their carriages, and remounting them, an exercise with 'a great deal of lashing, and cross lashing, and sailoring about it'.[60] The period at Futtehghur seems an almost pastoral episode, apart from the reprisals, with Indian servants for every need, including barbers who shaved their employers before they awoke. Captain Peel kept a hen, which every night retreated behind his portmanteau to present him with an egg for breakfast. Verney even had time to complain about the lack of reading matter. However, the idyll was soon over, the Brigade marching south on 1 February. Peel rode his grey horse, Selim, into Cawnpore six days later, to find the 2nd Company busy preparing 8-inch shells for the 68prs, and loading hackeries with rockets. Hoskins and his comrades had kept themselves amused with an odd mixture of church services, gun drill, and hangings, with a daily quart of porter and a dram of rum as spirituous consolation.

The entire Brigade set out for Lucknow on 12 February, over 430 strong. Hoskins thought their battery 'one of the heaviest and finest that ever the country presented'. It consisted of: eight 24pr and six 68pr guns, on the carriages from Futtehghur; two 8-inch siege howitzers; and eight rocket tubes. The Brigade's own hackeries carried 100 rounds per gun, with another 400 in reserve. The ready use ammunition for the 68prs alone required twenty carts. Peel reported the 68prs: 'sit better on the carriages than the 24prs, and we find them as easily handled and transported'.[61] He had not always been so sanguine. Hoskins was No. 8 on one of the heavy guns, responsible for bringing up powder from the tumbril to the gun-muzzle. Peel watched the twenty-man detachments working the guns 'with the usual quickness common to a sailor', and confessed to:

> a great deal of anxiety of late in thinking whether the guns would answer or that they would be too heavy to handle but that was over now as he could see we could handle them well enough.[62]

Such heavy guns had never before served in the field. The 68prs in the Crimea fought in a static siege rôle, only a few miles from the beach. The *Shannon's* heavy guns would march great distances, and display a remarkable level of tactical mobility in the fire-swept streets of Lucknow. Battery drill astonished the numerous soldiers who came to watch the sailors exercise their guns: advancing, retreating, and even forming square, as if the three-ton 68prs were so many field pieces. After gun drill there was time for a sports day with all the usual mounted events, as well as hurdling and sack-races. Sailors chased a pig with a greased tail, and raced water-buffalo, four or five to each bullock with another group hauling away at the tail.

The races marked the end of Campbell's lengthy preparations for his final blow at the heart of the Mutiny. By the end of February 1858 the Brigade was camped near the Alambagh, a British outpost on the southern outskirts of Lucknow. Sir Colin Campbell watched the Brigade at work, expressing his pleasure at how the sailors knocked their guns about the countryside. Campbell's interest was not just a matter of military aesthetics, for next day he ordered a night march to bring the Brigade up to the Dilkusha, which would again serve as the British forming-up area. The recurrence of names familiar from previous fighting at Lucknow lends this period an air of *déjà vu*, but Campbell's final offensive was not a simple re-run of November's relief of the Residency. His forces were much stronger now, some 20,000 British and loyal Indian troops besides Jang Bahàdur's 9,000 Gurkhas. The rebels had also gathered their strength, 120,000 of them congregating at Lucknow after the fall of Delhi. Neither Campbell nor his second-in-command, Sir James Outram, wished to throw away British lives. For this reason, they brought up a powerful artillery to prepare the way for the infantry, a tactical consideration that was understood even at the level of the Ordinary Seamen working the guns.[63] The Shannons' first task was to cover the bridging of the Gumti River for a right-flanking movement by Sir James Outram, to turn the enemy's prepared positions south-west of the city.

The gunners were told off into three reliefs before going into action. This allowed continuous operation of the guns, but complicates interpretation of the disjointed diary entries of men who saw action at different times and places. Operations began with a piece of bad luck: a round shot from the Martinière mortally wounded two men, including a boatswain's mate, 'the best man in the ship'. Luckily this was not a taste of things to come, although Lieutenant Salmon, recovered since his previous visit to Lucknow, thought the exchange of fire on 4 March 1858 the hottest fire of round shot he had ever seen. Outram crossed the Gumti on 6 March, taking in rear the rebel guns that enfiladed the approaches to the Martinière. Lucknow was now threatened on three sides: from the Alambagh, the Dilkusha, and by Sir James Outram beyond the Gumti. The 68prs finally saw action on the 9th. The men wore their blue frocks, white trousers and hats, halting at the Dilkusha to send the bullocks and their drivers to the rear, before dragging the guns into batteries built by the Sikh Pioneers:

> we could just see the Martinière through the dusk of the dawning day and the occasional flash from a gun told us the enemy were not all asleep.

The rebels opened fire from the Martinière and their riflepits at daylight. The 68prs 'answered admirably well', firing Moorsom shells, a new type of percussion shell which went off splendidly; the mud walls just hard enough to burst them:

> we kept up a pretty sharp [fire] on the left of the Martinière and a battery of foot artillery men kept up a sharp fire with mortars on the right of the building our battery was 700 yards from the enemy trenches about 11AM one half of the guns crews got their dinners then the others had theirs 12AM (*sic*) the orders came down to open as sharp a fire as possible on the outline defences (*sic*) as the troops were to storm it about one o'clock directly.[64]

When the storming party skirmished forward hardly a shot was fired: 'Our 68prs had done their work so well that there was not a man left in the building.'[65] Although British losses were few, the success was dearly bought. Sir William Peel was shot in the thigh, while reconnoitring a raking position for two 24prs. It was very hot, and the wound made the Captain weak and faint, so a bluejacket's broad-brimmed hat was brought to keep off the sun, while he was carried to the Dilkusha in a dhooli, under a sailor's shirt.

The event cast a gloom over the Brigade, which suffered no other casualty that day, but operations went on unchecked, directed by Lieutenant

Vaughan with his customary efficiency. The heavy guns pushed on, past the Martinière, to engage rebel positions beyond the canal. Overnight the gunners slept under their guns, rolled in their blankets, feeling well satisfied with themselves. Next day they began winkling out the rebels beyond the canal, dragging guns down paths cleared through the rubble by Indian Sappers, or hacking holes through garden walls to engage loopholed barricades beyond. On 11 March, Salmon and Hoskins were relieved. Verney's relief supplied the firepower that drove the rebels from their positions in the Kaiser Bagh, and the other palaces along the river bank past the old Residency. Soldiers of the 38th Regiment helped him run up a captured gun to blow in the Kaiser Bagh gate, a doubly hazardous position: heaps of loose gunpowder three or four feet high threatened by flames from the house next door, fired by retreating sepoys. Escaping these perils, Verney explored the captured palace. He gained little plunder, but sampled the contents of an Indian pharmacy, as if life was not dangerous enough.

On 17 March the last formed bodies of rebels left Lucknow, and the merchants came forward to ransom the city. Salmon thought there had been no fighting this time to compare with operations the previous November: 'few people I think have seen hotter work than that was'.[66] Nevertheless the onset of hot weather, and plentiful supply of corpses, bred a plague of flies:

> the moment one sits down they settle on every exposed part of the body; they drown themselves in the gravy, immolate themselves on the end of cigars, accompany to one's mouth all one's food, and render sleep next to impossible ... about sunset the mosquitoes relieve guard and the flies have their watch below.[67]

Salmon hoped the Brigade would soon go downcountry. Soldiering seemed 'dry work when there is nothing to do'.[68] The Admiralty's attitude had been in marked contrast to the obstructionism of the Crimean Board, but they now asserted their:

> earnest desire that the officers and men comprising the Naval Brigade may be returned to their respective ships as soon as the exigencies of the Service will admit.[69]

When that minute was drafted the Naval Brigade had already left for Calcutta. They handed their guns over to the Royal Artillery at Lucknow, where they remained until the 1950s, the name *Shannon* cut deep into their carriages. The carpenter prepared one of the King of Oudh's carriages for the wounded Captain, fitting it out in blue cotton, with 'HMS Shannon' painted over the royal arms. Chivalrous to the end, Sir William insisted on travelling in a dhooli, as a sick bluejacket might have done. On 8 April 1858 the 1st Company and Marines handed in their field equipment at Cawnpore, and set off downcountry by bullock train. Companies travelled separately with ten rounds of ball per man, for all the world as if they were in a country at peace.

MOPPING UP (APRIL–DECEMBER 1858)

The great centres of the Mutiny at Delhi and Lucknow had fallen, but the rebellion was so widespread that fighting continued for months after the fall of Lucknow. HMS *Pearl*'s men were in the thick of it, although the rebels rarely stood after Amorha, fading away like so many ghosts. Guerrilla tactics served the sepoys better than open resistance. Sotheby noted on 8 May that four men had died of fever and dysentery in the previous fortnight, more than had been killed in action at Amorha. Two days later the sick list was forty-five, about a quarter of his strength, with another two dead:

> we took every precaution to keep our men out of the sun but the heat and exposure to damp swamps – the frequent forced marches against parties of rebels who were constantly endeavouring to harass us but seldom waited to be attacked was telling on our men.[70]

The thermometer remained in the nineties throughout May, the wind like the draught from a blast furnace. Tents were poor protection from the sun, so the soil underneath was dug out and made into mud walls, the overall effect resembling a mausoleum for the living. Chappel's journal reveals the pressure felt by all ranks:

> The weather is very hot the thermometer 117 degrees outside and 98 degrees in the shade and not a breath of wind stirs the leaves on the trees on the boughs of which the tropical birds are perched panting with drooping wings for the breeze or the shower that is denied them. Our hospital is full and nearly all hands sickly while we are surrounded by enemies and we can hear their guns from morning till night they will not come out to fight us but harass us with incessant marching knowing the climate will take more effect on us than their bullets [sic].[71]

The rebels never exploited their superior numbers to cut the British lines of communication, although Rowcroft did beat a strategic retreat to a more secure position at Basti, which became the Naval Brigade's centre of operations for some months. Chappel's journal contains lighter moments, when he describes the parrots and monkeys that distinguished the sailors' camp:

Tame pigs may likewise be seen who have no objection to smoke a pipe if you will condescend to light it and place it in their mouths. The bluejackets themselves are scarcely less droll than their favourites being of all sizes and dimensions and are always ready for anything that may happen to turn up. fun and fighting for them coming under the same denomination and they might be frequently seen with a parrot perched on their shoulder going into action with as much indifference as if going to take a stroll for their own diversion.[72]

As in later counter-insurgency campaigns the result depended on who could win over the people of the surrounding countryside. The farmers grew tired of sepoys stealing their corn, and betrayed rebel movements. In response the rebels terrorised the villagers:

robbing them of all the little they possess putting those that had sold provisions to us to death ... whenever we halted at a village we were more a source of apprehension than safety to them for although they know that we would pay them for everything we got and that they were safe enough while we remained yet the moment we left they would be exposed to the mercyless (*sic*) fury of the rebels.[73]

Even when the rains made movement difficult, Sotheby had to send out parties to protect the 'honest people'. Villages nearest the Field Force soon recovered, their roofs rebuilt, and bazaars crowded with local inhabitants, as well as merchants driving a lucrative trade with the troops. The rains in late June brought cooler weather, and a much reduced sicklist. The Naval Brigade were snug in specially built barracks, with thick straw roofs against sun and rain, and a charpoy to every man. There was a covered skittle alley, and a portable library, with its own tent once mobile operations recommenced. In dry spells there were sports days, enlivened by donkey races, their nautical riders dressed as ladies of the previous century.

Conditions were less amusing when expeditions had to be mounted: roads washed out or waist deep in mud, guns and ammunition carried on elephants, and Jack wishing he had brought his boats. Typical detachments consisted of a couple of dozen sailors with a gun or rocket tube, some troops of cavalry, and a company or two of infantry, usually from Her Majesty's 13th Regiment who replaced the Gurkhas at the end of March. Drenched to the skin, Chappel chased rebels through flooded rice fields, levelling hedges to get the guns along, while the rain came down in torrents. On returning to Basti, there was scarcely time between marches to change clothes and complete with ammunition before setting off again. Sometimes flying columns outpaced their supplies and were reduced to eating Indian corn in its green state, washed down with river water. The besieged Sikh garrison of Bhansi, with generosity characteristic of Indian troops, cooked chupattis for their rescuers, 'a sort of thin cake baked on a hot iron plate', tasting something like sawdust.

Mobile operations resumed with the drier autumn weather. Brasyer's Sikhs, who had fought with the *Shannon*'s Brigade at Lucknow, reinforced the Field Force, the Pearls reverting to an artillery role. The rebels were on their last legs, but fought with the courage of despair. Near Jagdispur, a naval detachment was involved in a rare defeat, inspiring press reports that guns had been lost. Indignant correspondence ensued, the seamen anxious that the public should understand there were two things Jack never lost: his grog and his guns. The Field Force left Basti at the end of November driving the rebels north towards the Nepalese foothills, the Naval Brigade demonstrating their professional flexibility once more by taking over a siege train brought up from Lucknow. During the last serious action of the Mutiny at Tulsipur, two days before Christmas 1858, the heavy guns dropped out, but Sotheby, and his 12pr howitzers were well to the front:

> 'Come on boys,' said some of the soldiers and Jack limbered up, vowed he would go anywhere, and on he dashed, managing the horses and guns with such activity and readiness, that some of them said, using an expletive better suppressed, 'Well I'll believe anything about sailors after this'.[74]

In an hour-and-a-half the last rebel force in the field was broken, the sepoys hiding in the dense jungles along the Nepalese border. The Naval Brigade only once came across any fugitives, in a relentless pursuit without tents, baggage, or Christmas dinner:

> That was at the edge of the Terai (jungle), where we took them completely by surprise and actually found their pots on the fire, cooking. That was about the last shot the Brigade saw fired.[75]

On New Year's Day 1859 the war was declared over, and the Brigade ordered to return to Calcutta. The band of the 13th played them off, after Brigadier Rowcroft had addressed them, not unfairly ascribing his successes to their courage and discipline. Captain Sotheby went sightseeing, while his men proceeded by double marches to Allahabad, picking up detachments as they went. Sotheby visited the scenes of the Lucknow fighting, and saw *Shannon's* 68prs, now the main armament of the citadel. At Fyzabad he found the people perfectly paralysed:

> a few months since it was the rebels' headquarters after Lucknow was taken, now I went into the Temple not even with my shoes off.[76]

On 2 February 1859 the Pearls rejoined their ship at last. They had been ashore almost seventeen months, and seen twenty-six actions. The Shannons had passed through Calcutta rather earlier, but they too had been caught up in the turbulence that followed the fall of Lucknow. Scattered by companies around Bihar State, they saw little action to compensate them for standing guard throughout some of the hottest months of the year.[77] Hoskins' journal records almost daily funerals, including an old Exeter chum, and the Bandmaster, although in the latter's case 'it his supposed that the cursed rum killed him as he was a terrible drinker'.

A more widely felt loss was the death of Sir William Peel from smallpox at Cawnpore. He was travelling with another Victorian hero, Brevet-Major Frederick Roberts *VC*, later Lord Roberts of Kandahar, when the latter observed some suspicious looking spots about Peel's face. The Chaplain at Cawnpore, the Revd Moore, had befriended the Naval Brigade during their stay there in December, and at once took the sick man home, but, for all Mrs Moore's nursing, Peel sank rapidly, dying on 27 April. His insistence on using a dhooli infected by a bluejacket suffering from smallpox had proved fatal.

Peel was a remarkable character, whose hair-raising courage and sensitivity transcend the florid official tributes. Despite his calmness under fire, both Evelyn Wood and Roberts commented on Peel's underlying physical nervousness. A firm disciplinarian, Peel avoided using the lash, and objected to the barbaric treatment of prisoners at Futtehghur. In a materialist age he pursued a quixotic chivalry, once dismounting from his camel in the Sudanese desert to give water to a dying bird. He cared little for status. Old Turner recalled his saying in HMS *Diamond*, '"Every man must pull his pound in emergency no matter what his rank – Sergeant you clap on that rope"',[78] an attitude that endeared him to Everyman. The Sikhs at Lucknow gave Peel all manner of complimentary nicknames, sadly unrecorded, while years later Arthur O'Leary gave pride of place on his library wall in St Louis to a steel engraving of Peel, 'Leading the Naval Brigade into Action'. The news of his death caused almost as much sorrow among the 93rd Highlanders as the loss of their popular Brigadier, Adrian Hope. Verney wrote of the deep loss represented by Peel's death:

> the mainspring that worked the machine is gone. We have never felt our-selves to be the *Shannon*'s Naval Brigade, or even the *Admiralty* Naval Brigade, but always *Peel*'s Naval Brigade. He it was who first originated the idea of sailors going 1400 miles away from the sea, and afterwards carried it out in such an able and judicious manner.[79]

Hoskins waxed biblical, prophesying of Peel that 'his name will be num-bered among Old England's many heroes and spoke of by the bluejackets with praise'.[80]

The *Shannon*'s Brigade were relieved after almost a year ashore, arriving in Calcutta on 12 August. They received the sort of heroes' welcome that became common in the later nineteenth century, but would have been unthinkable before the Crimea. There was a triumphal arch, bearing the legend 'Welcome Hearts of Oak', and a large painting of Neptune, the streets were lined by East India Company sailors at the present, pretty girls threw flowers from windows, while several regimental bands all played at once: 'It was one continued cheer from the street down to the river'.[81]

They had more substantial entertainment on 1 September when 156 rank-and-file turned out in best white frocks and trousers for a civic reception at the Town Hall, decorated for the occasion with oil paintings of Neptune, Britannia, and vanquished sepoys. Hoskins' journal still encloses his copy of the menu, an astonishing catalogue of boiled and roast meats, beef and mutton, puddings and pies:

> every man had two plates, one of them a dessert plate, and two glasses one of which was a wine glass to drink the toast out of them, there was also a black servant to each man who brought in as much bottled ale and porter as he could stow away.[82]

The Boatswain's Mates piped for silence, the Loyal Toasts were drunk in brandy with loud cheers, and then a fourth in silence to the memory of Sir William Peel.

Despite their appetite for strong drink the men of both ships behaved well ashore, a pleasing reflection on their discipline at a time when most civilians expected sailors to be perpetually drunk. The Advocate General of Calcutta, who had professional reasons for knowing, compared the 'admirable steadiness, good conduct, and humanity' of both Naval Brigades favourably with that of the merchant seamen who volunteered for service ashore, contradicting claims in the *United Service Gazette* that *Shannon*'s Brigade had been the reverse of disciplined, the terror of friends and foes alike.[83]

Neither ship went back to China. *Shannon* paid off at Portsmouth on 15 January 1859, and the *Pearl* on 16 June. The rate of promotion was prodigious, three out of four watch-keeping officers in *Shannon* being now Commanders. The *Pearl*'s officers and men had similar steps, Lieutenant Turnour being promoted twice to Captain. Such promotions may reflect public relief at the outcome of events, rather than an objective evaluation of the campaign. Sir John Fortescue, the great historian of the British Army, suggested that the Mutiny should not be taken too seriously as a campaign, given the poor performance of the rebels on the battlefield.[84] Such a view is understandable in a work completed immediately after the carnage of the Great War, but it smells of hindsight. When Peel threw his handful of men into the struggle, Delhi and the Residency were still besieged, and the Mutiny's widespread nature made it appear a far more coherent affair than it was. For the men on the ground it had been no joke:

> fighting with a small force against vastly superior numbers, whatever they were made of. We never knew, especially in the early days of the Mutiny what a day might bring forth: we might even find our force annihilated . . . The rebels as a whole fought badly; but there were occasions when we were hard put to it – not so much by the actual fighting as by the state of unrest into which they put us. Then there was always the feeling that if retreat had been forced upon us we should have nothing to fall back upon: neither position nor reinforcements.[85]

British casualties in action were low, but tropical diseases and the climate took their toll. Only one Pearl was killed in action, but eighteen died from other causes, while a quarter of their strength were wounded, or invalided. *Shannon*'s losses were more considerable, 162 out of 520. Twenty died from enemy action, but an appalling eighty-three from disease.[86] Small wonder that Captain Sotheby, despite his own good health, was not sorry to give up soldiering. For him the best memorial to his men's work was a country once more at peace. *Shannon*'s Brigade subscribed £350 for a more tangible monument, now on the sea front at Southsea. Unfashionably classical in form, its design drew the marginal comment, 'surely this is too hideous even for Portsmouth', but it would not be the last Naval Brigade memorial to grace, or perhaps disfigure, the Royal Navy's home ports.

CHAPTER THREE

Terms of Reference

AN AMPHIBIOUS INHERITANCE (1660–1783)

EDMUND VERNEY credited Sir William Peel with an original idea in marching his sailors 1,400 miles into India, but it was nothing new for the Royal Navy to take part in operations ashore. A Colonel of Marines lecturing in 1903 on disembarkations compiled a table of 226 such operations over the previous 150 years. This should not be very surprising. The object of naval forces must be to influence the military or political circumstances ashore. Sometimes this can be done indirectly, as by the Allied blockade of Germany in 1914–18. More usually blockades escalate through raids into major amphibious operations, such as the siege of Havana in 1762 or the *coup de main* at Gibraltar in 1704. The fruits of sea power must be gathered ashore. The great French wars of 1793–1815 are best remembered for Nelson's wild chases and occasional climactic battles, but those years saw many operations not dissimilar to those that characterised the later nineteenth century. The Royal Navy's contribution to the defence of Acre in 1799 was a clear precursor to the Victorians' emergency use of maritime power, heavy naval guns and marines providing vital support for local Turkish forces at the decisive moment of Napoleon's adventure in the Levant. This was a striking success, showing the strategic leverage that maritime power could apply to the land war.

One can play antiquarian parlour games identifying the 'first' British Naval Brigades. Colonel Cyril Field, the erudite historian of the Royal Marines, awarded the prize to 500 English sailors landed to expel the French from Leith in 1560. A more useful starting point is the foundation of the British Standing Army in the 1660s, including the forerunners of Colonel Field's own Corps, the Lord Admiral's Regiment. Their formation in 1664 recognised the seventeenth-century differentiation of naval and military forces. Fighting at sea now centred around the heavy gun, a departure reflected in a succession of *Sailing and Fighting Instructions* issued from the Commonwealth period onwards. Seamen not only sailed their ships, they took the lead in fighting them, although ships still carried a proportion of marines, that is, soldiers raised for service at sea as marksmen or the nucleus of landing parties. The army developed its own expertise, as seen in the works of such drill masters as William Barriffe or Maurice of Nassau. British regiments might still serve afloat, several gaining battle honours at the Glorious First of June 1794, but the 1660s made a clear technical distinction between the services. The term 'Naval Brigade' before then is neither logical nor helpful, as there was often little difference between men serving at sea or on land.

The growing professional autonomy of the services did not preclude sailors from involvement in land operations in the later seventeenth century. British wars were inevitably combined operations, just as they had been at the Isle de Rhé in 1627 or San Domingo in 1655. There a battalion of sailors had covered the retreat of the ex-Royalists and Buccaneers who made up the unwilling majority of the soldiery. The sailors had made a point of drilling as infantry, in practical recognition of the growing gulf between the naval and military trades. In 1690 600 sailors and marines landed at Cork to build siege batteries and platforms, something of a naval speciality over the next two centuries. Six thousand seamen served ashore in Flanders in 1694, but the most dramatic contribution of the later Stuart navy to land operations was its part in lifting the siege of Tangier in 1680. The defences of this Portuguese outpost, acquired by Charles II on his marriage to Catherine of Braganza, were literally tottering when the navy arrived with reinforcements. Admiral Herbert landed some 500 seamen:

> composed of so many companies with a company of Granadiers (*sic*) with the compleat number of officers to each company, of the sea officers, and volunteers he made choice of Captain George Barthell who formerly had been a Captain in my Lord Dumbarton's Regiment, to command that battalion of seamen in quality of Major.[1]

The collective noun used for sailors fighting ashore at this time was battalion or regiment. Such units probably included both sailors and marines, as seventeenth-century sources did not distinguish between them. Later marine detachments always constituted a separate tactical unit from the seamen when ashore, even forming their own battalion if sufficiently numerous. This contrasts with the practice of distributing them amongst a ship's boats when these were manned and armed. The term 'Brigade' arose later, implying a self-contained group of units with its own headquarters staff and artillery. These could be bluejackets and marines from a single ship, or a composite force from several ships. Naval Brigades were rarely as large as military brigades, however. An RMA sergeant suggested in 1898 that the smallest Naval Brigade on record consisted of himself and a Lieutenant Beatty RN, with a good supply of Hales' rockets which they shot into the Sudanese camp on the Atbara. During the Indian Mutiny, HMS *Pearl*'s diminutive Brigade seems to have inherited the title from its Crimean counterpart, no particular word then being in use for a body of seaman landed for service on shore. The Press then applied the term to *ad hoc* groups of merchant seamen, in which case the *Pearl*'s chaplain argued, 'it need not be considered out of place to denominate a body of seamen and Royal Marines of Her Majesty's navy by the same name'.[2] The essential point is that the men should come from an existing ship's company. The term therefore should exclude such units as the RM Battalions formed at the Royal Marine divisional headquarters for service with the army, or the detachments of sailors formed for the local defence of naval bases in the emergency of 1940.

The seamen at Tangier, whether regimented or brigaded, repaired the battered defences, while Admiral Herbert and the more aggressive army officers planned a sortie to defeat the Moorish besiegers. The naval battalion formed part of the left wing of the little army, brigaded with Dumbarton's Regiment. Like their successors at Sebastopol they would not let the soldiers beat them into the enemy position. Their Major was rebuked, 'for allowing too forward and furious advancement, lest thereby they might fall into enemy ambushments'. In his defence he protested that he 'could lead them on but the furies could not bring them off'.[3]

The navy played a substantial part in the victory, contributing perhaps a quarter of the infantry. The Moors were so discouraged that they agreed a four-year truce, after which the British evacuated their indefensible North African foothold. The continuous competition between the maritime states of western Europe, however, ensured plenty of scope for the Royal Navy's amphibious capabilities. Sometimes they supported siege operations as at Cork in 1690 or at Barcelona in 1705, where 3,000 British and Dutch seamen built and manned the batteries. Sometimes they launched major raids, such as the descent upon Gibraltar in 1704 that won the Royal Marines their one representative battle honour.

There were many failures in the early days of this new form of warfare, with both services anxious to demonstrate their autonomy. The ill-fated attack on Cartagena in 1741 showed how not to run a combined operation.

The army admitted the gallantry of the Tars, who fought the batteries as well as building them, but poor naval discipline added to personal difficulties between the commanders. Admiral Vernon's second-in-command thought:

> it would by no means be advisable to trust the sailors on shore, as they could be kept under no command, and would soon disperse themselves in the woods; to which Mr Vernon (who sat in the gallery within hearing) added aloud that some of them would soon ramble into Cartagena.[4]

Disasters continued throughout the eighteenth century. Only 381 men returned out of 1,800 committed to the San Juan River expedition of 1781:

> an essentially foolish business which all but deprived this country of Nelson, [and] might be quoted as an example of how not to employ a naval brigade or any other force.[5]

Nevertheless lessons were learned. The Royal Navy mounted combined operations with a variety of military partners, from its own marines, through the regular army, to the North American militia who took Louisburg in June 1745. An anonymous army officer at Martinique in 1762 left a picture of sailors at work ashore that might have been drawn any time in the next 140 years:

> You may fancy you know the spirit of these fellows; but to see them in action exceeds any idea that can be formed of them. A hundred or two of them with ropes and pulleys will do more than all your dray horses in London. Let but their tackles hold and they will draw you a cannon or a mortar on its proper carriage up to any height ... It is droll enough to see them tugging along with a good 24pr at their heels; on they go huzzaing, halloing, sometimes uphill, sometimes downhill, now sticking fast in the brakes, presently floundering in the mire ... and as careless of everything but the matter committed to their charge as if death or danger had nothing to do with them.[6]

The siege of Havana in 1762 was a remarkable example of interservice cooperation. Each tried to outdo the other in their commitment to the common cause. As at Sebastopol a squadron, in this case Spanish, sought to defend a harbour, sinking block ships in the harbour mouth, and landing men and guns to reinforce the garrison.[7] In response the Royal Navy divided its forces into an offshore squadron, and another for direct support of the army, although as at Sebastopol it was found that direct bombardment from the sea was costly and ineffective. Nine hundred marines rummaged the guerrilla-infested woods, while seamen-pioneers cleared roads for the 24pr siege guns, made fascines and gun platforms, filled cartridges, and fabricated rope mantlets in such quantity that there was a shortage of cable. The navy stepped up its efforts when the Spaniards burnt the original British batteries, and sickness weakened the gunners. Reliefs of seamen manned 32pr guns taken from the battleships' lower gun decks, silencing the Spanish guns, and crowning the glacis of the key Spanish position at Fort Morro. The Admirals were hard put to balance the conflicting needs of the army and the fleet. The seamen ashore needed relief, 'but every ship taking their turn has many inconveniences attending it'. The rapid consumption of ammunition was another concern, requiring 1,000 cartridges a day:

> Our sea folks began a new kind of fire unknown or, at all events, unpractised by artillery people. The greatest fire from one piece of cannon is reckoned by them from eighty to ninety times in 24 hours, but our people went on the sea system, firing extremely quick, and with best direction ever seen, and in sixteen hours fired their guns one hundred and forty-nine times.[8]

The ships were reduced to thirty-two rounds per gun, below the level needed for a fleet action. Seamen did not join the storming party, but the army affirmed that their assistance could never be sufficiently admired. Never had there been such harmony between the sea and land service. However, success was not cheap. Despite the rapid conclusion of the siege, and the double proportion of medical stores taken, 800 seamen and 500 marines died, only eighty-six of them from enemy action:

> The seamen, who in all West Indian climates are healthy when they have no communication with the shore, partaking of our duties and fatigue partook also of our diseases.[9]

Other casualties were suffered in ways that justified Vernon's doubts about naval discipline ashore:

> The enemy's wild horsemen pick up straggling soldiers and sailors, but more of our profession than soldiers. I have, and continue to give, orders

to prevent our men straggling but, and as I hope when the *others* hear of their comrades suffering it will have some effect upon them.[10]

STONE FRIGATES AND STRATEGIC DEFILES (1793–1815)

Hostilities with Revolutionary France in 1793 changed the emphasis of amphibious operations. In this renewed bout between the Elephant and the Whale, naval missions ashore were limited in scope and duration, compared with the Seven Years War. Recapitulation of Chatham's colonial strategy during the 1790s failed to impress the hard men in Paris. Nelsonic Naval Brigades related more to the prosecution of the war at sea than to the pursuit of general strategic aims. Often the only area where the two sides could come to grips at all was along the European coast, which became the frontline in this asymmetrical contest.

The primacy of blockade, the only weapon available in the absence of British or Allied land forces able to withstand the Revolutionary armies, produced a rash of island strongholds. The administrative precursors of the 'stone frigates' of twentieth-century navies, these were an effective alternative to keeping ships permanently on station to interrupt coastal trade or deter privateers. The most unpromising scraps of real estate assumed quite disproportionate significance, most strikingly the Diamond Rock, a mile off Martinique. Diamond Rock was the perfect naval outpost, with sheer square sides 400 yards long. It, or perhaps she, was commissioned as a Royal Naval tender from February 1804 to May 1805, with a Commander RN and 121 men, including the appropriate warrant Officers. Rope ladders were required to reach the top, or for the timid an old cask slung from a cable, known as the mail coach or telegraph. A lookout on the summit could see the t'gallants of a frigate at forty-one miles, making the Rock invaluable when escorts were few. Armament included two 24prs hauled straight up in the air by the crew of HMS *Centaur* with a jack and purchase secured to a projecting piece of rock near the crest:

the word was given at the capstan to *heave round*; and to all the inspiring tunes the band could play, away marched the first gun up its tremendous and perilous journey of seven hundred feet from the level of the sea, and four hundred feet horizontally from the ship. The men at the capstan were relieved every hour; and commencing at half-past ten A.M. the gun was landed at the upper end of the stream-cable at five o'clock P.M., having been seven hours in heaving him up to the first landing place, when the party on shore parbuckled him up to his berth on the top of the rock with three cheers.[11]

The French tried to re-take the island in May 1804. They got close enough to see the light from the battle lanterns in the lower batteries before the current swept them away, but a more dangerous enemy were the fer-de-lances that infested the Rock. Over thirty men died during the fourteen-month occupation, only two in action. Despite this hazard, so attractive was a run ashore, that sailors returned onboard with reluctance, the sick conceal-ing their illness rather than do so. The officers had tents, but the men lived in large caves hung around with hammocks. Here sailors boiled up the abun-dant wild spinach, stirring the kettle with the branch of a tree and using another piece of wood, split at one end and a stone thrust into the slit, as a fork.[12]

The recapture of Diamond Rock in June 1805 was the only positive result for the French of the dash across the Atlantic that led to Trafalgar. The gar-rison of just over 100 held out for three days and two nights against a squad-ron led by two 74-gun ships, backed by 3,000 troops. Only want of ammunition, and fear of the massacre that might follow a night attack, per-suaded Commander Maurice to surrender at 5 p.m. on 2 June 1805, 'the unhappiest moment of my life'. His defence justified Sir Samuel Hood's opinion that thirty riflemen might hold the Rock against 10,000, the Royal Navy suffering three casualties to the attackers' thirty dead. However, the French skirmishers secured a lodgement under the overhanging cliffs, from where they pinned the defenders down, and after two sleepless nights the latter were exhausted:

> Their fatigue and hardships are beyond description, having only one pint of water during twenty-four hours under a vertical sun and not a moment's rest night and day, and several of them fainting for want of water and obliged to drink their own.[13]

Despite their losses, the French treated the prisoners decently, giving them fresh water and releasing most of them under cartel. Honourably acquitted by a Court Martial that expressed its admiration of his conduct, Maurice became an expert in naval islands. He was Governor of Marie Galante Island in 1808, and on promotion to post rank took command of a Danish island in the Skagerrak commissioned as HMS *Anholt* in July 1810. The island had been seized for its lighthouse in an almost bloodless coup the previous year, the one fatality allegedly being the Sergeant-Major of Marines, 'whom none regretted'. The subsequent garrison were almost all Royal Marines, but three divisions of seamen took part in the capture, a veteran's recollection of the affair providing a picture of the British seaman in action ashore that is morally convincing, if unconfirmed by more prosaic accounts of the affair:

> Front to front we stood there for a short time, giving and receiving a close and well sustained fire of musketry; until the untutored patience of the boarders being completely exhausted, they suddenly relinquished their muskets, and with a loud British cheer rushed upon the enemy, with a determination and an impetuosity that seemed to paralyse them.[14]

The fort itself fell to a leaderless party of sailors: 'determined to go to work in their own way, and get into the fort after their own fashion', they climbed through the palisades still under fire from the supporting British ships, to cutlass the Danish gunners. The Royal Marine garrison fortified the lighthouse with 70,000 specially imported bricks, enlisting the help of the islanders who were repaid with grog, although they complained they could not give the rum to their horses. The defences were ready just in time for a Danish counter-attack in March 1811, and by the end of the day the garrison had more prisoners than it could handle. The Danes had believed:

> that the garrison was disaffected at being obliged to remain on this barren island and a great part of them would lay down their arms on the first gun being fired. In this they were mistaken.[15]

A Marine shot down the Danish commander with the exclamation, 'take that pinch of snuff you s——', and his men found that after five hours fighting within pistol shot they were unable to retreat through the soft yielding sand.

The garrison had indeed been bored, despite dances with the local girls, and occasional fights amongst themselves. Maurice's predecessor, a Royal Marine Major known as 'Fighting Nicholls', had particularly distinguished himself in the latter field. An 1812 Court Martial reprimanded him for beating a Marine around the head with a bayonet, and firing into HM Gunboat *Grinder* from the lighthouse. Maurice avoided such extremities, but relations between the naval and military commanders on Anholt were not without difficulty. The despatch describing the action of 27 March 1811 is notable for its failure to mention the Royal Marine officers engaged, and the extensive deletions made by Admiralty clerks to remove excessive commendations for Maurice's own followers. Navy and marines conducted a bizarre competition to present the better sword to their man as a leaving gift, but Maurice was not employed again after 1812, when the 11th Veteran Battalion relieved the marines.

Sometimes the navy intervened directly in the land war. Defiles, where mountains or deserts hemmed in lines of communication against the coast, provided opportunities for the Royal Navy's cruisers to exert a disproportionate influence. The most decisive of these moments came at St Jean d'Acre in 1799, during the later stages of the French expedition to Egypt. A Turkish garrison thwarted young Bonaparte's bid for world power, via the overland route to India, with timely support from a British squadron.[16] Sir Sidney Smith's ships captured the French siege train before it could disembark, and prevented close investment of the tumbledown defences near the water's edge. Their seamen and marines made so effective a contribution to the defence that the French inspired several attempts to assassinate their leader. Marines headed the attacking columns during a sortie to pre-empt a French mine, clearing the way for demolition parties of seamen. Major Thomas Oldfield fell at the very entrance to the mine, provoking a macabre tussle for the body. The marines hooked him by the neckcloth to draw him off; the enemy at the same time piercing him with a halberd. The neck cloth gave way and the French succeeded in dragging the lifeless Oldfield to their works. The French Grenadiers kept Oldfield's sword, but buried him amongst their own dead with appropriate marks of respect.

Years later as HMS *Bellerophon* carried Napoleon into exile, he recalled this curious episode from his early career, with her Captain of Marines, who had fought at Acre as a subaltern. It was an appropriate theme for reminiscence at that point of Napoleon's career. When the French retreated to Egypt on 23 May, they left behind his dreams of overthrowing the Ottoman Empire and seizing India, along with their remaining guns. As world empires go, the price was low enough: ninety British dead or wounded and eighty-two prisoners, although an accidental explosion in *Theseus* doubled the British losses.[17]

French communications in Spain were also vulnerable to sea-borne interference, during the prolonged agony of the Peninsular War (1808–13). Three men-of-war held up General Reille and two divisions for almost a month at Rosas in late 1808 through the succour they brought the Spanish patriots who held out in the citadel, and Fort Trinidad to the east of the bay. They broke up Reille's attacks with hand grenades, a marine speciality, trimming fuses with axes, and measuring out powder in hats. Captain Bennet of HMS *Fame* was about to give up when Lord Cochrane arrived in HMS *Impérieuse*, fresh from a series of raids on the coastal road from Barcelona to Gerona. Cochrane reinforced Fort Trinidad with thirty marines and as many sailors, and took personal command. The reanimated garrison blocked up the breaches with palisades and barrels full of earth, entangled them with chains barbed with fish hooks, and hung live shells over the walls ready to be fired with quick match. Greased planks awaited any attackers unlucky enough to get inside, ready to slide them into a specially prepared pit. Cochrane's men only gave up after the citadel in Rosas had surrendered, slipping away down rope ladders. Cochrane and the Gunner were last to leave, blowing up the battered remains of the castle as they went.

Later the navy covered the flanks of the lines of Torres Vedras. The ragged armies of Ney and Masséna starved, while Sir Arthur Wellesley's army grew fat on supplies shipped in through Lisbon. At Sir Arthur's suggestion, a thousand men from the squadron in the Tagus marched up the left bank of the river to Santarem to disrupt French attempts to cross there. Later a battalion of Marines was sent out to replace the Naval Brigade, a Lieutenant RM being the first to report Masséna's retreat. The Admiralty objected to the employment ashore of so many of the ship's crews in similar terms to those they would use during the Crimea. Their previous criticism of Nelson's operations around Naples in 1799 provides a fair summary of the Admiralty's long-held views on the subject:

> although in operations on the sea coast it may frequently be highly expedient to land a part of the seamen of the squadron to cooperate with, and assist the army, when the situation will admit of their being immediately re-embarked if the squadron should be called away to act elsewhere . . . yet their Lordships by no means approve of the seamen being landed to form part of an army to be employed in operations at a distance from the coast where, if they should have the misfortune to be defeated, they might be prevented from returning to the ships, and the squadron rendered so defective as to be no longer capable of performing the services required of it.[18]

Their Lordships' views were not unreasonable. Nelson had committed a thousand of his best men to a siege fifteen miles inland, and had they met a regiment of good quality cavalry in the open the result does not bear contemplation. Sailors at this period learned only enough drill to move them from place to place, regarding such aspects of the soldier's trade as 'an amusing interlude in the serious business of war'.[19] This failure to take soldiering seriously may have extended to the officers as well as the ratings. In the early days of the Revolutionary Wars the army had refused to attack Bastia in Corsica. The navy took unilateral action, Nelson lost his left eye, and inter-service relations were soured for the duration. Even at the end of the Peninsular War, when the army had given abundant proof of its fighting abilities, naval men never ceased to regard the military officer as essentially wooden.

However, such an attitude never deterred naval officers from action on their own account around the more vulnerable sections of the French, Spanish or Italian coasts. Sir Charles Napier, who later commanded the Baltic Fleet during the Crimean War, even managed to snatch a troop of French dragoons from a sand-spit. The Commander-in-Chief's reaction to the signal 'Have captured the enemy's cavalry' was unsurprisingly crusty. Swearing that this time 'Mad Charley' had gone too far, Lord Exmouth ordered him within hailing distance of the flagship, allowing Napier to display a luckless cavalryman lashed to his kicking horse, 'fully accoutred and triced up . . . to the main stay'.[20]

THE FIRST WORLD POWER

It is a far cry from landing a handful of marines to kidnap a troop of dra-goons, to taking the majority of a ship's company into the middle of the Indian sub-continent. Nineteenth-century Naval Brigades differed from earlier examples in the sheer scale of their operations. The Crimean Naval Brigade was ashore for eleven months. It provided 40 per cent of the siege-artillery detachments, besides replacing the army's worn out 24pr guns with naval 32prs. They also landed 68pr smooth-bore and Lancaster guns, at that time the heaviest guns ever used ashore by the British armed forces. Major fleet units, such as HMS *Diamond* and *Sans Pareil*, were immobilised for months at a time to provide depot and hospital ships. So few men remained on board HMS *Shannon* at Calcutta that other ships had to provide hands when her services were required as a troopship. How could the Royal Navy of the 1850s afford to tie up its resources so literally, for so long?

The answer lies in the unique strategic situation that existed after the Napoleonic Wars. The Royal Navy's complete elimination of its rivals made such concepts as the 'struggle for command of the sea' meaningless. The usual criteria of naval strategy became largely irrelevant, and remained so for almost a century. Industrial and hence maritime power were concen-trated in Europe, so the Royal Navy's local command of the Channel and North Atlantic gave general command of the sea as far away as the Indian and Pacific Oceans. This strategic advantage was only lost with the emergence of the Japanese and American navies in the 1890s. Until then the British could control huge areas with symbolic forces.

For once such global pre-eminence did not conjure up forces to balance or even overthrow it. Throughout the entire century the only threat to the trade routes that stretched 1,500 miles from India to China arose from a brief squabble with the Dutch in 1830–31. Some of the credit for this is due to the British themselves who were careful not to cause unnecessary offence. They allowed the French to occupy Algeria, tolerated Gallic adventures in Mexico and Indo-China, and resolved disputes with the United States over slave-trading and the Civil War blockade of the South, by diplomatic means.

The Napoleonic Wars had left most European states exhausted and impoverished. They had no appetite for military adventures, setting the international stage for an unprecedentedly peaceful period of European history. European states had little incentive to challenge the Royal Navy, as the British Free Trade policies offered everyone a chance to grow rich, without the risk or expense of a naval arms race. A commercial free-for-all replaced the armed competition for overseas markets and colonies that characterised eighteenth-century international politics. Free Trade and the general pacific disposition fostered an easy acceptance of British maritime hegemony. The *Sailor's Home Journal* in 1862 noted the general support for British naval supremacy. It congratulated the Royal Navy on being:

> the most powerful agent for a policy the contrary of sentimental, but which, professing no interest beyond the interest of England, is the most moderate and just any great country has ever followed. The policy of England lies not in forcing her will on others, but in upholding peace and that good state of order which allows every other nation to develop its resources and provide for its welfare.[21]

In the middle years of the century, when a Bonapartist régime in Paris threatened the European balance of power, technological developments reaffirmed British naval supremacy. Self-sufficiency in coal and iron, the strategic raw materials of the day, allowed the British to build the most advanced metallurgical industries in the world. This left the Royal Navy well placed to exploit new developments in armour and naval artillery. When the French armoured wooden ships the British went a step further. They launched HMS *Warrior*, the first armoured iron warship, rendering obsolete every other battleship in the inventory. While HMS *Warrior* confirmed British pre-eminence in home waters, other weapon developments ensured success for British arms against less advanced opponents.

The disproportionate casualty returns of actions in the Indian Mutiny have already been noted. British losses were often in single figures, compared with hundreds of rebels. Such a disparity was typical of European encounters with less developed opponents throughout the later nineteenth century, thanks largely to rifled small arms: first the muzzle-loading Enfields of the 1850s, then breech-loading Sniders and Martini-Henrys in the 1860s and 70s. British smooth-bore muskets had few advantages over the weapons of their previous enemies. In April 1846 Barbary corsairs drove off a landing party from HMS *Fantome* with their longer ranging matchlock muskets. Rifles prevented such opponents coming close enough to inflict any harm with their own weapons. Often these were cast-off Tower pattern muskets, like those taken from T'ai-p'ing rebels by a Naval Brigade from HMS *Impérieuse* at Cholin in May 1862. The combination of strategic deterrence in home waters and tactical superiority over non-European opponents accounts in a nutshell for the Royal Navy's ability to send large numbers of men ashore for often extended periods. Serious naval opposition in distant waters did not exist, while local opponents could not withstand the firepower of naval landing parties with their rifles, light field guns, and rockets. The T'aip'ings were 'utterly powerless when brought within the range of British artillery'.[22] In 1863 even Japanese gunners gave up the unequal struggle against seaborne firepower, at Kagoshima and Shimonoseki.

A DEAFENING HUSH

It should not be thought that there was any systematic scheme to exploit British naval assets to gather the fruits of sea-power. British naval supremacy did not arise from the pursuit of any clearly articulated theory: it was a fact of life resulting from the French Wars. The Royal Navy's activities simply reflected the new state of affairs, placing less emphasis upon fighting for command of the sea, and more on exploiting the command it had already won. Nobody seems to have felt the need to justify the use of Naval Brigades in theoretical terms. Their development was pragmatic, driven by events, just as naval participation in the Indian Mutiny arose from Peel's fortuitous presence. The lack of debate is not surprising. The long peace and relentless pressure on naval budgets limited the mental horizons of those entrusted with the national defences. Officers selected to serve upon the

Board of Admiralty were often past their physical and intellectual best, thanks to promotion by seniority, and a Captains list swollen by the late wars. By 1843 the average age of admirals had risen to seventy-six, a considerable handicap in a physically demanding and rapidly evolving profession. Some senior officers were not overbright to begin with: Sir George Cockburn (First Sea Lord 1828–30) opposed the general issue of gunsights, thinking it enough to equip every other gun, or perhaps one broadside per ship. The whole tenor of British service life discouraged naval men from thinking about their profession:

> So far from bringing their professional and practical expertise to bear upon the real requirements of the navy and the duties that would devolve upon it in time of war, it was with the greatest difficulty they could be prevailed upon to entertain the subject at all, much less regard it from its various aspects and have it thoroughly thought out.[23]

Naval debates concentrated on technical issues, such as the effects of steam, armour, shells, rifled guns or torpedoes, rather than the relationship between the navy and national security. What few discussions there were about Naval Brigades also focused on practical matters, like the question of which side of their waterproof sheets the men should sleep on while ashore.

The political élite took little interest in service matters. The index of John Morley's massive biography of Gladstone contains not a single mention of the Royal Navy, despite its pivotal role in the Grand Old Man's eventual fall from office.[24] Even a level-headed statesman like Sir Robert Peel, father of the *Shannon*'s dashing Captain, accepted the popular view that the millennium was at hand, and the era of peace irrevocably established:

> War was looked upon almost as an impossibility: arbitration, the skill of modern diplomatists, finance, philanthropy, improved education, nineteenth century civilisation and above all the advance of science as applied to war would render the destruction of life so terrible as to ensure a continuation of peace.[25]

Politicians held naval men in low regard. A parliamentary committee on calculating longitudes, hardly a matter of naval indifference, included not a single naval officer. Parliamentary debates on Naval Estimates were notorious for their ability to empty the benches, MPs rightly anticipating a profitless wrangle about naval architecture.

Regardless of party allegiance, Victorian politicians much preferred hair-splitting arguments about tax reform, drains, or theology to the problems of imperial defence. Indeed there was no such phrase as imperial defence until much later when the changed circumstances of the 1880s refocused minds on the realities of power. Until then administration and economy appeared more important than the strategic ends such means might serve. Suppression of the Navy Board in 1832 overloaded the Admiralty with administration, to the neglect of policy, a state of affairs that did not bother the Cabinet at all, and still less public opinion:

> All were profoundly ignorant of the real requirements of the naval service, and were so impressed with the conviction that our naval supremacy was incontestable, that nobody took any trouble to ascertain the facts upon a subject so important to national greatness and prosperity.[26]

Such cocksure ignorance leaves little hope of finding a clear policy on the use, or otherwise, of Naval Brigades. The Admiralty's approach was generally to deprecate their use by over-enthusiastic station commodores or colonial proconsuls. Tension always existed between the forward policies of local commanders, and the more cautious attitudes at the centre, expressed in standing orders to commanders-in-chief prohibiting the misuse of landing parties. This conflict was particularly sharp during the Crimean War, but it re-emerged during the Zulu and Maori Wars. Senior Naval Officers on the spot soothing the nerves of the Board, like some querulous elderly relative.

One paradoxical result of economy was to draw the Royal Navy into military operations. The army suffered cuts every bit as savage as those inflicted on the navy, their parliamentary masters seeming to take disproportionate delight in disbanding such useful colonial formations as the Cape Mounted Rifles or the 3rd West India Regiment. Whiggish politicians had always disliked overseas garrisons as a constitutional threat to civil liberties at home, while pensions for the survivors of colonial garrisons provided a financial incentive to cut them to the bone. So committed were the Liberals to the idea of colonial self-defence by the 1860s that they withdrew New Zealand's garrison at the height of the Maori War! In all fairness naval defence of the colonies was often better value. In the early 1860s naval costs per man ranged from £86 to £106 per annum. The military garrison of Victoria in Australia, on the other hand, cost £157 per man, totalling £5.1 million per annum, enough to finance some 5,000 sailors with 500 guns, 'a most preponderating force'.[27] Garrisons were too scattered to be effective, and lacked fortifications able to withstand a regular siege. A naval squadron on the other hand could move to face threats as they arose.

Residual military forces remained only in such outposts as Malta or Hong Kong. Even the navy was cut back from 17,500 to 11,500 men on foreign stations. This turned out to be an irreducible minimum, despite Gladstone's dislike of a system that dotted vessels around the world, multiplying the chances of conflict without, in his view, adding materially to British strength. Gladstone's liberal pacifism, however, was only one strand in British imperial policy. Richard Cobden, the apostle of free trade, observed how Yorkshire and Lancashire manufacturers regarded India and China as fields of enterprise kept open only by force, a view supported by the *Sailor's Home Journal* commenting on the disadvantages of trading through Canton, which could not be approached by large warships: 'a great drawback, for in China our trade is always most secure under the guns of our vessels'.[28]

The unresolved contradiction between the liberal distaste for the military and free trade's dependence upon force placed the burden of imperial defence firmly upon the Royal Navy. Except in India, the army was primarily concerned with home defence. This reversed the usual British pattern of depending on the fleet for security at home, while using the army for offensive operations overseas. The confusion of traditional roles was deepened by the redbrick fortifications that sprang up along the south coast of England, as doubts spread about the navy's ability to secure the home base. By contrast the Royal Navy played an increasing part in land operations overseas. So far had this gone by the 1890s that there were serious proposals for the navy to take over the defence of all naval bases, replacing military garrisons in the Falkland Islands, Ceylon, Mauritius, and even Portsmouth.

MODELS OF INTERVENTION

Contemporary analysts had no clear view of the relationship between army and navy. They saw imperial defence as a series of local problems to be tackled piecemeal. It is helpful for us, however, to look at nineteenth-century naval operations in a more structured way. This has several advantages, apart from providing form for a dangerously broad subject. An explicit conceptual framework makes it possible to locate Naval Brigades within a range of operational possibilities. Their place within such a structure shows that Naval Brigades were not a misuse of naval assets, but possessed an operational validity of their own, comparable with such activities as enforcing a blockade, or shelling a barracoon. In general, contemporaries accepted that:

with our large Colonial Empire and enormous commerce all over the world, we must occasionally get into small wars, and the navy being on the spot must be the first to commence operations. Then of course if the matter expands they must be assisted, and when it comes to a larger affair the Army must take it up.[29]

Such statements recognised that naval interventions could take a variety of operational forms, depending on circumstances. These different types of action shaded into one another, to form a pattern of escalation, as shown below:

DEMONSTRATION →
BLOCKADE →
BOMBARDMENT →
LANDING →
RIVER OPERATIONS →
MILITARY EXPEDITION

The variety of conflicts in which Naval Brigades participated underlines the flexibility of general-purpose naval forces in the nineteenth century, and their ability to apply a level of force appropriate to a range of challenges. A century before Henry Kissinger popularised the concept, the Royal Navy pursued a strategy of graduated response, suiting its operational actions to the political circumstances in which it found itself.

At the more violent end of the scale were operations against recognised sovereign states, as happened during the Crimean War, or the China Wars. For the sake of analysis, these can be labelled 'offensive', their targets lying outside the British Empire, although many Victorians would have regarded them as defensive responses to external threats. These offensive naval actions usually formed part of an extensive military effort, requiring substantial land forces, and the presence of capital ships. This would be the case during the China Wars in the 1850s, or the intervention in Egypt of 1882, which drew in the Mediterranean fleet, and an army corps from the United Kingdom. Such campaigns did not usually result in long-term occupation of territory, the action tending to occur around the geographical periphery of the enemy, as at Sebastopol or Canton in 1857. Strategic objectives were limited even at this extreme end of the scale: the release of hostages from Abyssinia in 1867, or the assertion of trading rights in China or Japan. Only Burma suffered outright annexation in 1885, a result of sharper international competition rather than Burmese provocation.

A step below these offensive operations came wars of a more defensive nature, at least from a British point of view. These were fought in areas already within the Empire, as in New Zealand, or to defend existing posses- sions, such as the Gold Coast and Natal during the Ashanti and Zulu Wars of the 1870s. In these cases the Royal Navy's landing forces played a more significant role than in the offensive scenarios. The military forces available were limited, sometimes reduced by defeat, as in the Zulu War after Isandlwana. One of the most remarkable features of British colonial policy during the nineteenth century was its persistent failure to form a proper estimate of the opposition, despising Zulus for their simple weapons, and dismissing Boer marksmen as farmers. The richest nation on earth persis- tently embarked on military adventures with totally inadequate means, committing handfuls of infantry to hazardous expeditions with too few guns, improvised transport, and no cavalry.

The Royal Navy provided some strategic depth for these overstretched garrisons. Warships might bring the first reinforcements, as *Shannon* and *Pearl* did during the Indian Mutiny, or land their own men and guns to defend shallow coastal enclaves, like Cape Coast Castle. Naval guns and rockets played a disproportionate role as defence cuts left the British Army weak in artillery. Its ratio of gunners to infantry was even lower than in minor European armies, such as the Sardinians called upon to make up the numbers at Sebastopol. The technical skills of ship's crews allowed the Royal Navy to stand in for the Royal Engineers and logistical troops who were rarely present in adequate numbers in the colonies. Edmund Verney noted in the Indian Mutiny:

> how independent the Naval Brigade is compared with infantry regiments; the Naval Brigade can be sent anywhere with a small body of cavalry, but an infantry regiment must be accompanied by detachments of artillery, cavalry, sappers and miners.[30]

Verney thought every battalion should include a section of tradesmen: a wheelwright responsible for regimental and impressed vehicles, a ship- wright for bridging work, as well as a cabinetmaker, house carpenter, mason, armourer/blacksmith, and painter. The Naval Brigade at the Relief of Ladysmith in 1900 had a shipwright with every gun, well equipped with augers and coach-wrenches, able to replace shattered wheels or carriages. The natural presence of such skills among Naval Brigades made them more than just an additional source of bayonets. They represented qualitative as well as quantitative reinforcements, their long-service professionals readily switching from one role to another. After the Boers shot most of General Colley's gunners at the Ingogo River in 1881 the seamen gunners' training at Whale Island allowed the Naval Brigade to take over the Royal Artillery's 9pr field guns with as much facility as they had previously shown as riflemen. Acting as force multipliers in this way, Naval Brigades raised the operational effectiveness of British forces, enabling them to tackle tasks otherwise beyond them.

At the less intense end of the strategic continuum the Royal Navy found itself drawn into what might be termed police actions. The nineteenth-century world order was very different to that of today. In the 1990s legally established national governments are responsible for, or at least lay claim to, the entire land surface of the planet. A body of international law centred on the United Nations provides a means of addressing international issues peacefully. At the same time the loss of the Victorian sense of technical and moral superiority has eroded the will to act of most Western powers. In 1850 the will to act was alarmingly strong, while many areas lacked any recognisable authority from which legal redress could be sought for outrages against British trading or missionary interests. In some areas, such as Malaysia or the Arabian Gulf, piracy or gun-running were socially acceptable economic activities. Both coasts of Africa provoked intervention with the excesses of the slave trade and lurid tales of human sacrifice. In Central America infant republics struggled to establish their authority in the face of Yankee filibusters and homegrown revolutionaries. Royal Navy intervention in that area was as often supportive of local authority, as it was punitive. Captain Nowell Salmon, who won the *VC* at Lucknow, cooperated with Honduran troops in 1860 to foil an attempt by William Walker, a notorious filibuster, to establish his own republic there. The British Government preferred the restoration of peace and trade to the acquisition of new and expensive colonies, so short-lived interventions were more usual than permanent conquest. The Royal Navy's mobile units with their powerful self-contained landing forces were well suited to such operations which required prompt action rather than a persistent imperial presence.

Whatever the strategic level of naval power projection in the nineteenth century, one key feature runs through the subject like a dark blue thread. Technological and demographic developments ensured that major population centres and communication routes were vulnerable to maritime pressure. Often they lay near the coast or on major waterways such as the Peiho or the Irrawaddy. Until the internal combustion engine revolutionised transportation, steam-driven warships represented the most effective means yet devised of bringing massive fire power into range of these sensitive targets.

Most traffic still went by sea or river, despite the growing European railway network. Russia, the greatest land power of the mid-century with armies from Poland to the Caucasus, was brought low in the Crimean War by relentless pressure upon its Baltic and Black Sea coasts. The Tsar made peace in 1856 under the threat of worse to come, from a great armament of specialist gunboats and bomb-vessels. These never left Spithead, but the Royal Navy now had:

> the means of waging a really offensive war, not only against fleets, but harbours, fortresses and rivers – not merely of blockading, but of invading, and carrying the warfare of the sea to the very heart of the land.[31]

Naval Brigades were another crucial element in this application of seapower to events on land.

CHAPTER FOUR

The Kings Must Come Down and the Emperors Frown

THE 1850s and 60s saw a series of European interventions in three sovereign states in the Far East: China, Japan, and Burma. The Royal Navy took a prominent part in all these, as part of a general pattern of Western pressure upon societies that denied Europeans access to lucrative markets. Sometimes this denial was deliberate policy; sometimes Eastern governments were unable to prevent expressions of popular feeling against foreigners, as in Japan. French, Dutch, and United States ships often shared in the violent measures thought appropriate to the development of international trade. However, there was rarely any intention to annex large amounts of territory. Western action was meant to persuade local governments to provide a sound basis for trade free from the arbitrary exactions of government officials or private individuals regarded by Westerners as pirates.

OPENING DOORS I – CANTON (1856–58)

Western military historians divide the Anglo-Chinese hostilities of 1838–60 with misleading precision into the First, Second, and Third China Wars. The operations present no very coherent pattern, however, with frequent interruptions for diplomacy. The British had problems collecting sufficient forces at such a distance from home, and limited their actions, fearing the collapse of an already shaky Celestial Empire. Hostilities were rarely dignified by declarations of war, and often tempered by cooperation against common enemies, Imperial Chinese officials assisting in the Royal Navy's pursuit of pirates during inter-governmental hostilities.

The fundamental causes of conflict between China and the Western powers were economic. Until the eighteenth century China was self-sufficient, exporting luxury goods in exchange for hard cash. Then the importation of opium from India changed the balance of trade, draining China of silver and undermining the Chinese economy. The First China

War (1838–42) arose from the Chinese government's justifiable efforts to control the vicious import. Chinese refusal to acknowledge Westerners as political or military equals, however, led them into a disastrous blend of insincere diplomacy and ineffectual resistance. The more immediate cause of conflict was therefore the cultural clash between an inward-looking society, where merchants and soldiers were despised, and an aggressive trading nation, insistent upon its right to do business wherever it thought fit, however disreputable the commodity. The First China War ended after a British squadron had fought its way 100 miles inland up the Yangtse-kiang River, a fateful demonstration of the vulnerability of China's long coast, and great rivers to maritime pressure.

The Second and Third China Wars arose from British attempts to enforce the Treaty of Nanking of August 1842, but the fighting falls more logically into three geographical subsets rather than two legal ones. Operations began at Canton in the south, where Chinese seizure of an arguably British ship, the *Arrow*, led to a major Western assault on the Chinese provincial government there. This phase lasted from October 1856 to February 1858. There followed a series of attacks on the forts guarding the mouth of the River Peiho, which led via Tientsin to the Heavenly City itself. When the Treaty of Peking ended international hostilities in October 1860, British forces began a series of police actions around Shanghai in association with the late enemy against T'ai-p'ing rebels who overran much of central China during the 1850s. Operations in China employed a perplexing variety of warships, ranging from traditional men-of-war, with or without auxiliary steam engines, through modern steam corvettes like HMS *Pearl*, down to gunboats built for coastal operations against the Russians. Most of their crews saw action ashore at one time or another, showing how Naval Brigades formed as essential an ingredient of amphibious power projection as gunboats.

The brisk assertion of British control over the Canton waterways in October 1856 shows the flexibility of mid-nineteenth century naval forces. Rear-Admiral Sir Michael Seymour occupied all the defences of Canton between 23 October and 11 December, from the Bogue Forts near the river mouth up to the Dutch Folly and Bird's Nest Forts, overlooking the city itself. Casualties were few, despite the Chinese loading their guns to the muzzle with nails and scrap iron, for they built their defences square, without provision for flanking fire. The Chinese soldiers stood to their guns until the British entered the embrasures, but the Mandarins had boats ready to facilitate their own escape, abandoning their panic-stricken followers, who rushed into the water to be rescued by their erstwhile enemies.[1]

Yeh, the Imperial Viceroy at Canton, had a reputation for strongmindedness, and for having cut off more heads than any of his colleagues.[2] He refused to come to terms, despite the arrival around his *yamun* or headquarters of a steady stream of 10-inch shells from HMS *Encounter*'s pivot gun. Yeh responded with placards offering 300 dollars for any barbarian head taken.[3] Seymour resolved upon extreme measures to bring the situation home to Yeh personally. Civilians were cleared out of the line of fire to allow naval guns to breach the city wall, which they did on 29 October. Three hundred marines and small-arms men stormed ashore accompanied by two field pieces. The landing party spread out along the top of the walls, and blew in the gates, allowing Seymour and Mr Parkes the British consul to inspect Yeh's premises at close quarters. The only resistance was some sniping, which killed three marines, but at sunset the visitors returned on board, tacitly admitting that they were not strong enough to hold even part of the city. The Chinese underlined their defiance by capturing two American sailors who had gone along for plunder, and displaying their severed heads on the walls near the breach.[4]

The Chinese were not slow to exploit the weakness of naval forces when confronted with a determined land-based opposition. They repaired the walls with sandbags as often as British guns cleared them away, and exploded a bomb under the quarters of the garrison of the British factory. They floated fire rafts down on HMS *Barracouta* and exploded infernal machines alongside *Niger*. So taken were the Chinese authorities with *Barracouta* that they offered 50,000 dollars for her destruction, although her officers thought there was little danger of the reward being collected.

No troops were available from India, even before the Mutiny, so in January 1857 Seymour moved his ships downstream, to await reinforcements. The arrival of a fresh brigade of Royal Marines in December allowed him to resume hostilities. Seymour made careful preparations, a model of how a Naval Brigade might be organised. Almost his entire force was naval, except for Her Majesty's 59th Foot, including a brigade of French seamen. Throughout the autumn small-arms and field-piece parties were constantly ashore, drilling with their little brass 12pr mountain guns. In early December the landing forces concentrated on Honan Island opposite Canton, quartered in tea and ginger godowns. They broke open the tea chests, and drank the flowery Pekoe *ad nauseam*:

becoming perfect connoisseurs in aroma and flavour, almost qualifying for that sensitive profession, a tea taster ... I certainly could have had no nerves, for one drank enough tea, free of expense, to keep a fellow awake for the rest of his natural existence.

The marine officers built snug little rooms with the chests, the scent of tea leaves neutralising the unsavoury odours wafting across from Canton. They wondered whether the Chinese would really fight: 'all thought what hard lines it would be to have come so far for only a ransom and an abject apology'.[5]

Canton sat four-square on the north bank of the Canton River, its thirty-foot-high walls enclosing a dense labyrinth of streets. Their broad top formed an unbroken means of communication that put troops in possession of the walls in control of the city also. Beyond Canton lay a number of detached hills garnished with forts, in particular Lin's and Gough's Forts on the north-east. Seymour's plan was to concentrate naval gunfire on the corners to cut the defenders off from the east side where he intended to land. Before opening fire naval officers put up posters in Chinese warning of the impending attack. Joking crowds pressed around to read the proclamation, stuck onto a triumphal arch set up in honour of the British being kept so long outside the city.

Private William Baker RMLI was clearing his rifle, before embarking in one of the gunboats used as landing craft, when the warships opened fire, making the whole island shake. By nightfall Canton was ablaze, 'like our own Shropshire iron country at night – a plain of fire':

At first it appeared as though the besiegers were bent upon reducing the place to ashes; but little by little, as I gained . . . some idea of the scene as a whole the destruction was not without a plan. There was a great blaze at the north west angle of the city. The gate there is surmounted by a Chinese guardhouse, with the usual grotesque upward-pointed roof. Shells and rockets were poured in volleys upon this structure, and it became a sheet of flame through which the roof, the rafters, and the walls stood out in dark outline. By constant showers of rockets the flame was led up and down the city wall, and in an incredibly short time, the long thin line of fire shot high into the heavens, and then subsided into a smouldering smoke.[6]

The troops landed in waves at 7 a.m. on 28 December 1857, the Master of the flagship acting as beachmaster:

1st)	59th with Royal Engineers	800 men
2nd)	French Naval Brigade	950 men
3rd)	Royal Naval Brigade	1,829 men
4th)	Royal Marine Brigade	2,100 men

Sixteen different ships contributed to the Naval Brigade. HMS *Sans Pareil* sent eighteen officers and 267 ratings, almost half her complement. The Brigade was in three divisions, each about 500 strong, supported by HMS *Calcutta's* five field guns. The battery commander was a Lieutenant Goodenough, known as 'Holy Joe', but evidently a fighting man as he gave up command of HM Gunboat *Bittern* to lead a landing party.

The leading troops pushed north towards Lin's Fort near the north-east corner of Canton. At first the only sign of the enemy was the wailing and beating of gongs that echoed strangely across the paddy fields, but soon dead Chinese began to lie about, showing the effects of the ships' fire. Lin's Fort fell easily enough, but the 1st and 3rd Divisions of the Naval Brigade enjoyed an experience familiar to many infantry soldiers, fighting for the next day's start line. Then they settled down for a chilly night in the Criminals' Cemetery, sheltering from the cold wind between the burial mounds. Captain Cooper Key's coxswain made him some cocoa, but like a true Victorian hero he refused to drink it, as there was insufficient to go around.

The 1st and 3rd divisions of sailors took the right of the line, the *Calcutta's* field battery out in front in the place of honour. A provisional battalion of marines drawn from the ships of the squadron was in support behind them, while the 2nd division formed the centre with the French and 59th on their left. The 1,500 RMLI remained in reserve to bring up ammunition, guard the wounded, and cover the open right flank. The reserves were in action before the troops in front, marching off to Lin Fort next morning at 3 a.m. after a liquid breakfast of quinine wine and grog. William Baker described the action in breathless prose:

> we had to carry scaling ladders and it was enough to melt any one we advanced about one mile and a half where we was at once engaged we went in skirmishing order down a Plain and it was pretty sharp for the time . . . their was some on our left about a mile scaling the walls and they come round the wall Cheering on and then their was three hearty cheers from the whole and it was not long before the union jack and the french eagle . . . was soon flying on the height of Canton and to see the Chinese run and we laughing at them.[7]

Under cover of darkness the Naval Brigade had closed up to the city wall, and placed scaling ladders as close to the ditch as possible. One officer fell into a cesspit, swearing and smelling so horribly when he was hauled out that everyone agreed he could drive the Chinese off the walls on his own. Next morning at 8.30 a.m., the ladder parties rushed forward into the waterlogged ditch under the covering fire of howitzers and marine sharpshooters, followed by assault parties who swarmed up onto the covered way. One of Goodenough's seamen remembered him at prayer, 'standing with his face to the wall and sword in hand unsheathed', before hoisting his guns over the wall to meet a Chinese counter-attack:

> The Chinese came trotting up the hill, waving flags etc. . . . we had expended every shot and shell with the exception of three rounds of canister, with one of which our gun was loaded. After the discharge the rush at the foe was made, Lieutenant Goodenough singling out a big Tartar mandarin. When fighting with him his field glasses, which was slung round his neck, got in the way, and by sheer strength he broke the leather strap, and flung it away.[8]

French and British bluejackets raced north along the top of the wall, covered from the fire of Gough's Fort by the battlements, rolling up the defences as they went. Although the Chinese on the West wall held out until dusk, reversing their guns to fire into the city, it was clear the defenders had been taken unawares. No doubt they believed the height of the walls would prevent an escalade. They must also have been thoroughly shaken by the twenty-four-hour bombardment. A pond near the escalade 'was literally one mass of arms and legs, and heads', while surrounding villages were full of wounded Chinese, who had crawled there to die. Naval Brigade casualties were five killed and thirty-four wounded. Among them was a midshipman, mortally wounded by the heavy iron head of a spear rocket, whose deceptive zig-zag course made them one of the most dangerous Chinese weapons.[9]

Yeh remained obdurate until Captain Cooper Key's marines marched him off on board ship, but the Chinese military authorities were more amenable. They could not stand against western firepower and organisation, but it was impossible for the small numbers of Allied troops to control Canton, especially after the sailors withdrew on 12 January 1858. Popular resistance took the form of terrorism against the marine garrison:

> their was several of our men lost by going about they was very Barbarous People for they beheaded several of our men that was when their was one by it self for they are great Cowards.[10]

The Street of Benevolence and Love on the other hand greeted visitors with smiles, and bits of pink paper saying 'Welcome', and the Allies lifted the blockade on 10 February. The Royal Marines made themselves comfortable with the *Illustrated London News*, reclining in full Mandarin toggery under mosquito nets. Canton was reported, 'to have settled down very quietly', under an international commission assisted by Yeh's erstwhile military colleagues. Trade was lively; Chinese merchants anxious to barter their teas for foreign goods.[11]

THE TAKU FORTS AND THE PEIHO RIVER (1859–60)

Allied war aims escalated during the protracted crisis at Canton. Yeh's procrastination convinced Lord Elgin, the British plenipotentiary, of the need for direct representation at Peking, with access to the Emperor. This appalled the Chinese, who had no such rights themselves. In May 1858 British naval attention shifted to the Peiho River at the other end of China to Canton. The Peiho was unsuited to naval demonstrations. Except at high tide, the bar across the river mouth was dry, the shallows keeping major ships seven or eight miles offshore. The defences stretched for over a mile on both banks, which were piled to prevent landings. The defenders' morale was high, despite the poor social standing of Chinese soldiers, hired out by their officers as tea pickers, and their laughable weapons – wooden swords, bone-tipped arrows, and fantastically carved wooden helmets more fit for the nursery than a battlefield. Their cannon were better cast than at Canton, however, with good canister rounds and hollow shot modelled on the British pattern. When Lieutenant Goodenough reconnoitred landing places the locals admitted British strength at sea, but claimed they would be unable to cope with the Chinese on land.[12]

Chinese confidence was misplaced. HM Gunvessel *Cormorant* broke the boom at 10 a.m. on 20 May, followed by smaller steamers towing boats full of marines and small-arms men. Splashing ashore over fifty yards of mud to turn the upstream flank of the forts, they found the garrisons streaming away, led by their mandarins. However, not all Chinese gunners were cowards, or all British sailors heroic. Midshipman E.H. Seymour, later an Admiral of the Fleet, was among those towed past the forts:

I remember a shot passing through a boat close to mine, in which a young seaman had lain down under what are called the stern sheets; the shot must have narrowly missed him, and as he did not reply when called to I thought he was killed; examination showed he had escaped any injury, but was much frightened.[13]

[85]

Within a week the gunboats were at Tientsin, giving the mandarins no time to obstruct the river. Goodenough thought Tientsin 'a dirty wretched place', but it lay at the northern end of the Grand Canal, Peking's main route to central and southern China. Occupation of this sensitive spot led speedily to the Treaty of Tientsin, conceding all the Allied demands, including representation at Peking. The Tientsin merchants were pleased to accept payment for their fruit and flowers, but popular resistance only collapsed after some brisk crowd-control measures. Captain Roderick Dew was pelted as he walked along, making the best of his way off with the loss of his hat, and when a party of marines went up, the gate of the city was shut in their faces. However, half a dozen bluejackets got over the wall, and came down on the flank of the crowd, belabouring them with their cutlass scabbards, and opening the gate to the marines who marched round chastising some of the most impudent looking.[14]

Outrages against individual westerners continued. One technique was to wait up a dark alley with a long bamboo equipped with steel hooks, to catch a passerby round the neck, and drag him off to an unpleasant death. Walter White, who served in HMS *Scout*, tells of a French drummer whose boiled remains were found in a vat of oil. Other Chinese exploited the commercial possibilities of the Allied presence. Villagers swam out to passing ships with fruit, ice, and poultry, calling out '*Combien?*' and 'How much?' On Sunday afternoons Goodenough's men consumed tea and sponge cake at the Muslim baker's in Tientsin, while in the Street of Everlasting Prosperity, gambling for a hot dinner of chopped pork, shrimps, and seaweed reminded Walter White of the 'toss and buy' of pie sellers at home.

Once the Allies had withdrawn from Tientsin, Chinese officials resumed their evasions. A year after Seymour's capture of the Taku Forts his successor was back off the mouth of the Peiho. Rear-Admiral Sir James Hope had made his name raising the blockade of the River Parana in 1845 in command of the appropriately named paddle-steamer *Firebrand*. He would be less fortunate on the Peiho. The Chinese had repaired and improved the Forts, and matting obscured the embrasures, concealing the guns.[15] Four separate wooden booms bristling with iron stakes had replaced the flimsy bamboo obstacle of the previous year. Cross-lashed together, they formed a mass of timber, 120 feet wide and three feet deep. A narrow opening might have allowed a gunboat to enter, but the strength of the current would make such a passage exceedingly difficult.

Hope felt he had little alternative to a frontal attack, storming the forts after the gunboats had silenced their fire. The basis for his decision was flimsy enough. A surviving map of the forts drawn by Hope's Major Royal

Engineers on 20 June 1859, and possibly annotated by Hope himself, lists the information still lacking about the position of the high-water mark, the softness of the mud, and the nature of the ditches along the front of the Southern Fort. Some works were coloured red to show that their position was only approximate.[16] Hope had nine gunboats and two larger craft to tackle these uncharted obstacles. Bearing friendly sounding names such as *Starling* or *Banterer*, the gunboats displaced 235 to 250 tons, mounting a 68pr and 32pr apiece and a couple of 24pr howitzers, with a crew of forty. He also had a landing force of 350 marines, brought up from Canton as escorts for the intended mission to Peking, and a similar number of bluejackets from ships beyond the bar.

Two of the gunboats ran aground almost immediately, but four others, including *Plover*, the flagship, passed the first barrier at 2 p.m. on 25 June 1859. As they struggled with the iron stakes at the second barrier the Chinese opened fire with thirty to forty guns of all calibres from 32prs to 8-inch, their accuracy prompting stories of European gunners in Chinese pay. Hope himself suffered two severe wounds, his blood dramatically staining the map from which he was directing the action. Thirty-two of *Plover*'s crew were hit, and their commander sliced in half by a round shot.

Mr Ward, the neutral US minister in China, was watching from Commodore Josiah Tatnall's flagship USS *Powhatan.*

we could see from our vessels that the English were suffering far beyond their anticipations, and the Commodore said to me, 'Those forts cannot be taken with the force they have'. We could see the shot destroying the vessels, while the forts were hardly injured by the small battery of the English.[17]

Tatnall had fought the British in the War of 1812, but he was sufficiently moved to go aboard *Plover* to offer to evacuate the wounded. Waiting in the lee of the gunboat, the crew of his gig slipped quietly aboard to lend a hand with the forward pivot gun. However regrettable under international law, the incident became celebrated with the phrase, 'Blood is thicker than water', marking a new spirit of cooperation between the Royal and United States Navies.

Plover and *Opposum* dropped below the first barrier to refit, *Lee* took ground to avoid sinking, while about 5.40 p.m. *Kestrel* settled down, the water half-way up her funnels. Having accounted for half the British squadron, the Chinese guns fell silent at dusk, prompting the British to try storming the South Fort which had suffered most from the bombardment. Unable to tow up all the assault craft, they requested the help of the US Navy, who agreed, 'considering that the Chinese had forced them into their present position'.[18] No sooner were the British ashore than it became apparent the Chinese silence was a ruse, the defenders opening up with great guns, musketry, and stinkpots.

The term 'ashore' is misleading, the attackers walking 200 yards under heavy fire, before the water became even knee deep. Casualties were smothered in the mud, whole files swept away by round shot, and their ladders smashed. Perhaps 100 men were hit in as many yards. The marine officers suffered particularly, their red jackets standing out amongst the blue-clad rank and file. When the survivors reached the first ditch after an hour struggling through the mud, they discovered the significance of Hope's incomplete intelligence summary. Instead of finding the water knee deep, it was over their heads. Using ladders as bridges, the storming party got across somehow, to find a second 'dry' ditch full of soft mud. This took another hour to cross, the sights beyond all description:

> Now came the tug of war. We had crossed two ditches, and the third lay before us, not fifty yards from the wall. We had only three ladders left, and if we broke any of these it was all up with us, as none of our rifles would go off; the ammunition was wet, and the rifles also, besides being choked up with mud. Unless we could put three men up at a time on the wall (about thirty feet high) we should stand no chance, as we had nothing but cold steel to fight with . . .
>
> When I got on the bank there was a nice spectacle before me, the walls covered with men not more than thirty-five yards distance. When they saw me they gave a volley. I don't know how it was I escaped. My clothes were cut to pieces, and yet with the exception of a few scrapes here and there, I was all right. Was it not a pity all the ladders were broken? And here we were looking on while the enemy stood on the walls picking us off at their leisure.[19]

About 9.55 p.m. the boats began to remove the wounded, the last British personnel leaving the beach at 1.30 a.m. next day. Hope claimed that 'had the opposition they experienced been that usual in Chinese warfare, there is little doubt that the place would have been successfuly carried', but this reads like special pleading. The 25 June 1859 was the heaviest defeat the Royal Navy suffered during the nineteenth century, with a casualty list exceeding that of the Battle of St Vincent in 1797. Over a quarter of the gunboat crews became casualties, as did a staggering 44 per cent of the RM battalion.[20]

Narrow escapes were common. One man had no less than twelve arrow wounds, although none proved fatal. An officer having recourse to his brandy flask found the bottom had been shot away. Another, attempting to calm his nerves with tobacco after his trousers were riddled with bullets, found both his pipes choked with mud, although one more fortunate enjoyed a cigar in the front ditch. Walter White was among those who got away:

> As we lay huddled up round the funnel for warmth, covered with mud and being completely exhausted and disheartened by our defeat, I, and I daresay others as well . . . utterly broke down and had a silent though none the less bitter weep for nearly an hour. All round lay the wounded, whose cries and groans were terrible to hear, and the doctors working by lantern light, gave the appearance of a slaughter house.[21]

Once the British had gone, the Chinese went down onto the mud to pull out anyone left behind, sticking their heads up on the Fort walls. Three gunboats were lost, besides the human casualties, including *Plover* which took ground avoiding the crippled *Lee*. *Plover*'s funnels and steam pipes were so riddled that, despite their being patched up with hawsers and fearnought, she could not raise enough steam to get off again. For two nights volunteers pumped out her stokehold and threw guns overboard, before leaving her to be burned by the Chinese. A week later, after dressing ship in honour of Independence Day, American flags at the main, the squadron sailed for Shanghai.

When they returned next year, they were in overwhelming strength, with a large military force of French troops, and British units released by the end of the Indian Mutiny. The British commander was Sir James Hope Grant, a circumspect bassoon-playing cavalry officer. The most significant feature of his operations for the navy would be the absence of a Naval Brigade, despite initial reports that 'A naval brigade will probably be formed from the blue-jackets and marines who will act with the army'.[22] However, after the unopposed landings at Pehtang north of the Peiho estuary, Lieutenant Paget of HMS *Sampson* wrote:

> Everything still exceedingly monotonous . . . Everybody grumbling at not being home . . . The chance of a naval brigade seems quite to have died away and now nothing is left for the unfortunate Navy except dirty work and laying nine miles offshore.[23]

The Taku Forts fell to the army a few days later. Goodenough, who returned to China as Captain of HMS *Encounter* after the Peiho disaster, thought that the fighting was all over without any naval men, outside a few gunboats, hearing the whistle of a shot.

At least one naval detachment did see action ashore, unnoticed by Sir James Hope's laconic despatch. Lieutenant Percy Luxmore of HMS *Chesapeake* was pier master at Pehtang when he received orders to join the army with an armed boat's crew, two days' provisions, and some coils of rope. He had already lost a pair of boots in the mud dodging some Tartar cavalry. Now he was to assist 1st Division by spiking some guns on the other side of the Peiho which might enfilade the right flank of the army as it wheeled round to attack the Taku Forts from the rear. Dropping downriver in captured junks, his handful of sailors commandeered a sampan for their raid, the Royal Scots providing covering fire from the riverbank. Returning safely, despite fire from another battery, Luxmore found they had to do the job again. This time they took a couple of black-smiths across with their mauls, and knocked the trunnions off most of the guns. Luxmore and another man covered the blacksmiths with revolvers, trading shots with Tartar cavalry round the corners of the houses.[24]

Luxmore's party did not stay for the assault on the main forts. However, the ubiquitous Walter White describes the Second Fight at the Taku Forts in terms that closely follow other accounts: a brush with Tartar cavalry during the march from Pehtang to Tongku, the destruction of some junks under the guns of the Forts, and a pig chase along the beach, the gingall balls cutting up the ground rather closer than was pleasant. At the storming of the Northern Fort on 21 August he accompanied the 44th and 67th Regiments, supported by a Royal Marine Battalion. The ground all around was littered with crowsfeet, so constructed that, however they lay, two spikes pointed upwards. The marines, and possibly sailors, carried ladders down to the right angle of the Fort, where the fire was less intense, and put them across the ditch like bridges, men standing up to their armpits in water to support them while their comrades rushed across. The Chinese stood to the last, the gunners bayonetted around their guns. Others were impaled on *punji* stakes when they were thrown over the wall, or fell into their own traps as they retired.[25]

There followed a re-run of Seymour's waterborne advance on Tientsin. The wrecks of *Plover* and *Lee* could still be seen, while the 13-inch hawser holding the massive boom timbers end-on to the stream underlined Hope Grant's wisdom in taking the Forts from the landward side. Tientsin marked the end of active operations for the Navy, although Paget kept up his hopes:

our Naval Brigade [which] has been so much talked of has not yet been organised but if affairs do not shortly mend they will have to find men somewhere.[26]

The naval role for the rest of the campaign was logistical, including a bridge of boats built across the Peiho by men from the fleet. Goodenough impressed 200 salt-trade boats whose Chinese owners were astounded to be paid two dollars a day for their services. The armies went on to Peking to conclude a treaty on 24 October 1860, evacuating the Imperial city in November. The sailors who had suffered so much outside the Taku Forts were now quartered inside them. The river froze, and the skins of ration sheep were greatly valued in the intense cold. Barrels of porter appeared, the frozen ale served out in lumps to be melted over charcoal fires. It was wretched stuff to drink after so much trouble.

THE T'AI-P'ING REVOLT (1861–62)

The Treaty of Peking ended hostilities between the British and Chinese governments, but did not end Royal Naval activity in Chinese waters. The defeat of 1860 was catastrophic for the Manchu dynasty, whose ability to govern already faced a serious challenge from the T'ai-p'ing rebellion. Few ports in the central coastal provinces of Chekiang and Kiangsu remained in Imperial Chinese hands by 1861. Two of these, Shanghai and Ningpo, were also Treaty Ports. T'ai-p'ing moves towards them brought conflict with the western powers trading through them. Strictly the British and French were neutral, but in practice their neutrality was uneven. Sir James Hope grossly exceeded his orders not to use force against the rebels, 'except for the actual protection of the lives and property of British subjects'.[27] He began by helping the Imperial authorities keep the few cities they still held. Goodenough went to Ningpo 'to trace fortifications, plant guns and bully the mandarins into execution of their own cause, a much more difficult task than fighting'.

The incapacity of the Chinese government prompted Hope to more active measures. In February 1862 he launched a series of expeditions against T'ai-p'ing strongholds around Shanghai. The forces committed were small. The order of battle at the capture of Chepoo (17 April) was typical: 150 blue-jacket small-arms men, seventy-five more with three 12pr howitzers, another thirty acting as pioneers, and eighty Marines. The army contributed four mountain howitzers, a company from the 99th Foot, and two battalions of

Indian infantry. The French added a touch of the exotic, reinforcing their naval brigade with a battalion of Tirailleurs Algériens in cornflower-blue zouave uniforms trimmed with yellow.[28] Four hundred 'disciplined' Chinese troops were a reminder of the dubious company the Royal Navy were keeping – their commanding officer a one-time accomplice of William Walker the filibuster, who had been arrested by Captain Nowell Salmon *VC* in Central America, and shot.

The T'ai-p'ings usually stood on the defensive, behind formidable earthworks: rows of bamboo stakes three foot high, driven into the ground thick and close, heaps of boxes filled with earth and stones, coffins, bags of cotton, sandbags, tables and furniture. Outclassed in artillery, the T'ai-p'ings had plenty of modern small arms. A local newspaper remarked that the only trade they understood was arms smuggling, attributing heavy Allied casualties at Ningpo (16 May) to T'ai-p'ing possession of 'rifles and revolvers of the best foreign manufacture and charged with the strongest English gunpowder'.[29] Allied tactical success depended on exploiting their superior artillery, before coming to close quarters. The usual technique with the massive city walls was to demolish the flimsy brick parapet with field guns at a convenient point for an escalade, but heavier guns might be taken along, such as the two 32prs deployed at Kahding in October 1862. Small parties of marines infiltrated any cover near to the defences, ready to shoot in an escalade, or rush a breach cleared by *extempore* naval sappers. Often the artillery fire clinched matters, none of the defenders waiting for the final assault. At Chepoo the whole affair 'seems to have differed as far as the Allies were concerned, from a Volunteer sham fight only in so far as fewer people stood a chance of being hurt'. The T'ai-p'ing camp was well stocked with English-made ammunition still in its wrappers, dinners smoking upon the tables, and tea still warm in the cups.[30]

The T'ai-p'ings put on a better show at Ningpo (10 May), although even here British losses were under thirty all told. Walter White was among the landing party:

When we jumped ashore we found we were in for a hot time for in less than it takes time to tell Mr Hogg the surgeon was shot through the arm and Edward Cannon a Marine was dead with a bullet through his head. We formed up and with a cheer rushed for the walls . . . the first man up Davis was shot, fell back dead on us who were below. The next one down was Lieutenant Kenney who was shot through the chest and received a spear thrust as he was falling. Several men fell but we stuck to it and at last fought our way over the walls.[31]

The T'ai-p'ings suffered disproportionately heavy losses. Cut-off parties of bluejackets shot down fleeing rebels, a heartlessness reflected in Roderick Dew's comments on the 'verminlike nature of these rebels'. Chinese Imperial troops kept out of the way until the fighting was over, but made up for this afterwards by the most revolting atrocities. At Kahding, taken and then lost in May 1862, they killed 2,500 'escaping rebels', their commander offering to produce the ears as evidence. White believed the T'ai-p'ings had taken Ningpo recently, so blamed them for the horrible scenes he found in the streets there. In fact the blame lies with the pirates employed as Imperial officials, and with British officers who took sides in internal Chinese affairs.

The recapture of Kahding in October 1862 achieved Sir James Hope's aim of removing the T'ai-p'ings from an area thirty miles around Shanghai. Hope had been replaced by Vice-Admiral Sir Augustus Kuper, who had less patience with the excesses of such officers as Dew. The change of command combined with public outrage at home to end this unsavoury episode in British imperial history, which showed the dangerous possibilities of so powerful a weapon as Naval Brigades. Local commanders had pursued their own foreign policy, without proper consideration for international law, or the national interest. White and his messmates were delighted to get away from Shanghai, where they buried five men a day from smallpox, cholera, and dysentery. Their only regret was that so many who had come through the Mutiny and Chinese Wars should end their days in a sideshow, on the banks of some filthy river.

OPENING DOORS II: BEFORE THE RISING SUN (1863–64)

Disengagement from China did not end the Royal Navy's activities in the Far East. Commercial interest shifted to Japan, an island even more remote and mysterious than the Celestial Empire. The United States Navy had interrupted Japan's 300 years of self-imposed isolation in the 1850s, causing sharp conflicts within Japanese society. Popular xenophobia expressed itself in murderous attacks on individual Europeans, and shore batteries fired on passing steamers. Westerners were confined to Yokohama, doing business with their revolvers close at hand. Warships lay close offshore, their fires banked, ready for anything.

In August 1863 Vice-Admiral Kuper took half his squadron to the port of Kagoshima, in the southern Japanese island of Kyushu, the stronghold of the powerful Satsuma clan. A British merchant who pushed rudely through the Prince of Satsuma's entourage had been cut down, leading to demands for an indemnity and punishment for the Samurai responsible. The Prince considered the British demands unreasonable, and prepared to fight, his European-style batteries mounting over eighty guns, ranging from 10-inch to 18pr. Among the defenders were several young men who would rise to high rank in the Imperial Japanese Navy, including the future Count Togo and Admiral Inouye, whose ADC wrote a rare account of a naval bombardment from the recipients' point of view.[32]

The Japanese displayed their customary strategic inventiveness. A forlorn hope of Samurai rowed out to the squadron disguised as fruitsellers, hoping to take out the British officers as a prelude to the forts opening fire. Once on board, however, the Samurai found themselves too closely watched by marines with fixed bayonets to carry out their plan. As talks stalled, Kuper seized three steamers belonging to the Daimyo. When the British sat down for dinner at noon 15 August 1860, the hot-tempered Samurai took advantage of a squall to direct a hail of shot and shell upon the flagship HMS *Euryalus*. The British ships hastily weighed anchor, *Euryalus's* band playing 'Oh dear, What can the matter be?':

> The weather became worse, the air was misty, and a heavy sea was running. On shore men and horses were running hither and thither ... Everywhere there was excitement but especially onboard the *Perseus*, who being fired at suddenly by the Hakamagoshi battery, had no time to weigh; so she in much confusion, slipped her cables, and left her anchor, then came into battle formation with the remainder. The Japanese Samurai when they saw her do that all laughed heartily.[33]

Matters soon progressed beyond laughter as Kuper's squadron steamed slowly past the batteries at point blank range, wind-blown smoke making it hard to judge the distance, different sources giving 400 to 800 yards. The weather now being very dirty, the ships were unable to keep formation, allowing the defenders to concentrate on HMS *Euryalus*. One of her officers, a veteran of several smart storming expeditions in China, thought the action the warmest he had seen. One unlucky shell killed the Captain, as he was talking to the Admiral, and Commander Wilmot, scattering the latter's brains about the deck. One 10-inch shell exploded at the muzzle of No. 3 gun on main deck, killing seven men on the spot. Another came through the starboard waist bulwark and burst under the starboard launch, without hurting anyone, while a round shot carried away the starboard speaking tube on the bridge, breaking all the windows under the break of the poop.

British return fire was hampered by the weather, shells intended for the batteries starting numerous fires among the papier mâché houses. Despite this they silenced many of the defending guns. Admiral Inouye was one of a gun detachment firing red-hot shot, precariously insulated from the charge with green grass, when a bursting shell tore a piece from his thigh, and bent his sword like a sickle. The other gunners lay down, not to escape injury, but hoping to meet the landing they were sure would follow the bombardment. However, the worsening weather and Kuper's small force made such an operation impossible. To Japanese delight the squadron retired to ride out the typhoon that had set in. Kuper felt he had vindicated the honour of the flag, but in Japanese eyes the British had suffered 'an undreamed of defeat'.[34]

Kagoshima shows the futility of naval pressure applied without adequate landing forces. In the absence of a landing both sides could claim an indecisive exchange result as victory. Admiral Kuper had suffered 'unusually great losses': thirteen dead and fifty wounded, half of them in *Euryalus*. Commander Okuda by contrast recorded one killed and six wounded. The unusual casualty ratio is partly attributable to the failure of the technology that generally favoured the British. The vent pieces of the new Armstrong breech-loading guns jammed or split, while their carriages cracked with the recoil. Of eight 40prs in HMS *Euryalus*, one was unserviceable before the action and another five became so during it. The vent of her 110pr bowchaser blew out, knocking down the whole gun crew, who remained paralysed until roused by the captain of the gun shouting, 'Well, is there ere a b—— of you will go and get the spare vent piece?' Even the serviceable guns misfired repeatedly, 'a serious drawback to quick firing', as *Argus*' Gunner dryly commented. One officer blamed the sailors for cleaning the new shells too much, causing jams by scraping off the lead rings intended to grip the rifling.[35] The Armstrongs' poor performance at Kagoshima would set back the introduction of breech-loaders into the Royal Navy by almost twenty years.

The effect of the action upon the Japanese was quite different, the Satsumas becoming keen exponents of modernisation. The wounded Inouye remembered the battle as a dream, but his recollections in old age sum up the contrast between Japanese and Chinese reactions to Western intervention:

the squadron was very magnificent, a war vessel is indeed a brave object ... unless this country has these important engines of war, and it must be as soon as possible ... we cannot be independent among the world powers.[36]

The destruction of a city the size of Edinburgh had little short-term result, other than demonstrating the uselessness of Armstrong guns at 400 yards. Parliament and the press attacked Admiral Kuper's 'destruction of an ancient civilisation in the interests of commerce', and accused the Government of adopting the 'Yankee principle' of fighting every aristocracy not to its taste.[37] Nevertheless, eight companies of Royal Marines left Plymouth for Japan in December 1863, in HMS *Conqueror*, a line-of-battle ship with main deck guns removed to act as a troopship. The battalion marched up to Yokohama, with their band, accompanied by 'many dear little "musmees"', as Poyntz euphemistically called them, but the conflict between East and West was far from resolved.[38] Scowling assassins thronged the Japanese treaty ports where the times of Charlemagne met those of Louis Napoleon, and often had the better of it.

THE GIBRALTAR OF THE EAST – SHIMONOSEKI (SEPTEMBER 1864)

Captain Moresby of HMS *Argus* was puzzled by the contrast between the politeness of ordinary Japanese and their apparent ignorance of the laws of decency. Their temples and shops displayed items that at home might have appeared under lock and key in an anatomical museum. He marvelled at the exquisite beauty of Yeddo, the executive seat of the Japanese government, and ate sweets made from seaweed, but he was there for a more serious purpose: to agree joint action against Chosiu, a powerful Daimyo who prevented access to the Inland Sea through the Straits of Shimonoseki. Passage through this artery of trade was so dangerous that insurance offices would no longer cover the risk. During the winter of 1863–64 Chosiu isolated himself by attacking Japanese as well as Western shipping, providing an opportunity for international cooperation. When the Inland Sea expedition left Yokohama on 29 August 1864, it not only included a proper landing force in the shape of HMS *Conqueror* and her Marines, but also three French and four Dutch warships, while the USA chartered a civilian steamer to show solidarity.[39]

Shimonoseki had been compared with Sebastopol, but Kuper and his French colleague found its defences peculiarly ill sited:

A wooded valley some six or seven miles wide lay between two lofty bluffs, and along its foreshore, just above the high water mark, were ranged the principal batteries with groups of guns protected by a palisaded parapet. One small battery was placed on the northern bluff among the trees, and had the others been similarly hidden the result might have been very different.[40]

The Admirals agreed to attack on 5 September, as soon as the fierce tidal currents permitted. The Allied squadron formed three lines: seven corvettes off the western shore, with the larger flagships in the middle of the strait, further south. Five shallow-draught gunboats went inshore to the east, their bare-footed gun crews workmanlike in flannel shirts and trousers, rammers and trigger lines in hand. *Euryalus* opened the action at 3 p.m. on 5 September, with the 110pr that had caused trouble at Kagoshima:

> Most people imagined the Japanese would not show fight; but almost simultaneously with the first shot from the flagship their batteries returned the fire. It was a beautiful sight to see the flashes and puffs of smoke darting forth from the wooded sides of the hills, and very well indeed for a time were their guns served; many of the allied vessels were hulled, and several men killed and wounded; but Armstrong's and Krupp's, of heavy naval calibre, belching a hail of shot, shell, and rockets, were too effective, so by degrees the enemy's fire slackened, and eventually ceased.[41]

The marines in *Conqueror* were not to be left out, the RMA manning her pivot gun to lob shells over the gunboats. Japanese fire ceased by 5.30 p.m., too late for an immediate landing, although parties from HMS *Perseus* and the Dutch *Medusa* landed without orders to spike the guns of No. 5 battery: the one battery that did not resume firing next day. Kuper referred only to straggling shots fired at the gunboats towing in the landing parties on 6 September, but Moresby thought the Japanese fired with effect, showing how an assault needs to follow the preparatory bombardment promptly, without allowing the enemy time to collect themselves.

Otherwise the landing went in unopposed, covered by the ship's guns and howitzers mounted in men-of-war boats. The force consisted of small-arms men from *Euryalus* and *Conqueror*, the Royal Marine battalion, reinforced by Marines from the squadron, and battalions of French and Dutch seamen. Moresby thought it a marvel that the enemy had held out as long as they had for 'excepting the traverses between the guns there was not the slightest protection from our shell fire, which struck them full in the face'.[42] Kuper led the main body against the prime batteries, where they dismounted and spiked the guns, burnt the carriages and platforms, and blew up the magazines. The marines marched west along the beach, to the outskirts of Shimonoseki itself. While the men ate their dinners, Captain Poyntz and some other officers explored the empty streets. Revolvers in hand, they relieved a lonely samurai of his sword, and with more difficulty tried to make polite conversation with some young women left behind by the general evacuation.

Kuper judged it imprudent to remain ashore overnight, so at 4 p.m. he issued orders to re-embark. At this point events proved that withdrawal is the most dangerous moment for an amphibious force. No sooner were the French and Dutch battalions off the beach, than an outburst of firing began from the bush. At the same moment, by ill chance, HMS *Perseus* took ground under the silent guns of No. 5 battery occupied by the British Naval Brigade under Captain J.H.J. Alexander of HMS *Euryalus* to cover the right flank of Kuper's force as it moved along the beach. Japanese riflemen and light artillery had previously harassed them from the trees, but Alexander now decided he had to clear the valley before dark. Other sources attribute the ensuing action to a Japanese ambush, but Alexander's account leaves no doubt that the British took the initiative.[43]

Alexander requested support from Colonel Suther RM, agreeing to work up the left side of the valley, while the Marine brigade took the right.[44] The sailors scrambled over the intervening rice fields, and started up the narrow track on the left of the valley, Japanese shot and arrows whizzing about freely. The British advanced at the double, returning fire, until they arrived about 200 yards from a stockaded barrack at the head of the valley. Here they came under heavy fire which killed seven sailors and wounded twenty-six more, including Captain Alexander, disabled by a musket ball in the ankle. Most of the fire was directed on the sailors who turned out to be on the 'dangerous side' of the valley. The Brigade's colour sergeants were both hit, a midshipman taking over a tattered ensign, pierced by six musket balls.

Nevertheless the Naval Brigade and marines pushed on, swarming over the palisade, as the enemy ran out its open rear face into the woods, leaving behind a good many dead. Several of these were in armour, which the officers promptly appropriated. One company went astray in the difficult terrain, but Alexander found his sailors far steadier than he had expected from men together for so short a time. Indeed their only fault was their unnecessary recklessness, which did, however, bring them three *VCs*. The whole affair was over in minutes, but it was sharp while it lasted – had the attackers not made the most of the cover, their losses might have been considerably higher.[45] Setting fire to the defences, the force retired unmolested, embarking safely despite the violence of the currents. Moresby, whose ship took off the marines, thought steering alongside their parent vessels the most anxious job he had ever carried through, in impenetrable darkness, his decks covered with wounded men, the tide running at six knots, and the bridge occupied by senior captains making helpful suggestions. The indefatigable *Argus* rounded off the day at midnight by towing off HMS *Perseus*, the immediate cause of all the trouble.

Over the next few days, working parties demolished Chosiu's batteries, carrying off sixty-two cannon, including one 8-ton gun. The moral effects of the successful landing of 6 September compared favourably with the indecisive bombardment of the previous year. There was no interference with the work of destruction, and on the 8th Chosiu requested an armistice, saying that his samurai were tired now, but would happily carry on fighting after a couple of days rest. The result was a short but decisive treaty guaranteeing safe passage through the straits, and sparing Shimonoseki on payment of a ransom. The fleet were 'highly delighted with their little excursion', ended successfully at relatively small cost. The reticent Japanese never revealed their own casualties, but the lesson was not lost on other Japanese potentates. Moresby commented how much friendlier Yeddo seemed on his return.

In October Moresby attended a joint parade of 1,200 Royal Marines and an equal number of Japanese soldiers, half Samurai in armour and gaudy wigs, and half with Enfield rifles. Another witness thought the accompanying music, played on conches, was beyond a joke, but the parade was a sight never to be forgotten. The marines, 'a wall of massive men in red', dwarfed their opposite numbers but appeared lamentably prosaic beside the glittering swords and burnished armour. After the display the new order cheered the old, the Samurai receiving the applause with bowed heads. Moresby visited a factory at Nagasaki, where a Nasmyth steam hammer turned out parts for tubular boilers, giving him much to reflect upon. Although a Naval Brigade landed at Kobe in 1868, the Royal Navy saw no further action in Japan. Their brief but decisive part in 'opening up' the country contrasted as strongly with the protracted agony of the China Wars, as did the reactions of the local peoples themselves to Western intrusion.

THE IRRAWADDY FLOTILLAS: BURMA 1824–86

Unlike China or Japan, Burma exposed little coastline to British seapower. Its people and resources lay inland. The great rivers channelled access to the sea through a few key ports in the south: Rangoon, Bassein, and Martaban. In the intricate waters of the Burmese deltas the Royal Navy learned to play a new strategic role, as a brown-water navy. The Burma Wars show the stages by which this riverine capability developed. As steam power was applied to river craft the technological balance of power shifted in favour of industrialised naval forces, a shift reflected in the changing nature of Anglo-Burmese hostilities. The British embarked reluctantly on the First Burma War (March 1824–February 1826), in response to blatant Burmese aggression. They undertook the Second (April 1852–May 1853) more boldly, to protect trade much as they would in the contemporary China Wars, although a naval witness suggests that some drunk liberty men were the true *casus belli*. The Third Burma War (November 1885–January 1886) was provoked more by European power politics than the actions of the Burmese. A riverine blitzkrieg brushed their resistance aside, showing how far the navy's capacity for brown-water operations had progressed in the previous sixty years.

Geographical incentives to advance along the rivers were reinforced by the failure of successive Indian governments, responsible for running the Burma Wars, to provide adequate land transport. In April 1824 this was disastrous. The Burmese swept Rangoon clean of people, food, and transport, leaving the ill-equipped British holding a collection of dirty hovels in a swamp, infested by herds of pigs and hungry dogs, a sorry quarter for the imminent monsoon. By September 1824 750 British soldiers were dead out of 4,000 committed, with another thousand in hospital, a mortality not confined to the army. A quarter of HMS *Sophie*'s crew died, as did all but twenty-seven of the crew of Captain Frederick Marryat's sloop HMS *Larne*.[46]

In these grim circumstances there emerged a surprising spirit of cooperation amongst those 'roughing it out'. The unusual harmony between the United Services became a theme of general admiration, which was just as well, for the army depended entirely on the navy for food, stores, and transport. When the army did advance in early 1825, a third of the troops went by water, while the flotilla used every disposable man from HMS *Alligator*, *Arachne*, and *Sophie*. The navy provided more than logistical support, softening up innumerable Burmese stockades and dealing with their warboats. Some of these pulled seventy-six oars with a 9pr gun in the bow, but more terrifying were the bamboo fire-rafts:

> between every two or three rows of which a line of earthenware jars of considerable size filled with petroleum, or earth-oil, and cotton, were secured ... Many of them were considerably upwards of a hundred feet in length, and were divided into many pieces, attached to each other by means of long hinges, so arranged, that when they caught upon the cable or bow of any ship, the force of the current should carry the ends of the

raft completely around her, and envelope her in flames from the deck to the main-top-mast-head . . .[47]

Naval support continued throughout protracted negotiations in late 1825. HMS *Boadicea* and *Champion* arrived at Rangoon in September to add their men to the flotilla. When the Burmese launched a surprise attack in November 1825, 8,000 British faced their 50,000 attackers confident that the navy secured their retreat. More direct naval help took the form of manning 18pr guns ashore, and raking the attacking hordes with grape from ships' boats. When the defenders counter-attacked, the flotilla pushed upstream to turn the Burmese siege works, capturing 300 boatloads of munitions. Command of the waterways provided tactical as well as logistical mobility.

Throughout the First Burma War, the men-of-war's men preceded every movement on the water, leading the way into the hottest fire. Suffering from the same blazing sun and soaking dew as the soldiers, their small numbers afforded them little relief, as for weeks on end they watched out for the dreaded fire-rafts. Described by the Governor of Madras as 'the life and soul of the expedition, without whom nothing could have been achieved', the *Blues* took part in every battle but one, some remaining ashore for over a year.[48]

POTENTIAL UNREALISED: SECOND BURMA WAR (1852–53)

There was a crucial difference about the naval forces committed to the Second Burma War: in 1824 the squadron included a single steamer; in 1852 there were seventeen, one as big as an Atlantic liner of the day.[49] Calcutta was now two days' steaming from Rangoon, ensuring adequate supplies and ready evacuation of casualties. The campaign was an administrative master-piece, with a lower death rate among the troops than was normal in peace-time India. Militarily the war was disappointing. More was expected from the new technology than it could deliver. *The Times* claimed that a few steamers could transport an army from Rangoon to the Burmese capital in eight to ten days, instead of the two campaigns needed in 1826, but such opti-mism was misplaced.[50] Steam did reduce the physical effort of ascending the rivers, but much labour was still required to negotiate unknown and ever-shifting river channels, while early steamers were fragile and unreliable. A crucial relief expedition was delayed for hours while two steamers were repaired, one of which then broke its rudder head on the way.

Misunderstandings of Indian Government strategy compounded the failure to appreciate the limits of technology. The Marquess of Dalhousie, the Governor-General, believed that a policy of limited territorial occupation and blockade would soon bring the Burmese to heel. The force he despatched in April 1852 was less than half the number deployed in 1824–26.[51] The Burmese were not impressed. They had rebuilt Rangoon's defences since the previous war, an officer in HMS *Fox* opining that it 'would now cost a few the number of their mess before it was taken'. The Governor of Rangoon sent a saucy message to the blockading squadron that they should come in and fight at once, as he was tired of watching them swing at anchor, making mysterious signals to one another.[52]

The Burmese were soon disabused. Martaban fell after a ferocious naval bombardment on 5 April 1852, HMS *Rattler* earning the praise of General Godwin, the military Commander-in-Chief, for closing to a mere 200 yards from the batteries. Rangoon took a little longer, but the combination of naval gun fire and demolition parties was just as devastating. Godwin reported that the destruction of the town's river defences had been 'so effectually performed as to leave hardly a sign of where the stockades had stood'.[53] Rangoon itself fell on 14 April, after 120 sailors had dragged up 24pr howitzers to clear the infantry's way into the great Dagon pagoda. The main naval role ashore was the unremarkable but essential labour of landing troops, baggage, and stores, which went on day and night. Naval casualties were less than the anonymous pessimist in HMS *Fox* had feared: one AB was drowned and twenty-nine men injured, including one blown away from the after pivot gun in the *Tenasserim* which exploded while reloading.

The last piece of Dalhousie's strategy fell into place with the capture of the third Burmese port of Bassein by another combined operation, in May 1852. A field gun party from HMS *Fox* and her marines accompanied 700 soldiers sixty miles up the Bassein River to evict 7,000 defenders, with a loss of one killed and nine wounded, including the lieutenant in command of the field gun.[54] After the fight, which lasted all of forty minutes, *Fox*'s party pursued the retreating enemy forty miles upriver in the *Pluto*, breaking up their camp and driving them into the jungle. The locals, ethnically distinct from the people of the interior, received the invaders with delight, waving to passing ships, and providing intelligence and provisions. Thousands of civilians congregated round the British enclaves, feeling safer within sight of a steamer. In the countryside Godwin was not strong enough to impose British rule, leaving villagers at the mercy of marauding gangs of disbanded soldiery or dacoits. Naval forces could go more or less where they wanted along the waterways, but could not establish a permanent presence.

Naval officers were well aware of the problems of clearing the river banks.

Ambushed on the Irrawaddy, the fire-eating Commander Tarleton plied the banks with shell for an hour, but decided against landing:

> I have no doubt that we could have carried the work, by running one of the small steamers alongside, and throwing the small arms men on shore, but this could not have been performed without certain loss; and beyond spiking the guns, there was no object to be gained, the jungle . . . offering a secure retreat to the Burmese, from which they would have returned as soon as we had re-embarked.[55]

He pressed on upstream in a reconnaissance which, for all its brilliance, underlined the futility of river operations with insufficient military backup. Side-stepping the Burmese Army by following a creek containing two fathoms of water, Tarleton arrived in Prome with four steamers to find the riverside batteries deserted. Lacking infantry, all he could do was haul the guns off into deep water with a hawser made fast to the *Medusa*. Nervous that the Burmese might block the narrow channels behind him, Tarleton retired after two days, with little to show for his efforts apart from some highly decorated bronze gun barrels.[56]

Dalhousie realised that his economic strategy was ineffective against a regime whose absorbing interest was cockfighting. In August substantial British reinforcements arrived, including Henry Derry RM on the way home from hunting pirates in China. He saw a good deal of boat work chasing dacoits who had been 'trying to pop off the sentinels'. In old age he remembered the women, 'splendid walkers; mostly naked, only a loin cloth', and the snakes:

> On landing, a monster snake was coiled up right in the path of the man next to me, with his head elevated in the centre of the coil, and it was bolting little snakes by what appeared to us, hundreds. It would not move, but raised its head hissing, so he ran his bayonet into its mouth, and out through its neck. It knocked him down, and gave me a tremendous blow . . . It was full of young snakes, and was three yards long. We felt the sensation caused by the snake, for several days, and from what I could see, the place was swarming with all kinds. Black, yellow, spotted, some of them green, lying along branches of trees, after the birds and insects.[57]

Godwin moved forward in October 1852, taking Prome, and then Pegu on 21 November, the steamers hampered by lack of water in the narrow, twisting Pegu River. Godwin left a small garrison at Pegu, but the Burmese shut them up in the pagoda, and saw off an *ad hoc* naval relief attempt in paddle box boats with heavy losses. Commander Shadwell lost thirty-two out of 133 men, his cox'n being shot down at his side. The relief column took two days to reach Pegu, delayed by mechanical problems, but Godwin paid a glowing tribute to the navy's exertions, 'under the eye of that valuable officer Captain Tarleton'.[58]

His generosity must be remembered when considering a less fortunate example of naval-military cooperation. Dalhousie's strategy paid off in January 1853 when a *coup d'état* in the Burmese capital ended formal hostilities. However, the Burmese officials in the territories annexed by the British kept up a guerrilla war. Their most skilful leader was Myat Tun whose men shot up boats on the river, and burned down the villages in full view of British steamers. HMS *Winchester*'s boats were convoying river traffic in February 1853 when Captain Loch was asked to break up a concentration of Myat Tun's dacoits near Danubyu. Loch had commanded the Serapaqui expedition in 1848, engaging Nicaraguan gunners from his galley with a double-barrelled rifle. His luck ran out at Danubyu. Loch's 200 sailors and marines set off with 300 sepoys of 67th Bengal Native Infantry, slogging fifteen miles through paddy fields and dense jungle, in what they hoped was the right direction. They carefully placed pickets round their camp, but jitter parties harassed them overnight with horns and occasional shots. Next morning Loch pushed on until a deep *chaung* or water course suddenly blocked the path:

> The enemy at once opened a heavy and continuous fire of musketry on the advance guard of seamen and marines, from breastworks in which they lay concealed, while our men were completely exposed ... In such a narrow pathway, with an impervious jungle on each side, it was impossible to bring up the whole force at once to surround and storm the post, and nearly every man that approached the creek was shot down.[59]

The sailors had no choice but to retreat, spiking two small guns they had brought, and abandoning their dead in order to bring off the wounded.[60] Lord Wolseley, who fought in Burma as a subaltern, blamed Loch's rashness and lack of expertise for the disaster, which he claimed had degenerated into a stampede: 'The more I learned subsequently ... the more evident it became that this disaster was occasioned by Captain Lock's (*sic*) ignorance of military tactics, and of the precautions to be taken when marching through a strange forest occupied by an enemy.'[61] Only the steadiness of the Bengal infantry prevented the Burmese from cutting off the whole column.

THE KINGS MUST COME DOWN AND THE EMPERORS FROWN

Godwin ordered that all future operations ashore were to be commanded by the senior military officer present. The instruction may account for claims that the Commander-in-Chief was jealous of the navy, but Godwin never stinted in his praise of the 'sister service' on happier occasions, and his order seems a sensible enough allocation of responsibility. Wolseley commented that Loch should have allowed the Colonel of the Native Infantry to take command, and in general naval officers did leave overall control of military operations to army officers, who might well be junior to them in rank. When Captain Sotheby of HMS *Pearl* found himself the most senior officer present at Phulpur in February 1858, he told his senior army colleague it was a military affair, so the Naval Brigade should be under his orders.[62] In fairness to Loch, it took 1,200 picked infantry with howitzers and rockets to dispose of Myat Tun, and even heavier losses than those at Danubyu.[63]

THE CRUISE OF THE *PELORUS* (FEBRUARY–APRIL 1858)

The Indian Mutiny stimulated fears of Burmese revanchism, which it was hoped a naval presence might deter. A Naval Brigade from HMS *Pelorus* spent two months on the new Anglo-Burmese frontier at Myédé. The journal of Lieutenant Albert Battiscombe, their second in command, illuminates aspects of the Royal Navy's experience in Burma not depicted in the dry pages of the *Gazette*.

Like the Shannons in India, *Pelorus'* Naval Brigade went upriver in an iron flat under a canvas awning, daily routine following a similar pattern of drill, smoking, and watching the exotic birdlife.[64] Battiscombe feared the men would get as fat as pigs, with nothing to do and all night in bed, but they were well prepared for trouble:

We have taken our launch, pinnace, cutter, and Captain's galley; also two boat's guns, and a field piece, 89,000 rounds of ball cartridge, heaps of rockets, one month's provisions, and three months' rum – The ordnance at Rangoon supplied us with 40 Enfield rifles, and ammunition to boot so we are pretty well supplied, what with Cutlasses, Tomahawks, Guns, rifles, pistols, spades, picks, etc, etc, etc, we shall make such a formidable show that there will be no standing against us.[65]

The insects were unimpressed. Battiscombe claimed the Bassein mosquitoes could bite through the soles of your boots:

The mosquitoes tonight are dreadful, at dinner our mess place was quite black with them, they are larger than I have ever seen before, they bite through everything, our white trousers are no protection whatever, at this present moment my knees are one mass of little red spots, each of them smarting as if a needle were being pushed in.[66]

Myédé was fifty miles past Prome, and said to be the unhealthiest place in Pegu province, although one suspects Battiscombe's leg was being pulled. The officers of the 29th who saw the *Pelorus'* officers off with a bad dinner and insufficient wine, suggested they were meant to stir up trouble: 'if sailors go inland they are sure to get up a row somehow or other'.[67]

Leaving Rangoon on 5 January, the Brigade reached Myédé on 15 February, finding the fort 'beastly dirty, not whitewashed or cleansed, not fit for a dog to live in let alone a Christian'.

The Brigade settled down into a regular existence of cleaning barracks, assembly, cooks' bugle, and cutlass drill twice daily. Three POs and twelve seamen acted as guard, issuing the grog, and cutting up the meat, while the Chief Engineer kept full the water filter he had improvised from bread bags and charcoal. Every evening two men per boat crew went down to wet their boats, after which the men would shift clothing, and the officers relaxed over dinner, the men having eaten at midday. The routine varied on Sundays, with inspection of arms and divisions at 10 a.m., after which there was leave until quarters at six. A lucky few with a pass might stay out until 8 a.m. next morning.

Battiscombe found himself fighting a bureaucratic war reminiscent of Young Turner's problems at Sebastopol:

The people in charge of stores here seem to have a great objection to letting us have anything, throwing all sorts of impediments in our way, their war cry is 'Indent' if merely a stick is wanted, without an indent you may whistle long for it – And what is an indent? Nobody seems to be able to give a clear definition of the word, but one thing is certain viz, an indent is as well calculated to drive a man mad as anything I know . . .[68]

As the Burmese declined to start real hostilities, *Pelorus'* brigade returned on board 13 April 1858. Battiscombe had mixed views about the trip, feeling it would have been a capital cruise, if it had not been for the fearful sickness among the men. Four had died, and another went mad and jumped overboard. The dysentery had spoiled everything, but the deployment provides an early example of the navy's use as a strategic reserve, reinforcing threatened points around the imperial periphery.

RIVERINE BLITZKRIEG: THIRD BURMA WAR (NOVEMBER 1885–JANUARY 1886)

The Second Burma War reduced the Kingdom of Ava to its ethnic Burmese core. It now had to conduct relations with the outside world through the British, who had annexed all Burma's coastal provinces. The Burmese found this hard to accept, sending diplomatic missions to Italy and France in the 1880s. British statesmen were already nervous about French adventures in Indo-China, and the threat of Franco-Burmese military cooperation stimulated official support for commercial interests that coveted Burmese rubies, oil, and timber. High-handed Burmese action against the Bombay-Burmah Trading Company in late 1885 gave the British an excuse to remove a potential cause of conflict with their European neighbours. Burma itself neither threatened war, nor prepared for it.

Thanks to the telegraph, messages from Rangoon could now reach London in a mere two hours, allowing the *Naval and Military Gazette* to discuss the preparations for invasion before the British ultimatum had expired:

> The British force will comprise, as usual in our recent operations, a Naval Brigade . . . the steamers of the Irrawaddy flotilla are paddle wheel light draft boats of 500 tons burden, and tow a large flat on either side. These flats have large corrugated iron roofs, affording better protection against rain than sun, and can each carry several hundred men besides stores.[69]

The Government of India requested naval assistance on 22 October 1885: crews for twelve 25pr RML guns supplied by the ordnance department, besides help conveying the expedition upstream from Rangoon. The 444 strong brigade armed its flats with a variety of field guns and Nordenfeldt or Gardner machine guns, besides the 25prs, only ten of which could be manned, such were the other calls on the navy. The brigade took no special camping gear, as everyone had berths afloat. Mess utensils came from their own ships, which also provided supplies, a paymaster being appointed to ensure proper accounting procedures were followed for these. In view of Burmese pyrotechnic capabilities, a crucial part of the brigade was the 'torpedo corps', tasked with clearing underwater mines and obstacles with guncotton 'sinkers' in waterproof iron cases, each equivalent to 2,000lbs of black powder.[70]

The leading steamers crossed the frontier on 14 November 1885. The 'torpedo corps' led the way in the steam launch *Kathleen*, supported by the

IMS steamer *Irrawaddy* with the Naval Brigade's 25prs, and followed after a few miles by more sailors in the *Ngawoon*, to survey and buoy the channel. Then, came the HQ steamer, and seventeen others in single line ahead at two cables distance. Overnight the fleet closed up to one cable to anchor. Armed steam launches patrolled a mile upstream, with blue lights and grapnels, while other boat crews stood by to tow incendiary vessels clear of the flotilla. An empty barge trailing wires caused a brief panic, but the only resistance came from shore batteries, encountered at Minhla (17 November), Nyaungu (22nd), and Myingyan (24th), where gold umbrellas were seen in the stockades, amidst columns of Burmese troops in red and white. The latter fought their guns manfully, but:

> no troops in the world could remain passive under such straight shooting as we gave them, and after fourteen rounds from the big guns, and some shells from the siege train in the 'Yunan', and some from the 'Irrawaddy's' 20prs we could see them streaming away from their positions in hundreds.[71]

When the steamers ceased fire, two Burmese soldiers came down to the water's edge, where they danced about, waving their *dab*'s and making the most indecent gestures before retiring to the trees, rifle bullets kicking up sand all around them.

The main obstacle was the state of the river, now falling to its winter level. Large chunks of the bank tumbled into the water, so that a channel one day might be a sandbank the next. Experienced river pilots had taken French leave for the war, so naval officers conned the steamers. Meanwhile *Ngawoon*'s survey party kept ahead of the main body, 'making a running survey of the great Irrawaddy, with its constantly shifting sand banks, and difficult crossings . . . laying down a line of fairway buoys which enabled the column in line ahead to advance on Mandalay at the rate of six mph, against its rushing current without a check.'[72]

The advance was so rapid that HMS *Bacchante*'s landing party did not catch up with the flotilla until 27 November. Among them was an outspoken seaman, something of a sea-lawyer, called Richard Cotten:

> 10 o'clock we came in sight of the Ava forts whose earthworks were crowded with soldiers (Burmese) in fighting trim so we prepared for a bit of stiff work but when we arrived in line of the forts they hoisted the flag of truce so we gave them two hours to decide for a surrender. During this time we had dinner and were piped to clear in clean flannels and white trousers, but at 2 o'clock they surrendered.[73]

Next morning the squadron picked its way through the underwater obstacles to Mandalay itself:

> at 1 o'clock we landed all hands numbering 10,000 men and headed by the Naval Brigade we marched to Mandalay ... The city is surrounded by a large moat and a large thick wall of bricks and has got four gates which were entered at the same time by different divisions of our troops who disarmed the guards (*sic*) and marched into the palace with bands playing and colours flying ... a splendid place to look at but very dirty and neglected inside.[74]

King Thebaw was packed off on a steamer with the ladies of his household, and *Bacchante's* carpenter fixed a flag pole to the royal palace. The *Naval and Military Gazette* contrasted the rapid progress of the Third Burma War with the earlier prolonged and costly operations in that country, congratulating its inhabitants on their lucky deliverance from the French and King Thebaw. The invaders, however, were about to rediscover a truth forgotten since 1853. They might brush aside opposition along the rivers, but they could not pacify the interior. *Bacchante's* Commander Barlow led an expedition in mid-December 1885, showing the difficulties their military colleagues would soon have to face. The Burmese soldiery in their tattooed breeches and tin hats had no trade except pillage, and had suffered 'no punishment in action sufficient to inspire them with proper respect for British arms'.[75] For a week the sailors chased such 'dacoits' around the confluence of the Irrawaddy, and Chindwin rivers, covering 120 miles to little purpose. Cotten described their experiences succinctly:

> We got a 7pr gun and several bullock carts and started on our journey looking for dacoits and after 8 days marching without tents, blankets, etc, and laying at nights in the open air and doing about 26 miles a day in the scorching sun we arrived on board the *Tigris* on December 21st and started for Mandalay.[76]

Barlow was scathing about the futility of chasing dacoits with men on foot. Burmese officials were no help whatever, while the villagers would not assist a force passing through, for fear of being dacoited as soon as it left. He thought the number of dacoits exaggerated, as they were not borne out by the tracks left in the ground: 'Many of the so-called cases of dacoity were, on investigation, found to be the act of villages in the vicinity.' He refused to disarm the villagers, as this would leave them even more at the mercy of the dacoits, not to mention their neighbours.[77]

Barlow's men arrived back in Mandalay in time to take part in a final riverine excursion, to Bhamo near the Chinese border (19–28 December). Christmas was clouded by the death of Private James RMLI from cholera, although Cotten's account was laconic:

> we buried the poor fellow on the Riverside and we were lushed up to an extra tot of rum and salt pork and biscuit for dinner. We remained at Bhamo till the 31st of December – when we left for Mandalay amid the cheers of the troops and a friendly greeting from the general who flew a flag with the words A Happy New Year To All.[78]

Cotten's naval superiors had become restive. Vice-Admiral Richards, Commander-in-Chief on the East Indies station, had wanted to return his men to their ships soon after the fall of Mandalay. At the end of December he wrote:

> up to the present General Prendergast has not found it expedient to dispense with any part of the Naval Brigade placed at his disposal. I hope however by the end of the month I may receive some definite assurance on this head, as it is manifestly inexpedient that they should be retained indefinitely for operations against dacoits after the first object of the expedition has been accomplished.[79]

Men from the smaller ships, *Mariner* and *Sphinx*, had already returned on 16 December, and at Mandalay the Bacchantes received orders to do the same, much against their wishes. The Naval Brigade had all re-embarked by 13 January 1886. Twenty men from *Bacchante* were invalided home, although their generally good health contrasted with the horrors of the First Burma War. The daily sicklist ran at 1 per cent, with seven fatalities, generally from drinking dirty water or a native beverage called '*samshu*'.[80]

The Naval Brigade made a key contribution to the prompt resolution of a dangerous imperial problem. Had the campaign stalled like its predecessors, there could have been serious consequences in Europe. Prendergast's rapid advance paralysed the Burmese with a speed he attributed to the professional skills of the Naval Brigade. In the same theatre of war that had inspired a new spirit of naval-military cooperation in far less auspicious circumstances, the General wrote of the heartiness and thoroughness that characterised the Royal Navy's assistance. Just as in the First Burma War, the Naval Brigade had always been to the front, the eyes and ears of the fleet.[81]

CHAPTER FIVE

What We Have We Hold

Two centuries of overseas exploration, war, and commerce made Victorian Britain the sceptical owner of a string of maritime dependencies: islands, naval bases, or shallow strips of coastline. The Royal Navy provided strategic depth for such settlements, with few defensive resources of its own. Sometimes it did so in a purely maritime way, maximising the value of the few troops available by moving them to the appropriate place; sometimes Naval Brigades took the place of gunners and infantrymen.

THE UNDAUNTED MAORI: NEW ZEALAND (1860–64)

One of the first areas calling for such a defensive deployment was New Zealand, where Europeans had settled the edges of North Island, leaving the indigenous Maori population concentrated inland. The First Maori War in the 1840s involved half a dozen warships, some of which landed Naval Brigades. However, that conflict was resolved with limited forces, at most 1,300 soldiers. The Maori Wars of the 1860s were more extensive, drawing in thirteen warships and some 4,500 troops, furnished with all the means and appliances of modern science. It was a stubborn conflict, frustrating for army and navy alike.

Captain Cracroft of HMS *Niger* noticed the settlers' universal passion for gambling in land, well before hostilities began in 1860. The Crown monopoly of Maori land was a fertile source of distrust. Intended to protect the native peoples, it forced them to sell below the market price, especially as government officials were not above land-jobbing on their own account. When Cracroft took *Niger* to Taranaki province in response to sinister rumours about Maori opposition to a land deal, he did not share the Governor's faith in the deterrent effect of a visit from a warship. Threats seemed unlikely to intimidate men who, from childhood, had regarded it as a point of honour to shed their last drop of blood for their tribe's inheritance.[1] Nevertheless when the Governor requested help defending the straggling settlement of New Plymouth, Cracroft felt he could not refuse, despite the risks of landing a detachment on a lee shore, where he might have to put to sea at a moment's notice. Hans Blake, the First Lieutenant, took ashore fifty men with a 12pr howitzer, to reinforce the tiny garrison: twenty men of the 65th Regiment and a single bombardier of the Royal Artillery.[2] When Cracroft returned with ordnance stores from Auckland on 25 March 1860, he found his fears justified, with blood spilled on both sides. Three days later an expedition to escort some settlers into New Plymouth ran into trouble, providing the navy with an opportunity to score the first and, for some time, the only British success of the war.

As soon as the alarm was given, Cracroft landed every man fit for duty, and set off towards the rattle of musketry. The men were in high glee at the chance to do something, and marched along merrily, the carpenter-pioneers clearing a path for the bullock cart that carried their 24pr rocket tube. At Omata blockhouse they found Lieutenant Blake, shot in the chest. About a mile further on was a fortified complex, known as a *pah*, flying three flags, and surrounded by puffs of smoke from Maoris skirmishing in the ferns. Cracroft called his men together, and announced his intention of paying the enemy back for the loss the ship had suffered from the wounding of the First Lieutenant and the death of a marine, 'the quiet determined tone with which they uttered the words, "We'll go, sir", showing that they were all in earnest'.[3]

It was already evening when the force moved off. They fired rockets into the *pah* at 800 yards, but the men became impatient with being shot at from the bushes. Cracroft unrigged the triangle, formed his storming party, and pressed on, a young moon silhouetting their objective against the sky. The Nigers by contrast moved up a gully, able to see Maoris stood about in groups above them. 'Facilis descensus Avernis', thought their commander, but the die was cast, for the enemy had discovered his presence, and opened fire:

two men fell shot through the legs; three cheers were instantly given, a volley fired and the whole party rushed at the pah, entering simultaneously with some of the natives who were evidently not prepared for so sudden a movement. Panic stricken they retreated to their trenches, and not having time to reload, cut at the men with their tomahawks, inflicting very severe wounds on the legs. This was the expiring effort. The men discharged their muskets as fast as they could into the trenches, and the officers their revolvers, raking them fore and aft, so that it was almost impossible any one could escape alive.

Much to Cracroft's surprise only four of his men were wounded in the fight, but he had no time to contemplate his victory. His men were done up, faced with a five-mile withdrawal in the dark, before an enemy who might recover their nerve at any moment. The ship, swept clean of fighting men, lay in one of the most exposed anchorages in the world, with only the boys to look after her. Reforming his excited men with some difficulty Cracroft fell back, picking up the rocket party *en route*, to be cheered into New Plymouth by its relieved population.

Cracroft dressed his mastheads with captured Maori flags, which he presented to the Governor in Auckland to enthusiastic press notices, but Omata remained an isolated British success. Cracroft grumbled that never was a war rushed into by a government more ill-prepared. With a single battalion of the 65th to hold five stations, more men had to be found. Cracroft resisted suggestions that he lay up his ship at Auckland, and take the field with his whole company, but two other ships were immobilised to land brigades: HMS *Pelorus*, whose crew had recent experience in Burma, and HMS *Iris*.

Albert Battiscombe, First Lieutenant in *Pelorus*, described the hesitant development of the New Zealand campaign in his journal. At first the Maoris came right up to the town, 'murdering every soul who is fool enough to go half a mile outside the ramparts'. Refugees from Maori tomahawks huddled inside, rushing about during the frequent alarms, shrieking and getting in the way, 'so that if the town really had been entered by the Maoris, the butchery would have been something awful'.[4] Cracroft was disgusted by a strategy that allowed the enemy to roam the countryside at will, destroying farms and herds, but the army had good reason for caution. North Island was a mass of forest with ten-foot-high ferns and ferociously barbed brambles, penetrable only by Maoris. The one place the latter could be found was in the *pahs*, which they threw up with astonishing speed. Always in commanding positions, these were proof against shellfire, ingeniously constructued so that unless a shell burst in exactly the right spot it would be harmless. Underground galleries connected all parts of the *pah*, joining up the 'wharries' or dugouts, where the defenders sheltered from bombardments under a two-foot-thick layer of earth.[5]

A defeat at Puketakauere, near New Plymouth, on 27 June 1860 showed the problems such positions presented to a small force lacking artillery. A mixed force of sailors and soldiers waded out through a sea of mud, to attack a *pah* 'most fearfully strong, and surrounded by little gullies', but were themselves counter-attacked by three times their own number. The column fell back, after four hours under close-range fire from opponents hidden by ferns and embankments, leaving twenty-nine dead on the field. A safe distance from the fighting, the *Army and Navy Gazette* found it:

> astonishing and mortifying to learn that 347 British soldiers and sailors, led by experienced officers, and supported by the fire of grape shot and shell from regular artillery, were obliged to retreat before three times their number of men armed with tomahawks and fowling pieces . . .[6]

Captain Beauchamp Seymour of the *Pelorus* was among the wounded. He was certainly experienced, having spent his 1852 leave visiting friends on active service at Rangoon, where he earned several mentions in despatches for his part in the fighting. Puketakauere confirmed the defensive inclinations of the military. HMS *Iris* reinforced New Plymouth with 150 men and two 8-inch guns to keep *pah*-building beyond 2,000 yards. The town was under martial law, and drunkenness common. Battiscombe flogged a seaman found drunk on sentry duty. Cracroft returned to Taranaki in September 1860 to find the Naval Brigade quartered in tents:

> just behind the boat houses . . . which caution or precaution have converted into a miniature Gibraltar, with palisades, and ramparts, and ditches; and here our fine fellows have been fooling away their time, assisting in *important* garrison duties, instead of scouring the country, and making it hot for the natives. It is very humiliating![7]

However, the tide of the war had turned. *Pelorus'* Royal Marine detachment crept up on Puketakauere to find the *pah* empty, and occupied it against orders, the lieutenant of marines feigning deafness when ordered to wait. The enemy left little behind, except some blind shells, emptied of their powder, and the clay pipe of a man killed on 27 June. A new commander, General Pratt, began a regular campaign of sieges, to wear out the Maoris, without the risk of frontal attacks on their impregnable *pahs*. Battiscombe and twenty-seven seamen gunners went along with an 8-inch gun drawn by bullocks, the only animals able to cope with the 50 per cent gradients. The countryside was sadly changed: the houses burnt down, and deserted rifle pits commanding the road.

Arriving in sight of three *pahs*, Pratt dug in; just as well, for the Maoris fired into the camp, one bullet going close to Battiscombe's head, and another striking a man's cap. Next day the sailors laid a platform for their 8-

inch, while Battiscombe and the Colonel RE inspected the target at closer quarters:

> suddenly the natives opened the ball by firing a volley at us, and did not hit one soul, it is a caution if we did not run into the ditch pretty sharp![8]

Despite heavy small-arms fire, the guns were ready by midday, firing twenty-one 8-inch rounds into the *pah* before dusk, which persuaded the defenders to depart overnight. Cracroft wrote ironically of Pratt's 'safe and scientific' approach, but it turned the tables on the Maoris, forcing them to attack the British in their trenches. However, life in Taranaki remained a curious blend of danger and banality. The camp butcher was tomahawked out foraging, whilst Battiscombe read of Garibaldi's Sicilian exploits in the newspapers, and grumbled about gun-bullocks that trampled the peas and beans in his garden.

Pratt had developed a winning strategy. He moved upon Maori positions near New Plymouth at the end of December 1860 with 900 men, including a Naval Brigade of 125, mostly from *Pelorus*. Some Waikato chiefs told Battiscombe they were sick of the war, having nothing to eat but 'stinking Indian Corn', while European beef made them sick. None the less they defended their *pahs* vigorously. Pratt's riflemen fired 70,000 rounds in a twenty-hour firefight on 29 December, followed by a truce. Next day being Sunday, a missionary read prayers with the enemy, while his compatriots brought up two more 8-inch guns and heaps of ammunition. The Maoris then decamped, setting a pattern repeated throughout the first quarter of 1861, as Pratt gave them no rest. From 1 January Battiscombe was Assistant Engineer at 7/6d a day, 'not a bad thing at all', although he found positional warfare monotonous to an extreme. Frustration with the slow pace of the war was not restricted to officers. In January 1861, Cracroft organised an abortive operation to surprise some Maoris building a *pah*, the ship's company receiving the plan with intense satisfaction: 'They all feel the degradation daily and hourly accruing here', and volunteered accordingly.[9]

The Maoris talked peace throughout March 1861, while collecting spent bullets to replace the hard-wood plugs to which they had been reduced. Battiscombe suspected the enemy preferred fighting, regarding it as a good lark, but peace was agreed in April. Cracroft shipped *Pelorus'* crew back to their own ship in Auckland. He objected to the Maoris keeping their arms. They could build another *pah* and resume the war whenever they pleased, or when the spring weather (in October) made fighting in the open air more agreeable.

Further violence in 1863 showed Cracroft was right. Pratt's successor, General Cameron, pursued a more mobile strategy, with flying columns of picked men to scour the bush. His success, however, depended on logistical support from a flotilla of flat-bottomed barges operated by the seamen and marines of HMS *Harrier*: 'without the aid of such boats, operations up the Waikato could not be carried on as there is no road on either side of the river'.[10] Six armoured gunboats joined the barges, the first steamers ever to navigate the shoals of the Waikato. The strangest was the *Pioneer*, constructed at Sydney, and towed to New Zealand by HMS *Eclipse*. She had iron cupolas fore and aft, loopholed for musketry, and a 12pr Armstrong gun. A gruesome novelty was a perforated pipe running round the gunwales, and connected to the boilers, so that any canoe laying alongside could be sprayed with scalding hot water.[11] The armour proved its value during a reconnaissance at Mere Mere and Rangiriri on 29 October 1863 when *Pioneer* lay at anchor for two hours under close-range fire, her crew sustaining no losses despite repeated hits on the vessel.

This operation foreshadowed a more active combat role for the navy. Commodore Wiseman responded to a request for help from Cameron by landing as many of HMS *Curaçao*'s crew as could be spared. They took with them the diving apparatus, with its enormous leaden-soled boots, for use in the besnagged Waikato: '"I'm blowed if the chap who wears these pumps will be in like marching order, Bill"', was the generally expressed sentiment in reference to the invention. The press were inclined to stand 'carpenter's crew' a drink, encumbered as they were with saw, axe, cutlass, revolver, blanket and rations, but hesitated under the Lieutenant's eye. Meanwhile fifteen more seamen clapped onto the drag ropes of their 6pr Armstrong, and before the reporter could calculate how many men equalled the drawing power of a horse, let alone how many ordinary men equalled one sailor, he had to give over mental arithmetic to join in the cheering.[12]

British command of the river allowed them to turn Mere Mere on 1 November, as they had done similar defences in China and Burma, but an attack at Rangariri three weeks later brought heavy casualties. Cameron trapped 200 Maoris in the *pah*'s central redoubt, where they twice drove off the army. Ninety revolver men from the squadron tried their luck, but were twice repulsed despite a bombing party throwing grenades from the ditch. Next day 185 Maoris surrendered for lack of water. Commander Mayne of *Eclipse* was among the unnecessary casualties, shot so close to the enemy position that unburnt grains of gunpowder were found in his wound.[13]

Cameron had driven the Waikato Maoris so far upriver by spring 1864 that *Pioneer*'s cupolas were removed to reduce her draft. The Waikato Naval

Brigade redeployed to Tauranga Harbour on the east coast of North Island against a strong *pah* at Pukehinahina, known as the Gate Pah.[14] The sailors spent 27 and 28 April landing an impressive array of artillery, including a 110pr Armstrong, possibly the largest gun used ashore anywhere before the First World War. The 68th Regiment infiltrated round the *pah* to cut off the defenders' retreat, while the heavy guns softened them up. The naval and military commanders thought this had been done by 4 p.m., when the Maoris began to slip away as usual. An Auckland correspondent of the *Army and Navy Gazette* was doubtful:

> the practice of the Armstrong guns . . . particularly the 110pr was a signal failure; nearly every shell burst many yards beyond the pah, and some as far as half a mile. The only really good practice was made with the 24prs.[15]

No wonder some die-hard gunners wanted a return to smooth-bore muzzle-loaders! The 43rd Regiment formed the storming party, with the Naval Brigade: 150 of each in the first wave and the rest in support. The mixture of soldiers, sailors, and marines has attracted criticism, but there is much to be said for attacking in depth, so that successive waves come from the same unit. As for not using the Naval Brigade in this way, they were the second largest unit available, and the 68th were already committed. What seems more questionable is the decision to make any assault at all, rather than strengthening the cut-off parties to take a good toll of the enemy as they retreated. Cameron had not learned the lesson of Rangariri, one that Pratt had understood.

The four-deep column paused at a fold in the ground to draw breath, before rushing into the work. Their cheers were premature for the work was 'such a complication of traverses, rifle pits, and underground holes that it was difficult to get along at all, and impossible to move in numbers'. Invisible Maoris, firing double-barrelled guns from their fox holes, shot down all the officers. Captain Hamilton of the *Esk* fell cheering on his men; his last words: 'Follow me!' The supports came up, but were themselves driven out by the retreating remnants of the storming party.[16]

Partisans of both services blamed the other. The *Army and Navy Gazette* claimed the men, 'got a panic, fairly bolted, and could not be rallied'.[17] The *New Zealander* alleged the seamen had deserted their officers, provoking the crew of HMS *Esk* to surround the editor's office, and prepare to 'down house'. The Commodore declined to intervene, his infuriated subordinates not retiring until promised a special edition retracting the story, and putting the blame on the 68th instead. Any 'panic' had been limited, as the survivors dug in on their start line, 100 yards outside the *pah*. After 20 per cent casualties, over half from the Naval Brigade, it is hard to see what the survivors could have done except retire, once the impetus of their rush was spent. Next morning John Colenutt, an AB from HMS *Harrier*, found the Maoris gone, leaving twenty dead and six wounded.[18]

Gate Pah was the last naval engagement in New Zealand. All naval personnel, with guns and stores, were back onboard by 4 May 1864. The Maori Wars ran down after the 43rd defeated the over-confident victors of Gate Pah in June 1864. Battiscombe's letters from home had disapproved of the war, 'thinking the natives were in the right', and domestic pressure brought a rapid disengagement. The last imperial regiment left New Zealand in 1870. Captain Edmund Fremantle took over HMS *Eclipse* soon after Gate Pah, and found the ship somewhat demoralised, 'as is often the case after seamen had landed'.[19] She reverted to a purely naval role, landing only in pursuit of intelligence, or perhaps the local wildfowl.

THE GRAVEYARD COAST – SECOND ASHANTI WAR (1873–74)

The West coast of Africa had a terrifying reputation in the nineteenth century. Its deadly climate prevented European traders going far inland, so the coastal peoples acted as middlemen in the exchange of gold and slaves from the interior for European cloths, guns, and strong drink. The Fante of the British Gold Coast protectorate, now part of Ghana, used their position to restrict the supply of European goods to the Asante further inland, a dangerous game, as the Asante sustained their military pre-eminence with massive imports of smooth-bore muskets and ammunition.[20] In 1872 the British purchased Elmina, a Dutch trading post which had supplied most of the Asante arsenal. The threat to their arms trade combined with internal political rivalries to provoke Asante military action against the Fante.

Fante refugees crowded into their insanitary entrepôt at Cape Coast Castle. The only troops available for their defence were a few sailors and marines, and 500 soldiers of 2nd West India Regiment. Throughout 1873 these slender forces sustained a messy defensive campaign consigned to obscurity by the absence of a well-known commander or regiments with famous names. The Admiralty objected strongly to deployments ashore in so unhealthy a spot. The fate of two detachments of Royal Marines sent out at the height of the Asante threat shows that their Lordships' fears were not groundless.

Captain Edmund Fremantle had returned from New Zealand to take command of HMS *Barracouta*, an ancient paddle gunboat he had last seen in China in 1853. In response to the Fante's latest defeat he was sent with a special detachment of 110 Royal Marines to take command of the ships off West Africa. As soon as Fremantle arrived he moved to assert British control at Elmina, where the king was still selling arms to the Asante. Commander Luxmore, last encountered on the banks of the Peiho, went along *en amateur* to watch. When the population refused to be disarmed peacefully, he took charge of a party sent to burn down their houses, rockets from the boats outside and bullets from *Barracouta*'s men coming rather too close to be pleasant.[21] Most of the landing party had withdrawn to the boats for dinner when 3,000 Asante counter-attacked across open ground, only to suffer heavy losses from the breech-loading Snider rifles of the British. Fremantle, firing his revolver into them at eighty yards range, was much struck by Asante discipline. Like European troops, their skirmishers systematically reformed behind their main body when the British fire grew too hot, but, contrary to all expectations, they would not run away.

The political authorities at Cape Coast Castle resented Fremantle's action, but he thought a war with the Asante was inevitable, and at least he had begun it successfully. Unfortunately the rainy season stopped further activity. The weather was appalling even by West African standards. The rain brought down the roof of the smallpox hospital in Cape Coast Castle, allowing the patients to escape, while Colonel Festing, the marines' CO, was turned out of his bedroom by a stream running through it. Sickness accompanied the rain, even Festing's African clerks falling ill. Within six weeks of his Marines landing at Elmina on 9 June 1873 two had died, and eighty-seven were invalided home in the *Himalaya*. Ten more died at sea, and fifty-eight sent to the military hospital at Netley on arrival. Many of the rest were too weak to walk to barracks. Half the *Himalaya*'s main deck became a hospital, her surgeon describing conditions aboard in terms that lose none of their horror for the antique medical terminology. The main complaints were dysentery and remittent fever, often together, with headaches, delirium, and vomiting which left the tongue coated with a brown fur, as if painted with chocolate: 'Those who died succumbed seemingly from pure exhaustion or asthma, worn out by loss of rest and wearying pain.'[22]

A second batch of 110 marines sent out in August suffered similar attrition: by December 1873 just fourteen were still serving, although they were all specially picked to withstand the rigours of the Coast. One hard case left over from the first batch was known as 'the Fossil'. Some looked at *Barracouta*'s steamy interior, and blamed conditions in the ships that took them out. Others blamed salt pork: 'poison to men suffering from diarrhoea', although, as the Deputy Adjutant General RM pointed out, thirty staff officers had also fallen sick, who had probably not dined on pork.[23] Festing and a devoted few hung on, hampered by rows with the Colonial Office, ants nests in limbers, mildewed and rotten weapons, and an elusive enemy.

In August 1873 the crisis deepened. Commodore J.E. Commerell VC, Fremantle's superior and last man off the beach after the Peiho River débâcle, took over direct command. After an ugly palaver, throughout which Luxmore kept his hand firmly on his revolver, Commerell led a reconnaissance up the Prah River, seeking a route into the interior. Everything seemed quiet when a tremendous volley was poured into the boats from the bank, closely followed by a second, hitting Luxmore in six places, and leaving scarcely anyone else unwounded. The steam cutter towed off Commerell's bullet-riddled party, but another disaster threatened downstream, where ostensibly friendly villagers had attacked an unarmed beach party. Their cutter capsized, and in the confusion a sailor and two native policemen were caught and beheaded according to custom, before a rocket from a second boat frightened off the attackers.

This affair set the whole coast ablaze, outside a few previously British villages:

> for about fifty miles west, the black sweeps would cut all our heads off if they had a chance. It is no war at all worthy of the name, but as much mischief has been done as if it was one, and the worst of it is we can do but little harm in return. If we do burn their coast towns, the black sweeps can go in the bush, and their clothes don't trouble them much.

The midshipman responsible for this acute strategic analysis took charge of the Dutch fort at Sekondi:

> a tumbledown old affair, but quite strong enough to keep all the niggers from here to the Mediterranean out of it, and I have two good guns, a 20pr Armstrong, and a little bronze mountain gun, both from ships. The remainder are of the shakiest description, old Dutch things, out of which I fancy the shot would roll if they were at all depressed. I speak in gunnery terms as you know.[24]

The *Army and Navy Gazette* bewailed the ignominy of burning 'the wigwam homes of the defenceless wretches to whom we offered "protection"',[25] but there were few military alternatives. The departing Commerell had left Fremantle orders not to land or go up rivers, as: 'the loss of one human life from our forces but very inadequately compensates for any amount of injury we may do to the savage natives'.[26] Knowing his man, Commerell copied his instructions to the other Post Captains, to tie Fremantle's hands. The arrival of Sir Garnet Wolseley on 2 October 1873, tasked with clearing up the mess, allowed Fremantle to launch a series of raids against Asante camps near the coast: at Essaman 14 October, Assayboo 26–28 October, and Abrakrampa 5–6 November. Combined with losses from disease and lack of food these persuaded the Asante to depart. Fremantle had no doubt about the value of his operations, claiming the enemy had been 'forced into the bush and by paths where they must die of starvation'. However, he had to address fears of another disaster like that suffered by Festing's luckless marines. He wrote that he and Wolseley were 'deeply sensible of the necessity for taking every care of the Europeans'.[27] They hoped to prevent disease by limiting time spent ashore and providing boiled filtered water in sealed containers. However, Wolseley insisted on supporting the locally raised black troops with Europeans.

There was little fighting, but much slogging down jungle tracks in single file, deep in mud or over jagged rocks. Local levies skirmished around, catching the occasional Asante scout or a starving Fante slave, 'logged' to prevent their escape. The climate was the main enemy. Few marines had sun helmets, while the sailors only had caps with white covers:

We stopped for five minutes every quarter of an hour notwithstanding which the men fell down by threes and fours with sunstroke, many being quite insensible; but water, shade, and loosening their clothing soon brought them round.[28]

Fremantle's old shipmate Commodore William Hewett *VC* arrived to replace Commerell on 14 November 1873. The defensive stage of the war, of which the brunt had fallen on the navy, was almost over:

Sir Garnet Wolseley may own without reserve that his late successes could not have been achieved without the force of Bluejackets and Marines supplied from Her Majesty's ships present. These appear to have shown how thoroughly qualified such a body is for this peculiar warfare, and to have called forth the admiration of all for the ready way in which they adapted themselves to a military *régime*. Sailors have this peculiar faculty, while their perfect discipline, when allied to those powers of endurance which their life engenders, render them in a wild country equal to the best troops.[29]

Laird Clowes was less sanguine. He blamed the home government for leaving the protectorate without white troops in face of the Asante invasion, obliging the navy to undertake work ashore that it was never intended to do.

HMS *Barracouta* went to St Helena to shake off the malaria that riddled her crew, including Fremantle:

> I tried staying on deck, but to shiver under a large boat cloak over flannels with the thermometer at 84 degrees speaks for itself; so to my cot I went, and then the reaction, the burning fever like a furnace inside me till I could bear it no longer; and about midnight I jumped up having a vague idea of getting into the main top to be cool.[30]

One of the few officers still able to stand put him back to bed, with a temperature of 105. Returning to the West Coast in January 1874, the Barracoutas found a new phase of the war begun without them. Their exclusion from Hewett's recently landed Naval Brigade so incensed Fremantle's men they went onto the quarter deck to complain, although after their recent experiences they might have known better.

THE MARCH TO KUMASI

The new Commodore had responded readily to a request from Wolseley for a Naval Brigade. Hewett was one of the great characters of the Victorian navy, winning the *VC* at Sebastopol, running contraband into the Confederacy, and leading a diplomatic mission to Abyssinia, quite apart from a more orthodox naval career, culminating as Commander-in-Chief of the Channel Squadron 1886–88. Wolseley needed to keep up pressure on the Asante, although the first regular British troops would not arrive on the Coast until January 1874. To show his appreciation of those who had borne the 'heat and burden of the day' so far, the Naval Brigade would be the first to enter Asante territory.

Hewett issued detailed orders on 22 December 1873. Captain William Hans Blake, wounded at the Omata stockade, would take 215 officers and men from the squadron to link up with another fifty already ashore, representing about a sixth of Wolseley's European troops.[31] One of the most intractable problems in a country devoid of horses or railways was transport, so a particular attraction of the Naval Brigade was its labour force of Kroomen, black sailors recruited on the Coast. Almost 200 were available to carry the brigade's spare kit and reserve ammunition, besides 'spirits authorised to be sent to the front'. These would be a more precious luxury than usual. Wolseley meant to run a dry war, and asked Hewitt to stop the issue of spirits once the first British soldiers reached the front.

Preparations for a Naval Brigade had been in hand for a month, the navy's skilled men making up for the army's logistical deficiencies: 'making tents, cots for the sick, and many other things for the Control Department. Boats continually employed landing stores, provisions, etc. Cut up studding sails for covering huts, etc'.[32] A more dubious job was press-ganging Africans to carry the army's baggage to Kumasi, the Asante capital. As in many colonial campaigns the navy played an enabling role, without which operations ashore might never have begun. Despite the hectic activity, Lieutenant Pipon of HMS *Active* found time to write home at Christmas:

I thought after prayers this morning of what was going on at home ... I fancied you all walking up to church, and wished myself with you. This day does not seem like Christmas Day, making active preparations for landing, and reading General Orders ... to the ship's company, without any of the merriment, etc. usual on that day, taking all the pleasant associations away from it.[33]

The Brigade landed on 27 December 1873 after a special breakfast of fresh soup to ward off chills, and set off 'with the cheery swing of a set of men carrying on a duty which had to be performed in the shortest period of time'.[34] A concertina played during the afternoon halt, two bluejackets 'dancing an uncommonly good "trois temps" to the accompaniment of the ammunition in their pouches which rattled tremendously'. White and black sailors sang in their own fashion, the bluejackets mimicking the Kroomen so the forest rang with shouts of laughter. They set a good pace:

taking into consideration the amount each man had to carry viz. rifle and sword bayonet, 70 rounds of ball cartridge, waterbottle, filter, and haversack, as well as all the belts to which the pouches were attached, and which impeded a man's movements, and breathing considerably.[35]

Every stop showed Wolseley's careful preparations: good huts and latrines, water filters invented by Captain Crease RM, and quinine issued after the breakfast cocoa. Blake and Luxmore shared a hut:

A rat or lizard would at times crawl over Blake or myself, and then whoever felt it first kicked it over to the other, not a difficult job as our beds were not far apart. To prevent catching chills I always slept in everything except boots, but sometimes when it was unusually hot and sultry I took my coat off. Trousers always tucked inside socks, and a veil over my face.[36]

The brigade reached the frontier at the Prah River without losing a man. Here it starred in a diplomatic demonstration before some Asante envoys, firing off three drums of Gatling gun ammunition, and marching down the road to Kumasi singing loudly. More practically, carpenter's crew set about bridging the Prah. Despite leaving the 'deadly miasma of the coast', disease soon appeared. Among the sick was Blake who worked on despite chronic diarrhoea. His final journal entry for 17 January 1874 reads:

> Sent special runner with telegraph to Commodore ... to report that I am too ill to continue in command of the Naval Brigade, and that I should return tomorrow. One hour after, in consequence of feeling so much better, sent another telegram to say that I should await his arrival.[37]

Blake had left it too late, for he died at Cape Coast on the 22nd.

The much delayed invasion of Asante began on 20 January, the Naval Brigade waking everybody up at 3 a.m. with the noise of their preparations. Luxmore, their temporary commanding officer, remembered that morning as the most trying yet, stumbling about the pitch dark forest, but next day the Commodore arrived with comforts: 'potted meats, etc, and above all Liquor, all most acceptable'. Wolseley's teetotalism did not seem to apply to officers. Soon the column passed the Adansi Hills, catching a tantalising glimpse of the country beyond. Thick fog hid an immense forest, while here and there hilltops appeared above the mist, like islands in an inland sea. White threads hung between the trees along the road, like a child's idea of telegraph wires, bits of white calico lay across the path, while a complete skeleton impaled on bamboo guarded a huge 'fetish pit' full of skulls and bones.

Asante strategy had denied Wolseley the prompt victory that he sought. Now his white troops were falling sick. The Naval Brigade lost forty-eight men out of 250 during its first month in the field. However, the unrelenting advance left the Asante with little choice but to fight. The first skirmish was a reconnaissance on 29 January 1874, where HMS *Active*'s bluejackets won the force commander's praise for their steady rearguard action. Two days later the column met the main Asante army at Amoafo, in a well chosen position across the road to Kumasi. The Asante line formed a reversed arrowhead, threatening the flanks of any attack directly along the road. These were effective tactics against the Asante's usual opponents, but less successful against trained infantry deployed in depth. The 42nd Highlanders charged straight down the road behind their pipers, trusting other units to cover their flanks. This was the job of Wood's and Russell's irregulars, supported by the Naval Brigade. As the latter had to fight on both sides of the road, it split into two wings of some ninety men each. Captain W.J. Hunte Grubbe (Blake's replacement) took the left of the road and Luxmore the right. The remaining British infantry covered the rear, the whole force forming an irregular extended square.[38]

Luxmore's wing had orders to clear a path 300 yards eastwards into the bush before turning north, parallel to the road, but they were pinned down after only a hundred:

> the Kossoos were keeping up a tremendous fire on the bush where they supposed the enemy was – My men lying down to escape the enemy's storm of bullets and slugs, and there we had to remain over four hours without being able to advance . . . We ourselves fired into the 23rd Regiment once I afterwards found out, but the bush was so dense that one could scarcely see one's own men . . . The whole day I only saw one living Ashantee about 50 yards from me, and as I was in the act of going to snatch a rifle out of a man's hand, he saw my movement and hid.[39]

Another officer noted how the Asante gave away their position by using horns to control their movements:

> had they moved silently they could have harassed the English force fearfully, but as a rule we knew nearly the exact direction in which to aim, though from the very broken nature of the ground, we had to make guesswork of elevation . . . We fought steadily up the path gaining ground but going very slowly, and suffering a good deal, especially as the Ashantees got so close to our flanks, and for an hour we made hardly any advance, keeping cover and maintaining a hot fire, no object to aim at but right into the bush, on the chance of hitting.[40]

Asante resistance slackened after the 42nd took Amoafo, allowing Luxmore to push on. There were pools of blood in the hollows, but few bodies. Hunte Grubbe's wing worked around to the left in much the same way. Heavy fire killed the Lieutenant RE in charge of the cutters, forty yards from the road, but the bush was so thick that Hunte Grubbe never saw his opponents. Once back on the main road, his wing formed line along it, exchanging occasional shots with Asante who had closed in on the left flank, while Luxmore's wing swung right through the Asante camp, fires still burning, and full of bundles made up like pillows for carrying on the head.

The Brigade reached Amoafo at dusk, the officers going to sleep on the mud floor of a hut, as close as they could stow. They were glad of a respite from the continuous firing, but had nothing to eat, as the enemy had cut off the transport. Just out of bed from an attack of fever, Luxmore hardly knew how he had got through the day. The victors buried 1,600 Asante killed in a desperate battle that no one had expected. The Naval Brigade had no fatal casualties, but thirty-two of them were wounded.[41] The Asante scored numerous hits, but their ammunition was so poor, including pebbles and snail shells left over from making soup, that they had little effect. It was lucky the Asante did not have Sniders!

The advance resumed on 2 February, the Naval Brigade acting as rear-guard, a most fatiguing duty, as they felt every delay in the extended column. Luxmore broke down fourteen miles from Kumasi:

> My thirst was unquenchable, and having, while still marching, emptied my own water bottles had to beg from Pipon, who goodnaturedly supplied me. I knew I was utterly used up . . . and could not go a step further, although I much wanted to, being so near Coomassie . . . It was most disappointing.[42]

Like the other sick, Luxmore was carried back to the coast in stages. Caught in a tropical storm the bearers lost their way in the pitch darkness, falling about and howling fearfully. Luxmore's cot filled with rain, obliging him to cut a hole in it with his penknife, to let the water out.

Conditions at the front were no more comfortable, as the expedition closed up on the River Dah, the last obstacle before Kumasi. In their cheerless bivouac nothing was heard except the dripping rain and the constant hails of the sentries, doubled for fear of a night attack. Next day, 4 February, the 150-strong rearguard shepherded forward 2,000 carriers, who went naked except for a layer of oil to stop the Asante grabbing them, while another battle raged a few hundred yards ahead.

At 1.45 p.m. word came that the road to Kumasi was open, the final advance through knee-deep water encumbered with dead Asante and murdered slaves, their heads ritually twisted away from the invaders. Kumasi was not much better: water everywhere, but none fit to drink, everyone exhausted, and the stink of innumerable sacrificial victims. There was little rest, with double sentries and impromptu fire fighting, thanks to Fante prisoners paying off old scores. The Naval Brigade counted heads in the morning, 157 left out of the 250 that crossed the Prah, while the General waited in vain for the King of Asante to give himself up. A stream washed furniture down the main street, while torrents of rain built up a foot of water on the slush and mud of the innumerable courtyards.

Colonel Festing had argued in the summer for the necessity of reaching Kumasi, not with a small band of weary soldiers, but with sufficient force to impress the native mind with British power and resource.[43] For all his preparations and energy, Wolseley had failed to do this. After a day and two fearful nights he withdrew, the Naval Brigade leading the reversed order of march. Previously dry ground was now submerged, cut up by swollen streams which forced the bearers to wade neck-deep with their loads. The bridge over the Dah was two feet under water and falling to bits, as was the expedition. Even the sailors' physique, which had impressed observers at Cape Coast Castle six weeks before, showed the ill-effects of their recent exertions. Many fell out along the march, while the exhausted Kroomen quarrelled interminably over their loads.

There was no further contact with the enemy. The Brigade re-embarked on 19 February, the squadron dressing ship and firing a royal salute in honour of the fall of Kumasi. The navy's sick rate was 95 per cent, the worst of all the European units committed. The Naval Brigade had been ashore longest, and many sailors had been exposed to malaria earlier in the war. They invalided 39 per cent, compared with 10 per cent from the black regiments. The obvious lesson was to make better use of local troops. The Third Ashanti War of 1895 was fought mainly by black regiments, with no Naval Brigade, to the disgust of naval correspondents of the *Army and Navy Gazette*.

Luxmore preceded his comrades by a week, but his feelings must have been similar to theirs:

Never have I been so glad in all my life to see the blue water again – Worn out by the journey, heat, noise of the bearers, and illness, only getting a little pressed chicken, and wine as medical comforts, it was quite time to get afloat again . . .[44]

He had succeeded Blake as Captain of HMS *Druid*, so after a substantial breakfast, including a very good bottle of Moet et Chandon, he went out to his new ship to experience the delicious sensation of a clean linen shirt and a hair cut. He had been ashore fifty days, and was one of two Naval Brigade officers not invalided home, although as he remarked he should have been!

A CONSPICUOUS EXAMPLE: THE ANGLO-ZULU WAR (1878–79)

The Asante were not the only African people under-estimated by British statesmen in the 1870s. The Zulu severely tested the British military machine in South Africa in 1879, demanding a familiar deployment of Naval Brigades, first to defend the frontier of the British coastal enclave in Natal, followed by offensive operations in Zulu territory. The British defeat at Isandlwana affected only one sailor directly: William Aynsley, Signalman 2nd Class of HMS *Active*, last seen backed against a wagon wheel defending himself with his cutlass. However, the disaster threw the whole British plan of campaign into confusion, demanding long-term naval commitments ashore. Naval Brigades featured as beleaguered garrison and relieving force, as they would at Ladysmith twenty years later. At the end of the war, they lent an unexpected maritime twist to the story, showing the strategic value of a Naval Brigade in operations near the coast.

It is hard not to attribute the Zulu War to the mismanagement of the colonial authorities at the Cape, who provoked conflict with a Zulu king anxious to be their ally. Eight British battalions were available to defend a 200-mile frontier against some 40,000 Zulus, and not a single regular cavalry regiment. As always in such emergencies the army turned to the navy, Lord Chelmsford asking for as many men as could be spared.[45] Taking into consideration the serious aspect of affairs, Commodore F.W. Sullivan, Commander-in-Chief of the Cape of Good Hope squadron, immediately landed HMS *Active*'s Brigade on 19 November 1878.[46]

The people of Durban cheered, while the ship's band played *Hearts of Oak* and *There's Nae Luck About the House*, in honour of Commander H.J. Fletcher Campbell. The sailors carried revolvers and Martini Henry rifles, their thickset forms and resolute bearing greatly impressing the local newspaperman. The brigade marched north to the frontier on the Tugela River in capital spirits, pitching their tents like hardened campaigners, although the rivers were supposed to be full of crocodiles, to the terror of cooks seeking water for a brew. The Admiralty was unenthusiastic, complaining of the harm done to naval efficiency by landing half the ship's company, complaints reiterated a fortnight later when HMS *Tenedos* reinforced the Actives, leaving some small gun vessels the only effective units in the Cape squadron.[47] However, the local commanders' wishes prevailed. Chelmsford felt he:

> should not like to give up one man of those landed ... as their armament and general efficiency would be absolutely necessary to the success of Colonel Pearson's column.[48]

The Tugela River gave them the chance to justify Chelmsford's assertion. It was 200 yards wide, usually up to the armpits except after rain when it became a foaming torrent. Much encumbered with sandbanks, the river posed a serious problem for a force with no bridging train. Campbell's solution was to lay a five-inch wire hawser across the stream, anchored at one end, with a purchase at the other, the fork of a tree supporting the wire above the water. The hawser passed through two freely moving iron thimbles secured to a large flat-bottomed boat or pont, so that teams of oxen could haul it back and forth, two or perhaps three times an hour. The work was hard and often dangerous. Floods swept the whole lot away, including a 9cwt anchor, with the loss of a promising young seaman. The sailors worked through the night under the direction of the boatswain, 'an old and valuable officer', who had served in the trenches at Sebastopol, a quarter of a century before. By the end of the war the single haul-over pont, on its much spliced hawser, would ferry 5,000 men, innumerable wagons (each with sixteen oxen), and hundreds of tons of stores.

Sufficient material had crossed by 18 January 1879 for Pearson's column to proceed, leaving HMS *Tenedos'* detachment to secure the crossing. The first contact came four days later, just after fording the Inyezane River. The head of the column had halted for breakfast at the foot of a pass dominated on both sides by steep crests, when they were attacked by Zulus concealed in the bushes. Pearson at once closed up two companies each of the Buffs and Naval Brigade to a knoll half-way up the pass where they engaged the Zulus with rockets and 7pr guns, reinforced by a Gatling, somewhat delayed by its disselboom carrying away. The Buffs cleared the Zulus to the right of the trail, while Campbell began a turning movement against the commanding heights at the top of the pass. Under heavy fire, the small party of seamen drove the enemy back step by step for about three quarters of a mile:

> By this time four men of the Naval Brigade had been sent to the rear badly wounded, and another temporarily stunned by a bullet passing through his helmet, when the arrival of a company of Buffs under Colonel Parnell enabled the attack to be very rapidly pushed to within a

hundred yards of the Zulu position. A final rush was then made, headed by the Naval Brigade, and the position carried . . . The first unmounted man in the enemy's position was Thomas Harding, Ordinary of HMS *Active*.[49]

Campbell did not record that he preceded Harding on his horse. Contrary to the usual image of massed Zulu charges, the enemy restricted themselves to skirmishing, ducking behind cover to reload. Nevertheless the three-hour fight on the Inyezane cost them at least 300 dead compared with twenty-six British casualties. The navy lost seven wounded in its attack, 'one of the finest incidents of the war', breaking through the right horn of the Zulu Army, to clear the road to Pearson's objective: the old mission at Eshowe.

The victory at Inyezane was the last good news the Admiralty would receive for some time. The simultaneous disaster to Chelmsford's main column at Isandlwana wrecked the British invasion of Zululand, isolating Pearson at Eshowe and exposing Natal to a possible counter-invasion. Commodore Sullivan's first incomplete account of heavy losses near Rorke's Drift also reported that HMS *Tenedos* had been damaged by an uncharted reef during a demonstration off the coast of Zululand. He concluded with masterly restraint: 'Further reinforcements, in my opinion, urgently needed.'[50] The excitement and terror in Durban baffled his pen. HMS *Boadicea* arrived with Sullivan's replacement, Commodore F.W. Richards, but she had smallpox onboard, so went straight back to sea. Sullivan had to do his best to calm public fears: advising on defensive measures, landing 12prs from *Active*, reinforcing the frontier with HMS *Tenedos'* field guns, and despatching torpedo warheads, wires, and batteries for fougasses or command-detonated mines. Help came unexpectedly, providing a dramatic illustration of naval flexibility and initiative. HMS *Shah* called at St Helena, on her way home from the Pacific, after fighting the Royal Navy's first action against an armoured ship, the Peruvian *Huascar*. Hearing of Isandlwana, her Captain changed course for South Africa with 161 soldiers from the island's garrison, besides her own Naval Brigade:

At such a moment the unexpected appearance of a magnificent man-of-war bringing, as it were from out of the ocean, a large and complete body of well trained and seasoned fighting men, had a most valuable moral effect on all nationalities, classes, and professions. There was not, I am convinced, a single man or woman in Natal who did not experience a sense of added security when they heard the news.[51]

Even the Admiralty would endorse Captain Bradshaw's judicious action, although they can have been less happy about HMS *Active*'s brigade, besieged at Eshowe. The garrison expected a night attack, although the Zulus: 'never come near in large numbers, but creep among the bushes, and take a quiet pop at anyone who comes close enough'.[52] Pearson had sent useless mouths back to Fort Tenedos, so there was plenty to eat, albeit stringy trek oxen. Boredom was alleviated by messages passed by native runners and makeshift heliographs, 'like an old fashioned bedroom looking glass, to show upright for a flash, and horizontal'.

Campbell smuggled out a 'semi-official' journal on tissue paper, asking for an account of the Brigade's situation to be published in British newspapers. He might get a message through, but 'None of the men can write'. Nevertheless:

> The conduct of the men is exceptionally good if the Kroomen are not considered, and seem quite cheerful, notwithstanding the great amount of rain. They are without tents, and have only a kind of shelter made of waggon covers . . .
>
> We get on very well with all the military, but I shall be glad when it is over. We all want a change. Sickness is increasing, despite the most careful arrangements. Please tell them to say where they flash from. Can't make it out.

Meanwhile a relief force gathered on the Tugela, with detachments from HMS *Tenedos, Shah,* and *Boadicea.* There were so many bluejackets that the Naval Brigade provided 20 per cent of its European strength and all the artillery, shared between the column's two brigades.[53] Sailors not employed as gunners were told off as escorts, with orders to defend the guns to the last. Two of HMS *Shah*'s Brigade left journals: Commander J.W. Brackenbury and William Jenkin, Captain of the Main Top, whose scepticism provides a colourful alternative to the prosaic account of his Commanding Officer.[54] Like Captain Cracroft of HMS *Niger*, Brackenbury was a mixture of piety and practicality. He took an infantry officer's interest in his men's feet, and formed an *ad hoc* band to entertain them on the march. When he double marched them past the day's camping ground, he bought everyone a beer to apologise.

The Eshowe relief force moved off on 29 March after standing all night in the rain. Waggons stuck fast in the mud, needing double teams of oxen, while sailors cut brushwood to throw under the wheels. There was no sign of the enemy except for some kraals burning in the distance, but overnight the column went into laager, the waggons in square with the fighting troops in a trench outside, cattle and native auxiliaries inside, Naval Brigade with guns and rockets on the corners. The defensive precautions paid off at Gingindlovu on 2 April when large numbers of Zulus appeared all round the laager, advancing in extended order through the tall grass and clumps of trees. However, the Gatlings worked admirably, while the 9prs and rockets broke up more distant Zulu formations:

> in three-quarters of an hour the attack was virtually over – the cavalry and native troops sallied from the laager, and pursued the flying foe.[55]

William Jenkin's account was more circumstantial:

> Stood to arms 4 a.m. Had been raining furiously previous night, there being four feet of water in the trenches. Zulus thought our ammunition would be wet. The enemy sighted by our scouts 6 a.m. Order 'man the trenches' every man in his place in three seconds. Zulus commenced fire at 6.30 p.m. advancing in horseshoe formation, estimated number of Zulus 1,500 to 3,000. Gatlings and 9prs opened with shell at 800 yards (should have waited till nearer, but the thought of 'Isandula' made all anxious to get at them). Enemy advanced courageously and ignorantly to within thirty yards of our trenches, one man throwing his assegai at a Gatling gun.[56]

The enemy regrouped for a final attack, 'in splendid skirmishing order, but were again repulsed with immense loss ... falling like corn before the scythe'. The Naval Brigade lost seven wounded, including HMS *Tenedos*' surgeon:

> It was a 'hot corner' at Gingindlovu, where the cart containing our appliances was stationed ... I was looking after a poor fellow from the 99th ... when I was myself disabled – I cannot say I was placed *hors de combat*, for, as I have said the place we were in was hot, and continued to remain so.[57]

Jenkin's breakfast was another casualty. His kettle remained outside the perimeter, suffering several direct hits. He roasted a mealie pod, his first hot food for twenty-four hours, and wrote:

> I hope during my stay in Her Majesty's Service I shall never again be similarly situated, and if it should again fall to my lot to form part of a Naval Brigade or Relief Column, I hope it will be better organised.[58]

Part of the column went on to relieve Eshowe, while Jenkin buried dead Zulus, forty to sixty in a grave. Afterwards he walked over the battlefield, where the sights were better imagined than described. There was all sorts of spoil: assegais and shields, British rifles and belts taken at Isandlwana. The Eshowe garrison were in poor shape, with 200 sick and twenty-eight fresh graves in the neat burial ground, including five from the Naval Brigade. Midshipman Croker, whose disselboom had given trouble at Inyezane, was amongst them. Most of the graves had simple wooden crosses, but *Active's* men had thought Croker 'one of the right sort', and roughly carved him a stone memorial decorated with a broken anchor, strewing it with wild flowers before they left.

The remainder of the Naval Brigade's campaign was an anti-climax, as the strategic focus shifted to Chelmsford's advance on the Zulu capital at Ulundi. The months after the relief of Eshowe saw the Actives recuperating at Fort Tenedos, while the Shahs and Boadiceas built roads, and stocked forts with supplies to be sent on to Ulundi, once it had fallen. This static role, with large numbers of men camped out for weeks in the same confined quarters, soon affected their health. By 15 May, out of 769 naval personnel still in theatre seventy-five were in hospital with another fifty-nine on the sick list.[59] *Tenedos'* detachment returned onboard reluctantly, to take their crippled ship home:

> 'We have had no fighting yet', said one bronzed and burly tar, 'for we have only been defending ourselves.' – a singular commentary on the campaign.[60]

One of his officers, writing under the pseudonym of 'Nemo', must have spoken for all, rather than no one, when he wrote home:

> This extraordinary, 'As you was before you was', is most heartbreaking, and the same cry is in everyone's mouth, 'I wish they'd either go on or go home out of this'. They say they are waiting till they mass supplies in front, but somehow to my idea do not seem to be straining a little bit of nerve to get them there. And when we have burnt the king's kraal (which he can rebuild in three days), and massacred a few thousand more wounded Zulus (this I may tell you is the use of the Native Continent) – Cui bono?[61]

The Admiralty became anxious for their half-manned ships in the approaching winter, and suggested moving them to Simonstown, but Commodore Richards would have none of it:

In keeping these ships at this anchorage where ... their presence has been almost indispensable, I have given the question of their safety my most anxious consideration, and have myself examined the records at the Post Office, which clearly show that the finest weather in Natal is experienced in the winter season, and that gales from the eastward are of very rare occurrence.

The ships are always prepared to slip, and put to sea on a heavy sea setting in, but we have now thirty weeks experience of Her Majesty's ships continuously lying in these roads without this having once been necessary.[62]

At the end of June the Naval Brigade concentrated at Fort Chelmsford, once more under Fletcher Campbell's command, 545 strong, and armed to the teeth with three 9pr guns, six rocket tubes, and five Gatlings: 'everyone very discontented, wishes to advance to finish up the affair'.[63] Their impressive armament saw little use, however. The projected move had a deeper strategic purpose, to open a seaborne supply route into the heart of enemy country, through Port Durnford, which lacked any of the facilities usually associated with the term. There was a good anchorage about a mile out, but the open beach was exposed to the full force of the Indian Ocean. The navy moored three buoys outside the breakers, attached by strong hawsers to sand anchors buried above high water. The bight of the hawser passed through timber rollers in the bow and stern of purpose-built surf boats, which slipped along the wire to the beach, using the force of the waves to take them in, and the backwater to return. Two thousand tons of stores were landed in this way, and 600 sick evacuated. Fletcher Campbell was surprised at the good effect on his men's health of the holiday combination of sun and salt water, although they worked from dawn to dusk, wearing only their flannels. It beat digging trenches, which made them ill.[64]

Among the reinforcements rushed out after Isandlwana was Sir Garnet Wolseley, 'our only general', to replace the popular but unlucky Chelmsford. Hoping to snatch the latter's glory, Wolseley appeared off Port Durnford, but the weather was unfavourable:

All hands were pleased he could not land as that night we had news of Lord Chelmsford being within sight of Ulundi, and we hoped he would be in and finish the campaign before the landing of Sir Garnet.[65]

Chelmsford's victory on 4 July 1879 ended the war, so many Zulus surrendering at Port Durnford that they formed working parties on the beach. The

Zulu King Cetewayo remained at large until 30 August, but Wolseley lost no time in 'wiping out' the naval element. The Brigade loaded their artillery into lighters for the trip back to Durban, and marched up to be inspected by the new Commander-in-Chief. Wolseley complimented them on their efficiency and noble service in the field, regretting that he was not out sooner to share their honours: 'Quite surprised', Jenkin commented. 'I thought he was a man against Naval Brigades'.[66]

Then they rode out through the surf to return to their ships, in rather less time than it had taken to reach Port Durnford:

22 July: Arrived at Natal at daybreak and embarked on board our own ship amid loud cheering (the ship keepers manning the rigging), and never was I so glad to get on board ship in my career in the service.[67]

The ships' parties might well cheer their shipmates' return. The ships rolled continually through 30 degrees, while to ensure the safety of a shorthanded warship through the equinoctial gales, on a coast lacking secure anchorages, called for as much labour and anxiety as facing the Zulu. The naval contribution to the campaign was remarkable:[68]

SHIP	DATE LANDED	MONTHS ASHORE	OFFICERS	MEN	LOST DEAD
Active	19 Nov '78	8	10	163	11
Tenedos	1 Jan '79	4.25	3	58	1
Shah	7 Mar '79	4.5	16	378	4
Boadicea	18 Mar '79	4.5	10	218	3
TOTALS:			39	817	19

Simple numerical comparison with the 16,000 soldiers employed in the war does not reveal the Naval Brigade's full contribution:

composed as they were of seasoned and hardy, well trained and disciplined men, accustomed to turn their hands to any sort of employment, and to work in small detachments; these were far more serviceable than unseasoned troops, and immature recruits.[69]

Bartle Frere was not just being polite. Many of *Active*'s men had signed on for a second commission with Hewett, after the Ashanti War, and then taken part in the Kaffir War of 1877–78 near East London. The attack at Inyezane was one of the few successful offensive actions of the war. The

navy provided all the artillery for the Eshowe Relief Column, the reinforcements from *Shah* and *Boadicea* making that operation possible. The
navy built and operated the pont which allowed the army to pass its stores
and transport over the Lower Tugela, while the operations at Port
Durnford dramatically shortened the army's lines of communication. The
most impressive tribute came from the *Natal Mercury*, taking up six column
inches in the *Army and Navy Gazette*, compared with one-and-a-half for
Wolseley's farewell speech. The Zulu War had provided a conspicuous
example of Britain's naval pre-eminence, the navy being associated with
none of the campaign's disasters. The *Active*'s brigade had secured the frontier in the early days, while HMS *Shah* had stabilised the situation after
Isandlwana:

> Whatever shortcomings may have been discerned in other services . . .
> nothing can be, nothing has been said in disparagement of the Naval
> forces in connection with the war . . . As colonists we are proud to be
> identified with a country that can produce a service so efficient – whose
> supremacy at sea is preserved by men so worthy of national respect and
> honour . . .[70]

A CERTAIN STAIN: THE TRANSVAAL WAR
(DECEMBER 1880–MARCH 1881)

The other African people under-estimated by the British were the Dutch-
speaking white farmers, or Boers, of the Transvaal. They had only
accepted British protection for fear of the Zulus. The Anglo-Zulu War
removed this threat, allowing the Boers to give full expression to their
hatred of outside interference. They ambushed a British column at
Bronkhurst Spruit in December 1880, and blockaded garrisons in the
Transvaal, while their main force closed the obvious route for a relieving
column at Laing's Nek in northern Natal. The war that followed was short
and inglorious, but illustrates how the tactical superiority enjoyed by previous Naval Brigades over such enemies as the Chinese or Asante was
starting to wear thin.

British forces assembled for the Zulu War had dispersed. Major-General
Sir George Pomeroy Colley, Governor and Commander-in-Chief of Natal,
'having regard to the smallness of the force at my disposal', asked the navy
for help. However, he refused the offer of two 9pr guns, as he felt he already
had 'sufficient artillery in proportion to my forces and means of transport'.[71]

Commodore Richards had loaded warlike stores at Simonstown on first hearing of Bronkhurst Spruit, and landed a Naval Brigade of 130 men as soon as HMS *Boadicea* reached Durban.

Events soon showed that Colley, 'a man who had only moved leaden soldiers',[72] was not the man to shift the Boers. At Laing's Nek on 29 January 1,200 British troops launched a frontal attack on twice their number of Boers in a prepared position with breech-loading rifles. Much to their surprise the British were repulsed, their retreat covered by naval rockets infiltrated into a mealie patch in front of the Boer position. When the infantry fell back, the sailors found themselves under a brisk fire. The carts and mules used to move the rockets were shot up, and two seamen killed.[73]

Richards landed another sixty men with two field guns, although the Admiralty insisted on his own return to Durban, a decision which may have saved his life. They sympathised privately with his desire to be at the front, 'but if anything happened to you we should be in a mess'. They also complained that Richards had not used the telegraph to consult them before landing reinforcements. The Board were not just spoilsports: they needed HMS *Dido* on the Gold Coast, where the Asante were stirring, but did not like to move her with three dozen of her crew ashore in South Africa: 'You ought to have asked sanction for landing men. We should not have refused *Boadicea*, but should have stopped *Dido*.'[74]

Neither naval detachment took part in Colley's next reverse, at the Ingogo River, although *Boadicea*'s men cleared the battlefield. Commander Romilly noticed how Boer marksmen had crept within thirty yards of the British position:

> average distance of the Boers was 200 yards; their skirmishing, and shooting beautiful . . . many 60th were shot through the ornament of their helmets.[75]

Colley had now lost so many men he could hardly defend his camp below Laing's Nek at Mount Prospect. Naval signallers set up heliographs in case the Boers cut the telegraph wire, while Romilly enciphered messages, as most of Colley's staff had been killed. Morale was shaky. When a nervous sentry fired on a patrol one night, 'bugles sounded various calls indiscriminately. Some struck tents, others did not.' The sailors kept their heads, and awaited orders.[76] Religion provided poor comfort: The chaplain preached on the efficacy of death-bed repentance, while, in a macabre piece of class distinction, the officers killed at the Ingogo were disinterred, to be buried separately from their men:

Who had this morbid piece of sentimentality carried out I do not know. Everyone seems to condemn it; but I believe it was owing to a telegram from the relatives. We have had quite enough funerals in camp without having double ones. Heavy rain in evening.[77]

Reinforcements arrived on 23 February, Highlanders of the 92nd Regiment, and two mule-drawn 9prs from HMS *Dido*. This made it possible for Colley to redeem a promise made to the Naval Brigade after the Ingogo River, that he would employ them next. Colley did not, however, use the complete fresh battalion for a concentrated blow supported by the so far undamaged Naval Brigade with its collection of guns. Instead he took a few companies from each of his battered regiments, destroying their unit cohesion, and added a handful of naval riflemen.[78] He meant to scale Majuba Hill, hoping to turn the Boer position at Laing's Nek. The column moved off at 10 p.m. 26 February 1881 in the greatest secrecy, Colley explaining his intentions to no one. They ascended the precipitous mountain unopposed, but with difficulty, the men carrying greatcoats and waterproof sheets, three days' rations and seventy rounds a man. The sailors at the rear of the column reached the top early next morning, some deploying around the top of the path, the rest remaining in reserve.

The unreconnoitred hilltop proved to be a trap, too far from the Boers' camp to shoot at them, while the steep slopes prevented the defenders firing down without showing themselves against the skyline. The Boers exploited this, moving up in the dead ground, keeping the defenders' head down with a continuous fire. This caused few casualties among the seamen who were 'lying down under good cover, firing seldom, as the Boers did not show in force on the left, and generally kept out of range'.[79] Commander Romilly, however, was hit by an explosive bullet, 'the first mention . . . of the employment of these barbarous missiles by the Boers'.[80] About midday, there was a lull in the firing, followed by a rush of Boers firing so rapidly that only their rifles could be seen through the smoke. Dr Mahon the naval surgeon was in the thick of the fight, as the Boers poured across the top of the hill, towards his dressing post. He held up a white flag, 'but it was almost immediately shot away, and a hot volley poured all around us'.[81] Sick Berth Attendant Bevis was shot twice through the helmet so both men lay down until the rout had passed, before surrendering successfully. The younger Boers wanted to shoot everyone, especially Romilly whom they took to be Sir Garnet Wolseley, but the older men prevented them, bringing water for the wounded, and bandaging their wounds. Sub-Lieutenant Scott, the one naval officer to survive the action, was at the rear of the hill when the general panic

A quiet day in the batteries: sailors before Sebastopol
with 32pr guns, the left one still on its naval truck carriage.

RMA officers at Balaklava, only recognisable by their
swords and cap badges.

HMS *Pearl*'s Brigade in a frenzied attack at Amorha;
a limbered field gun in the background.

Assault Landing Techniques 1858: Royal Marines leave a Gunboat at
Canton. A boat carried thirty marines or twenty soldiers.

The Taku Forts after their capture in 1860, scene of
the Royal Navy's worst defeat of the nineteenth century.

Naval Brigade and Royal Marines in action at Shimonoseki,
the image reversed by the engraver.

Breakfast on the road to Kumasi:
white neck cloths provide extra protection from the sun.

Marching into Prahsu: the little boy at the head of the column
was 'Mixed Pickles', the Brigade mascot.

HMS *Active*'s Naval Brigade on the Tugela: two companies of bluejackets (in caps) flank marines (in helmets), with Kroomen extreme left; 12pr RBL and Gatling in front.

HMS *Shah*'s bluejackets in action at Gingindlovu, sketched by one of their officers. Friendlies wait inside the square, ready to pursue the defeated Zulus.

All warships carried small arms: cutlasses hang above Lee Metfords
with bayonets in HMS *Alexandra*, a veteran of Alexandria.

Aiming Practice: Boy sailors from HMS *Cambridge* learn to use the Lee Metford.

Prepare to resist cavalry: an obsolete manoeuvre by 1896
but an impressive spectacle at reviews.

'Make believe field gun exercise on a narrow strip of deck':
HMS *Camperdown*'s 7pr RML; obsolete but a handy little weapon.

Instructors at HMS *Excellent* with a Maxim on naval
field mounting; a weapon still in service in the 1920s.

Skylarking in an Egyptian battery at Alexandria. The parapet
protecting the only modern gun (left) has suffered a direct hit.

Armoured train at Alexandria:
firing the 40pr Armstrong RBL gun.

Field Service dress of the 1880s at Sawakin: blue serge
and blanket rolls make no concessions to the Sudanese sun.

The Naval Brigade hard at it with Gatling and Gardner guns
at El Teb; Sir William Hewett VC well to the front.

(Top) Bluejackets at Mwele in 1895: others rest under the awning (bottom left), ready to turn out at a moment's notice.

(Above) A stiff piece of work: 12prs under fire at Colenso.

(Left) One of many unlikely positions reached by naval guns: a wheeled 4.7-inch during the relief of Ladysmith. Infantry can just be seen, following the shell bursts beyond the ravine.

(Top) A platform-mounted 4.7 takes a rest from shelling Pieter's Hill. Boer War Naval Brigades wore military khaki with sennet hats.

(Above) From Ladysmith to Peking; HMS *Terrible*'s 12pr 12cwt gun rigged for shore service.

(Left) HMS *Orlando*'s Nordenfeldt detachment: some of the men who fought at Tientsin, wearing the bandolier equipment.

How to land a 4.7-inch gun, as specified in the 1910 Landing Party manual; probably photographed at HMS *Excellent*.

The Navy provided specialist artillery during the First World War: a 2pr pom pom of the RM Anti-Aircraft Brigade, on an Arrow Pierce armoured lorry.

Pillaging Canton in 1858: seamen in sennet hats, marines in havelocks, and Chinese of the 'Bamboo Rifles'

swept his party away, scattering them down the almost perpendicular sides of the mountain in a hail of bullets. As one survivor put it: 'We took three mortal hours to get up that blooming hill, but we come down in three bloomin' strides.'[82] Scott waited out of range for stragglers, but only twenty came in, most without their rifles. The troops left in camp were in total confusion:

> Fugitives now reaching camp by dozens, great excitement prevailed. Men were sent nearly to distraction by contradictory orders. The Naval Brigade, now under a third commanding officer, was ordered to get their guns into a small fort in front, water and provision it for two days, and build up the entrance. It was scarcely done when the whole thing was reversed. Everything was wrong until the arrival of a senior colonel who had been out with a reconnoitring party. When he came the confusion ceased, and the camp at once became the camp of an English army.[83]

The Boers allowed walking wounded to return to Mount Prospect, unwounded prisoners carrying others down until a thick evening mist prevented further evacuation. Mahon had enough blankets and waterproof sheets to cover the wounded still on the summit, but nothing to give them except water and opium, the Boers having drunk all his brandy:

> It now commenced to rain heavily, and continued to do so without intermission during the whole night, which much aggravated the sufferings of the wounded. It also became bitterly cold towards morning. The darkness was so intense that it was almost impossible to attempt to alleviate the sufferings of the wounded without stumbling over them. We had neither lantern nor matches.[84]

Four died before stretcher parties arrived from Mount Prospect in the morning. Romilly was found under a bush 'not much the worse', but died three days later of peritonitis. The whole Naval Brigade attended his funeral, an AB writing that they had lost their best friend and counsellor, 'his loss being felt as deeply on board as in the Naval Brigade'.[85] The Boers lost two dead and four wounded, compared with 285 British casualties out of 365 present at the start of the action. The losses included Colley and thirty-three of the Naval Brigade: half their number.[86]

Richards had requested another fifty bluejackets from home, 'in view of the possible exigencies of the service', although he cannot have expected them to be needed so suddenly. They left Durban on 4 March to reinforce the survivors at Mount Prospect whose hands were more than full with continuous outpost and hospital duty. Military reinforcements were also on hand, making Colley's half-baked escapade the more inexcusable. His successor Sir Evelyn Wood, an inspired fighting man, negotiated an armistice on 24 March that effectively conceded the Transvaal's independence. The Naval Brigade returned to Durban where they enjoyed three days' leave before embarking on 19 April 1881. Despite the campaign's disastrous outcome the inhabitants turned out *en masse* to bid them goodbye:

> respectably dressed men on the wharves eagerly asking anyone to get a cargo of grog on board. Being told it was against discipline, they purchased all the fruit the vendors had for sale, and disregarding the remonstrances of the officers, distributed it to the men with a handshake.[87]

Such a defeat inspired the wildest allegations. Critics attributed the Naval Brigades' heavy losses to their carrying revolvers and cutlasses, or to their having no bayonets; both assertions untrue. The *Standard*'s correspondent claimed panic-stricken seamen had swept away the 92nd, and questions were asked in the House of Commons. The *Army and Navy Gazette* derided the idea:

> What sort of compliment is it to the gallant 92nd to suggest that they were carried away by the 'flight' of eighteen men of another command . . . an extraordinary thing to suggest that the alleged wavering of these few sailors should put to flight a force of over 700 officers and men, largely comprised of picked troops from seasoned regiments. The fact is the seamen were cut to pieces.[88]

The immediate reasons for the defeat were inadequate fields of fire, the lack of defensive depth to the position with no satisfactory location for the supports, and the exhausted state of the men.[89] Individuals of both services had behaved heroically:

> A Boer Commandant pointed out [to the burial party next day] . . . the bodies of George Hammond, and Samuel Witheridge, Gunners, as men who remained to the last, and died at their posts. Lieutenant Trower's body was also found on the extreme ridge, shot through the chest, temple, and with left hand shattered.[90]

The Boers had shown their tactical superiority throughout the war. Trained to the rifle from boyhood, they fought like modern infantry, covering every move by fire, or ground. For the first time British forces had met an enemy as well armed as themselves, but able to use their breech-loading rifles to better effect. Boer fire and movement called into question the British Army's established tactics and training, and by extension those of the Royal Navy also.

CHAPTER SIX

Mechanisms of Intervention

THE military skills of the Naval Brigades that fought in the Crimea and South Africa varied widely. Naval training and discipline improved dramatically during the mid-nineteenth century. Naval Brigades ceased to depend on the whim of individual captains. They became the subject of official doctrine, laid down in printed manuals, and taught centrally at newly established gunnery schools. Such institutional developments were evidence of a new spirit of professionalism that affected all aspects of the service.

The term 'profession' implies an externally recognised group in unique possession of a codified body of non-trivial expertise, such as the law or healthcare. A hierarchy of experienced practitioners controls access to that expertise, and monitors its development. The Royal Navy that triumphed in the Napoleonic Wars was not a professional body in all these senses. The exclusion of naval officers from the committee on calculation of longitudes shows how their expertise lacked external recognition, perhaps because it had never been codified. Naval officers scattered around the world in remote locations had no standard operating procedures to lend consistency to their most routine activities. The Admiralty failed to provide gun powder for practice, while the gallant old seamen who received warrants as Gunners were 'usually the persons on board least conversant with artillery'.[1] The only gunnery system known in the post-Nelsonic Navy was that every captain had his own way – the very opposite of professionalism. As for the *arme blanche*, a frigate's boarding party was a joke, 'sticking in the hatchways, like Greeks at the straits of Thermopylae, unable to move themselves, and threatening destruction to all who dare approach them'.[2]

Meanwhile the French, heartened by British defeats against the US Navy in 1812, began a systematic training programme in naval gunnery for all officers, gun-captains, and half their ratings. The Royal Navy could not afford to continue in its old 'rule of thumb' methods, so in 1830 the Admiralty established a 'temporary' school of naval gunnery in HMS *Excellent*, a hulk moored at Portsmouth. Guns could still be fired 'without danger or inconvenience' within the harbour itself, although practice had to be at high tide to stop mudlarks scavenging shot under fire. Royal Marine artillerymen acted as instructors until 1868, underlining the navy's lack of equivalent expertise. The men they taught, however, formed the nucleus of a professional force. The Captain of HMS *Excellent* was allowed to recruit seamen gunners for a fixed, renewable term of continuous service. This was a revolutionary step, for sailors had always served one commission at a time, returning in between to civilian life. The Gunnery School was thus at the forefront of the most important social change to affect the Royal Navy during the nineteenth century, a change that contributed to the solid discipline of later Naval Brigades compared with the seamen who rambled the woods around Havana or Cartagena.[3] Some officers objected to making sailors into soldiers, although the peculiar difficulties of naval gunnery, with its complex tackles and breechings, and necessary precautions against wind and spray, plainly showed the need for a gun drill as automatic as the manual exercise of a regiment.[4]

Their Lordships showed their own opinion of the value of HMS *Excellent* in their choice of captains, who included such leading figures as Astley Cooper Key, John Fisher, or Percy Scott. All were destined for some degree of greatness, and many were veterans of Naval Brigades. The above officers served in China, Egypt, and West Africa: Scott in all three. The purchase in 1859 of a mud bank in Portsmouth Harbour, for rifle practice, underlined the permanency of the Gunnery School. Spoil from new dockyard basins augmented the mud bank, known as Whale Island, which acquired a pier, drains, rifle ranges, grass, a parade ground, and living accommodation to replace the hulks scrapped in the late 1880s. The Admiralty even built roads, after Scott gave the Board a miserable afternoon trudging through ankle-deep mud. Generations of seamen learned gunnery and tactics at Whale Island, where HMS *Excellent*, in her terrestrial incarnation, is still a major Royal Naval training establishment and home to the Portsmouth Field Gun Crew, the lineal descendants of the original seaman gunners.

TACTICAL DOCTRINE

Intellectual developments matched material ones, although as late as 1886 'one of the old school' grumbled after a gunnery paper at the *RUSI* that, 'we try to educate the young officers too much'.[5] Not only did seamen value the educational possibilities at *Excellent*, teaching themselves to read, write, and cypher, but a coherent body of technical doctrine emerged, despite the professional antipathy to 'scientific bosh'. One of the first printed manifestations of the trend was *Questions and Answers in Naval Gunnery* by Lieutenant Farrant RMA, published soon after HMS *Excellent*'s permanent establishment in 1835. Aspiring gunnery lieutenants recorded their verbal instruction in handsomely illustrated notebooks. Gunnery at this time covered all military aspects of the naval profession, so notebooks document 'Cutlass and Pike Exercise', 'Questions at the Rocket Boat', and 'Field Piece Manoeuvres', besides the use of great guns. Students hammered bullets into unwieldly Brunswick rifles, whose kick bruised their shoulders, built fieldworks worthy of Laurence Sterne's Uncle Toby, and then blew them up. Sometimes they stormed the poopdeck with tomahawk and pistol in an uproarious drill known as 'toggle and mount'.

Instructions for the Exercise and Service of Great Guns, and Shells on Board Her Majesty's Ships 1848 laid down the Manual and Platoon exercise for naval infantry, that is, the movements for handling unloaded and loaded firearms respectively. A *Field Exercise and Instructions for Landing* manual appeared in 1854, just in time for the Crimean War. Comparison with Gunnery Notebooks compiled in 1851 and 1853 shows how the printed manuals formalised verbal instructions, with identical sections on skirmishing, rockets, landings, and field guns.[6] The navy's first free-standing field exercise appeared in 1859, following major Naval Brigade deployments in Russia, India, Burma, and China. It is hard to see the formal separation of the field exercise from pure gunnery at such a moment as coincidental. *Instructions for the Exercise of Small Arms, Field Pieces, etc for the Use of Her Majesty's Ships* described every aspect of naval operations ashore, in a logical sequence, placing those old chestnuts the Cutlass and Pike exercise after more essential matters. Headings included:

Organisation of Seamen for Landing
Instructions for Landing Seamen and Marines
Manual and Platoon Exercises
Formations for the Company
Field Exercise for a Battalion of Seamen
Light Infantry Movements, including patrols and advanced guards
Musketry Instruction, and care of the Enfield rifle
Exercises with Cutlass, Pike, and the Colt or Adams revolver
Field Piece Exercise
Assault on a Field Fortification

The *Instructions* were the culmination of an evolutionary process, much of their substance reflecting earlier printed manuals, or Gunnery Notebooks. However the 1859 authors left no doubt about their work's significance:

As the efficiency of Seamen when landed in any considerable number depends most materially upon a proper system of organisation, and training *previous* to their being landed, and without which they are inefficient, the following system is to be strictly observed in all Her Majesty's ships.[7]

Captain Fletcher Campbell echoed these sentiments after the Zulu War: 'too late to think of drill when a campaign has commenced!'[8]

The other natural source of the *Instructions* were the equivalent military publications, whole chunks of which were repeated verbatim.[9] The main difference between the services was the simple, direct language used by the naval instructors, who specified the required effect, without spelling out the method in mind-numbing detail. They omitted the more esoteric aspects of military drill, remarking that all unnecessary and complicated movements should be avoided. Instead they concentrated on the open-order tactics that formed the basis of mid-nineteenth century combat. Land tactics had evolved in response to the increasing lethality of weapons, so that, by the 1850s, most firefights were conducted by skirmishers. Infantry still manoeuvred in columns and fought in lines, but, as we have seen in the Indian Mutiny, a screen of sharpshooters kept the enemy at a distance. The *Instructions* laid down that there should be two lines of skirmishers, a firing and support line of similar strength, with about half the force in reserve further back. HMS *Active*'s detachment had been well grounded in the official tactical system before they used it at Inyezane. Fletcher Campbell believed that 'to attack an enemy in position without supports and reserves should rarely be attempted, and only as a dernier ressort, as if unsuccessful it will surely lead to repulse and disaster'.[10]

Some close-order work was still necessary, if faced by cavalry, or masses of fast moving spearmen. William White remembered how smartly the marines formed square when menaced by Tartar cavalry, compared with the bluejackets who formed more of a heap. The squares used in 'savage warfare' bore little resemblance to the packed battalion squares of Waterloo, however. Against the Maori, Lieutenant Albert Battiscombe formed an extended square of skirmishers six paces apart: 'somewhat on the principles of Maori warfare every man working for himself'.[11] Half the force remained inside, with a 12pr howitzer, to give support wherever needed. Such dispersed formations bore only a semantic relationship to the solid traditional squares that appeared at reviews to delight audiences, and confuse historians.

The nineteenth-century revolution in weapons technology had just begun, so the authors of the navy's early manuals did well to pick out the points that became crucial with the spread of rifled small arms. They emphasised marksmanship and effective use of ground. Sailors had to learn to judge distances and take deliberate aim at a specific object when brought to the present, even if this meant painting circles on the side of the ship. They were not to jerk at the trigger, or fire hastily, as: 'efficiency is not estimated by the number of shots fired . . . but by the execution performed'.[12] Such views were revolutionary, after the crude methods used with the percussion musket. Now skirmishers had to use cover, selecting their next position before moving:

> ever bearing in mind that the grand requisites in skirmishing are a sure quick and steady aim, together with that ready tact in seizing at a glance those local advantages which enable a man to do the utmost injury to his enemy with the least exposure to himself.[13]

Naval riflemen were often referred to as 'light infantry', a distinction underlined by their adoption of a short Enfield rifle similar to those used by Light Infantry regiments. The shorter weapon was handier for boatwork, and suited the irregular warfare in which Naval Brigades found themselves engaged.

A peculiarly naval part of the manual dealt with assault landings. This changed little until specialist landing craft appeared during the First World War. Boats lined up one length apart, in waves corresponding to the three tactical divisions: skirmishers, supports, and reserve. The lightest craft went in front with gunboats on the flanks to provide close fire support from brass howitzers mounted as boat guns, on slides between the oarsmen. Carriages and wheels were stowed in the bottom of the boat, and a limber in the stern sheets. Skirmishers landed as the boat guns cleared the beach, the main body in succeeding waves: 'fast pulling boats with Medical Officers will attend in rear of the line'. Artillery tactics were basic. Guns were not to fire together, but continuously at a named object in front. Batteries were to conform to the movement of associated units, remembering not to move with loaded guns; necessary injunctions for gunners used to someone else taking care of station-keeping when at sea. During withdrawals guns stayed with the troops nearest the enemy for maximum effect, rapidly falling back on the supports when pressed.

TRAINING

However admirable official instructions might be, their practical value depends on how they are put into practice. Anecdotal evidence suggests a major improvement in naval drill between the 1850s and 1880s. Members of the Crimean Naval Brigade were never reconciled to the technicalities of soldiering:

> beyond the 'manual and platoon', a little squad drill, 'forming fours', we were not, in the Navy, in those times adepts at soldiering so that the handling of a regiment of six hundred was no easy task. To be sure, we had with us two or three 'educated men', gunnery officers from HMS *Excellent*, who 'knew radius' and everything else . . . but that was of little use when scarcely anyone knew how to obey them.[14]

Small-arms men and field-gun crews brushed up their drill and musketry, when there was a prospect of work ashore, a practice favoured by the gentle pace of early Naval Brigade campaigns.

The crack Mediterranean Fleet of the 1880s on the other hand fielded battalions 'quite equal to any line regiment',[15] while later wars demanded a more immediate response than was acceptable in India, or China. During the Zulu War 'every man that could possibly be spared was wanted for other purposes. There were no men to be spared for drill, or anything else'.[16] The inference must be that HMS *Excellent* and the Devonport Gunnery Ship, HMS *Cambridge*, were making their influence felt. A veteran of the Maori Wars thought few things marked off the old navy from the new so much as the advances made in service ashore:

> Nowadays [about 1900] a Naval Brigade is better disciplined and organised, in the strict military sense, has more cohesion, is better provided, and is better equipped than brigades of soldiers. In my day when we landed at Taranaki, we simply transferred the deck of our frigate to terra firma.[17]

The improvement was achieved through a combination of training afloat and ashore. Regular practice was expected of the landing parties of seagoing ships in the 1880s: 'As one forenoon in each week is devoted to perfecting all the arrangements which would be required in action on board the ship, so another should be employed in perfecting the organisation for fighting on shore.'[18] In 1890 Sir Edmund Fremantle's flagship HMS *Boadicea* exercised her Landing Parties and Small Arms companies more often than she beat to General Quarters.[19]

Only so much could be done at sea, so training ashore became part of naval life, although one eccentric officer did try marching his men over the cables in lieu of ploughed fields. Marines and seamen from the Mediterranean Fleet landed at Malta, or friendly ports like the Piraeus:

> Our ships have been keeping the D—— out of Jack's mind by landing the small arms parties and marines from each ship every Thursday, and you can form no idea of how it is looked forward to by them, and what a magnificent show they make . . . As an old soldier observed to me, 'They are equal to regulars'.

Landing parties preparing to attack the Taku Forts in 1860 practised on each other so enthusiastically that they suffered several real casualties. Such outings were accepted as good for morale, as well as for exercise. When the Queenstown guardship marched her company through the Irish country-side, drums beating and colours flying, her band playing 'St Patrick's Day in the Morning', the *Army and Navy Gazette* remarked:

> Landings of this sort cannot be too highly encouraged, as they are highly useful to the men in a Service point of view, and promote among them an *esprit de corps*, which is so necessary for the wellbeing of the Navy.[20]

The Cape squadron of the 1890s trained ashore every Tuesday, the long days in the country 'a welcome change to both bluejackets and marines'.[21] They studied the lessons of recent West African campaigns, adopting a modern 'herring-bone' pattern of all-round defence, or clearing the cover around villages before moving through them. The hills outside Simonstown provided room for modern fire tactics under realistic condi-tions, the Kopje fighting a fair sample of what would happen in the South African War.

An appreciative correspondent remarked, 'One so rarely gets a chance at home of operating against a real farm.' Some runs ashore were less useful. A cynic remarked that a four-day exercise in Malta was 'chiefly remarkable for the large number of staff officers employed'.[22] Sometimes the instruction was interspersed with music and even dancing. In an age starved of entertain-ment, crowds gathered to watch Jack at his evolutions, and, in the case of the daughters of Erin, to provide dancing partners. A Grand Review at Yokohama preceded the attack on Shimonoseki, winning high praise from spectators surprised to see bluejackets manoeuvre in a manner worthy of the 'boys in red':

> On landing they formed into line, flanked by the batteries, fired a number of rounds, formed squares, prepared to resist cavalry, dismounted the batteries, taking the wheels and other gear off the guns inside the squares, then fired several volleys of musketry, remounted the guns, formed columns of companies, and marched off the ground through the settlement.[23]

Some objected to such displays as a waste of time. An anonymous officer regretted the lost simplicity of naval training:

> Some few years ago the Navy possessed a short manual of 'Rifle Exercise', containing all the instruction it was then deemed advisable to give to seamen. It embraced some dozen simple manoeuvres, besides the ordinary instruction for using the rifle. It is not too much to say that it was nearly perfect of its kind.

He blamed the drill makers, who elaborated an extraordinary number of different ways of doing the same thing. Naval officers resented such pointless complexity. Trusting to luck, they found themselves unable to carry out the simplest company movements. Ratings were better prepared for work ashore than their officers who:

> ignore all that the continuous service system and years of careful drill have done for the seamen of the fleet; and shut their eyes to the radical changes which have been effected in land warfare.[24]

The tactical changes caused by rifled small arms emphasised individual fighting skills, favouring the natural self-reliance of the sailor. Even the shift from sail to steam helped by persuading him to wear boots, 'the beginning if not the end of foot soldiery'. Fletcher Campbell's experience in the Zulu War supported the view that there was an inverse relationship between rank and capability. He declined to comment on the sufficiency of his men's training, but felt, 'there can be no doubt that the training of officers is very much behindhand for the purposes of landing'.[25]

Experience of Boer snap-shooting at Majuba coincided with criticism of naval musketry. *The Army and Navy Gazette* had commented at length on poor shooting in an international rifle match in 1879: 'seamen are provided with weapons, the best that science can produce, but singular to say they are not taught to use them'. Bright brass work and spotless whites counted for more than the probability that 'out of a crew of 500 to 800 men, not a dozen of them could hit a haystack at four or five hundred yards'. The other problem was the inadequate allowance of practice ammunition, 100 rounds a year:

> False economy is the order of the day. Spend millions on useless ships, and equip them with a body of men who cannot make even a decent score at the butts, simply through want of a few extra rounds of ammunition.[26]

Lieutenants Ferris and Lowry voiced their complaints in the *RUSI* Journal. They blamed the training process for the low standard of naval shooting. Only the Mediterranean Fleet with its permanent facilities at Malta allowed enough time for musketry. Other stations suffered 'constant interruptions, indifferent rifle ranges, and too often a general carelessness as to the training of the seamen'.[27] It was not uncommon to find Ordinary Seamen 'so afraid of their rifles, as to miss the target repeatedly at short distances from sheer nervousness'. On distant stations without rifle ranges men might complete ten years' service with no musketry instruction beyond that received as boys, in the training ship. HMS *Espiegle*'s crew on the Australian station did their preliminary drills two months before the annual course, which was then hurried through in a week: 'men came off leave, acted as markers or boat crews in the forenoon, and shot in the afternoon'. The results were so poor that the writer suggested abolishing musketry training altogether.

Weapons technology had left naval training behind. There was a growing gap between the short ranges of most training and the long ranges of modern rifles. The annual exercise was conducted entirely within 400 yards, the men never raising the flap of their sights, although the Martini-Henry rifle was sighted to 1,450 yards. Judging distance was neglected, while individual instruction was 'utterly unlike anything encountered on actual service'. Only ten rounds a year were allowed for collective firing, although its distractions of smoke and noise most nearly resembled firing in action.

Lieutenant Lowry had looked at the subject in some depth. He quoted German military regulations, and had compared notes with French officers in the Pacific, but his paper was read to a small and not very appreciative audience who confused marksmanship with drill. Perhaps one should not make too much of the deficiencies of particular ships. Naval Brigades were usually picked men, who presumably could shoot straight. Much would depend on the commitment of the Gunnery Lieutenant, and his ability to rub along with the Captain, or First Lieutenant. The high standards displayed at the Piraeus in 1863 were attributed to Lieutenant Inglis of HMS *Marlborough*, 'whose whole soul is in this service, and the military training of the bluejackets'.[28] The old school may have had a point, given the opposition faced by most Naval Brigades:

> In Africa I have been called upon to fire when we could not see what we were firing at. There were fellows firing at us, but there was so much bush that we could see nobody, and we could only fire at the smoke.[29]

In such circumstances discipline was as important as marksmanship. Lord Chelmsford complimented the Naval Brigade after Gingindlovu on the steadiness of their fire, compared with that of some of the soldiers, 'which was proved by counting the dead which lay in heaps in front of our position'.[30]

ORGANISATION AND METHOD

Armed forces need more than appropriate doctrine and training to be effective in the field. They need an organisational structure cemented by discipline and directed with competence. They also need equipment suited to the conditions that they face. Naval Brigades possessed a distinctive culture reflected in their organisation and weapons.

Officers responsible for Naval Brigades always emphasised how their proceedings conformed to the usual customs of the service. As far as possible routine mirrored that on board ship. Bluejackets in New Zealand kept ordinary sea watches with a lieutenant of the watch and half the men under arms, ready to spring out with as much alacrity as if they had to shorten sail in a squall:

> Boatswain's mates went about with their whistles and shouted orders in their stentorian voices; bells rang regularly every hour and half hour sea fashion; lights went out and rounds took place with the ordinary routine to which we were all accustomed.[31]

No one thought of going out of camp without leave. HMS *Active*'s brigade in Zululand maintained the strictest discipline and uniformity of dress, with a general inspection every forenoon, the same as on board ship. If any irregularity were detected in a tent the inmates were brought to order by striking their tent and keeping it down all day. There was always extra work for individual defaulters, digging latrines being their special province. Eight months saw one case of corporal punishment: a stoker who took a bottle of brandy from a sutler's wagon. The Admiralty had already suspended flogging in peacetime, and would soon stop it under war conditions, so discipline depended on more positive means than the lash, for example allowing more leave to men of proven good conduct. Peel and Sotheby inflicted floggings during the Indian Mutiny, but discipline owed more to good management than severity. HMS *Shannon*'s Master at Arms, the Petty Officer responsible for discipline, had been 'very much respected by the ship's company'. When he died of dysentery the burial party dug his grave particularly deep to stop the jackals digging up his body.[32] There were no disciplinary repercussions at Sebastopol when the ineffectual efforts of a newly arrived officer to move a 32pr gun provoked one of the working party to ask loudly: 'Will somebody send that damned fool away and put a man there as knows how to do it?'[33]

Naval Brigade organisation reflected that of a ship's company, with gun crews, port and starboard watches of seamen, and detachment of marines: 'Each division of quarters to have its company, sub-division, or section of small arms men commanded by its own officers and petty officers.'[34] Each ship's detachment was complete in itself, ready to land independently, or as part of a brigade landed from a squadron. A typical Naval Brigade structure was two small battalions of bluejackets and one of marines. The latter were an integral, but often neglected, component of such forces:

> 'it makes me mad to hear so much about the Mutiny', grumbled Henry Derry, 'and not a word about the Joeys. Why if we had not taken those guns and made that hole in the wall for those bare-legged Johnnies to get through, I'm thinking a different story would have been told.'[35]

Exact numbers depended on the size and number of ships involved. The old style men-of-war had large complements, which reduced as steam replaced sail. The 1859 *Instructions* specified companies of eighty men commanded by a lieutenant with a couple of mates or midshipmen and three petty officers. A ship of the line might land two such companies, a frigate one, and a sloop half. More men were available in an emergency. Commodore Wiseman landed 220 men from HMS *Curaçao* at Auckland in 1864. He left ninety shipkeepers, with orders to keep their rifles loaded, the upper-deck Armstrongs cast loose, and powder ready, in case of a Maori descent. Later company strengths varied between eighteen and twenty-five file (thirty-six to fifty men), with the same number of officers as before. Captain Blake organised his bluejackets into four companies of twenty file each, although they came from five different ships, with another two of Royal Marines. In Zululand companies were fifty strong. They had five tents per company, a tent corresponding to a mess onboard ship. The men stacked their rifles round the tent pole, worked and ate together, the cook being excused other duties.

A variety of specialists accompanied the small-arms men: pioneers, stretchermen, spare ammunition numbers, armourers, signalmen, and buglers. Naval tradesmen had shown their value in the Crimea and India, and their skills were always useful on campaign: carpenters bridging the River Prahsu, armourers checking native auxiliaries' rifles in Zululand, sailmakers fabricating tents almost anywhere. Naval officers had to be alive to unfair exploitation of naval skills, one Admiral writing to his SNO ashore: 'Let the general understand our men are *not* for coolie work.'[36] Sometimes stokers might do the physical jobs, but the manuals warned against depleting the engine-room strength on which a ship's mobility, and hence her safety, depended. Few stokers were trained to shoot, and a man without a rifle was a liability in the vicinity of Zulus or Maoris. The proportions of tail to teeth are shown by the following analysis of the Brigade in Burma 1885:

Officers RN	30
Officers RM	1
Seamen gunners	280
Royal Marine O/Rs	60
Rocket party	8
Torpedo Party	18
Pioneers	6
Signallers	3
Armourers	7
Musicians	4
Commissariat	2
Ambulance	18
Ammunition Party	5

Totals: 31 officers, 351 RN, 60 RM.[37]

The pattern persisted throughout the period. A battleship like HMS *Centurion* in 1900 might land a self-contained unit of 450 men: 80–100 Royal Marines; 200 bluejacket small arms men in four companies commanded by lieutenants with two midshipmen; two Maxim-gun crews of twelve men each; two field gun crews of eighteen. In addition there would be the usual headquarters, technical, and medical staff including a stretcher party of stokers trained in first aid.

COMMAND

When several ships formed a brigade, a senior captain or commander took command, usually with a second-in-command, and a lieutenant as adjutant or brigade major. Naval Brigades, with their small companies, were heavily officered compared with equivalent military units. The brigade that marched to Kumasi had sixteen officers, including the midshipmen and gunner, to command 163 seamen and forty-five marines. Two infantry companies would have had only six or seven officers, so naval officers found themselves doing jobs that NCOs would have done in the army. This contributed to the high standards of discipline maintained by Naval Brigades and the care they took of their men, but it looks a poor bargain from the taxpayer's point of view, even allowing for the low rates of naval pay.

The high proportion of officers with Naval Brigades was increased by their taste for touring battlefields before the original owners had finished with them. The battle of El Teb in 1884 was conveniently near the Sudanese coast, so unofficial naval onlookers followed at a respectful distance, the general having declined permission for them to advance with the square. Captain Arthur Wilson 'walked out in the morning as a loafer, just to see the fight', and ended up winning the *VC*. He broke his sword on a spearman's ribs, and fought six Arabs with his fists, receiving a cut through his pith helmet that sent blood running down his face and clothes: 'I had no business to go, but it would not do to miss such a good chance of learning one's trade, and it was a most enjoyable day.'[38] Not for nothing was he known as 'Ard Art'!

The anxiety of naval officers to learn their trade contributed to a growing neglect of their most obvious source of expertise in land operations. Royal Marine officers almost never found themselves in command of mixed forces of bluejackets and marines, although it was admitted that many naval officers were ill-equipped to do so. Experienced RMOs might find themselves under the command of quite junior gunnery lieutenants, in the absence of anyone more senior who 'knew the drill'. Disagreeable letters to the press punctuated every campaign, complaining about the marines' poor treatment:

It is only when landed from ships as a portion of a Naval Brigade in but small numbers, and often without their own officers to command them, that they have an opportunity of showing their worth; and even then the old jealousy will show itself, the Marines on every possible occasion being kept in the background.[39]

Certainly HMS *Shah*'s detachment was left behind to garrison Durban when her brigade marched up to the Tugela. Royal Marine officers feared that reductions in the Corps were the 'thin end of a wedge which year by year will be driven further home until as a body it shall cease to exist'. Some naval officers doubted the value of marines. Militarisation of the seamen following the advent of steam appeared to make the sailor/soldier redundant. Nevertheless Royal Marine detachments retained a distinctive tactical role throughout the late nineteenth century. They exploited their superior weapons and marksmanship in earlier conflicts to act as sharpshooters, skirmishing ahead of the bluejackets who followed in support. As the seamen's drill improved through the efforts of HMS *Excellent* and *Cambridge*, the seamen often took the lead, the marines being held in reserve, where the steadiness of the trained infantry soldier might be invaluable in an emergency. It was the RMA who rallied the broken square at Tamai, in response to their Major's bull throated appeal to the Portsmouth men to stand firm.[40]

INTER-SERVICE RELATIONS

Naval officers' relations with their opposite numbers in the army were usually more harmonious, perhaps because inter-service boundaries were clearer than those within the navy. HMS *Shah*'s Captain outranked every military officer in Natal, except Lord Chelmsford, so he remained at Durban to avoid friction. In the same campaign, Admiral Sullivan described press speculation that he disagreed with the conduct of the war as presumptuous.

Commanding Officers of Naval Brigades routinely received orders that exhorted them to follow such directions as they might receive from the military officers commanding the army, emphasising the need for hearty cooperation. Lieutenant Blake's orders at Taranaki in 1860 went further:

as it is of the utmost importance that you should act unanimously, it would be better to give way a little should any difference arise in opinion, rather than run the risk of preventing the most cordial cooperation between you and the other forces.[41]

In India Naval Brigades were very much at home with the army. The Shannons parked their guns with the RA, their band played the Rifle Brigade march, *I'm Ninety-Five*, and the 93rd Highlanders greeted them in turn with *Auld Lang Syne*. When the 93rd observed a naval funeral in progress the battalion suspended its drill session as a mark of respect, the men spontaneously joining in the obsequies.

Occasional diary entries reveal private undercurrents of inter-service suspicion. Albert Battiscombe commented:

> The more I see of the soldiers the less I like them, they are a backbiting set and never lose an opportunity of sneering at a person, they are superbly lazy themselves and cry down anyone who tries to exert himself and raise himself above their standard.[42]

The great exponents of Naval Brigades – Lord Lyons, Peel, Hewett, and Richards – were all notable for their ability to rub along with the military while maintaining close personal control of their forces. Richards travelled up to Mandalay in 1885, and would have accompanied Colley into the Transvaal, if the Admiralty had not recalled him. Hewett had a positive appetite for powder. At Amoafo the Asante nearly broke into the clearing occupied by Wolseley's headquarters. The affair looked ugly for a moment, but sword in hand, the Commodore rallied the left division of the Naval Brigade, driving the enemy back into the bush. He 'was indeed a man to be relied on in an emergency'.[43]

SMALL ARMS

Anecdotes of senior officers mixing it with the enemy, sword in hand, are a reminder of how personal combat was, despite breech-loading rifles and machine guns. Cold steel remained a significant part of the nineteenth-century sailor's armoury. HMS *Royal Sovereign*, a modern battleship of the 1890s with 13.5-inch guns and torpedo tubes, also carried 120 boarding pikes and forty tomahawks. Sailors still carried cutlasses for personal defence. These were a hybrid weapon that could serve as a sword, or fit onto a naval service rifle as a bayonet, although in Zululand cutlasses saw more use chopping down brushwood. They were an awkward compromise. Heavier than a sword bayonet, their long scabbard flapped between the knees, and got in the way when kneeling down. Sailors in the Sudan scrounged bayonets from dead soldiers, while the soldiers preferred naval sennet hats to their own helmets.

If side arms changed little, fire arms underwent a revolution in range, ease of use, and rapidity of fire. When HMS *Excellent* was established in the 1830s the standard infantry weapon was the smooth-bore muzzle-loading musket. These had hardly changed since the Marlborough Wars, although they would soon acquire a more reliable percussion lock with obvious advantages at sea. A second innovation was rifling: a spiral groove inside the barrel that made the bullet spin, improving accuracy. The Royal Marines received a number of rifled 1842 pattern percussion muskets in 1851. These became the first sea service rifles, firing a massive .731 inch Minié bullet with a hollow base that expanded to grip the rifling.

It seems likely that Royal Marines used these makeshift weapons in the Crimea, alongside the army's 1851 pattern rifle and the 1842 smooth-bore musket, both rifles described as Miniés. All three were soon overtaken by a group of very superior .577 calibre weapons known collectively as Enfield rifles. First issued in 1855 these replaced the old weapons during the Indian Mutiny. HMS *Pearl*'s seamen received theirs in February 1858. The Admiralty ordered its own sea service pattern of Enfield with a 33-inch barrel, six inches less than the army's version. The result was the Pattern No. 1 Naval rifle of 1858 sighed to 1,100 yards, altered to take a cutlass, and with brass fittings against rust. The barrel was heavier than the military short rifles already used by the Royal Navy, and shot much better, although, inter-service rivalry delayed issue until 1861. Royal Marines, being infantry, used the full-length Enfield with a triangular bayonet. The Enfield multiplied the range of small arms by at least five, and dramatically improved accuracy compared with the smooth-bore musket. It formed the basis of British tactical superiority in India, China, and Japan. Only the dense terrain and Maori guerrilla tactics limited their advantage in New Zealand.

So far the rate of fire was unchanged, but the Prussian victory at Sadowa in July 1866 demonstrated the advantages of breech-loading rifles. The British promptly converted their existing stock of Enfield rifles to breech-loaders, with Snider rolling-block breech mechanisms. After the introduction of the brass Boxer cartridge, these shot even better than the original muzzle-loaders, more than doubling the rate of fire, while allowing the user to reload lying down. The navy used short rifles converted into Snider carbines in Abyssinia in 1868 and against the Asante in 1874. The two services had agreed a new rifle by then: the .45 inch Martini Henry adopted in 1871. The naval representative in the discussions was Captain Arthur Hood of HMS *Excellent*, a veteran of the Crimea and Canton Naval Brigades and later a First Sea Lord. The Martini Henry had a falling breech, hinged at the back so that it dropped forward to expose the breech, ejecting the spent cartridge case ready for another to be inserted by hand. The new rifle went through fourteen test models, including the Type 12 Naval pattern, but in the end the navy adopted the same Type 14 as the army. Naval-issue weapons were distinguished by a letter 'N', but no longer required brass fittings, as they were browned to prevent rust. The navy kept their cutlasses, the blade fixed horizontally, the edge and knuckle guard away from the rifle. The weight of the cutlass ruins the aim, but the Martini Henry was an excellent rifle, serving Naval Brigades in Zululand, Egypt, the Sudan, and Burma.

All the above weapons used black powder as a propellant, and were of large calibre. The next step in the small-arms revolution was the introduction of a magazine rifle of reduced calibre using cordite, a new smokeless propellant. This gave much higher muzzle velocities, producing a flatter trajectory and a deeper danger space for the target. The .303 Lee Metford magazine rifle replaced the Martini Henry during the 1890s, small-arms companies bound for the 1897 Benin Expedition learning to use theirs during the voyage from Malta and the Cape. There was no special naval pattern of Lee Metford. *Royal Sovereign* carried 345 of the Mk II version for use with bayonets by seamen and marines alike. Cutlasses were relegated to the foot of the masts, for use by boarders.[44]

The traditional accompaniment to cutlasses had always been the single-shot pistol, replaced during the 1850s by the Adams or Colt revolver. Trainee seamen-gunners of the 1860s fired twenty rounds from one of these, compared with sixty from the rifle. Like all hand guns, they posed more of a threat to the user's friends than to the enemy, although a New Zealand journalist thought them the very weapons for boatwork or storming rifle pits. In the Crimea revolvers were thought too dangerous for sailors, as they had a taste for discharging several barrels simultaneously. There were so many accidents in the Zulu and Transvaal Wars that revolvers were kept unloaded. They were commonly issued to gunners or rocket parties who might find the rifle an encumbrance, but Fletcher Campbell condemned the practice of landing men with swords and pistols: 'the idea of taking men into action so armed should not be entertained for a moment'. Officers, however, should carry revolvers of the latest pattern in a holster attached to their belt. Safety had been a concern with the Enfield rifle which appeared fragile beside the old muskets. Sailors were taught not to sling weights on the barrel, as it bent, or to run the muzzle into the ground lest the earth thus rammed in burst the barrel when fired. Above all: 'If a man suspects that his barrel is bent, he should report it immediately.'[45]

Standard rifles in use by the Royal Navy 1851–1899:

Designation	Date Issued	Barrel Length	Calibre (inches)	Rounds/ Minute	Sighted (yards)
Sea Service	1851	39	.731	2	900
English Minié	1851	39	.702	2	1,000
Enfield	1855	39	.577	2	1,100
Naval	1861	33	.577	2	1,100
Snider	1867	–	.577	5	1,000
Martini Henry	1875	33	.45	7	1,450
Lee Metford	1892	30	.303	10	2,800

NB: The Snider's barrel length depends on the original type of Enfield converted.

FIELD GUNS

Most nineteenth-century warships carried a field gun or two on the upper deck, complete with limbers. HMS *Shannon*'s brigade, renowned for deploying siege guns in the skirmish line, also landed their ship's 24pr howitzer, but it was soon lost to sight. Having short barrels for use as boat guns, these smooth-bore weapons were outranged by military field guns: HMS *Pearl*'s brigade acquired two brass 9prs from the Gurkha Army to put themselves on a level with the rebels.

Not long after the Mutiny, revolutionary new field guns appeared, in the shape of 9pr and 12pr RBL guns, the lower end of a range of guns designed by William Armstrong of the Elswick-on-Tyne Engineering Works. These had rifled barrels made from concentric hoops of wrought iron, and were phenomenally accurate for their day. Midshipman Edward Bayly fired a 20pr Armstrong along the beach at Sekondi in 1873:

> The black devils thought they were alright there, but I undeceived them by firing a shell at them from the 20pr, which it seems persuaded one fellow to stop where he was, and freshened up the others considerably. The range was very long, 2500 yards, but they must have been sold considerably. I could count the beggars with a glass, but they only looked like little black dots on the sand to one's eye.[46]

Armstrong guns soon replaced smooth-bore howitzers in HM Ships. HMS *Pylades* undocked at Chatham in October 1862 with two RBL boat guns, a

12pr 8cwt and a 9pr 6cwt, and a 12pr 8cwt RBL field gun. Her one smooth-bore gun was a brass 6pr used for short-range practice.[47] Her main armament included four 40pr RBL guns and a 110pr on the upper deck. These heavy breech-loaders were notoriously unreliable, but the small-calibre RBL guns saw extensive service in Japan and New Zealand, without any problems.

The deficiencies of large RBL guns reflected on the smaller field guns. RML 7pr and 9pr guns replaced Armstrongs after 1871, the Naval Brigade in Zululand having a mixture of all three. Muzzle-loaders were in theory a backward step, but the new 9pr was more accurate and more reliable than the RBL gun it replaced. There were 6cwt and 8cwt Sea Service 9prs sporting different sights to the military version. HMS *Royal Sovereign* carried two, although RML guns were hopelessly obsolete by 1897. The C-in-C of the Cape squadron was scathing about HMS *Tartar*'s 7pr, the only naval gun lost during the Boer War:

> An absolutely useless weapon . . . which would be completely outranged by the Mausers of the Boers, besides being in itself a disgrace to naval gunnery . . . It should never have been sent into action.[48]

The 7pr mountain gun had one advantage: mobility in difficult terrain. A powerful stoker, supported by a shipmate on either side, could just carry its 200lb piece across a West African creek on his shoulders. For all its deficiencies, the weapon would still feature in the 1910 *Landing Party* manual.

The obsolete equipment used by the RMA at Eastney astonished the Kaiser during a visit in 1890, and soon afterwards a new breech-loading naval field gun was introduced. The 12pr 8cwt was a quick-firer with fixed ammunition, but it lacked a recuperator. A rope toggle between the wheels and the handspike brackets at the trail eye limited the recoil, but the gun still jumped five feet backwards when fired. The 12pr 8cwt was designed for boat and field work, with a lower carriage than its military equivalent, so its detachment could manhandle it with the ease demonstrated annually by Field Gun crews at the Royal Tournament. It should not be imagined, however, that Naval Brigades dragged their guns everywhere by hand. Fletcher Campbell thought it

> out of the question that guns can be dragged by men on a march, or spare ammunition be carried by them; they should be reserved in all their strength and vigour for fighting purposes, and taken into action as fresh as circumstances will allow.[49]

Naval Brigades were adept at exploiting local resources. They accumulated 400 transport animals in Zululand. Each 9pr needed eight oxen, with another dozen on the two ammunition wagons that followed each gun. The field guns used by both services had insufficient range for the South African veldt in 1899. In response to the Boers' long-range artillery, naval craftsmen mounted powerful ship's guns, never intended for use ashore, on an inspired lash-up known as the Scott carriage. These 40-calibre 12prs and 4.7-inch Q/F guns became the most celebrated naval field guns of all, overshadowing the navy's standard field guns.

Standard field guns in use by the Royal Navy 1851–99:

Designation	Years in Use	Type	Range (yards)
12pr 6.5cwt howitzer	1850s	SB	1,050
24pr 12.5cwt howitzer	1850s	SB	1,350
12pr 8cwt	1860s–70s	RBL	3,700
9pr 6cwt SS	1870s–90s	RML	3,760
7pr 200lb Mtn Gun	1870s–90s	RML	3,000
12pr 8cwt Q/F	1890s–1920s	RBL	6,000

ROCKETS

Rockets were an elderly weapon system derived from the Congreve system of the Napoleonic Wars, but falling out of favour in the 1850s. Compared with guns, rockets project a large volume of fire from light, portable launching platforms: a simple tube mounted on a bipod, or lashed alongside a ship's launch. They are an attractive source of firepower in areas impassable to orthodox artillery, as many twentieth-century guerrillas have found, making them a natural choice of weapon in the jungles of Malaya or Africa: 'it is next to impossible to transport any naval service gun in such country, and also some villages are so constructed that field guns have little or no effect on the gates'.[50]

A naval rocket battery accompanied the expedition to Magdala in 1868, through mountainous terrain where elephants carried the field guns. In more open country they were 'not a desirable weapon to accompany an army on the march, although they may be used with advantage in fortified positions'. Two tubes and fifty rockets weighed the same as a field gun and thirty rounds, a poor exchange as rockets were 'calculated to frighten rather than hurt'. Rockets were very much a terror weapon. During the Benin expedition of 1897 native carriers ran away when their own side fired rockets.

Shannon's brigade cleared the way to the Lucknow Residency with an infernal machine made from four rocket tubes lashed onto a hackery. Asked whether the device made good practice, Peel replied that if it frightened the enemy half as much as it did the men firing it, there would not be a rebel left in Lucknow by evening.

HMS *Excellent* taught that the rocket's stick should be screwed on tightly: 'if much precision is required care should be taken not to use sticks that are bent'. Boat crews were supposed to retire 'abaft of the stanchion, and sit with their backs to the bow when firing', which may have been less frightening. One boat was blown up by its own rocket during an attack on Viborg in the Baltic in 1854, while rockets fired at Frederickshavn accidentally set the next town on fire as well. Various range tables were in use for 3pr, 6pr, 12pr, and 24pr rockets, extending to 1,300, 1,700, 2,700, and 3,500 yards respectively. Much shorter ranges must have applied in the field. HMS *Active*'s Gunner at Inyezane shot rockets into a kraal at 400–500 yards, 'scattering the defenders in fine style'. The Hales rocket replaced the Congreve pattern in 1867, in time for the Abyssinia expedition. Hales rockets sought to control the missile with spin instead of a stick, their well aimed fire at Magdala nearly killing King Theodore who cried out, 'What a terrible weapon! who can fight against it?'[51] The Perak Naval Brigade fired Hale rockets at Malay stockades from wooden troughs, with paper primers stuck into a hole in the base and lit with a common match. The opposition always fled 'in good time to save themselves from what they most dreaded – the rockets'.[52] Safety became a concern. The Admiralty suspended rocket training in 1880 until a more 'trustworthy' missile could be supplied. However, ships still carried rockets for war use, mainly in Africa, until their final withdrawal from service after the First World War.

MACHINE GUNS

Unlike rockets these were a new weapon, destined to become the main source of infantry fire power, although the War Office might be forgiven for not realising the great future ahead of the clumsy apparatus peddled by Messrs Gatling, Gardner, and Nordenfeldt. Weight mattered less on board ship, so the navy bought them for use against torpedo boats. Soon Lord Charles Beresford could claim before an audience of gunner officers that 'the Navy has had more actual experience in the working of machine guns in the field than any other branch of Her Majesty's service'.[53]

The 1880 *Gunnery Manual* divided machine guns into two classes: the rifle calibre *mitrailleur* used against people and the 'machine gun proper' which fired 1-inch shells, for use against *matériel*. Naval Brigades used the former, in particular the .45 calibre Gatling and Gardner; Nordenfeldts were initially anti-boat weapons. Early machine guns were operated by turning a handle. This fed cartridges into a multiplicity of barrels fired in succession, unlike modern gas-operated machine guns which use the energy released by the gun to load and fire successive rounds from a single barrel. The early weapons were very heavy, 444lbs in the case of the Gatling with its ten barrels revolving in a wrought-iron gun frame. The *Gunnery Manual* claimed the Gardner gun's special characteristics were 'lightness combined with considerable rapidity of fire and simplicity of mechanism'.[54] This must have been true as the authors said it twice, but the two-barrelled version still weighed 290lbs.

Nobody seems to have thought about the use of machine guns ashore before 1884. There were 600 rifle-calibre machine guns in service, but only two dozen official field carriages, with very small wheels and thoroughly inconvenient. At Sawakin the Chief Engineer of HMS *Sphinx* improvised carriages from the ship's 7pr field guns, adding a plate to raise the gun clear of the wheels to permit traversing. The weapons looked like artillery pieces, pulled by limbers. The aggregate length caused chaos on coming into action, and prevented guns from closely accompanying their supporting infantry, which may explain the ease with which machine guns were overrun in the Sudan.

Ammunition was poor, the guns' extractors pulling the base off discharged cartridges, leaving an empty cylinder in the breech. Arab spearmen rarely allowed time to unscrew the feed plate to remove the lock and clear the barrel. Like all new weapons, however, it is important not to exaggerate the lethality or unreliability of early machine guns. The Gardner that jammed at Abu Klea in 1885 subsequently fired all afternoon without stopping. Fletcher Campbell reported that Gatlings had been used at Inyezane and Gingindlovu 'with considerable success, and no difficulty whatever was found in the working of the machinery'.[55]

Machine guns seem to have been regarded as psychological weapons, rather like rockets. A naval Gatling demonstrated its powers for some Asante envoys, but was left behind at the Prahsu. A similar display was laid on for some Zulus seeking terms in 1879: 'Gatling made them stare as they are very superstitious. They fancy there is some witchcraft attending to it, that to touch it would be instantaneous death.'[56] Nevertheless Sir Garnet Wolseley, not a man noted for his enthusiasm for Naval Brigades, thought it worth landing naval Gatlings in Egypt in 1882, 'having for years past entertained a very high opinion of this arm in the field'.[57] Captain A.K. Wilson *VC* at El

Teb reckoned the Gardners were worth 100 rifles each at 900 yards, their great advantage being the ready control of their fire:

> in comparison with the rifle fire of both soldiers and bluejackets. The men were at this time very excited, the noise and general confusion preventing orders being heard; mounted officers rode up and down the line with little effect, while the bugles almost continuously sounding 'Cease Firing' seemed only to add to the noise; but the machine guns were under perfect control. Orders quietly given to 'search out that clump of bush', 'keep your gun bearing on that corner of the wall', or 'cease firing till they show again', etc, were carried out with the greatest regularity.[58]

The navy converted their machine guns to .303 calibre on the introduction of the Lee Metford rifle, adopting a standard cartridge for rifles and machine guns. This had not been possible previously, although they were all .45 calibre, as Gatling cartridges stuck in the breech of the Martini Henry, threatening to spike every rifle in a regiment. The Maxim gun signalled the end of the mitrailleur. Naval Brigades used the new weapon, but the army's adoption of the Maxim in the 1890s removed a specific role, as machine-gun battery, which for twenty years had been a naval monopoly.

CLOTHING AND EQUIPMENT

Lieutenant Caspar Goodrich USN witnessed Naval Brigade operations in Egypt in 1882, recording his observations for the US Naval Intelligence Department. His account opens on a wistful note:

> The equipment of men landed from British ships of war for military operations is not a matter of individual taste or caprice, but is uniform and efficient. As a consequence it is possible to assemble squads, companies or gun crews from a number of vessels, meeting for even the first time, into a homogenous military organization which is not open to criticism as a laughable combination of heterogeneous elements.[59]

There had been little standardisation in the early days of Naval Brigades. One senior officer of the Black Sea fleet in 1854 declared that as far as he was concerned, officers could paint themselves black and go ashore naked![60] By the 1880s, dress was expected to be blue. A naval officer in Egypt in 1882 nearly came to grief on the lances of some Indian cavalry, who confused his whites with the white uniform of the Egyptian Army. William Jenkin grumbled that whites were 'a beastly rig for shore', while Fletcher Campbell urged that whites should be stained brown as hostile marksmen had easily picked them out at Inyezane. Turn-of-the-century Field Exercise manuals explained how to improvise khaki with Gambier Dye, Condy's Fluid, or tea. In warm climates a white cap cover was worn with an optional 'havelock' or flap hanging over the shoulders to protect the neck from the sun. The men preferred the sennet or straw hat, as lighter and cooler, besides shading the eyes. Contemporary illustrations show both worn interchangeably. In Abyssinia seamen had white helmets with a puggaree, but these were never popular, the men working better in their caps. George Crowe, Master-at-Arms in HMS *Terrible*, condemned the seaman's service dress on the basis of experience during the Nile expedition of 1884–85 and the Boer War. Serge wore badly, dried slowly and chafed the skin. Duck was cold and clammy, especially when wet. The straw hat wore out quickly ashore, unless painted, when it became heavy causing sore heads. The cap provided no protection against the sun. He preferred military khaki, either wool or cotton, and colonial felt hats.

Naval Officers ashore wore helmets or white caps with much the same clothes as they used on board, 'a single breasted pea jacket, with stand-up collar buttoning up close to the throat, and having distinguishing lace on the sleeves'.[61] This was ill-adapted to tropical service. 'Perspiring Executive' complained of the horrors of watch-keeping in such a rig at Aden where the temperature was 98 degrees in the shade, 'when even the lightest and thinnest of cotton or linen fabrics are felt to be an encumbrance'.[62]

A rolled blanket continued in use, to carry a shift of clothes, soap and towel, the bight over the left shoulder, and the ends meeting under the right arm. Military greatcoats were often used, as were waterproof sheets, which turned out to be more effective against fever when placed underneath the sleeper. Kit issued to the Abyssinia brigade included: 100 helmets, 100 pairs of gaiters and 200 of ankle boots, 200 blankets, 100 waterproof sheets, seventeen tents, ten camp kettles with lids, ten baking dishes, and ten tea strainers. Water bottles resembled small coopered barrels, covered with grey felt, with a wooden plug in the drinking hole. Cheap and strong, they contained little water in proportion to their weight.

Boots were a problem. Men were seldom allowed to wear shore-service boots on board ship, certainly not with nails or plates on the soles, while a sea-service boot exposed to damp decks would not survive a day's hard marching. George Crowe found military boots more adaptable to the feet, but even they did not last long in the Sudan:

leather perishes at once, unless . . . soaked in oil and that one hasn't got in any quantity, and during the day the rocks, which are of black granite and syenite, and the sand gets so hot you can't touch them. The result is that the nails soon drop out of one's boots, the stitches crumble away, and off come the soles.[63]

All naval ranks had leggings made of stout tanned canvas. Bound with leather and coming well above the calf, so they would not slip down when wet, George Crowe thought they did not compare with army puttees for comfort, although nice for parades. The old pattern of cross belts proved inconvenient on the march, so by 1881 new leather accoutrements had replaced them. These consisted of a waist belt with braces which went over the shoulders, and crossed behind, with an enormous number of buckles allowing the wearer to adjust the equipment to suit himself. An 'S' clasp at the front of the belt easily came undone during short halts, to relieve the weight on the wearer's waist. An ammunition pouch of soft black leather hung on the waist belt at the rear, while more cartridge pouches could be strung onto the belt as needed. Fletcher Campbell complained these were not deep enough. Many cartridges fell out in the heat of action, when no one could stop to button up their pouches. This was a serious matter as the standard 70 rounds per man were soon expended. He suggested that Kroomen should bring up fresh ammunition, returning to the rear with the wounded, as no one should leave the ranks for that purpose. During the 1890s bandoliers were adopted, one across the body, another along the waist belt. These allowed ready access to cartridges during fire fights, but were uncomfortable on the march, preventing the passage of air inside the men's jumpers.

The weight of a naval rifleman's equipment in marching order was similar to that carried by a British infantryman in 1914:[64]

	lb.	oz.
Martini Henry Rifle	9	0
Bayonet	2	8
Haversack with 2 days' rations	4	8
Water bottle	2	8
Belt, 3 cartridge pouches, frog	6	0
120 rds of ammunition	13	0
Blanket and other personal items	7	8
Total:	45	0

The uniform and equipment of the Royal Marines conformed to those in use by the army, with local modifications. HMS *Alarm*'s Lieutenant of Marines was thought a great swell during an expedition of Nicaragua, wearing his scarlet coatee buttoned up with nothing underneath. Marines were often last in line for more up to date items. The detachments who suffered so horribly in the Ashanti War never received helmets, making do with white cap covers and havelocks. White helmets, now the trademark of Royal Marine bandsmen, became standard issue for ship's detachments in 1879; HMS *Active*'s marines were photographed in theirs on the Tugela. There was little practical difference between Red and Blue Marines, apart from their badges. Often both wore the blue serge tunics introduced in 1861, as they would in Egypt, where they boiled their white helmets and belts in tea to make them less conspicuous:

We were dressed in tight blue uniforms, with heavy uncomfortable helmets of a foolish shape, pressing on the temples, and giving no shelter to vital spots from the sun. We had always worn thin Wellington boots with our uniform, and had been obliged to fall back on the stiff hard leather 'ammunition boots' commonly called 'Pusser's crabs' which we managed to draw in our ships ... The men wore heavy buff leather (pipe-clayed) equipment, with stiff shiny black pouches to carry their ammunition. They could only open the covers of the pouches with great difficulty when lying down, and much of the ammunition fell out when they got up. The haversacks were made of thin linen, easily worn through by their contents, and worst of all the water bottles were small wooden ones of inferior design ... and that in a thirsty desert![65]

Campaigning wore out men and equipment alike. An RMLI Sergeant wounded during the Boxer Rebellion was unrecognisable on returning to his ship:

I had a full beard and was much thinner. My helmet was smashed, as also some of my equipment, and my trousers were in rags. It is remarkable into what a dilapidated condition men can get who are on active service when there are no regular supplies.[66]

Royal Marines' tropical uniform from 1875 was 'fine white duck', despite demands for khaki, which was easier to wash and harder to see. A witness of an exercise in Malta observed that, while the Naval Brigade were clearly visible, especially the marines in their white helmets, the soldiers in khaki could only be picked out with powerful field glasses: 'taking into consideration the deadly effect of modern firearms when the object can be distinctly seen it is simply murder sending us out to fight clothed as we are at present'.[67] The Boer War Naval Brigades used military khaki, but the navy still had no standard-issue khaki uniform at the outbreak of the First World War. The Royal Naval Division at Antwerp wore dark blue, while ship's detachments in the Persian Gulf conducted experiments with potassium permanganate to produce a degraded sort of khaki: 'I have rarely', wrote their CO, 'seen such an awful looking collection of pirates as we appeared when wearing these garments'.[68]

CHAPTER SEVEN

On the Banks of the Nile (1882–85)

Bᴿɪᴛɪꜱʜ involvement in Egypt and the Sudan during the 1880s came at the high water mark of Victorian imperialism. Its demonstration of the value of seapower provoked major shifts in foreign perception of British imperial policy, undermining the conditions that had made Naval Brigades a viable strategic option. Except for a little unfinished business in Burma, Egypt would be the last of the Royal Navy's autonomous interventions against an independent sovereign state in the style of Canton or Simonoseki.[1] The bombardment of Alexandria caught the public eye, but naval units contributed more to British control of Egypt by their amphibious assault on the Suez Canal a month later. The Egyptians could not have held their last outpost on the Red Sea, at Sawakin, in 1884–85 without the guns of HMS *Dolphin*, or the Royal Marines in the perimeter blockhouses. Sailors helped to stem the full flood of the Mahdist Revolt, as artillerymen, machine gunners, boatmen, and even camel corps. The campaigns in Egypt and the Sudan would illustrate every aspect of Naval Brigade operations.

The opening of the Suez Canal in 1869 had set British strategists an insoluble problem: how to secure access to the new route to India and Australia, without taking direct responsibility for its defence. For the Egyptians, cruelly taxed to pay for it, the canal was an added burden. Egypt's titular ruler, the Khedive, was subjected to an Anglo-French system of Dual Control, intended to reform Egyptian state finances. This foreign intervention, however honestly undertaken, inspired inevitable suspicions that Egypt would go the same way as Tunis and Cyprus, recently detached from the Turkish Empire by the French and British. When Colonel Arabi of the Egyptian Army moved against the Khedive in early 1882, he had behind him a justifiable popular agitation. On 11 June 1882 a devastating riot broke out in Alexandria. Arabi's troops did not step in until 150 Europeans had been killed, including the Engineer of HMS *Superb*. Thousands of refugees fled on board the warships gathered to protect their nationals. HMS *Monarch* took 280, troops of giggling girls invading the midshipmen's chest room, while half dressed snotties hid behind the chests.[2]

British diplomacy was ambivalent, unwilling to abandon British financial and strategic interests, but unready to defend them. Armies of Egyptian labourers worked day and night on Alexandria's defences, 'strengthening and repairing or building new works, and mounting more guns every hour . . . as busy and thick as bees'.[3] The Commander-in-Chief of the Mediterranean squadron objected to these threatening preparations, but the Egyptians denied their existence, even when the ships' searchlights caught them working by night. They might have been less inclined to trifle with Sir Frederick Beauchamp Seymour had they known of his record in Burma and New Zealand. On 10 July Seymour announced that he would open fire next day, unless the Egyptians immediately disarmed their works. The stage was set for another chapter in the sorry tale of Western relations with the Arab world that started with the Crusades, and continues with cruise missiles directed on Baghdad.

THE CATASTROPHE OF THE CENTURY (JUNE–JULY 1882)

Alexandria's defences were of poor quality: extended along the waterfront, their grotesque trace provided little head cover. Above the parapets barracks and magazines were clearly visible, the latter identified by conspicuous lightning conductors. Lieutenant Goodrich USN watched with professional detachment from USS *Lancaster*. He thought it wonderful that 'any of these ingeniously designed man-traps could have escaped destruction during the bombardment, or by accidental explosion at any other time'.[4] The Egyptians had almost 300 guns, but the defence rested on forty-four rifled guns, mostly 7- to 10-inch Armstrong muzzle-loaders, the rest being obsolete smooth bores. The British outnumbered the defenders by more than two-to-one in modern heavy guns. Fortunately for the British, the Egyptians lacked the expertise in 'torpedo warfare' to mine the harbour, much to Goodrich's professional regret.

The British ships had been regularly clearing for action, improvising extra protection from rope mantlets, and stopping chain cables to bolts every few yards along their sides. In HMS *Monarch* even the galley hot-plate was unshipped for machine-gun shields. Charles Hickman, a seaman in HMS *Invincible*, 'Fighting Flagship of the Mediterranean', recorded heavy gun drill every day aiming at the forts, although on 1 July 'Captain had all hands aft and told us that if he should sound for action and commence firing we was to be careful not to damage the town'.[5] Opinions on board were divided over the likely outcome. HMS *Sultan*'s Captain 'seemed to think we are in for a good row evidently to his intense delight', although his Lieutenant (G) did not believe it.[6]

At 7 a.m. on 11 July 1882, Lieutenant Mostyn Field found he was wrong, as HMS *Alexandra* fired the challenge shot: 'immediately along the whole line of forts down came the mantlets, the ramparts swarmed with men and every gun opened fire'. Since the Royal Navy's bombardment of Kagoshima in 1863 naval *matériel* had undergone a revolution. Ranges had quadrupled: Seymour's ships engaging at an average of 2,400 yards compared with 400–800 at Kagoshima. Despite the power of the new guns and the excellence of their practice, silencing the Egyptian forts proved a slow business. *Sultan* anchored to improve fire control, firing single shots at specific embrasures, a chain of midshipmen calling down the results, as the voice tubes to the fighting tops were all shot away: 'It came like a revelation to me', wrote her Gunnery Lieutenant, 'that a fort is invulnerable except through its embrasures and every individual gun on shore must be *hit* in order to silence it.'

The defenders were technically outclassed, but fought back with astonishing bravery. Whole gun crews were swept away, but fresh men instantly leapt to replace them. A 10-inch shell hit one of *Sultan*'s main battery guns, a large piece passing under Mostyn Field's arm, spoiling his old frock coat, while another burnt his neck. So far the seamen gunners had thought it all a fine lark, but casualties brought a change of mood:

> seeing men down and wounded, gave me the first realisation of being in action – I had even been pitying the unfortunate Egyptian soldiers opposed to us – but now I saw, and so did we all I think, that it was no child's play we were about, but downright grim earnest and that they *must* go down, and the sooner the better.[7]

Fort Ada blew up at 13.30, 'a wonderful sight, and one not to be forgotten', after which it was 'only killing dead dogs'. Mostyn Field had time to feel bored, his disengaged gun crews drinking buckets of water with gallons of lime juice, sleeping on the deck, or playing cards, 'against all the old rules'.

British losses were 'insignificant', while the Egyptian losses were never accurately ascertained, perhaps a third of the 2,000 men in the forts, plus 150–200 civilians, according to their own Chief of Police.[8] The material results of the bombardment were disappointing: the British won by attrition, killing the gun crews rather than demolishing their forts, suggesting that

'Recent high powered guns are not adapted to bombarding earthworks'. Goodrich thought ships should be armed with howitzers for shore bombardments, as modern guns did not elevate sufficiently. Defective ammunition further reduced the attackers' effectiveness: 80 per cent of the percussion fuzes exploded prematurely, or not at all. An 8-inch shell was later found intact in a magazine surrounded by 400 tons of gunpowder.

Not only had it taken all day to silence the forts, it had used up most of the available ammunition. *Inflexible* had only forty rounds of 16-inch battering shell left, while *Sultan* could not have continued the action for another hour. Nevertheless damage to the ships was slight, despite the irresponsible wishes of *Monarch*'s midshipmen:

> We were hoping that we should get a few honourable scars. The gunner believed we had been hit once, but it was always disputed whether the dent had not been made by an anchor in the previous commission ... when the gunroom compared notes that evening it was universally agreed that it had been both an exciting and an enjoyable day.[9]

All were ready and eager for action next day. However, the garrison had been 'whipped and thoroughly whipped', and evacuated the city overnight. Unfortunately Seymour does not seem to have looked beyond a demonstration of firepower, despite the Invincibles sharpening their cutlasses on 3 July. As at Kagoshima, there was no landing force ready to exploit the moral effect of the bombardment. The day after the battle the weather deteriorated, and Seymour was shy of committing his limited numbers of seamen riflemen and marines to the tangled streets in the face of Arabi's 9,000 soldiers. So demoralised were the latter that Goodrich thought with hindsight that a few hundred men could have seized the city on 12 July, preventing 'one of the most shocking, wanton, and deplorable catastrophes of the century'.[10] When the first landing parties went ashore on 13 July the lawless elements of the population had already taken advantage of the absence of the armed forces of either side to burn and pillage their own town. The European quarter suffered enormous damage, its fine buildings gutted, and the streets blocked with rubble.

Twentieth-century bombardments customarily cause widespread collateral damage. By comparison, most of the damage suffered at Alexandria was social in origin, rather than explosive. A report in the *Army and Navy Gazette*, telegraphed at 1/9d a word so deserving credit, contradicted early reports that the Royal Navy had demolished Alexandria: 'it would not be in the nature of things if large shells did not set buildings on fire', as was proved by the huge holes in the walls of the burnt out parts of the Ras-el-Tin palace, 'but all things considered, the damage done by the projectile was small compared to that which was the work of incendiaries and robbers.'[11]

Bluejackets occupied the Arsenal and Ras-el-Tin palace as 'safe havens' for refugees, while warships covered the approaches to the city with their guns.[12] Patrols dealt out summary justice to looters, including three local policemen caught robbing their own countrymen. Lurid contemporary engravings show bluejackets clearing the streets with Gatling guns, but these were fired over, rather than into, the mob. The frightening new weapons deterred more serious opponents. An Egyptian officer later admitted: 'That he knew no army which could face machines which "pumped lead", and that all the gates were defended by such machines as well as having torpedoes under the bridges.'[13]

Some of the Royal Naval detachments around the city's defences might have welcomed such reassurance:

> The first night on shore was an anxious one for all engaged – for if Arabi had known his business he would have driven our small force into the sea, for we were only about 1,200 seamen and marines ... the whole Egyptian army in front of us, and the vast hostile native population in rear of us – on the other hand they were for the time being thoroughly cowed, and had had all they wanted, while our men were in high spirits, and as they always do when landed looked upon it all as being the best lark in the world (until they realised the situation) ...[14]

Behind this slender screen, the Provost Marshal, Lord Charles Beresford, restored order with his customary lack of inhibition, co-opting the Egyptian commander of Fort Marabout onto his staff, and proclaiming that looters and incendiarists caught twice would be shot. Working parties collected at bayonet point set to clearing up the streets, naval artificers crewed the city's fire engines, while trigger-happy Europeans acting as if they had personally silenced the forts were disarmed, and put in irons for shooting at inoffensive Arabs. Charles Hickman spent five days on police work, searching refugees returning to town: 'the orders being that if any Arab is found with loot in his possession ... he is to be lashed up and have six dozen with the cat'. After two days on board Hickman landed again 'as Fire Brigade, regular London Fireman Steam Engines we had, we carried our cutlasses and rifles wherever we went. Very hot. Houses falling'. The fire station was a disused theatre: 'we are very theatrical you bet'.[15]

The arrival of a battalion each of the South Staffordshires and King's

Royal Rifle Corps allowed the army to take over the external defence of the city on 18 July. This relieved the strain on the landing parties who were exhausted, if only by the attacks of fleas and mosquitoes. The only previous help had come from a source as novel as it was portentous: sixty US Marines landed from USS *Lancaster*. They barricaded themselves inside the Club Building in the Great Square, but left the front doors wide open in the hope of tempting some desperadoes inside.

The strain was not only felt by those on shore. Shipboard duties had to be done shorthanded, especially when the heavy ironclads shifted their moorings, weighing anchor and hoisting in the boom boats. Mostyn Field found he was needed in two places at once: ashore with *Sultan*'s landing party as was the perquisite of her Lieutenant (G), and onboard to operate the searchlights, and drill idlers to take the places left at the guns by the trained seamen gunners who also made up the landing party. The organisational conundrum posed by the unique skills of the Gunnery Lieutenant make it the more surprising that the Royal Navy did not make better use of Royal Marine officers, who had all the expertise needed for operations ashore.

Seymour withdrew his bluejackets on 18 July, but the navy continued to play an integral part in the occupying forces, acting as 'judges, lawyers, policemen, engineers, diplomatists, in addition to their ordinary business'.[16] So constant were naval movements to and fro that Goodrich denied that there was a Naval Brigade 'as meaning a fixed organisation'. The demolition experts from HMS *Hecla*, the torpedo depot ship and floating arsenal, ensured that the contents of the Khedive's magazines could not be used against his protectors, holing the mine cases at Fort Mex with pick-axes, tipping hundreds of tons of gunpowder into the sea, and detonating small charges of guncotton at the muzzle of scores of guns, distorting them sufficiently to prevent the introduction of a shell. Many of the damaged guns seen in contemporary photographs were the result of this vandalism, not the bombardment.

Mostyn Field found himself ashore on the staff of Captain John Fisher of HMS *Inflexible*, commanding officer of all naval forces in Alexandria. Hauled out of the mud at the Peiho River disaster, Fisher had gone on to become one of the Royal Navy's leading technical officers, with a spell as Captain of HMS *Excellent*. Field's post was 'no sinecure of a billet – in the saddle all day riding round the different posts, and writing and organising in the evening'. Characteristically Fisher told Field he wanted heads of Department whom he could hang if anything went wrong. Living quarters combined luxury and barbarism: 'deal tables, tin plates, and bottled candles, hardly matching with beautiful carpets, gilt mirrors and chandeliers, with here and there a big shell hole through the walls'.[17]

Field was kept busy, for 'it was both sides doing a Plevna', digging in for a siege: 'we put up a gun, Arabi put up another; we built an earthwork, Arabi promptly built two; we ran an armoured train, as soon as he conveniently could Arabi did the same'. Charles Hickman was on the train during a skirmish at Mallaha Junction. Besides a 40pr in the bow, the train carried two naval 9prs hoisted in and out with a crane:

> Was rather warm work indeed and a picturesque sight though saddening. We took several prisoners the two I saw were hale hearty fellows and I think they enjoyed it. They laughed a great deal as we took them back to the train.[18]

HMS *Invincible*'s 9prs were returned onboard having insufficient range for siege work. The Gunnery Lieutenant of HMS *Inconstant* made up for this by extracting some 7-inch RMLs from the wreckage of their fort. As Captain Percy Scott he would play a key role in fielding heavy naval guns during the South African War. Now he contrived complex devices for unmounting the massive Armstrong guns, and skidding them and their carriages across the yielding sand to Ramleh. The sand was too soft to hold the pivot bolts of the gun-slides, so Scott fitted them into the bore of a 32pr gun buried muzzle upwards. A cable shackled onto two blind 16-inch shells from *Inflexible* secured another gun, although the witness did not state whether the bursting charge had been removed or not!

Much of the garrison's activity was intended only as a diversion, 'something of a playing at soldiers'. Sir Garnet Wolseley, the newly appointed military Commander-in-Chief, did not intend to advance on Cairo from Alexandria, but through the back door, via the Suez and Freshwater Canals. Hickman noted on 18 August, 'everything going on in haste for coming blow – no one knows where it will be struck'. The troop transports formed up in Aboukir Bay, but on 20 August everyone realised they had been sold: 'a steamer load of visitors and newspaper correspondents arrived from Alexandria to see the battle of Aboukir, and found nothing but two ironclads lying peacefully at anchor'.[19] Wolseley and Seymour had used command of the sea to turn Arabi's strategic right flank, simultaneously seizing the main British objective of the war: the Suez Canal. When the army arrived off Port Said, the northern entrance to the maritime canal, on the morning of 20 August 1882, they found the entire waterway already in the hands of the British Navy.

SECURING THE CANAL (AUGUST–SEPTEMBER 1882)

This brilliant combined operation was the work of a squadron that had lain off Port Said since 5 August, supported by another at Suez, the canal's southern end, under Wolseley's old comrade Rear-Admiral Sir William Hewett VC. Three more British warships had been at Ismailia, the mid point of the canal, since 26 July.[20] Despite the obvious presence of British warships, the simultaneous movement along the whole line in the small hours of 20 August achieved complete surprise. The Bimbashi in command at Port Said was absent, his sentries asleep, and their rifles unloaded. One crucial element in the British success was their ability to exploit the divided loyalties of many Egyptians. The landing parties were not to load their rifles without orders, and all concerned were impressed with the need to keep up amicable relations with the local population, white or Arab.

HMS *Monarch* landed almost 500 men at Port Said, so silently that a French ironclad moored to the same buoy heard nothing. While bluejackets sealed off escape routes, marines surrounded the barracks, covering the entrance with a Gatling. Other parties occupied vital points such as the reservoir and the customs house.[21] Meanwhile HMS *Ready* moved down the canal to seize the dredgers and telegraphs needed to operate the waterway. The narrow canal only allowed one-way traffic, so parties dropped off in small steam craft to keep merchant shipping tied up in the gares or passing places. The only resistance came from the Captain of a French steamer, who affirmed that 'the first man stepping on board would be the signal to let go the anchor, and leave the ship in his hands'. The *Army and Navy Gazette* huffed and puffed, but the naval officer on the spot remained calm, avoiding unwelcome international complications.[22]

Admiral Hewett had already sealed the southern end of the Maritime Canal. Marines from his East Indies squadron occupied Suez on 2 August to prevent its imminent destruction, along with its Christian population, by the local Bedouin. Hewett's naval forces were too weak to secure both town and canal, so he commandeered a battalion of Seaforth Highlanders, the advance guard of reinforcements called up from India. HMS *Seagull* and *Mosquito* carried 200 Highlanders up the canal to Shaluf, where 600 Egyptian infantry were found, their heads sticking over the railway embankment north of the Freshwater Canal. Their strong defensive position was of little help against the dash of the Highlanders, and covering fire from the Gatlings in the ships' fighting tops. A hundred of the elderly Egyptian reservists were killed, many wearing the chains in which they had been sent down from the interior. Reduced to firing their rifles blindly over the top of the embankment, they only succeeded in wounding a couple of sailors from the landing party. More important than the tactical success was the closing of the lock gates, securing drinking water for Suez, and the Indian troops expected on 21 August.

The British forces at Ismailia were in a more exposed position, in the heart of the enemy's country, cut off from reinforcements until the canal was cleared from Port Said, almost fifty miles away. Lieutenant Pitcairn-Jones was in the corvette HMS *Carysfort*, his diary recording daily drill onboard for *Carysfort*'s 'A' and 'B' companies, interspersed with seine-net fishing in Lake Timsah. Only on 16 August does he first refer to the 'enemy', after the Khedive's representative at Ismailia fled to HMS *Orion* in a washerman's boat. On the 19th preparations were made for landing, the Gatling and 7pr lowered into a lighter, and live ammunition issued: 'Then off belts and place them where they stood ready to fall in at two in the morning.'[23]

This was done in such perfect silence that the telegraph and railway stations were seized without resistance. The Arab town was more noisy, both corvettes firing five rounds of common shell at the guard house before *Carysfort*'s small-arms men skirmished through to occupy the outer wall. Nervous tension was high. The scattered bushes on the horizon looked like skirmishers in the mirage, while the right half of 'A' company expended a good deal of ammunition on a couple of Egyptian vedettes:

> After waiting for some time and finding the enemy did not attack we proceeded to entrench ourselves by barricading the streets, loopholing the houses on the outer faces, building up sandbag batteries, and making a platform of doors, etc for the guns to work on, the men working very well. Alfred Wager Ordinary Seaman got sunstroke and died the following night.[24]

During the day *Orion* and *Carysfort* shelled the railway station at Nefiche to dissuade the 3,000 Egyptian troops there from attacking the 565-strong Naval Brigade.[25] The target was out of sight from the guns, so Lieutenant Royds directed fire by azimuth from *Carysfort*'s fighting top, jamming the line with wrecked waggons, and putting one shell through the station window. Shelling continued through the night at half-hour intervals, searchlights illuminating the target: 'It was very pretty to watch the shell coming over *us*, and bursting over *them*.' At 6 p.m. 340 Royal Marines arrived from Port Said to thicken up the defence, but the expected night attack never came, perhaps as the result of a bogus telegram sent in the Governor's name advertising the presence of 5,000 British troops. Next day the army relieved the Naval

Brigade: 'us unhappy sailors being sent back to our ship . . . henceforward to drudgery and lumping on the wharf'.[26]

Having seized the canal the navy now set about defending it. *Seagull* and *Mosquito* patrolled between Ismailia and Suez, steam picket boats operating further north. Landing parties with Gatling guns dug in at the gares, and covered the isthmus west of Port Said with trenches armed with naval field guns. A reserve of 500 bluejackets and marines backed them up in the Dutch Hotel, commanding the entrance to the canal. The Royal Marine battalion at Ismailia joined General Graham's 2nd Brigade, becoming known to the enemy as the 'blue devils', in contrast to their red-coated comrades. Formed from the Royal Marine establishment at home, they acted as regular infantry for the remainder of the campaign, rather than as part of a Naval Brigade.

There was a genuine naval presence at the decisive action at Tel-el-Kebir on 13 September 1882, in the shape of a naval machine gun battery. Wolseley may have had doubts about using sailors away from their natural element but the army had no machine-guns. He drew therefore upon the weapons of the Fleet, although the Admiralty insisted on their going no further than Tel-el-Kebir. The battery landed at Ismailia on 10 September, moving up by rail to join General Macpherson's Indian brigade at Kassassin.

The main army, including the Royal Marines, was to assault the Egyptian entrenchments north of the Freshwater Canal under cover of darkness, while the Indian Brigade with the Gatlings covered the left flank south of the canal. They moved off at 3 a.m. on 13 September, after the main force. It was frightful work in the pitch darkness, the narrow gun wheels sinking into the soft sand. The seamen cursed the authorities responsible for such lumbering, clumsy weapons, but worked with a will lest they missed the fight. Day broke as they approached the Egyptian positions, gun flashes directed against the main attack lighting up the horizon. A maize field appeared to the left front: 'Bluejackets deployed at the double, and were amongst the stalks in no time. No game was started; the covert was drawn blank. The battery continued its advance.' Some hostile cavalry turned tail before a hail of lead, and at last the battery was within easy range of the Tel-el-Kebir earthworks, 'a living line of fire above them':

Nothing daunted, the order 'Action Front' was given, and was taken up joyously by every gun's crew. Round whisked the Gatlings, 'rrrrr rum, rrrrr rum, rrrrr rum!', that hellish noise the soldier so much detests in action . . . The report of the machine guns as they rattle away rings out clearly on the morning air. The parapets are swept. The embrasures are literally plugged with bullets. The flashes cease to come from them. The Egyptian fire is silenced. With a cheer, the Bluejackets dash over the parapet, only just in time to find their enemy in full retreat. That machine gun fire was too much for them . . .[27]

The Naval Brigade pressed on to the Egyptian camp, where they 'set to work cooking their breakfast most methodically', unlike the marine battalion who breakfasted off biscuits and muddy canal water. Both stayed behind to clear the battlefield while the Cavalry and Guards pressed on to Cairo to finish off the war. On 17 September the machine-gun battery returned to Ismailia, leaving the Royal Marines to go on to Cairo by train.

The Khedive's return to his capital on British bayonets caused much grumbling about 'the manner in which the Naval service is invariably treated by those in authority'.[28] Sir Beauchamp Seymour's absence from the ceremony was attributed to the Admiralty's mean-spirited refusal to let the navy share in the fruits of victory, despite the combined nature of the campaign, which exploited good personal relations between Wolseley, Seymour, and Hewett dating back to the Burma and Ashanti Wars. As it turned out, the naval part in the campaign did not go unrecognised. A 350-strong naval detachment, including *Carysfort's* Gatling detachment, took part in a victory parade at Cairo on 30 September 1882. Mostyn Field was adjutant, planning the manoeuvres with a coloured diagram, to the amusement of a Prussian military observer with whom he travelled up to Cairo. Bluejackets and Egyptian soldiers had jointly repaired the railway, and demobilised Egyptians crowded the train, 'chin-chinning everybody, being evidently only too glad to get home again to their mud huts, cotton fields, ditches, and water buffaloes – Fighting was not their business'.[29]

Mostyn Field inspected the review ground, and drilled his men: 'carefully rehearsing those movements, and those movements only, which would be required in the afternoon'. The Naval Brigade marched in its proper place, at the head of the infantry, with splendid views of the richly decorated British and Indian cavalry, and the ladies of the Khedive's harem. The Prussian baron was so impressed he stood Mostyn Field lunch at Shepheard's Hotel, although the Cairenes were less enthusiastic, watching the display in gloomy silence. When the tired and thirsty sailors arrived back in camp the *sowars* of the Bengal cavalry fetched them water in their own drinking vessels, an exceptional gesture for high-caste Indians. Next day the Brigade had a fine time roaming the city, whose bazaars were in full swing, as if there had never been a war. Three hundred bluejackets visited the Pyramids, on hired donkeys: 'a curious looking but quite orderly species of

cavalry riding in sections of four'.[30] Mostyn Field found the indistinguish-
able features of the Sphinx disappointing. He sat on top of a Pyramid thinking how little the ordinary Egyptian's lot had changed, except that now they
had to dig the Suez Canal or trenches at Tel-el-Kebir. To all appearances
the Egyptian war was over. The Royal Marines, who had taken more than
their fair share of hard knocks, went home to astonishing scenes of public
excitement, the crowds outside Stonehouse barracks jamming the street
solid. A leader in the *Army and Navy Gazette* eulogised the versatility and hard
work of the men-of-war's men who had prepared the way for the victory at
Tel-el-Kebir.[31] Neither branch of the naval service, however, had finished
with the Land of Bondage, where their efforts had sown the seeds of fresh
turmoil.

THE NAVY AND THE MAHDI (1884–85)

South of Egypt, between the arid Red Sea coast and the jungles of
Equatoria, lies the Sudan, conquered by the Egyptians during the 1820s for
its slaves, ivory and ostrich feathers. Nationalist feeling in the oppressed and
over-taxed Sudan was already strong when the British occupied Egypt in
1882. A Dongolawi boat builder named Mohammed Ahmed had won several
skirmishes against Egyptian troops, tactical success combining with his
piety to mark him out as the Mahdi, the expected deliverer from 'Turkish'
oppression. In October 1883 his followers, the Ansar or servants of God,
destroyed a complete Egyptian army. Much against their will, the British
found that occupation of Egypt implied less congenial responsibilities than
financial reform. Egyptian military weakness not only encouraged the
Mahdiyya, but forced the British to take military action to prevent destabil-
isation of Egypt itself. The primacy of water communications in a desert
land ensured the navy would be part of that military response: first along the
eastern Red Sea flank of the Sudan, and then up the Nile, into the heart of
the country. The Ansar were a different proposition to Arabi Pasha's brave
but inept soldiers. Seven lieutenants RN would die in action in the Sudan,
compared to one at Alexandria.

ALL HOT SAND AND GINGER (FEBRUARY–MARCH 1884)

The flashpoint was at Sawakin, an island harbour on the Red Sea coast,
where an erstwhile slave dealer Osman Digna inspired the Hadendoa tribes-

men to revolt. The British sent warships in November 1883 to support the beleaguered Egyptian garrisons, and a force of Egyptian gendarmerie, but the Hadendoa killed most of them at El Teb on 4 February 1884. The whole coast threatened to fall into Mahdist hands, perhaps encouraging some other European power to take an interest in a region dangerously near the route to India. Rear-Admiral Sir William Hewett *VC*, Senior Naval Officer in the Red Sea, was not the man to allow that. He had wanted to send 200 bluejackets and marines with the Egyptian gendarmerie, which might have resulted in a different outcome to the fight, though probably not in the way that the *Hampshire Telegraph* correspondent who supplied the news item might have wished. On 10 February 1884 Hewett landed 150 seamen and marines at Sawakin to stabilise the situation, pending the arrival of reinforcements. A marine battalion and five machine guns from the Mediterranean Fleet set the pattern for Hewett's Naval Brigades in the Sudan: seamen gunners with machine guns, and Royal Marines fighting as infantry. Hewett had told Wolseley, after the Ashanti War, that nothing would induce him to land bluejackets as riflemen: 'I will always give you as many as you want to fight guns as artillery, but never again as foot soldiers.'[32]

Hewett's prompt action at Sawakin demonstrated the naval capacity to react quickly in an emergency. The navy's part in the Sudan operations resembled its defensive operations on the Gold Coast or in Zululand, holding the ring, then providing technical support and extra firepower. Critics took a dim view of the Government's makeshift policy of fighting a war on the cheap. The Admiralty had diverted paid-off crews and marine detachments, homeward-bound from China, to reinforce Hewett, sending them 'where neither honour nor profit can accrue to them, but where hard knocks will be plentiful'. This was not the way to entice recruits into a naval career![33]

An Egyptian outpost south of Sawakin at Tokar was at its last gasp, so a joint naval-military relief force landed nearby at Trinkitat, under General Graham of the Tel-el-Kebir campaign. Hewett's civil and military powers within Sawakin caused some confusion at the War Office, but Hewett's sense of duty prevented inter-service squabbling.[34] Half Sawakin's Egyptian garrison were in open mutiny, but he denuded his ships of seamen to land a machine-gun battery, and of field guns to equip a Royal Artillery camel battery. Besides the Royal Marine Battalion, he strengthened Graham's force with the York and Lancaster regiment, earmarked for Sawakin's defence. Altogether Hewett furnished a quarter of Graham's rifle strength, and all his guns.

The machine-gun battery consisted of three Gardners and three

Gatlings, the five weapons from the Mediterranean joined by one from Hewett's flagship, HMS *Euryalus*. Each gun had a double crew of thirty, a lieutenant in charge and a gunner's mate. The manpower was extravagant, but necessary to drag the weapons through the sand. Battery transport was three camels, three riding ponies, and a dozen ammunition mules with army drivers. The administrative tail was: two armourers, two carpenters, three cooks, and a couple of sick-berth attendants with a junior surgeon. The latter had a crash course in the revolver, for the Hadendoa had no respect for non-combatants.[35] Hewett chose Commander Rolfe of *Euryalus* as Commanding Officer, 'for his tact, coolness under fire, and knowledge of native warfare'. He had acquired the latter in West Africa, as Naval ADC to Wolseley during the march to Kumasi, so how useful his experience was in the treeless wastes of the Sudan is debatable. Such disparate conditions, however, were usual for British officers in the nineteenth century, hence the *Gunnery Manual*'s emphasis on suiting Naval Brigade tactics and organisation to specific conditions. Armchair critics may grumble about 'improvisation', but the variety of imperial small wars made explicit regulations inappropriate, and potentially disastrous.

Graham's battles at El Teb and Tamai (29 February and 13 March) were less one-sided than British advantages in weaponry might suggest. The Hadendoa were on top fighting form, utterly reckless of their own survival, their reactions as sharp as the ironmongery in their fists. The British fought in large squares, or rather oblongs, each several battalions strong, the machine guns remaining inside while on the march. In action they were run out at the corner, or in the centre of the front face. They did well enough at El Teb, silencing Osman's captured Krupp field guns with a stream of bullets, although Rolfe's report gives no hint of the desperate close-quarter fighting that ensued, as he pushed his guns forward to provide close support for the infantry. The whole battle might have been a cold-blooded exercise in fire control, although he did admit using the men not engaged at the guns as a covering party.[36]

The reality was considerably more confused: Gunner J.T. Wilkinson RMA thought the Mahdists meant to serve the British as they had the gendarmerie, 'but luckily for us we had the pleasure of disappointing them, for they got as hot a reception as they would have done in H in U':

> it was something grand to see their dauntless bravery for they came up and tried to get hold of the bayonets and pull them off but two of them even rushed up and jumped on top of a Gatling gun but did not live to look round the place he (*sic*) so much coveted to get into.[37]

The Hadendoa killed three marines, including one pulled into their gun position, and cut about beyond recognition. The RMA had their revenge, turning a captured Krupp on the retreating enemy, 'fetching them down like rabbits' with case shot. Afterwards a dozen sailors volunteered to carry *Carysfort*'s wounded gunnery lieutenant back to Trinkitat, thinking he would be more comfortable onboard ship. He died, despite their efforts, and was buried at sea. His shipmate, Pitcairn Jones, took comfort from this: 'he will rest peacefully let us hope among the coral reefs, nine fathoms beneath the blue water until the sea gives up its dead'.[38] So anxious were the stretcher party not to miss the advance on Tokar, they marched back at 4 a.m. next morning, after just five hours' rest.

The *Army and Navy Gazette* sneered at the fight, reflecting on the discredit had a British force wavered before 'the onslaught of naked barbarians armed with primitive swords and javelins'. Naval casualties were too high for any purpose achieved: Tokar was a miserable mud village and its inhabitants convicts. The paper had a point, for it was impossible to hold the place. Graham evacuated its starving garrison, and the Naval Brigade arrived back at Trinkitat on 4 March 1884, a detachment of Hussars dragging the guns.

Graham's second battle, at Tamai, was still less successful. Osman Digna had learned the futility of charging several hundred yards under rifle and machine-gun fire, so he lay a trap not unlike the one that would catch the 21st Lancers at Omdurman, thirteen years later. Osman's riflemen occupied a line of thorn bushes screening the edge of a deep wadi, steeply banked like a railway cutting on the near side. The majority of his men, with their antique swords and spears, lay inside the wadi. Arab riflemen knocked the Marine's MO off his mule, persuading others to dismount. Inside the squares staff officers on foot could see neither the wadi nor the masses of spearmen concealed within it.

Graham's troops were in two mutually supporting squares, 1,000 yards apart: the Marine Battalion and Naval Brigade in the leading square on the left, machine guns behind the front face, marines along the rear. Detailed accounts of the action vary. Some say the whole front face of the leading square charged the bushes, leaving gaps on either flank where the sides failed to keep up. Others say that only the Black Watch, the left front and side of the square, charged; the York and Lancasters to their right not having received orders to do so. Either way, the Naval Brigade doubled forward, one half battery on the right of the Black Watch, the other filling up the left angle of the square. The machine guns opened fire at once, but the smoke blew back in the gunners' faces, hiding a large body of spearmen to their right: these charged the battery in flank, killing many of the men at the guns, which all fell into enemy hands.[39]

Legends have attached themselves to the affair; in particular claims that the Gardners jammed. None of the contemporary reports, however, refer to ammunition problems, while the Royal Artillery officer in command of the camel battery believed the reverse was tactical in origin: 'I do not think they had fair play there; they were dragged onto the edge of a ravine close to the enemy, and could not be fired at any but a very short range.'[40] Sub-Lieutenant G.A. Ballard of HMS *Hecla* was in charge of the Naval Brigade's camels, naval cap ribbons tied to their headstalls to prevent the Marines stealing them. His personal observations from just inside the square suggest the front face had no time to develop its fire, before it was overwhelmed:

> a sudden loud shout ran along our front line, with a staggering break in their ranks accompanied by about five seconds outburst of furious musketry, more like a ragged volley than anything else, throwing up an instantaneous curtain of dense white smoke, through which burst a close-packed swarm of bounding fuzzy heads and upraised spears, seeming to appear from nowhere as thick as bees.[41]

The whole front face lurched back onto the transport. Some did their best with rifle and bayonet. Others thought they had been let down, and did less well. One Petty Officer was court-martialled afterwards for 'not doing his utmost to engage the enemy'. Graham had calculated on the Royal Marines as a last reserve, but even they were swept along in the general confusion. The whole mass shuffled backwards for ten minutes until they came alongside the other square, who shot down the Arabs from the flank. Hardly a quarter of an hour had elapsed since the square first went to pieces.

The square had become lost in a straggling line of exhausted men, three to eight ranks deep. The six machine guns stood as left, three turned uselessly towards the square; one of the limbers on fire. After a pause to refill ammunition pouches, both squares moved cautiously back to the wadi over a gruesome carpet. The mutilated bodies of all three lieutenants lay around the guns of the right half battery. Their swords were sticky with blood, and every chamber of their revolvers empty. Of the five ratings who crewed each machine gun in action, almost half were dead or severely wounded, but, even as they were cut down, they had disabled their guns. Graham's despatches referred three times to the incident:

significant proof of the coolness and gallantry of the officers and men of the Naval Brigade, that in all the heat and excitement of the enemy's desperate charge, when three officers and seven men were killed beside their guns, not one of these guns was allowed to fall into enemy hands before it had been secured by the safety keys from being turned against us.[42]

A few Hadendoa die-hards had run one limber into the wadi as bait for an ambush, sprung when a party of bluejackets went to retrieve it. The ambushers got two of the covering party before they themselves were all shot down, but in the confusion the marines fired into the other square, putting a bullet through the ear of General Buller's horse, the only touch of comedy in a grim day. Next morning Admiral Hewett sent up 200 bluejackets to evacuate the wounded, and the column withdrew, reaching Sawakin on 18 March.

The chief memory for many must have been thirst. Two pints of water per day did little to moisten tongues cracked and bleeding from plodding through clouds of dust at the rear of a square. The machine-gun drag-rope numbers were quite done. The gunner officer quoted previously thought it wrong to haul such weapons by hand:

I have never witnessed such a sight as the sailors drawing their machine guns. The pluck they showed and the work and labour required to drag those guns along for more than twenty miles was very great. I am sure if I had not seen it, I would not have believed it.

George Aston, an RMA lieutenant, borrowed a tiny basin of water after El Teb. It was as thick as pea soup, but before he finished shaving, his Corporal interrupted to ask him not to splash too much, as six other men were hoping for a rub. Aston dreamed of sitting in a bath with a pint of champagne and soda water, the ice tinkling against the glass.

THE FEVER BATTALION (APRIL–OCTOBER 1884)

The British Government persuaded the Khedive to abandon the Sudan, and recalled Graham's troops. Only the marines from the Mediterranean Fleet remained at Sawakin. Marines could man cannon and machine guns in the forts, or fight as infantry, and were less noticeable than high-profile Highland regiments. In April a fresh Battalion RM replaced those originally landed. One of the new arrivals asked who this Mahdi was that they had to fight, and was told with an element of truth, 'Oh, he's a sort of Salvation Army Captain, that's what he is.'[43]

Sawakin in the summer was not such a joke. One of the Royal Marine officers was Lieutenant Alfred Marchant RMLI, whose sister Emmie kept his letters home:

> Really this place is an awful hole, and it is generally asserted that for the three worst months of the year no white man stays here, but yet they keep the Marines here. We have lost fourteen or fifteen by death and the number of sick who have gone to Suez is astonishing. A company goes there for relief and it is a hard matter to distinguish who is well and whom is sick.[44]

The worst time was at night when the Arabs came down to snipe the out-posts. They rarely hit anyone, but kept everyone awake. Sometimes a few got inside the defences, spearing and stabbing anyone in reach before disappearing with equal rapidity. HMS *Dolphin*, a gun vessel stationed at Sawakin to support the garrison, caught some Arabs with her searchlight, the rays momentarily confusing them. Several were shot as they shielded their eyes with their hands, before the rest broke away. Once the Arabs learned how to escape its beam, the searchlight proved more of a nuisance to the defenders, destroying their night vision or silhouetting their position. A better use of electric light was for emergency treatment of men wounded during these nocturnal affrays, HMS *Dolphin*'s surgeons working on her quarter deck under a cluster of light bulbs.

Lieutenant Marchant and his friends formed a band with ocherina, pannikin, and comb and paper, the racket drawing a barrage of shoes and bad language from the Major in the next tent. A sort of café sold inferior vermouth and soda at the exorbitant price of one shilling. Marchant hoped to save money as there was nothing else to spend money on, except a photographer and the Sawakin Recreation Cricket and Lawn Tennis Club. On a pitch made from pegged-down coconut matting the Marines played the world, and won by ten wickets. Autumn brought cooler weather, only 98 degrees in the shade, but the rain spread dysentery. Marchant described reinforcements as 'candidates for the fever battalion', and accompanied a party of sick to Suez, where he slept between blankets, and was delighted to see English ladies dressed in all their finery. He played donkey polo which left him stiff, and covered his hands in blisters: 'I haven't enjoyed a game so much for months'. Three of the sick died during the trip, one of them 'like a living skeleton when he was taken off the ship'.

In October 1884 the battalion supplied four officers and 102 marines to form a camel company, the ultimate variation on the theme of Horse Marines: 'some say this is a bribe to keep us quiet down here'. The Royal Marine Camel Corps was not for use around Sawakin however. They were to join one of the great setpiece Victorian adventures, the relief of General Gordon at Khartoum.

THE RACE TO KHARTOUM (SEPTEMBER 1884–MARCH 1885)

The only certainty about British policy in the Sudan in the 1880s was Mr Gladstone's objection to defending it, although his Government's intervention had stopped the Egyptians doing so for themselves. General Charles Gordon was sent to evacuate the Egyptian garrisons, but was trapped in Khartoum, the Sudanese capital. Why the Royal Navy should have become involved in rescuing Gordon from the middle of Africa is not immediately obvious. The most direct route is across the desert from Sawakin to Berber (250 miles), and then up the Nile to Khartoum (210 miles), but Lord Wolseley at the War Office in London overruled the men on the spot. His Red River expedition in Canada in 1870 convinced him that a river-borne relief column would be better, although the distance from Cairo to Khartoum was almost four times the distance via Berber. Wolseley imported Canadian *voyageurs* and Kroo boatmen, limiting the navy's role to surveying the River Nile, and helping craft up the cataracts that disrupt its navigation. Given the navy's expertise in riverine warfare, it is a pity that he did not make more use of their services. The *voyageurs* themselves were astonished by how quickly the few sailors on the Nile could sail their deeply laden whalers.

The last telegram from Gordon, in April, suggested he could hold out until mid-September. At that date an eighty-strong party of bluejackets were working twelve-hour days to haul a steamer up the Second Cataract at Wadi Halfa. Gordon's would-be rescuers were only a third of the way to Khartoum, and the river level was falling rapidly, soon to make the Cataracts impassable. One of the naval officers was Lieutenant Rudolph de Lisle, a devout letter writer and artist, several of whose cataract sketches appeared in the 'Illustrated'.[45] Twice the current swept de Lisle down the rapids, dashing his boat against the rocks. Three bluejackets were drowned in another incident, their bodies recovered by native swimmers, and buried in one grave. The accident had a disastrous effect on morale, de Lisle grumbling that the men would watch officers doing tasks they should have risked themselves: 'together with the rotten boat we have to work in, they hate the water and the work too'.[46] A month later the cataract party was still at Wadi Halfa, where the first of Wolseley's specially built whalers arrived on 14 October. De Lisle thought they looked too slow:

> More disgraceful boats I never saw, old hulls, leaky, sails frequently in shreds, yards sprung (nearly broken), some without rudders, others without masts; so we had ample opportunities of dismantling the wrecks to get the lame ducks along.[47]

It took another six weeks to track enough boats up to smoother waters. By then the fifty-seven surviving bluejackets of the original detachment had become an official Naval Brigade commanded by Lord Charles Beresford, Wolseley's naval ADC. De Lisle had no doubts about their contribution to the campaign so far:

> Without the *Alexandra*'s and *Monarch*'s – in other words the Cataract party – there would have been no Naval Brigade at all ... Without the bluejackets what they would have done fitting the boats out I can't think.[48]

The sailors soon showed their boat-handling skills after leaving Wadi Halfa on 6 December. They rigged their whalers as men-of-war's boats, and sailed in line ahead, passing the rapids at Dal in a day, where every other boat spent three days tracking. The soldiers cheered them as they went by:

> There was not a scratch on any boat, nor a drop of water in any of them. Every cargo was complete in every detail, including machine guns, ammunition, oil and stores.[49]

De Lisle was amused to hear soldiers talking about the sailor's superior skill, as if ships spent every day shooting rapids. He had a better opinion of Wolseley's boats now, or at least their camping equipment, 'all provided with the most wonderful forethought'. Everyone was covered in insect bites, but there were no cataracts, and it was heavenly sailing along with boat awnings set as spinnakers, making twenty-two miles a day.

The Naval Brigade reached Wolseley's headquarters at Kurti on 5 January 1885, their ninety-day 'Nile store' intact, even the three bottles of medicinal brandy. It was more than three months since Gordon had estimated Khartoum would fall. There was no time to pursue the Nile around the great uncharted bend from Kurti to Berber. Wolseley had foreseen this, forming a camel corps from detachments of the Guards and Cavalry: 'London society on camels'. The Naval Brigade was to accompany the Desert Column in a dash from Kurti to al Matamma, to take over the 'penny steamers' that Gordon had sent down to meet his rescuers. For once the Naval Brigade included a proportion of engineering ratings whose boiler plate, rivets, and oakum Beresford insisted on packing onto camels. Many would owe their lives to his foresight.

Sailors learning to steer ships of the desert provided amusing newspaper copy, with plenty of port and starboard, steering small, and running aboard. A soldier who watched camels spilling sailors into the sand was less impressed:

> What's the British Army a-coming to? . . . It's a-turning it upside down Lord Wolseley is, and a-metamorphosing everything. First he makes sailors of us infantry; then he turns the cavalary into infantrymen, and I'm hanged if he ain't a-making cavalry of the sailors![50]

Events would soon show that his distrust of Wolseley's methods was not just an old soldier's grousing.

The first leg of the Desert Column's shortcut was to the wells at Jaqdul, moving in the cool of the night. De Lisle found the soldiers wonderfully civil, while the sailors did as well on their camels as many who had expected to see them landed off their backs. The desert provided plenty of material for the artist, but his sketchbook fell apart in heat so intense that bone knife handles crumbled, and De Lisle's camel caught fire. His hands were still blistered from boat work, but he thought he could hold a sword if necessary. Two days after leaving Jaqdul on 14 January, the Desert Column saw the first sign of enemy, near the wells of Abu Klea. Next morning the fighting part of the column, 1,300 strong, formed up in square to force a passage to the wells, leaving most of its camels in a *zareba*. The Naval Brigade were in the centre of the rear face of the square, Beresford's instructions allowing him to deploy the Gardner on whichever flank was attacked.

As always in the Sudan the attack came with terrifying swiftness. The square halted 400 yards from a mass of flags sticking up out of some tall grass, when 6,000 Ansar suddenly rushed the square in a V-shaped column. Their mounted leaders came on at a hand-gallop, the lightly clad spearmen keeping pace with them. Beresford ran out his gun five paces from the left side of the square, and opened fire, but this time the Gardner did jam. The extractor of the second barrel from the right pulled the base off an empty cartridge, preventing the next round being forced home. Beresford and William Rhodes, Chief Boatswain, unscrewed the feed plate to clear the barrel, when the enemy was upon them, instantly killing Rhodes and the armourer next to him. Beresford was struck on the head with the feed plate and knocked down, then swept back against the square:

> The crush was so great that at the moment few on either side were killed, but fortunately this flank of the square had been forced up a very steep little mound which enabled the rear rank to open a tremendous fire over the heads of the front rank men; this relieved the pressure and enabled the front rank to bayonet or shoot those of the enemy nearest them.[51]

None of the enemy got into the square at that point, the surviving Ansar calmly turning, and walking back to the cover where they had started their charge, before Beresford could bring the Gardner back into action. Somehow he escaped with only a spear scratch on one hand, but Lieutenants Pigott and de Lisle were less fortunate. Their bodies lay twenty yards left rear of the gun, where the crush had taken them. The Naval Brigade had lost eight dead and seven wounded from a battle strength of forty, a much higher percentage than any other unit. Apart from the débâcle of the Gardner gun, the sailors had been caught up in the collapse of the rear face of the square, which never formed properly, thanks to the camels dragging behind. The dismounted cavalrymen there moved back involuntarily, as they fired, not being trained to stand rigidly in line, taking the handful of seamen-riflemen with them. A military observer thought the sailors' training to fight in ships did not prepare them 'to stand shoulder to shoulder in a square like grena-diers. Their officers died, disdaining to move from their guns, as they did at Tamai'.[52] With hindsight, the irreplaceable sailors, needed to man Gordon's steamers, should have remained in the *zareba*, where the Gardner would have been less exposed, and more effective.

That was its role in the battle of the Abu Kru, fought three days later to win through to the Nile at Gubat, the Gardner giving covering fire from a *zareba* built from camel saddles and biscuit boxes. The enemy lacked the ferocious determination of Abu Klea, but Ansar riflemen mortally wounded Sir Herbert Stewart, the column's commander. When four of Gordon's penny steamers appeared on 21 January it was impossible to carry out the original programme. Beresford, the only naval officer unwounded, was crip-pled by saddle sores. So desperate was the situation that Mr Webber, Boatswain in HMS *Monarch*, took command of the seamen involved in a reconnaissance towards al Matamma, an unprecedented departure from naval custom.

Not until 24 January did Colonel Charles Wilson, the senior officer still on his feet, set off for Khartoum in two steamers, an ERA in each engine room. Laird Clowes criticises Wilson's failure to replace the Egyptian crews completely, but Gordon had warned against doing so, and none of the naval officers were fit. Wilson's approach triggered the end of the siege, the Ansar overwhelming the exhausted garrison on 26 January 1885, two days before he arrived. Subsequent critics have condemned Wilson's delay after reaching Gubat on 20 January, but more significant delays occurred in England, where the first boats were not built until August 1884, and along the Nile where Wolseley under-estimated the navigational difficulties.

These nearly finished Wilson during his return. Both his steamers were wrecked thirty miles south of Gubat. This accident and the arrival of the Naval Brigade's 2nd Division on 30 January allowed Beresford to show how much better real sailors could manage river steamers. The only remaining vessel was the *Safieh*, barely capable of two-and-a-half knots heading upstream, but Beresford manned it with the best of his bluejackets and twenty picked marksmen, placing two Gardners amidships and a 7pr brass howitzer in a wooden redoubt at each end. Believing Wilson's steamers lost through treachery, Beresford handcuffed the *Safieh*'s Egyptian pilot to a stanchion watched over by a Quartermaster nicknamed Punch, who stood 'grim as death at his side revolver in hand quite ready at the slightest sign of treachery to carry out his orders'.[53] Luckily for the pilot there were no accidents, but just south of where Wilson was waiting for a sight of the White Ensign lay the Mahdist battery of Wad Habeshi. Beresford ran past it as fast as he could, sharpshooters and machine-gun crews keeping Ansar heads down as the *Safieh* crawled past at slow walking pace. The machine guns could not fire astern, however, allowing the defenders to put a single shot into the boiler, just after the steamer had passed. Steam flooded the engine room, scalding both the ERAs until the flesh of their hands and faces hung down in strips like boiled chicken.

As the *Safieh* came to a stop on the other bank, a Gardner was moved into the stern to prevent further shots from the fort's upstream embrasure. Bluejackets rebuilt the after gun platform to fire one 7pr astern, then sawed off its carriage to fit the cramped platform. Luckily Mr Benbow, the Chief Engineer, and a Leading Stoker were on deck when the boiler was hit, and between them they could patch the three-inch hole in the casing. Beresford's insistence on bringing his engineering stores now paid off. Benbow cut an oblong iron plate sixteen by fourteen inches, drilling holes in it for bolts, with corresponding holes in the injured boiler plate, accurate to a fraction of an inch, threading his nuts and bolts by hand.

Meanwhile rifle fire rattled against the crazy little ship's makeshift armour like hail, occasional rounds finding their way inside. Reliefs of marksmen and gun crews returned the fire, even the Surgeon taking a turn with a rifle. The Gardners belied their reputation for mechanical unreliability, firing 5,400 rounds in a thirteen-hour firefight with no stoppages. The boiler was still too hot at sunset, despite pumping cold water in and out of it, so one of Gordon's black crewmen was bribed to cover himself in tallow and climb inside, on the dubious assumption that a skin proof against sunburn would offer some protection against hot boiler plate. At first the Sudanese shot out faster than he went in, but went back after some argument to offer up the bolts for Benbow to fix and caulk.

Overnight deception measures persuaded the Ansar that the British had abandoned the steamer. No lights were shown, the sailors lighting their beloved pipes at a slow match hidden in a bucket. Draught plates lowered to prevent telltale sparks, steam was raised at 5 a.m., escaping notice until furious shouts from the bank showed that the game was up. Before the Ansar guns came into action, Beresford had weighed anchor and was heading upstream, away from the fort. Safely out of range he turned to run back, this time with the current, blazing away at the embrasures. Picking up Wilson's men two miles downstream, the *Safieh* was back at Gubat the same day. Beresford was so tired he slept until rats ran over his face.

The Naval Brigade had finally justified their presence, but the expedition had failed. Gordon was dead, and the Desert Column, deep in enemy territory, faced large numbers of triumphant Ansar released by the fall of Khartoum. The *Safieh* was falling to pieces, despite the Naval Brigade improvising a dry-dock to mend her rotten timbers. It was decided to fall back upon Kurti, scuttling the steamers after throwing the guns overboard, and removing the eccentric bands from the engines. So many camels had died that the Naval Brigade marched, barefoot for lack of boots. Every man carried his rifle, cutlass, and seventy rounds, but none dropped out. Years later one of the scalded ERAs admitted to Beresford how his heart sank when the bearers put down his stretcher, as firing started between Gubat and Abu Klea; but the alarm was a false one. The column reached Jaqdul on 26 February. The surviving camels' humps were so full of holes they had to be made watertight with shot plugs, prompting official correspondence on the antiseptic qualities of tar. The Naval Brigade reached Kurti on 8 March, to disperse down river, after appropriate compliments from Wolseley.

The Ansar may have been happy to let the British escape. Egyptian intelligence sources later revealed that the action at Wad Habeshi had deterred a 30,000-strong force of Ansar from attacking Gubat, saving the whole Desert Column. Benbow was promoted to Inspector of Machinery.

Beresford thought he deserved the *VC*, but instead Benbow received a unique award: Wolseley's silver cigarette case.

MACNEILL'S *ZAREBA* (MARCH 1885)

Popular outrage at the death of Gordon compelled even a Liberal Government led by Gladstone to take action. The Nile Campaign had shown the river's deficiencies as a line of advance, so the operational focus shifted back to the Eastern Sudan and the projected Sawakin-Berber railway. General Graham returned to Sawakin, cheered enthusiastically by the Royal Marine garrison. Graham had 13,000 men, a much larger force than the previous year, reducing the significance of the navy's role. The squadron's main function was to secure the base. Ships constantly had men away in boats, or covering the causeway between the mainland and Sawakin with machine and field guns. By day the Arabs kept away from the long-ranging naval guns, but they had no accurate way of judging distance. Sometimes they strayed within range, especially when the clear air of early morning betrayed their movements. All hands would roll ship to extend maximum range from four to six miles by firing at the top of the roll. However, naval etiquette required permission to fire from the SNO, and the enemy soon learned to take cover when they saw the signal flags.

Graham resumed his strategy of driving Osman Digna away from water sources near Sawakin. The Marines had 'a thoroughly exciting sporting day, if somewhat hot', evicting Hadendoa from the wells at Hasheen, and two days later (22 March 1885) a Naval Brigade landed with machine guns. HMS *Dolphin* sent her senior lieutenant, nine ratings, and two Gardners, as did HMS *Carysfort*, to join a force going to establish a supply depot at Tofrek, to be known as Macneill's Zareba. The Hadendoa struck before the thorn hedges were finished. The RMLI had just piled arms to draw their rations when there came 'a roaring noise just like the sea makes in a squall', and Osman Digna's men appeared to arise from under their feet. *Dolphin's* machine gun crews were in a sandbag redoubt on the extreme southern corner of the position, still removing the upper tier of bags for the muzzles of the guns to point over. The Arabs were among them before they could open fire.[54] Lieutenant Seymour and four ratings were killed, and two wounded; all picked men that a small ship could ill spare. *Carysfort's* machine guns did better, mowing wide gaps in the Hadendoa ranks as they charged past the redoubt at the northern corner of the *zareba*, where the marines were fighting for their lives:

It is really wonderful the way these fellows come on, they fear nothing . . .
I saw one fellow who had forced his way into the zareba, going along at a
sort of jog-trot, brandishing his sword, receive three bullets in his body,
and then it took another before he fell.[55]

The Hadendoa suffered their usual frightful casualties, including boys of ten
or twelve, but the marines' losses were not insignificant: ten dead and thirty-
five wounded out of 540, among them a sergeant killed when a swordsman
cut his arm clean off. The temperature was 100 in the shade: 'rather terrific,
so you can imagine campaigning in this country is not skittles!'[56]

In May 1885 a Russian war scare gave the Government an excuse to
abandon the game. Railway equipment rusted on the beach, 'a mournful
record of indecision and failure'.[57] The soldiers and sailors who fought at
Sawakin might have welcomed some explanation of why they had been sent
there to kill people whose vitality and courage they admired. The Royal
Navy had shown its usual gallantry and adaptability, but paid a high price
learning how to employ machine guns in the field. Machine guns can be as
dangerous to their users as to the enemy, unless deployed with secure flanks
and a clear field of fire, preferably over an obstacle.

Naval Brigades had met another enemy able to resist their superior
weapons and discipline. Sudanese and Boer nationalism were a sign that
conditions were changing. The conspicuous demonstration of sea-power in
Egypt prompted other Western countries to build up their own maritime
strength, and shocked the Near East. A Turkish officer angrily rebuked visitors when HMS *Sultan* visited Smyrna after the bombardment of
Alexandria: 'How can you go aboard that ship, which has overthrown Arabi,
and whose guns and rifles are red with the blood of our brothers?'[58] British
maritime supremacy had at last provoked a hostile response, one that would
eventually undermine the viability of Naval Brigades.

CHAPTER EIGHT

The World's Policeman

Most Naval Brigades represented less significant commitments than those in Egypt and the Sudan. Single ships or small squadrons frequently acted at the lower end of the strategic continuum described in Chapter Three, as a kind of maritime gendarmerie. The challenges they faced, and the responses they evolved, form a pattern, of which Naval Brigades were an integral part. Their activities can be seen as a significant step towards today's world order, where the spread of Western legal and commercial standards around the globe has made such interventions less necessary, as well as less acceptable.

THE CHALLENGE

In between campaigns serious enough to be dignified with their own medals, the Victorian Royal Navy carried out three routine tasks: imperial policing, trade protection, and low-level operations on the imperial fringes. The first of these might be no more than its name suggests. During the 1860s, Sergeant William Joy RMLI chased Red Indians and whisky traders in British Columbia, and guarded a British Consulate in Mexico against 'Rebels (so-called)'. Diplomatic protection was a common mission for Royal Marines throughout the period: in 1909 HMS *Spinx*'s RM Maxim detachment reinforced the Consular guard at Shiraz, 180 miles inside modern Iran. Four years later the same vessel heard of a pearl merchant murdered by his crew on the Arabian side of the Gulf: 'we went and steamed around about the alleged locality to show the flag, but with no hope getting forrader as the news was about a week old'.[1]

Sometimes civil unrest in old-established colonies exceeded the capabilities of the local police. HMS *Cordelia* landed twenty-eight marines at St Kitts and Nevis in February 1896, resulting in: 'serious encounters with the mob who fired on our men, and used very large stones to throw at them'. Two marines returned on board wounded, and several houses were burned.[2] Captain Edward Bayly of HMS *Mohawk*, first met as a Midshipman at Sekondi, was pelted with stones while aiding the civil power in Dominica during what he described as 'a copy of an Irish row'. The incident was appropriately set off by an eviction, and rendered complete by an Irish Catholic Bishop, 'always against the government', with whom Bayly shared a drop of whisky in the interests of crisis resolution. In Belize Horse Marines from HMS *Lancaster* chased a Mexican general suspected of recruiting *chiché* workers from the chewing-gum plantations to take part in a revolution.

More serious naval actions took place against slave traders on both coasts of Africa. These had dwindled by the 1890s into *Boy's Own* style chases in sailing boats after Arab dhows off Zanzibar, but a major amphibious assault was needed in 1861 to destroy the barracoons at Porto Novo, the King of Dahomey's principal slave depot. Even slave dealers suffered from his tyranny, one being carried into the royal presence rolled up like a cigar. Instructions to a Naval Brigade in 1890s Gambia still requested the destructions of slave depots, if found, and the return to Bathurst of any slaves for formal liberation.

Gun-running became a problem in the Arabian Gulf, where Afghan arms dealers waited on the Persian coast for rifles bound for the North West Frontier of India. Tangistani tribesmen, 'the worst offenders in this matter', murdered pearl fishermen who informed on their activities, leading to the destruction of their village at Dilwar by a joint Royal Navy/Indian Army force in lieu of 60,000 rupees compensation.[3] Modern weapons also contributed to instability in the Horn of Africa. Royal Naval vessels imposed an arms embargo on Somaliland's 'Mad Mullah' in 1906. Hired dhows armed with 3pr Q/F guns established a wholesome fear amongst the Arabs of Djibouti, who were as anxious to sell arms, as the Mullah was to obtain them.

The decline of the slave trade did not end naval interventions on the West Coast of Africa. The British encouraged legitimate commerce as a substitute for that in black ivory, but the appetite for trade ran ahead of the legal and economic framework needed to sustain it. Commodore Sir Frederick Richards burnt the Biafran town of Batanga after its inhabitants held a white seaman hostage to blackmail his employers into opening a factory there. Richards regretted such an 'ignoble species of warfare', but thought it inevitable: 'while traders continue to push their way everywhere along the coast, outrages by the natives will but too surely be repeated'.[4]

The Commodore knew that dubious commercial practices were not a monopoly of the indigenous African population, describing the Brass River Blockade of 1879–80 as 'a salutary lesson to others besides the natives'. The Brass River pilot had deliberately run a schooner aground, and the United African Company's employees knowingly bought its cargo of palm oil below the market rate, forty cases of gin a puncheon instead of fifty-six. The Brass men, 'a very bad set', were in trouble again in 1895, attacking the factory of the Royal Niger Company in response to the company's extortionate business practices. The fortuitous arrival of a company steamer saved the white employees, but sixty Kroomen perished on Sacrifice Island, 'according to the horrible rites of the Brass men's religion'.[5] The Juba River affair of 1893 also featured the rescue of a trading company's agents, this time from their own private army.

Trade with less developed societies caused problems elsewhere. The inhabitants of the Pellew Islands looted a wrecked British schooner, releasing the passengers. The latter lodged complaints at Hong Kong, leading to a visit from HMS *Comus* to seek compensation: tortoise shell, copra, and bêche-de-mer. Looting wrecks was one step away from the more serious business of piracy, an important sideline for fishermen in the China Sea, around the Malay Archipelago, and off the Congo River. Mpinge Nebacca was a Congo pirate sufficiently notorious to be known to the sailors as Pinch of Tobacco. In 1870 he carried off the crew of an English schooner, with its cargo of rum and gunpowder, attracting retribution from HMS *Growler*'s energetic Captain Seymour, who had hunted Chinese pirates as a midshipman.

The lack of recognisable political authorities able to provide legal redress seemed to leave little alternative to armed reprisals in such cases. There was also a tradition of Great Powers acting together or singly to maintain what were perceived as reasonable standards of behaviour on the part of weaker states. As the ubiquitous representative of the only world power, the Royal Navy had its fair share of such interventions. Latin America remained unstable throughout the Victorian period, revolutionary leaders needing frequent reminders of their obligations towards neutrals. There was much good-natured cooperation with the United States Navy, the officers sharing operational command, and the marines swapping uniform buttons. Captain St Clair of HMS *Champion* made a stand, with the French and American Rear-Admirals, in front of Balmacedist machine guns to prevent a massacre of civilians at the end of the Chilean Civil War in 1891. RN and USN ships cooperated at Blewfields, Nicaragua to prevent serious loss of life, disarming the losers in a civil war, and getting them a free pardon. HMS *Lancaster* went from Belize to Haiti, where the fifth revolution in two years was in progress – rather a tame affair: the victors fired off their spare ammunition, and went home, selling their rifles for 4/6d each.

Great Britain took an interest in a succession of disputes in strategic areas like Zanzibar, which then included much of the coast of East Africa. The sudden death of the Sultan in 1896 precipitated a coup, and one of the shortest wars on record. The bombardment of the pretender's forces started as the palace clock struck nine, and ended when their red flag came down thirty-seven minutes later. The exchange of fire followed days of Cold War style brinkmanship: sentries tramping their posts in full view of each other, gunners lying beside their pieces, occasionally glancing over the sights, a Zanzibari machine gunner seated on a chair behind his Maxim which he kept trained on the English Club, ready for any emergency. When the target was less accessible than a waterfront palace, more strenuous efforts would be necessary, such as the Naval Brigade that marched thirty miles into East Africa to overturn a 'usurper' at Mwele in 1895. Some actions had flimsy justification, for example the Anglo-American intervention in the Samoan Succession dispute in 1899, a conflict where few British interests were at stake, and neutral arbitration later found against the two powers.

All too often conflict seems to have arisen from mutual incomprehension, a theme evident in earlier confrontations in China, Burma and Japan. Negotiations for the return of property taken from the Niger River steamer *Sultan of Sokotto* were stymied by the local inhabitants' refusal to talk at all:

> after a while a man came from behind the huts, where they had taken shelter at first sight of a man-o-war, after a few words the interpreter went on shore to palaver with the chiefs, but could not come to any arrangements as they said they did not want anything to do with a white man. The captain thought he would teach them to be civil so he gave the order to open fire.[6]

Sometimes the other side was too hasty, as when the King of Benin added a British Consul to his other human sacrifices.

The collapse of the Turkish Empire provided strikingly modern opportunities for peacekeeping. Ships and landing parties took part in international action in Crete in 1897, to evacuate Turkish civilians from villages surrounded by Greek insurgents wanting to settle scores going back to the Middle Ages. Just before the First World War Royal Marines occupied Scutari, in what would soon become Yugoslavia, to protect the Muslim inhabitants from ethic cleansing by Montenegrins. Sometimes it seems as if nothing ever changes.

THE RESPONSE

One undoubted reason for the use of Naval Brigades to meet these minor but widespread challenges was the responsiveness of naval units. Ships in commission have to be ready for immediate action, if only to face the hazards of being at sea. Victorian army units, on the other hand, were under-strength and unprepared for war. Sir John Fisher, no friend of Naval Brigades, recognised that, by the time a military force could be organised, 'the moral effect of swift retribution would have been lost'.[7]

The army's inability to respond to the Benin outrage in less than three months, when the rains would prevent movement, left no alternative to naval action. In twenty-nine days a force of 1,200 men was collected from up to 4,000 miles away, organised, and landed. Benin fell thirty-four days after the Admiralty issued the orders, and forty-five after the murder of Consul Phillips. Preparations at ship level reflected the same urgency: HMS *Theseus* received orders for West Africa at nine in the morning. Empty of stores for a triennial inspection, and half her men ashore on the rifle range, she was ready to sail at midnight. Response times at the tactical level were even sharper. HMS *Philomel* and *Thrush* reacted to the Zanzibari *coup d'état* 'with a promptness characteristic of the British Navy', their landing parties 'landed, ready armed and equipped within fifteen minutes of the first sign of the disturbance'.[8]

Similar alacrity characterised the departure of Royal Marine battalions. The prompt despatch of 500 marines to Sawakin in 1884 suggested to the *Army and Navy Gazette* that 'Ready-aye-ready' would form an appropriate addition to the Corps motto: 'It is this mobility that renders the Marine Corps so valuable, and one that can always be relied upon to move without delay.'[9] The Corps always had men ready for sea service at the three RMLI depots, and the RMA barracks in Eastney. These included a good propor-tion of experienced men, as Royal Marines continued to serve up to twenty-one years after the army introduced short service under the Cardwell Reforms of 1868–74. Every marine sent to Benin in the S.S. *Malacca* was over twenty-seven years old. The home battalion of an infantry regiment, drained of its best men for service in India, would not have had such reserves of seasoned manpower.

Earlier in the period such actions as that at Zanzibar were unhindered by detailed instructions from home. The absence of worldwide telegraphic communications allowed naval officers to use their initiative, and seek approval afterwards. Admiralty replies to Captain's Proceedings commonly expressed *post facto* concurrence with action taken. This had advantages: offers of armed support for the Kaimakan at Jeddah if he punished the instigators of a massacre of Christians were bluff. The Commodore had no such orders, but it worked. SNOs might still ignore London's views when telegraphic communications were established. Commodore Richards resisted Colonial Office opposition to the Brass River blockade: losses to British trading companies would have 'the beneficial effect of making them ... more careful in the selection of their employees'.[10]

By the 1890s the telegraph made it possible to agree action in advance, at the highest level. Vice-Admiral Sir Edmund Fremantle's expedition against Fumo Bakari, the Sultan of Witu, was taken 'in accordance with instructions received from Her Majesty's Principal Secretary of State for Foreign Affairs'.[11] Such consultations did not always result in better decisions. The Sultan was blamed for the murder of nine Germans on the evidence of their surviving friends. Roger Keyes, a participant not widely regarded as a liberal pacifist, thought the Germans had themselves attacked the Sultan's troops. Promised a fair trial, the Sultan would not take the chance.

Faced with endemic violence, it is not surprising that naval officers took extreme measures. Fremantle's successor explained another collision on the grounds that, 'It seemed inevitable if the lives of the Englishmen (sic) ... were to be saved.'[12] Nevertheless, they often moderated the violence of their actions. It was usual to give the inhabitants of towns threatened with bombardment time to remove their families. Sergeant Joy's dealings with Red Indians were preceded by one round from the ship, which failed to explode. The officer responsible for a second expedition against Witu in 1893 began his advance, 'hoping to settle things peaceably, but ready to fight if necessary'.[13] Orders for disarming the people of Birkama in the Gambia the following year distinguished between the peaceable inhabitants and the local resistance leader. The latter was believed to occupy a separate quarter of the town, which it was hoped to destroy without harming the rest, and in any case the people were to be given time to remove their grain stores and other property. Such habits died slowly: HMS *Minerva* landed fire-fighting parties at Akaba, after the outbreak of war with Turkey, to stop fires started by her own shells spreading to civilian property.

Sometimes violence took a ritualistic form. HMS *Comus'* landing party burnt the houses of the Pellew Islanders' chiefs, sparing the rest:

> The people of this village fled to the woods but as the rearguard appeared they came out of the woods again armed with spears and guns (mostly Snider rifles) in a menacing manner. The Marines faced about and came to the present (but strictly obeyed the orders that had been given them not to fire) and the natives retreated.[14]

Commander Sotheby experienced a similar scary moment, up a proverbial creek, with just the six men of his gig:

> I had no sooner shoved off than the natives emerged from the jungle armed with muskets and pointed them at us, and were only prevented from firing by an old woman beating the muskets down by a stick. The war drums immediately sounded and we were followed down the creek . . . I must say I was excessively glad when I got out of the creek.[15]

SHIPS AND MEN

The ships employed in these minor operations bore little resemblance to the ironclads that overthrew Arabi Pasha. The Cape squadron usually included one modern cruiser, like HMS *St George* in the 1890s, but most of its ships were better adapted to police work:

> the sort of vessel dignified by the name of a 'bugtrap' . . . barque rigged, extremely handy under steam, not a bad steam boat, and good for rivers, drawing only nine feet of water. But though you could tack and wear her, as I often did, Neptune himself could not have made her work decently to windward under sail.[16]

Fisher mocked such ships as too weak to fight and too slow to run away, but they carried appropriate weapons for the challenges they faced: a 65pr RML in the bow, a pair of 12pr Armstrong RBLs on the beam, and a couple of brass howitzers. Later gunboats, elevated to 3rd class cruisers, tended to have three 4-inch or 6-inch BL guns on either broadside, with machine guns for close defence.

Seymour painted *Growler* yellow with a red stripe, but conditions on board were less attractive. Condensed drinking water was plentiful, but took hours to cool, its metallic taste thinly disguised by rum. A well-meaning reduction in the rum ration moved a WO to write scathingly of the iced and fizzing drinks of London clubmen:

> We would like to see Mr Trevelyan taking a pull at a can of water fresh from the condenser in the Persian Gulf or on the Coast, and ask him what he thought of the refreshment.[17]

The term 'bugtrap' was literally true. Cockroaches blackened the bulkheads, laid eggs in the soup and died in the mustard pot. Bed bugs lurked in cot crevices, scorpions beneath books, and tarantulas, whose bite drove men mad, amongst the bedclothes. Floating islands in the mouth of the Congo might contribute snakes and other fauna, anxious to disembark before being swept out to sea.

These bug-infested warships supplied the nearest approximation to fully autonomous Naval Brigades operating under exclusive naval command. On the fringes of the Empire, they depended almost entirely on themselves. Fremantle thought the Witu expedition 'the first occasion within my knowledge in which a campaign of such short duration has been undertaken by Naval resource alone, the whole of the Transport and the Commissariat having been organised and arranged by Officers of Her Majesty's Navy.'[18] His exhaustive orders show a degree of thought and care that refutes claims that Naval Brigades were slipshod improvisations. Technology abetted such thoroughness; hektagraphed copies of preliminary orders for the Benin expedition were posted on the lower decks, and distributed to all officers and WOs going ashore.

Fremantle covered every aspect of the anticipated operations: weapons and equipment, organisation, transport and supply, disembarkation, and tactics. Personal equipment was standard, although midshipmen were to replace their dirks with cutlasses, and sailors to fill their bottles with cold tea. Numbers approximated to an infantry battalion. Fremantle's eight ships landed 500 rifles: HMS *Phoebe* and *Alecto* less than 200 for a reconnaissance in force at Brohemie in 1894, about two rifle companies. They followed the traditional pattern of two small 'battalions' of naval riflemen and one of marines, although the Benin Naval Brigade was more complex. Its two 'Divisions' each had two seamen companies and one marine (220 per division), supported by a separate 'battalion' of 120 marines from the *Malacca*. A company of seventy bluejackets guarded the carriers, or at least stopped them running away. Local auxiliaries often supplemented Naval Brigades, for example the 320 Haussas who accompanied the Benin expedition, or the Zanzibaris and Indians who featured at Witu and Mwele. Such units stood the climate better, but were not always trusted in a fight. Sailors took the lead for the last push on Benin, as white troops were thought better for a dash. Weak in rifles, Naval Brigades carried a high proportion of heavy weapons: rockets, 7prs, and machine guns. Fremantle had four of each, absorbing 171 men, a fifth of his strength. The 7pr limbers were fully packed with twelve shrapnel, and twelve empty common shell, to be filled with petroleum to make primitive incendiary rounds.[19]

Transport was a problem away from the water's edge. As a Major in the Naval Intelligence Department, George Aston compiled the official analysis of the Benin expedition. He commented on the: 'great difference between the relationship between time and space by water and ashore in a country of this nature'.[20] Climate and topography forced African expeditions to depend on carriers. Fremantle needed 400, but 'as in most African expeditions the question of porters was the greatest difficulty'. The local people exaggerated the dangers, and refused to serve against their co-religionists at Witu. Fremantle was saved by a freelance caravan leader, and Zanzibari soldiers who agreed to serve as carriers. He also made liberal use of 'Seedies', the East African equivalent of Kroomen. Seedies and other carriers wore a red distinguishing mark, to avoid understandable mistakes, the former armed with cutlasses as far as possible. British sailors, however, were responsible for the camp kettles containing tea, sugar, and cocoa.

Sir John Fisher mocked naval stores' unsuitability for movement ashore, recalling the distressing sight of six stokers, 'trying to insinuate a salt beef cask slung on a couple of oars, along a jungle track'.[21] Tinned food and professionalism made a dramatic improvement. The Benin porters carried standard 55lb loads, equivalent to four days' water for themselves and two fighting men, or twenty-four complete rations. Uneaten portions were thrown away, and the carrier sent back. The expedition employed over 2,000 carriers, although smallpox hampered recruitment in Sierra Leone, and none could be had on the Gold Coast without compulsion, which was prohibited, a change from the pressgangs of 1873–74.

Nevertheless the commissariat collapsed, the marines at Benin 'living on wind': a daily helmet full of biscuit between forty.[22] Water was a major problem. Wells were scarce, while water is heavy and easily spilt. Fremantle asked officers to: 'impress upon their men the absolute necessity of the most rigid abstinence and care in the consumption of water, there being no water between the sea coast and Witu';[23] a distance of thirty miles. He took sixty gallons, pairs of porters carrying a ten-gallon barricoe between them on a pole. Paraffin cans were used in Benin, but they sprang leaks if dropped, as was likely during an ambush. The Benin expedition nearly failed for lack of water: fighting men were reduced to four pints a day, and the unfortunate carriers to two, insufficient to stop them collapsing from dehydration. Fortunately there was no counter-attack after Benin city fell, as everyone was utterly done in. No more water could be found, and in reserve was only two pints a man. The heat was terrible, the sights ghastly, and the stink from human and other sacrificial victims awful, sentries fainting from the smell.

Poor intelligence made logistical planning difficult. The distance to Benin was unknown, as few visitors had lived to tell the tale. Local people had no units of distance, and gave pleasing rather than informative replies. Native guides were notoriously unreliable. The three taken to Benin were questioned separately to prevent collusion. Some old carriers who had traded with Benin put together a plan of the city's main compounds on a hut floor, with corks and string, but scientific methods were no better. HMS *Theseus'* navigational instruments could not shoot the sun through the forest canopy, while paths were too winding to count paces marched.

Inaccurate assessment of water availability contributed to a disaster in Gambia in 1894, where a 204-strong Naval Brigade lost a staggering 35 per cent casualties. Among them was the Captain in command, who condemned the:

> want of knowledge of the state of the country. I have also a very strong opinion that the guide who was sent to me was one of the enemy ... it is impossible for a force to march through such country with thick bush and no water, having to fight every yard of the way, without serious loss of life.[24]

KEEPING THE PEACE?

Captain Gamble wrote in a state of shock, but he raised an important question: how could Naval Brigades operate in such a hostile environment, at an acceptable cost in casualties? Part of the answer must be that it was unusual to penetrate far into the interior. Naval Brigades with objectives a day's march inland, like Gamble's, entailed far greater effort and risk than most power-projection exercises. As suggested in Chapter Three, these ran from blockades, through sometimes ritualised bombardments, to amphibious operations along the water's edge. Only occasionally did they culminate in full-blown Naval Brigades.

On the surface at least, a blockade is the least violent of these forms of pressure. Commodore Richards' orders for the Brass River blockade of 1879–80 prohibited landing for hostile purposes. Boats were to remain within range of the ship's guns, the Brass men having numerous war canoes, well-armed with smooth-bore cannon in the bows. The arms embargo in the Gulf, on the other hand, required a mixture of amphibious measures. Armed cutters watched the coast, supported by cruisers on a fixed beat, stopping every dhow they encountered. Landing parties searched for consignments that slipped through, as at Pishkan in 1910, where HMS *Perseus'* marines found the foothills and wadis an ideal place to try out their field training. They netted 850 rifles including: 'new 1909 Lee-Speed B.S.A. Rifles with the stock cut away behind the aperture sight to receive the B.S.A. sight so much favoured by our Bisley shots last season'.[25] Such successes cost the Afghan dealers £20–£30 per rifle, and might lead to reprisals against British-operated telegraph stations along the Persian coast. In 1908 HMS *Proserpine*'s marines reinforced forty sepoys at the Jask telegraph station, occupying an old fort 'kindly lent by the Persian authorities'.[26]

The threat of bombardment remains a favourite nostrum for those seeking international influence on the cheap, but it is a clumsy device. The threat may not impress men of violence with little to lose themselves, while international forces may lack the resolve to open fire. The Greek insurgents in Crete in 1897 despised the international squadron there for its failure to impose a ceasefire, until HMS *Camperdown* opened up with her 13.5-inch guns, perhaps the heaviest weapons ever used in peacekeeping operations. In Africa there were fewer inhibitions. Rockets and howitzers were the accepted means of setting a village alight. Direct fire with solid shot did little damage to green-wood stockades at Lagos in 1851, but more scientific methods were in use by the 1890s. HMS *Phoebe* fired 1,100 4.7-inch shells into the town of Brohemie, invisible behind its mangroves. The Lieutenant (G) directed fire from a thirty-foot pole above the fore-topmast: 'laid for elevation by Watkin's clinometer and for direction by standard compass, and the results were very satisfactory'.[27] Only three blinds were recovered, and hardly a building escaped some sort of perforation. At Dilwar in 1913 the naval fire support 'was rather a fiasco', nearly hitting some trees where the landing forces were resting:

> some time before we could get a signal out to the ships and stop them. The shells made a deep hollow whistling sound and one couldn't help wondering whether the next one would fall in the plantation.[28]

The natural follow-up to a bombardment is a landing to finish the job. Swampy ground might have absorbed the rockets and shells:

> after bombarding the place for about twenty minutes, the landing party went on shore. They kept up a continual musketry fire onto the thickest part of the bush where the natives had taken shelter, and destroyed everything of value and then set fire to the place, the ships keeping up a cross fire of shell and rockets the whole time.[29]

That attack was not wanton destruction, a subsequent visit found property taken from the *Sultan of Sokotto*, whose people the villagers had murdered two years earlier.

A logical step once ashore was to press on to destroy military *matériel* like the Spanish cannon cast in 1703 that served as a symbol of kingship at Brohemie, or to release hostages. Seymour led a three-mile dash to rescue the crew of the *Loango*, who had been seized by Congo river pirates: 'the village was so hidden in the forest that without a guide I should never have found it, and probably no white man was ever there before. Like rabbits the inhabitants jumped up and fled.' Wanting a prisoner, he chased a group through the eight-foot reeds, until one fell over near enough for Seymour to fling himself on top of them. They rolled over in the grass and his captive's only garment came off, leaving Seymour in a highly compromising position with a young woman.

The attacks on Brohemie were reprisals for Nana's smooth-bore guns firing at HMS *Alecto*'s cutter in the Benin River, but inland waterways might be dangerous for other reasons. The Congo's seven-knot current swept three of HMS *Encounter*'s seamen out to sea in a pulling boat. Hippos abounded, and might upset the boats, which, as the river was full of alligators, might be serious. An ant's nest, twice as big as a man's head, fell into a boat from a tree, causing a hasty disembarkation. Snipers could pick off a boat's crew exposed in mid-stream. One shot Seymour in the leg, the sensation exactly as if someone had hit him very hard with a big stick. Artificers armoured the exposed decks of larger craft with sheet iron to prevent disasters like that on the Prah where Commerell was ambushed in 1873. The Cape squadron's base at Simonstown held stocks of armour plate, along with spare boots, onions, stout, Bovril, and cyclostyles.

Rivers were essential highways into the African interior. The initial advance to Benin was by steamer, 'firing into the bush all the way with Maxims'.[30] HMS *Alecto* penetrated to Aboh, 100 miles up the Niger River in 1883: 'It all looked so beautiful that it was hard to believe that we were travelling through a country poisonous with malaria.'[31] The Brass River expedition of 1895 was conducted entirely by river. Nimbi, the chief town of the Brassmen, lay sixteen miles inland, accessible only through a network of creeks, whose tree-lined banks might conceal any number of riflemen. The artificers of HMS *St George* and *Barrosa* riveted steel plates along the sides of their steam pinnaces, and armed them with a 3pr Hotchkiss in the bow and a Maxim astern. The miniature ironclads scouted ahead of the ship's boats, signalling progress with blasts on their steam whistles. The Brassmen boomed the creek at Sacrifice Island with long baulks of timber, two feet thick, secured by forked trees well driven into the bottom, but were surprised by the navy's rapid advance. Their canoes only appeared, war flags flying and tom-toms beating, after the torpedo party had blown the boom.

King Koko, the chief of the Brassmen, declined invitations to palaver, so the expedition pressed on to Nimbi, war canoes and stockades unable to withstand Messrs Hotchkiss and Maxim. The armoured pinnaces were not entirely satisfactory; a round shot bent the corner of a Maxim shield, killing Lieutenant Tayler. Another penetrated a cabin, decapitating a domestic, while an AB lost his foot.

Most of these Nelsonic casualties came during the assault on the stockades before Nimbi, and explain the care usually taken to avoid opposed landings. One great advantage of amphibious forces is their ability to launch surprise attacks on undefended beaches, and extract themselves before large-scale resistance develops. Unlike Rear-Admiral Sir Michael Seymour, who stuck up warning notices on the gates of Canton, late Victorian naval officers customarily exploited surprise. Fremantle's preliminary orders for Witu stressed the importance of not mentioning the true direction of his advance, hoping that preparations elsewhere would 'lead the enemy to suppose that the attack will be delivered by the usual road'.[32] A squadron raiding the Mad Mullah's arms dump at Illig in 1904 approached the landing beach in the dark, guided in by the lights of HMS *Mohawk* anchored offshore the previous day. A naval officer had sketched the beach eighteen months previously so there was no sudden flurry of activity to arouse suspicion. The landing place was three miles north of the target, a choice approved by a participating infantry officer: 'there is no doubt that had the force landed on the beach at Illig it would have met with a very warm reception, and it would have been no easy job to scale the heights and take the position by a frontal attack'.[33]

To maintain surprise the landing began before dawn, displaying more of the seamanship that had allowed the squadron to concentrate under cover of darkness without showing any lights. A covering party of 150 bluejackets occupied the cliffs 100 feet above the beach, covered by boats armed with field guns and Maxims. The whole force of 540 men and four machine guns took two hours to land. Steam pinnaces towed in ship's boats, which anchored and swung stern on to the beach, the troops wading ashore through the surf sometimes up to their necks in sea water.

The use of a covering party supported by armed boats was standard doctrine, laid down in the Admiralty manuals. At Dilwar in 1913, the Naval Brigade landed first, occupying the sand dunes to cover the disembarkation of 200 Rajput infantrymen, packed like sardines into four big dhows. Fremantle covered his Witu landing with two companies and the field battery. A beach master and his assistants guided in the remaining companies and the transport with flags displayed on boarding pikes: fleet numbers for each ship or initial letters for Ammunition, Provision, or Water parties.

Naval Brigades faced a variety of terrain beyond the beach, from a solid rock plateau at Illig, devoid of vegetation, to the slippery mud of west African mangroves where Seymour writhed snakelike among the roots, or waded deeply like a man shrimping. The East African bush lay between these extremes:

> For more than a mile from Kipini, we had to march through heavy sand with high scrub on either side; thence for about a mile along a level plain which forms a marsh at high water, spring tide, and after heavy rains; thence through a grassy country interspersed with palm trees for two miles; then the clumps of bush got thicker and the grass higher . . . being in places over men's heads, making marching more difficult.[34]

Further inland the ground was sufficiently open for Witu to be seen from a hill 1,200 yards away, a distance unimaginable in West Africa or Malaya, where Naval Brigades met conditions familiar to later generations of British servicemen:

> For nearly a month the brigade under Captain Buller had nothing to eat but preserved meat, supplemented occasionally by wild buffalo – no veg- etables or bread; the men were constantly wet through by rain, they had frequently to wade through water and mud over their waists. For the last three days of their advance on Kinta they had to thread their way in a thick jungle, which during the whole of that time, allowed them no sight of the sky.[35]

In such terrain the standard enemy tactic was the ambush, preferably at a turning in the path, blocked by fallen trees entangled with bushes. West Africans cut ambush paths parallel to the line of advance, but this worked against them as British advanced guards doubled forward along both paths. Bush warfare was a weird business, with hardly a living enemy seen during the four-day advance on Benin, although their presence was palpable enough: 'At each clearing the proximity of the enemy could be seen, the fires not yet out, the water gourds upset in their hurried departure'. Benin's defences were magical as well as material:

> As we proceeded the human sacrifices became more common. At length we came to a very big and well placed stockade with a large gun on the

top about four inches across the muzzle, as we came up a man got up, and with a great piece of wood lighted a long train of gun powder which eventually fired the gun, but as it was pointed nowhere in particular, the shots went somewhere in the bush to our right, and the gun went backward over the stockade.[36]

Only near Benin did the jungle open out into a broad avenue, about thirty yards wide and a mile long: 'It did seem glorious to get out of the bush into the open and see the sky overhead.'[37] As always in bush warfare, an open space spelled danger, the enemy opening fire as the advanced guard lay about, glad of a rest:

It was now that we saw the enemy for the first time in the open, and it was now the maxims were especially needed, so they took it into their heads to go wrong; one having its sight shot off and the other jamming . . . The enemy had some small cannon that they got to bear on us, but they must have had a squint in their aiming powers for they never hit us.[38]

The snipers in the trees did better, so the marines' machine gun section propped the front tripod legs on ammunition boxes to increase elevation, and cleared the trees, 'not a shot coming from that quarter afterwards, though they still kept it up slowly from the bush'.[39] Dr Fyfe was shot dead attending to the wounded, who were terribly in want of water. None could be spared for the Maxim's water-jackets, so lime juice was substituted, with good results![40]

East African tactics were more aggressive, leading to several attacks on Fremantle's *zarebas*, but he adopted an equally offensive response, 'as this has been found to be the plan which most disconcerts savages'.[41] Less overgrown terrain permitted a more conventional deployment, a rough square on the march opening out for the assault: marines in the centre, bluejackets on the wings, and the Indian Police in the centre of the now skeleton square in case of a counter-attack. Artillery and Gardner guns kept the enemy's heads down from a convenient knoll. Two 7pr rounds fired at close quarters made little impression on Witu's massive gates, so Mr Jennings, in charge of *Boadicea*'s gun-cotton party, blew them up in a great cloud of dust. As the Naval Brigade charged in the gate the enemy ran out the back, leaving behind diverse curios that would be thrown away on the return march: shields and spears, old guns and ammunition, the Sultan's state chain, and a framed photograph of the Kaiser.

The ground at Illig was so open that standard Whale Island tactics could be used: waves of skirmishers, supports, and reserves. The left flank rested on the sea, exploiting dead ground to approach the Somali position with few losses, while bluejackets on the right swung wide of the enemy flank, carrying their machine guns with them: 'a marvellous performance of dogged courage'. The advance continued by short rushes until the fire of the seamen endangered the left of the line, when the Flag Captain ordered the charge, 'and in an instant the whole line of the Naval Brigade surged like a sea over the walls'.[42] Some of the enemy escaped along the cliffs, pursued by 4.7-inch shells from HMS *Fox*, but others hid in the village, sniping at the wounded on the beach. Three held out in a cave, until Captain Hood himself dashed through a wickerwork screen to kill two of them with his sword and revolver.

Such obstinate resistance was unusual. A naval officer in the Gambia during the 1860s thought it a matter for comment when the Mandingoes stood a bayonet charge:

> The enemy, however, had no alternative but to stand as they could not get out of the stockade. The fighting became very desperate, and the blacks so determined that they unshipped the sword bayonets from our men's muskets, but were knocked down and over powered before they had time to use them.[43]

Most opponents were more dangerous when following up a retreat. Only a quarter of Fumo Bakari's men were engaged, but Fremantle was 'convinced that had any check occurred we should have had 3,000 or 4,000 to deal with'.[44] Such reinforcements would have been doubly dangerous, as the returning Brigade were exhausted: 'being cramped up in a ship for so long, many of the men were not in very good marching order . . . often suffering from sea-cuts or swollen feet'.[45]

Captain Gamble's decision to abandon his advance in the Gambia encouraged the enemy to an unaccustomed boldness, justifying Fremantle's apprehensions. Single shots started almost as soon as the retreat began, the fire becoming hotter once fairly into the bush. Men soon began to fall, the removal of the wounded causing delay and confusion:

> The men got crowded together and to a great extent disorganized, which I fear was unavoidable under the circumstances, the carrying of the wounded, the passage of the field-gun, combined with the narrowness of the path, and the heavy fire poured on us by our unseen enemy, making it difficult to keep in any regular formation without crowding.[46]

Disaster came at the water's edge. Low tide prevented immediate evacuation, so the enemy closed in on all sides, keeping up a heavy fire from bush too thick for a counter-attack. Only after two hours did the rising tide allow boats to approach the beach. Lieutenant King-Hall of HMS *Magpie* was one of the last to leave, fighting with a wounded man's rifle:

> As soon as I saw the steam-cutter was clear and the boats pointed fairly well in the right direction, I ordered 'cease firing', told off the remaining men into two parties, one for each canoe, and ordered them to retire. All this time firing was being kept up, though not as hotly as at first, which was probably due to their ammunition running short, and also, I trust, to their losses.[47]

He left several of the dead and the 7pr whose removal might have cost another dozen casualties, a risk King-Hall preferred to avoid.

Embarkation was dangerous even when unopposed. Commodore Richards was shot accidentally leaving the beach at Batanga. Nerves were at full stretch after two men had been killed earlier:

> Just as the first boat was going off there was an alarm on shore and everyone began easing off their rifles anyhow, and a great many rushed back into the water. Soon after this, Fox the quartermaster, firing his rifle without looking, hit the Commodore, luckily on the front button of his jacket; it followed along his breast and lodged in the lining of his coat at his shoulder, only bruising him.[48]

The surf at Illig beat HMS *Hyacinth*'s steam cutter to pieces, while taking men off the beach, provoking criticism from Sir John Fisher. HMS *Mohawk*'s men returned to the beach in the dark, after aiding the civil power in Dominica, to find the surf too heavy for ship's boats. They embarked three at a time in a canoe, illuminated by the ship's searchlight, and were fortunate not to lose anyone, the surf rolling several men on the stony beach.

PROS AND CONS

The perceived value of these low-key operations depends as much on the viewpoint of the observer as their own merits. Not all service opinion was favourable. A naval officer criticised the navy's treatment of King Jaja, deposed on behalf of the palm-oil traders: 'Honesty is the best policy, even with African kings.'[49] A midshipman who sketched Witu for the *Illustrated London News* took a cynical view of Zanzibar's declining place in the world:

> The Sultan is now king in name only, the rival British and German commercial companies having stolen from him, by continual bullying, the whole of his mainland possessions, and he would probably now have to pay duty on his arms, etc, if he landed in his own country.[50]

Albert Battiscombe witnessed the executions that followed the Jeddah massacre. They delighted the Arabs, as the leading rioter had been 'the terror of the place', but Battiscombe spent the rest of the day very unpleasantly, 'the bodies of the victims rising up to my eyes every moment, and reminding me of the bloody though necessary deed I had witnessed in the morning'.[51] It seems likely that lower-deck opinion was less fastidious. Seymour overheard a marine in the Congo averring that he had killed two and murdered two, and would have liked to ask him where he drew the line:

> How many were killed I cannot say; but it is a well known fact that the British sailor or marine, and I believe soldier, is not very squeamish about taking life when once he is thoroughly excited.[52]

Richard Cotten thought HMS *Comus'* bloodless visit to the Pellew Islands:

> An emphatic proof . . . that European traders must be regarded as sacrosanct both in person and goods. Above all king Arracklye and all those under him have been taught a smart lesson which may impress upon their minds the fact that solemn promises made to the British Government cannot be set aside with impunity.[53]

Captain Bayly, whose men shot four rioters dead in Dominica, thought the lesson 'badly wanted, and might have been more severely taught later on'. He blamed the French priest for encouraging his parishioners to attack the Governor's small party with rocks and cutlasses, never imagining the bluejackets would open fire: 'I don't think he chuckled so much when the business was over. It is wretched business all this, but it is duty and must be done'.[54] The Niger expedition of 1883 inspired similarly mixed feelings:

> When our men had time to reflect, they felt somewhat disappointed at the one-sided fight and said very little about it. Certainly it was not much to

be proud of; but we had taught the chiefs that it did not pay to maltreat missionaries, and that was what we came for.[55]

The horrors at Benin left little doubt in anyone's mind about the validity of intervention there. One sailor commented with remarkable restraint that it was just about time someone did visit the place. Within months the city of blood was transformed with a postal service, new trade in copal and rubber, a council of chiefs for local affairs, and a golf course. The release of hundreds of starving slaves from Nana's compound at Brohemie, to be fed naval rations by bluejackets, cannot easily be condemned. The world still has no effective answer to humanitarian disasters inflicted by rulers on their own people.

CHAPTER NINE

Reprise: from Ladysmith to Peking

THE Naval Brigades that took part in the Second Boer War of 1899 and the Boxer Rebellion in China a year later are deservedly two of the best known. The navy made up for the army's material deficiencies in the early stages of these remote campaigns, providing strategic depth in a crisis, as it had in the Crimea and Mutiny. In a striking demonstration of naval flexibility HMS *Terrible* featured in both campaigns, her 12pr gun carriages boasting the inscription 'Ladysmith to Peking – Immediate'. However, at the very height of their success, Naval Brigades reached the limits of their usefulness. The lengthy operations against the Boers, and the heavy losses suffered at Graspan, the Naval Brigade's only action in South Africa as infantry, showed that under modern conditions even a bunch of farmers demand a proper military response. Roger Keyes, a dashing destroyer commander in 1900 and a 'thrusting' Admiral in the Great War, thought it impossible for a handful of seamen and marines to make war on China, however bad its army. The future usefulness of Naval Brigades was in question, for all their gallantry and the lessons in mobile firepower provided by their long-range guns.

THE SOUTH AFRICAN WAR (1899–1900)

The British approached their second war with the Boers with astonishing complacency, although the Transvaal and Orange Free State were heavily armed and known to be intent on driving the British out of South Africa. Rear-Admiral Sir Robert Harris, Commander-in-Chief on the Cape Station, met British traders operating in the Transvaal, while shooting hippopotamus near Lourenço Marques in August 1899. They told him the Boers boasted openly that, when the grass came in October, there would be war. Cape Town would fall into Boer hands by Christmas. Events would show this was 'not altogether an absurdly sanguinary aspiration' (*sic*).[1] On the other side, naval and military officers alike longed to wipe out 'A Certain Stain': the British defeat at Majuba in 1881.

When the squadron returned to Simonstown from its diplomatic and sporting cruise in East African waters, Harris made immediate preparations for the coming struggle.[2] Ships went into dock, and seamen and marines practised landing drill:

> skirmishing up the rough hills encircling Simon's Bay, holding sham fights, dragging up guns – storming the Red Hill against time and each other – with much the same rivalry of ship against ship as drills aloft.

Harris' apprehensions were not universal:

> the unbelievers said it would be a walkover, a mere soldier's picnic and no business of the officers and men of the Royal Navy, who were much too costly to be expended in shooting down a few semi-civilised Boers.[3]

Harris offered stores and munitions to a complacent army: 'Very many thanks, but I do not think we want anything.'[4] Percy Scott criticised Harris for not making more extensive preparations, but it is hard to see what more the C-in-C could have done without a formal request for help. This was an essential pre-condition for active naval participation in land operations, as in the Crimea or South Africa in the 1870s–80s. Harris' orders were to defend the ports through which reinforcements would come, while inhibiting the Transvaal's arms imports through the neutral Portuguese port of Lourenço Marques. It had not mattered in previous wars in South Africa, if ships were immobilised by the absence of their crews. This time the blockade would be hard, thankless work. Ships remained at sea until they ran out of coal, refilling their bunkers at Durban, and returning to sea with no leave, and no chance of action to stimulate their energies. It was undesirable for Harris to weaken his ships by landing guns or men, whatever the traditions of the service to which Scott appealed, and of which Harris himself was well aware.

Military optimism was too much at odds with the darkening situation to last. On 20 October Harris landed 300 marines and two field guns under Commander Ethelston RN and Major Plumbe RMLI to defend the railway junction at Stormberg.[5] This force was the thin end of the wedge. The Royal Navy's contribution to the Boer War at its peak rivalled that in the Crimea, totalling 1,400 officers and men and over sixty guns. These ranged

from a 6-inch BL Gun to a 3pr Q/F mounted in an armoured train,[6] suggesting the naval C-in-C was not the pro-Boer some made him out to be.
So outrageous were the comments of one Cape newspaper that a group of
naval officers threw its editor off the Admiralty House pier. Humour was
much rougher then. Press comment focused on their colleague's aversion
to washing rather than the brutality of his assailants, whose £1 fines were
paid by the patriotic ladies of Rockhampton, Queensland.

HMS *Terrible* docked at Simonstown on 14 October 1899, two days after
20,000 Boers crossed the Natal border, outnumbering the British defenders
two to one. *Terrible's* Commanding Officer, Captain Percy Scott, was unfashionably keen on gunnery, and despised such bureaucratic niceties as not
spending the Navy Vote on the army's work. He turned his inventive mind
to countering the Boers' modern field guns which outranged the standard
British 15pr field guns. The 12pr 8cwt naval field gun was no better than these,
so Scott mounted one of his ship's 12pr 12cwt guns on a field carriage improvised from two Cape waggon wheels, and a fourteen-foot baulk of timber
bought to make a towing target. Firing the same ammunition as the 8cwt
weapon, the 12pr 12cwt was designed for use at sea. It was much longer, forty
calibres as against twenty-eight, and had a correspondingly greater range of
8,000 yards. It was also a true Q/F gun. The gun barrel recoiled within its
mounting, resulting in greater accuracy and rate of fire when bolted onto the
timber trail. A complete Scott 12pr weighted in at 25cwt compared with 19cwt
for the less effective 15pr.

Scott admitted that the result looked amateurish, and it was prone to
capsize on rough ground. He had difficulty persuading anyone to take it seriously, but his chance came on 25 October when Sir George White *VC*, the
often maligned defender of Ladysmith, telegraphed:

> In view of heavy guns being brought by General Joubert from the north,
> I would suggest the Navy be consulted with the view of their sending
> here detachments of bluejackets with guns firing heavy projectiles at long
> ranges.[7]

Harris immediately offered two 4.7-inch guns, comparable to the Boer 6-
inch Creusot siege guns, but his flagship's Gunnery Lieutenant was unable
to design carriages for them. Scott, however, saw no more difficulty in
mounting a 4.7 than a 12pr, and by the following evening two 4.7 platform
mountings were ready for trial, the carpenters breaking their rule of 'only
working days (except on coffins)'.[8] These first 4.7-inch mountings were not
mobile, the ordinary ship's gun mounting bolted onto four pieces of timber

arranged crosswise. The parts travelled on waggons to be assembled where required, a lack of mobility that would not matter in the place they were destined to serve. On the evening of 27 October 1899 HMS *Powerful*, the sister to HMS *Terrible*, sailed for Durban with the two platform 4.7s, and three 12pr 12cwts on Scott carriages, with orders to take them up to Ladysmith.

THE SAVIOURS OF LADYSMITH (OCTOBER–NOVEMBER 1899)

Not everyone was overjoyed by this turn of events. *Powerful* had been on her way home, her men: 'as motley a collection as ever sailed consisting of chiefly men who had been three years on the China station'. Among them was Petty Officer Joseph Withecombe, who had joined the ship from a river gunboat employed on anti-piracy duties. His account of the beginnings of HMS *Powerful*'s Naval Brigade lacks the triumphalism of those written at a safer distance. The voyage from Mauritius, where she was diverted via the Cape, had been 'very interesting though a sad one', as arms and accoutrements were mustered, swords sharpened, and khaki suits run up from cloth provided at Captain Lambton's own expense. Recalling an earlier South African emergency, Lambton had also transported Mauritius' infantry garrison to Durban.

There the chances of war seemed to have diminished, to Withecombe's relief: 'What a load of anxiety seemed to have been lifted off each mind . . . everybody seemed glad enough to lay down their weapons', which made the return from Simonstown the more poignant:

> our minds are now filled with the awful reality of war with no other alternative this time. Many a poor fellow tried to put on a cheerful exterior but to one who is accustomed to human nature's mysteries it is impossible . . .

The *Powerful*'s Brigade went forward from Durban by train, packed into coal and cattle trucks that still bore their peacetime trademarks. Cheering crowds saw them off by torchlight, whilst 'four of the gentler sex held "The Flag that braved a thousand years the battle and the breeze"'.[9]

The Naval Brigade reached Ladysmith in the middle of the battle of Lombard's Kop. They detrained the three 12pr 12cwt guns under shellfire, and lashed them behind ox-waggons, moving off past a stream of ambulances and dhoolies that belied assurances of victory retailed by an ASC sergeant at the station. Hardly had the guns taken up a concealed firing position behind Limit Hill than came the 'hardly credible intelligence' of retreat:

> Our condition was critical in the extreme. There we were with our guns hitched up to bullock waggons . . . The shells were falling thick and fast around us and in fact the whole battle field was a ball of fire; every moment seemed like a century especially when the oxen would stop dead and shake their heads and bellow, as much to say they were going no further.

Pretoria's prison camps stared our heroes in the face, as a Boer shell blew the wheel off one of the 12prs, wounding three of the crew. However, the other two guns found a new firing position, and hit back at their tormentors, Gunner Sims silencing the gun on Pepworth Hill with his third round of common shell at 6,000–7,000 yards:

> This had the effect of dampening the enemy's ardour for the fray for their fire grew less severe and changed the whole aspect of affairs. It was the means of Ladysmith continuing in the hands of the British.[10]

More exalted witnesses than Withecombe took the same view. The semi-official historians of the Naval Brigades in South Africa had no doubt 'the sudden appearance of long range guns capable of paying the enemy back in his own coin . . . caused him to reflect and pause in his intended swoop on the town'.[11] Sir George White's last telegram before the Boers cut the line read: 'Your long 12-prs have been very useful to me today. Could you send as many more as possible to Pietermaritzburg and Durban with detachments to work them?'[12] Their immediate influence on the Boers, however, was limited to the Long Tom crew on Pepworth Hill who remained out of action all day. The failure of the Boers to follow up their success owed more to the natural caution of General Joubert who ignored the pleas of younger Boer leaders to 'Los jou ruiters'.[13]

The 4.7s with their platform mountings were unsuited to a fluid battle, and remained at the station until evening. It took two days, or rather nights, to install them in commanding positions on the north side of Ladysmith, where the Boers were expected to attack:

> These guns attracted much attention from everybody even our own artillery who wondered however Jack would mount them and many enquiries were made if the 12-inch shot ML (of which we had thirteen for

building the foundations) were to be fired from the guns. Rather a comical question.[14]

One of the 4.7s stayed in its original position throughout the siege. The other moved to the southern perimeter whenever relief looked imminent, until it became 'a sort of bird of ill omen and faces fell directly there was the slightest suggestion of moving it'.[15] The more mobile 12pr 12cwts shifted about in response to perceived Boer threats, while the 8cwt was relegated to close defence of the 4.7s. Lambton controlled naval operations from the 'Conning Tower', a redoubt on Gordon Hill above the Naval Brigade's camp, connected by telephone to White's HQ and the gun positions. At night seamen extended their originally modest parapets into huge sandbagged structures, piled up to the height of a man's head, with magazines and barbed-wire entanglements that even the builders could not negotiate.

After the siege, Sir George White paid especial tribute to the 4.7s, without which 'the guns of the Boers would have been brought into position very much nearer to my defence. That would have enormously embarrassed my power of resistance and would have added enormously to the mortality of the garrison.'[16] A letter captured during a sortie on 7 December 1899 shows that at least one Boer agreed:

It is very dangerous to attack the town. Near the town are two naval guns from which we receive very heavy fire which we cannot stand. I think there will be much blood spilt before they surrender, as Mr Englishman and his damn sailors fight hard . . .[17]

LORD METHUEN'S BLUNDER (NOVEMBER–DECEMBER 1899)

While HMS *Powerful*'s brigade became the stuff of legend at Ladysmith, Ethelston's brigade was kicking its heels at Stormberg. Recalled to their ships in mid-November, hard-bitten seamen wept with frustration at not having had a shot at 'they Boers', and two asked permission to disable their guns before handing them over to the Royal Artillery. Harris was playing his cards close to his chest, to mislead Boer sympathisers at Cape Town. A new Naval Brigade under Captain Prothero of HMS *Doris* set off immediately to join Lord Methuen's advance into the OFS. Just as the Transvaal Boers had stopped at Ladysmith, so the Free Staters sat down around the diamond town of Kimberley. The war resolved itself into British attempts to relieve the two towns.

[219]

Inexplicable optimism still infected the participants, Fleet Surgeon Porter writing that the expedition was urgent, 'for might not Methuen be in Kimberley ahead of us?'[18] Methuen, however, was plodding along the railway, with insufficient cavalry or imagination to outflank a succession of Boer positions covering the siege. Prothero's Naval Brigade first saw action at Belmont on 23 November after a confusing night march with uncooperative mules. It was nearly daylight before the guns were in range of the Boer position:

> Shelling began at once but with the first streaks of dawn our infantry already in position were to assault, and artillery fire had to cease after a few rounds. There was no time for our guns to 'prepare' the kopjes before the infantry advanced to what was known afterwards as the deadly frontal assault.

Fortunately for the victims of Methuen's tactics, the medical machine had improved since Peel's men carried wounded soldiers off from the Alma, 'every requirement of aseptic surgery was waiting ready to hand' at Belmont schoolhouse. The only naval men needing medical attention were two victims of sunstroke aggravated by: 'long abstinence – a night's march followed by a fight – and no breakfast till the bivouacs were reached in the afternoon'.[19]

Methuen appeared to regard a night march followed by a frontal attack on an empty stomach as the ideal battle plan. The Naval Brigade officers were dining off tinned kidneys and muddy water two days later when they received orders to lead the next attack:

> A thrill of excitement ran through the Brigade. 'By Jove, what sport!' said a midshipman. 'What luck!' said an officer of marines. 'Is it true, sir?' asked a company sergeant, radiant with the anticipation of an infantry job; everyone felt a sense of subdued joy and satisfaction that *something* was going to happen tomorrow.[20]

The attack at Graspan on 25 November was in the best Victorian tradition of heroism regardless of cost; 105 out of the 385 seamen and marines were hit.[21] Methuen's despatch attributed such heavy losses to the men bunching through inexperience, but the fault was his own for launching a frontal attack across a plain as flat as a billiard table, swept by sheets of Mauser bullets. Over half the men taking part were Royal Marines, long-service infantry who had practised kopje fighting around Simonstown under the officers who led them into action. It is hard to believe their training was inferior to that of the erstwhile garrison of Mauritius who formed the supports. The only two RMOs to survive the action both denied that the average extension was ever less than the original four paces. The men were a haphazard selection from several ships on the station, but they behaved like picked men, carefully lowering their sights as they closed the range. Many had to be held back to maintain the line's cohesion:

> The wounded fell silently – it was rare to hear even a moan – it was a blind rush on – then fall flat under the hail for a minute or two to draw breath then another rush – the natural feeling is to go forward to the invisible foe – never to go backwards – That would always be a deadly move with a second line of skirmishers advancing to take up the music.[22]

The Colonel of the King's Own Yorkshire Light Infantry, whose men supported the attack, thought he had never seen anything so magnificent in his life, but Admiral Harris was appalled. He had believed Methuen wanted artillery, and the marines had accompanied the guns to save Methuen's overstretched infantry providing escorts. However, Methuen made no better use of his artillery at Graspan than he had at Belmont. He deprived the naval 12prs, his most effective guns, of their mules, confining them to the railway some miles from the fighting. Lieutenant Dean was left in an exposed position under accurate fire that spattered his guns and ammunition waggons with shrapnel. Unable to drag his guns away without heavy casualties, he stood fast, making all hands lie down when the Boer guns flashed, until he had silenced his opponents.

Despite the strain thrown upon his depleted ship's companies, Harris sent up his Flag Captain, J.E. Bearcroft, with 120 replacements to take over command. All the naval officers with the brigade had been hit, so Captain A.E. Marchant RMLI, last met at Sawakin, took command, the first Royal Marine to command a mixed Naval Brigade of seamen and marines. Admiralty drafts filled up the smaller ships on blockade duty, but *Terrible* and *Powerful* were laid up for lack of men. The most powerful cruisers in the world were white elephants, too large for blockade work and enormous eaters of scarce coal.

Methuen made no particular use of the Naval Brigade at the Modder River and Magersfontein battles which rubbed in the tactical consequences of magazine rifles, smokeless powder, and an invisible enemy. A single 4.7-inch on a wheeled Scott carriage shelled the Magersfontein trenches, but could not silence the hidden riflemen. The Kimberley relief column ground to a halt close enough to its objective to signal to the defenders with another of Scott's inventions: a searchlight rigged on a railway truck with its own dynamo. The Naval Brigade settled down to lobbing a few shells into Boer trenches before the mirage built up in the morning, fighting with sand devils, and waiting for boiled water, the colour of pea soup, to cool. A man's most precious possession was his personal canvas water cooler.

NOISES OFF

The casualties at Graspan provoked unprecedented criticism, albeit: 'a dispute which happily died down early'.[23] A *Times* leader questioned the desirability of draining away naval personnel in military operations hundreds of miles from the sea, and received unusual support from the *Army and Navy Gazette*. The latter recognised the pressing need that had drawn Ethelston's brigade to the frontier and Lambton to Ladysmith, but accepted the argument that:

> our skilled seamen gunners and marine artillerymen, educated at great expense for a specific purpose, ought not to be wasted in assaulting positions with rifle in their hands, when less highly trained men would, in all probability, perform this kind of work equally well.[24]

The debate drew in one of the few parliamentary figures with relevant expertise. Sir John Colomb MP used *The Times* to protest at the 'growing practice of robbing warships of efficiency' by landing their crews as Naval Brigades. He had raised a question in the House of Commons about Ethelston's Brigade, but had been fobbed off. Colomb surmised that 'the Admiralty regarded the act of depriving Her Majesty's ships of effective fighting power as such a matter of routine that the First Lord himself was not sure to what extent this had been done':

> the habit of employing naval officers and seamen as land troops is now so common that the Admiralty did not think it worthwhile to find out the total number of officers and men sent away from the ships . . . or even what prospect there was of being able to recall [them] to the ships if necessary.

Colomb even mocked Scott's field carriages:

We hear much of the 4.7 and 12pr naval gun. They inspire awe and wonder in the uninitated, and music halls cheer the men who:

> 'Work their way to heaven
> To the tune of four point seven.'[25]

Unfortunately for Colomb's case, which deserved proper discussion, his letter was less a reasoned critique of using sailors ashore, than a partisan attack on the under-use of Royal Marines, in which corps Colomb had served. This confused the issue, but not before 'A Naval Officer' joined in to ask: 'What would the country have thought...if guns and men had not been sent in answer to an urgent request?'[26] Colomb's anti-naval agenda became apparent when he published extracts from a letter written by Major Plumbe, who had fallen out with Ethelston at Stormberg. Such use of a private letter so soon after both men died at Graspan seems insensitive even today, despite Ethelston's transparent pseudonym. Plumbe's letter, however, illustrates how inter-service strains could arise:

> 'A' is trying the same old naval game, ignoring everything we do well and taking all the credit. I try to be as polite as possible but it is a cursed service that places an old major of 42, grey and experienced, to work for a young naval officer of 34...Never have I cursed the Corps as I do now.[27]

Lieutenant W.T.C. Jones RMLI, himself wounded at Graspan, regretted that such letters should appear, 'some of which were not in good taste, and which tended to arouse a spirit of jealousy which happily did not exist. Do not Marines and Bluejackets making up a Naval Brigade belong to one and the same service?'[28] Some good may have come of it. The Cawdor 'New Scheme' of 1902 laid down that whenever naval work was on hand ashore, the senior officer should command, whether RN or RM.

Despite its personal overtones the debate revealed a pragmatic consensus on the use of Naval Brigades. It was admitted to be a very serious thing to cripple the two most powerful cruisers afloat by stripping them of their people for service ashore. On the other hand, 'Necessity has no law':

> the conditions on which Naval Brigades can be and ought to be employed in land warfare must not be too rigidly defined. In the last resort the question must be determined not by routine and red tape, but by common sense...All that we are concerned to insist is that the element of emergency ought to be regarded as one of the essential conditions.[29]

THE TUGELA FERRYMAN (DECEMBER 1899–MARCH 1900)

The element of emergency was certainly present in Natal after the Boers slammed the door shut on Ladysmith. Harris agreed with Sir Redvers Buller *VC*, the recently arrived Commander-in-Chief South Africa, that no more guns should be sent in response to White's last telegram, lest they fell into enemy hands. However, the two Commanders-in-Chief did send HMS *Terrible* to secure Durban. By 8 November, Captain Scott had imposed martial law, encircled the town with naval guns, prepared to barricade the streets, and sent a bluejacket to chalk the word 'Shut' on the door of a seditious newspaper. Never one to pass up a testimonial, Scott relates how years later the Boer leader Louis Botha told him that, but for those guns, the Transvaal's Vierkleur would have flown over Durban's Town Hall.[30]

Scott's guns also impressed Buller: on 7 November he requested a 'small naval brigade' armed with two 4.7s on 'travelling carriages' and four 12pr 12cwt guns. The most blimpish looking of the British generals in South Africa, Buller would make better use of his naval guns than any of them, developing a pattern of infantry-artillery cooperation that would be commonplace in future wars. Unfortunately for Buller's reputation, it took him some time to develop the new technique. His first attempt to breach the Boer lines along the Tugela River, covering the siege of Ladysmith, collapsed at Colenso on 15 December, four days after Methuen's defeat at Magersfontein.

Eight more 12prs had reinforced the Naval Brigade, which fought as two six-gun batteries.[31] Captain Pitcairn Jones of HMS *Forte*, an unofficial spectator at El Teb, commanded the two heavy guns with four 12prs on Gun Hill on the left, while Lieutenant Ogilvy took six 12prs forward to support Colonel Long's RFA brigade on the right. Gun Hill opened fire at 5.20 a.m. on a lovely cloudless morning so still that many thought the Boers had gone. Soon after the infantry went forward at 5.40 there was no question whether the Boers were there or not, as they 'opened a tremendous fire from every imaginable direction, from miles of rifle pits along the river . . . and from guns placed everywhere . . . commanding every approach'. These were hard to locate even with the 4.7s' telescopic sights, being 'beautifully concealed and firing mostly smokeless powder'.[32]

Jones had a relatively quiet time, as the Boers fired at more immediate targets, but Ogilvy was caught crossing a donga. Two guns jammed in the drift, the wheels of the waggon-limbers locked together, and the oxen turned round in their yokes. However, all six guns came into action, although it was 'a stiff piece of work'. Unlike Long's RFA they remained so, being 300 yards further back:

We tried to crush the trench-fire, but what could two lyddite guns do when there were numberless trenches? . . . In some cases we silenced the Boer guns absolutely, but there were some so placed that we could not see them. The naval guns did good work, but their hands were too full. We wanted many more long-range guns. But even so without taking Hlangwani Hill (*sic*), it was an almost impossible position to get through.[33]

Several naval officers criticised the lack of heavy artillery. Scott claimed that half a dozen 6-inch guns would have opened the road to Ladysmith three months early, and blamed Harris for their absence. The Admiral would have been happy to take 6-inch guns from his two white elephants, rather than stripping his blockading squadron of their main armament of 4.7s, but he thought 6-inch guns too heavy for field work.[34] The one 6-inch used on the Tugela front required triple teams, and only achieved maximum range by sinking the trail in a hole, limiting choice of targets. Such weapons could never have achieved the tactical mobility of the 4.7s, which were themselves quite capable of finding soft patches of ground, or falling through bridges.

There was little to do until sufficient reinforcements arrived to force the Tugela. The naval guns were the only British unit able to hit the Boer positions. Naval officers measured ranges from Gun Hill, studied the country through their long telescopes, and harassed the Boers at odd hours. It is doubtful whether they did much physical damage, Boer working parties diving for cover when they saw the gun flash. Jones thought their guns had alternative positions, keeping out of harm's way until needed: 'Except on the 15th during the action I myself have never seen one gun since we have been here.'[35] Even naval guns shot poorly at ranges of 7,000–12,000 yards, but they moved one Boer to threaten to crucify 'those straw-hatted gunners'. On the British side, Gun Hill became a social focus, known as Liar's Hill for the monstrous rumours started there, while soldiers and journalists queued for their first glimpse of a live Boer through a naval telescope. There were three of these, with a magnification of forty diameters. Naval observers honed their skills until they could pick out the raised leaf of the back sights on Boer rifles silhouetted against the skyline at 2,000 yards. Ogilvy felt they would rather have lost a gun than injured their telescopes.

On 10 January 1900 Buller moved west from his railhead at Chieveley, to seek the Boer right flank at Spion Kop and Vaal Kraantz, west of Colenso, on the north bank of the Tugela. The Naval Brigade's part in the abortive series of battles that followed was slight, although they had a ringside view of the fighting from their position on Mount Alice, a thousand feet above the river. Daily they shelled the Boer positions, and watched the enemy through their long glasses:

> At one end of the hilltop . . . perhaps thirty Boers. Fifteen of them sitting with their rifles between their knees and their backs against the boulders, screening them from our infantry. The rest were beautifully under cover, picking off and driving back our men. Why will not our Tommies do as the Boers do? – crawl on hands and knees and do anything to get cover and shoot from cover.[36]

Lieutenant C.R.N. Burne took two 12prs across Potgeiter's Drift, the pont repaired by bluejackets, to support the troops on Spion Kop:

> We ourselves were all dead beat, but had to be up all night with searchlights working on the Boer main position; but what of poor Warren's force after five days constant marching and fighting?[37]

Next day came the depressing news that Spion Kop had been evacuated:

> Incredible! But the long glass confirms it. The Boers are there, many with two rifles, gathering up water bottles, leather gear, and trophies of that sort.[38]

A pair of naval 12prs had set off on the roundabout route to Spion Kop after the Royal Artillery refused to take guns up there. The Naval Lieutenant, by contrast, 'would go anywhere and would have a try anyway. He was quite sure that if he could get to the top of the hill he would knock out the Boer guns, or be knocked out by them', a logic it is hard to deny.[39] Luckily for him, he met Spion Kop's defenders coming down before he reached the top.

A diversionary attack by the King's Royal Rifle Corps the day before the evacuation had demonstrated a more hopeful style of infantry-artillery cooperation:

> They took about two hours climbing up, our guns keeping down fire and throwing shells over the hills towards the enemy position. A fortunate shot by Lt Hunt burst a lyddite shell on the conical top and cleared it just before they made their final rush to the summit.[40]

All naval guns now carried telescopic sights allowing precise aiming. The crosswires had obscured such narrow targets as a trench at 5,000 yards, so

strands of cobweb were stuck on with torpedo compound. The guns themselves, however, began to show signs of wear. None of them were new when
landed, having generally fired 300–400 rounds, half the normal barrel life.
The constant use of full charges at maximum elevation wore out the barrels.
They fired so many rounds during the stalemated battle of Vaal Kraantz (5
February) that one 4.7 became 'most erratic owing to the gun having become
eroded, there being a difference of as much as 1,000 yards with the gun laid
at exactly the same elevation'.[41] Nevertheless the naval guns began to get the
better of the Boer guns, the long range of hills beyond Vaal Kraantz ablaze
with their shells, lurid and desolate. Burne's men were exhausted when
Buller gave up his stalled offensive on 7 February. Asleep on their feet, they
covered the retreat across Potgeiter's, still strangely confident that the C-in-
C knew best.

Back at Chieveley, the Naval Brigade was reinforced to its peak strength
with a 6-inch gun, so heavy it bent its railway truck, and three more 4.7s, two
on platforms and one on a railway truck. The only human reinforcements
were fifty men with the 6-inch and another dozen with the 4.7s, so Jones
made up gun crews from the Natal Naval Volunteers, whose local knowledge proved invaluable on trek, with soldiers as ammunition numbers. The
Admiralty recognised the urgency of the army's demands for naval guns, but
instructed Harris not to land any more bluejackets.

Buller at last realised the weakness of the Boer left, where Hlangwane's
defenders had their backs to the river. Barton's brigade with Ogilvy's 12prs
began knocking away the props: Hussar Hill, Cingolo, Monte Christo.
Fighting was so far from Gun Hill by 18 February that Jones could hardly
hear it. His report to Harris on the vexed question of ammunition supply
broke off dramatically:

> 10a.m. – I have just received wire from the General that our troops had
> captured Cingolo and advanced down the neck and are now about to
> attack Monte Christo. Heavy gun fire is now going on.[42]

Jones' next report came from Ladysmith, after ten days' heavy fighting in
which naval guns played a key role: 'all our guns being used to keep their [i.e.
the Boers'] fire down'.[43] The advance of the Naval Brigade, from one gun
position to another, 'over fat boulders, over bushes and young trees, crash-
ing along like elephants'[44] showed why 6-inch guns would never have done.
When Hlangwane fell on 19 February they marched over the mountain itself,
'one of the worst pieces of ground it is possible to imagine, bad enough in
the day time, but a thousand times worse at night . . . a good test of the

strength of the gun carriages'.[45] The Boers abandoned Colenso, allowing two 4.7s and four 12prs across the river to support the Irish Brigade's abortive frontal attack on Railway Hill on 23 February. Jones took the big glass forward to look for Boer guns, 40pr shells falling around him. His coxswain lost half his thigh, torn off by a pom-pom shell: 'fortunately it did not burst as there was a little knot around the glass where an officer was pointing out the position of a gun to me'.

Buller now had plenty of artillery, with eighty guns in action around Colenso and Hlangwane, including four RGA 5-inch guns and six 5-inch howitzers besides the six heavy naval guns. He made his winning move on the night of 25/26 February when the Naval Brigade emplaced two platform 4.7s on Hlangwane, dominating Pieter's Hill, the army's next objective:

> not wishing to do it in daylight as we were only 2,300 yards from the enemy's highest position . . . It was very heavy and tiresome work in the dark, a glimmer of light to the front always produced some sniping on this as on every occasion.

In the morning the RE threw their pontoon bridge over the river again, ready for a determined and well-planned attack next day: 'on that great day the *27th* I not only saw every detail of the fight from relatively close to, but also saw the finest shooting I have ever seen in my life . . .' Once set up and ranged in, a platform mounting could achieve shipboard rates of fire and accuracy. Jones watched Patrick Cashman, 'a born gunner', put three lyddite shells into the embrasure of a troublesome Boer gun in one minute.

The great contribution of the naval guns was to shoot in the infantry in a way that had never been done before. The Royal Irish Fusiliers advanced past the gun positions at 7.30 a.m., their colonel pointing out the line of advance across Jones' front: 'The battle was half won before they started.'[46] Pieter's fell by 2.30 p.m., Ogilvy's six 12prs firing 190 rounds in the last fifty minutes of the attack, some landing fifteen yards from the advancing infantry. There followed a tremendous bombardment of Railway Hill. Jones thought it 'a wonderful sight to see our men in the open creeping up to the trenches':

> The naval people with their powerful glasses could follow every detail of the fight, and could be perfectly sure of what they were doing. Besides we thoroughly knew the plan of attack . . . rather took the bit between our teeth and went our own way, confidently knowing the general's wishes.

Messages came from the staff officers saying that our fire was dangerous and did we know what we were doing? We did and we meant that until Tommy was right up and on top, the Boer riflemen should not have a chance. The closer we got the more lyddite we poured into them, till white flags began to wave in the Railway Hill trenches. Then we saw the final rush and the bayonet at work.[47]

Unable to stand the coordinated pressure of infantry and guns, the Boers broke, and Buller's army finally breached the Tugela line. The German military attaché said it was a wonder, and he does not seem to have exaggerated. Burne inspected the intricate Boer trenches above Colenso. Blasted out of six to eight feet-thick rock, with loopholed stone conning towers dominating the road, they were a revelation compared with the modest 'prepare to dig trench' exercise of the drill book. Buller's whole force advanced on Ladysmith, after a day refitting for further fighting, but the Boers had all gone. Jones rode ahead to see Lambton, finding him and all his brigade 'looking very ill and worn – all his Lieutenants but one in hospital and many men sick'.

The siege had not lived up to the drama of its opening. The Boer distaste for heroics made it more of a blockade, to be resolved by hunger and disease, rather than active siege operations. Casualties from enemy action were few, although the death of Lieutenant Egerton on Monday 2 November had a sobering effect on those inclined to regard the siege as 'a sort of land picnic'. Mournful Monday was an unreliable portent of what was to come, although a returning PO told the *Hampshire Telegraph* that 'all through the siege the big Boer guns paid particular attention to the Naval Brigade', forcing them to move camp twice. The Boer gunners would 'watch for the arrival of a barrel of ginger beer which used to be brought into camp, and when the men congregated around it to get a drink a shell would be discharged at it'. Rations were issued in proportion to the perceived chances of relief, falling to three quarters of a pound of horse per day, sometimes disguised as sausage or 'potted tongue', and one and a half pounds of bread. The anonymous PO brought a piece of Ladysmith siege bread home for Portsmouth's City Museum. Made from ground mealies stuck together with starch, and surprisingly heavy for its size, the bread looked like sandstone, and easily crumbled to pieces. The only fresh vegetable was wild spinach gathered on the hillside around Ladysmith: 'boiled up with rock salt it proved a most acceptable dish to men pining for some variety to the everlasting horse and bread'.[48]

The *Hampshire Telegraph* also published the diary of Yeoman of Signals

A.C. Bradley.[49] This provides a unique record of the siege from a lower-deck point of view, as Withecombe's journal breaks off before Mournful Monday. Suet, sugar, and milk were luxuries by the end of December, a dozen eggs fetching a sovereign: a week's wages for a working man at home. The tea ration was interrupted in January, particularly disheartening after news of Spion Kop. Everyone was played out towards the end of the siege, their rifles an unwelcome burden. Nevertheless, after their liberation, the men marched from Pieter's Hill to Colenso, where the railway began again, dragging their 12pr 8cwt and four Maxims down a long dusty road marked by wooden crosses and the stench of dead horses. The people of Durban and Simonstown did their best to feed up their deliverers, giving them enough fruit and stout to last the voyage home. Our PO put on fifty pounds, but some of his shipmates were too sick to enjoy the luxuries provided for them. Fleet-Paymaster W.H.F. Kay, a veteran of the Zulu War, who had bought up the last beer in Ladysmith for £30, died of enteric at Ascension.

Others, too weak to travel, remained in the neutral hospital set up outside Ladysmith. Captain Jones visited them on 13 March, 'some looked dreadfully ill and all longing to get away'. Twenty-seven Naval Brigade personnel died of disease during the siege, compared with six killed and five wounded, including two bluejackets blown up dismantling an unexploded 6-inch shell. The river water was much to blame for the sickness, a copious draught having the same effect as four ounces of Epsom salts and half a pint of castor oil mixed. Perhaps the most significant naval contribution to the outcome of the siege was clean water. Chief Engineer Sheen and his artificers improvised condensers from corrugated-iron tanks, 500 yards of coiled water pipe, and some locomotive boilers, producing 1,500 gallons a day, until coal ran out in January.

The enemy restricted themselves to harassing fire: 'Even the cattle regard the Boers with contempt.'[50] The only Boer offensive was at Waggon Hill on 6 January. By chance the Junction Hill 4.7 had gone there to cooperate with an imaginary relief effort. Most of the fighting fell upon the Devons and Gordon Highlanders, but Gunner Sims and a dozen bluejackets twice restored the situation at critical moments directed by Sims in his best fo'c'stle voice. The *Hampshire Telegraph*'s sub-headings to Bradley's diary after Waggon Hill reveal the tedium of a siege where the only news came from the *Ladysmith Lyre* or the imaginations of black runners: 'Depressed And On Short Rations', 'So Near And Yet So Far'. Even the jokes in the *Lyre*'s competitor, the *Bombshell*, were stale: 'The Convent is now empty: Nun left'.[51]

TOWARDS GUERRILLA WAR (APRIL–OCTOBER 1900)

The siege of Ladysmith ended just after the relief of Kimberley and the surrender of a complete Boer army at Paardeburg. Lord Roberts had superseded Buller as Commander-in-Chief after Colenso, leaving the latter with only the Natal front. Roberts began his drive through the Boer Republics on 11 February with far more troops than Buller or Methuen ever had. He asked for two more 4.7s, but he did not depend on the coordinated use of infantry and artillery.[52] The flat open veld of the OFS allowed wide outflanking movements around the Boers' defensive positions, and there was no call for massed gunfire to blast them out of their trenches. At Paardeburg the Naval Brigade competed with the RA's howitzers in demolishing Boer waggons, but caused few casualties among their owners, safe in their dugouts.

Bearcroft's Naval Brigade clocked up some astonishing mileages during Roberts' advance but never played the pivotal role of Jones' Brigade on the Tugela, where Buller had said, 'it would never quite be known how much the success of the assault was due to the naval gun fire'.[53] Bearcroft's exhausting marches showed just how mobile big guns could be, strolling away from the RA's 6-inch howitzers. The navy's marching powers were a revelation, one detachment of 4.7s travelling thirty-seven miles in twenty-five hours:

> If the naval guns have done nothing else than this they would have left an indelible mark on the campaign, and indeed in all probability, upon military tactics. No longer will military powers be contented with 12 and 15prs as field guns, since British seamen have shown them that even a 100pr can be made to accompany the passage of an army.[54]

Disappointed in their hopes of 'a show', the Naval Brigade's bilious yellow guns at Bloemfontein and Pretoria were a powerful reminder of the sea-power that had made it possible for a British Army to reach the heart of the OFS and Transvaal.

The fall of the Boer capitals did not end the war, however. Many Boers refused to recognise defeat, and attacked British forces around Pretoria. Grant's guns supported counter-insurgency operations around Lindley and Heilbron in May and June 1900. Boer commandos swarmed around the supposedly victorious British, the 4.7s moving and firing alternately to keep the enemy at a respectful distance. Heilbron had to be evacuated, the Naval Brigade on the last train out, a leading inhabitant on the locomotive praying loudly for his own safety and that of his captors. Hoping to scotch this people's war, Roberts pursued the fugitive Boer Governments east, towards Portuguese Mozambique. Two of Bearcroft's 12prs were in at the end of the regular campaign at Koomati Poort in August, travelling further east than any other naval guns. They covered ninety miles in nine days, the powerful ten-mule teams requiring the most careful seamanship to negotiate the hairpin bends in the Kaap Mountains. In the Crocodile Valley, masses of partially destroyed arms and ammunition lay beside the railway, the heat from blazing truckloads of mealies, sugar and coffee making the stifling atmosphere almost intolerable. The main Boer Army had escaped across the border.

The relief of Ladysmith did not end the fighting in Natal either. The RGA took over most of Jones' guns, and the naval detachments followed *Powerful*'s men back to Durban, releasing *Terrible* for the China station. Jones's attenuated brigade of two 4.7s and four 12prs shared with Bearcroft the opening moves of a guerrilla war that would continue until May 1902.[55] The Boers had already shown new fight at Elandslaagte, north of Ladysmith, shelling the British camp from the surrounding hills. The naval guns calmly spread out and returned fire, the native drivers earning Jones' admiration for the cool way they inspanned their grazing oxen amidst the shells. The Brigade had a last opportunity in June to demonstrate their skills in close fire support. Buller moved north to join up with Roberts' forces, but had to force strong Boer positions in the Drakensberg Mountains to do so. To reach their firing positions at Botha's Pass, the Naval Brigade dismounted their guns and dragged them up in waggons behind triple ox teams, all in darkness and mist:

> General Hildyard was good enough to say it was the record performance of the campaign and I think it was (except getting them down again).

The Boers were astonished to find British guns in a position they themselves had failed to occupy. Much was heard throughout the war of the superior mobility of Boer guns, but they invariably used much easier routes to reach their firing positions than it appeared from the front. Jones never saw a Boer gun position that he could not have occupied, and claimed to have reached many more difficult ones. General Coke, the brigade commander, thanked Jones for his support at Botha's Pass, and again at Alleman's Nek, where the Naval Brigade searched the dongas and ridges up which the infantry had to advance:

but for it their casualties would have been doubled – we kept on shelling a little in advance of our leading troops and where we saw the Boers thickest until they retired.[56]

The Admiralty were pressing Harris to withdraw his men, now the emergency was over. Asked to fill Bearcroft's vacancies he replied: 'Cannot be done. Naval Brigade should all be sent back to their ships the moment the Field Marshal can spare them.'[57] The Foreign Office wanted ships for Zanzibar, Accra, and Lagos. Buller released his Naval Brigade without delay. Burne thought Jones did not know whether to be glad or sorry: 'Such is the Naval Service, here one day and off the next.'[58] General Hildyard, with whom Jones had worked since December 1899, asked to see him before he left, the General being ill in bed.

He said he had been proud to command us, that the Naval Brigade had always been so thoroughly reliable. Wherever and whenever the guns were wanted they invariably got there, often in the face of great difficulties. They have got their gear into positions where people said it was impossible to get them. Never in the course of the campaign have I been disappointed in their getting wherever wanted.[59]

HMS *Forte*'s men rejoined their ship on 25 June leaving two small detachments in Natal with the 12prs. Burne had asked to stop and see it out, although his appetite for soldiering was much diminished by jaundice and other ills of the flesh. From a vantage point on Grass Kop he watched ineffectual British attempts to catch Boer laagers which only dispersed them, providing the fuel for 'a guerrilla warfare of small actions and runaway fights at long range', which furnished few discoveries for Naval gunners. The Admiralty stepped up their efforts to regain control of Bearcroft's scattered Brigade. They asked Harris to report which ships were still inefficient through men landed for Naval Brigades: 'No ship actually inefficient, but I fear good order and discipline may suffer from continued absence of officers.'[60] In mid-July he reported there were thirty officers and 337 men still ashore, and most of them stayed there until October 1900. One seaman, drafted into a troop of light horse, only reappeared when he rejoined his ship voluntarily in January 1901. Men could disappear quite easily in wartime, when even a railway waggon of lyddite shells might vanish for weeks.

COMING HOME

The Admiralty's slowness to distribute rewards to the South African Naval Brigades was at odds with the enthusiasm that greeted HMS *Powerful*'s return to Portsmouth on 11 April. Not a single naval officer appeared in the Queen's Birthday honours in May 1900:

> 'Thank God', exclaimed a distinguished Admiral in the 'Senior' on Wednesday, 'they've left the Navy out altogether this time; now perhaps some notice will be taken of the matter'.[61]

Even some of the Board were alleged to be embarrassed by such shabbiness. By contrast, hundreds waited on Southsea beach, despite the drizzle and chilly wind that swept over the Solent, to see the big cruiser, dressed rainbow fashion, enter the Harbour. The entire garrison lined the fortifications, while HMS *Victory* and *St Vincent* manned their tops and rigging. The Queen reviewed the Brigade at Windsor, Lloyd's of London gave them dinner, arms piled in the Royal Exchange, and Portsmouth provided a magnificent reception. One of the subscribers was old Admiral Raby who had won the *VC* at Sebastopol. Such celebrations were not without precedent. The same committee at Portsmouth had organised a reception for HMS *St George*, after a commission that included Naval Brigades at Mwele and Benin.

What was unusual was the level of public excitement, verging on hysteria. Portsmouth was decorated as never before, even for the Diamond Jubilee. The streets were a mass of red, white, and blue. *Powerful*'s own white ensign that had flown throughout the siege was displayed at the naval recruiting office by the Hard. Even the ugliness of the railway bridge was temporarily concealed by wreaths of honour. Inside the Town Hall incandescent electric lights formed the letters RN in patriotic colours. Children from the Royal Seamen's and Marines' Orphans Home sang '*Home Sweet Home*' and '*The Lads of the Naval Brigade*', followed by little Miss Lillian Albert reciting '*The Handy Man*', in a wonderfully accurate manner. Before the toast of the evening, boys dressed as sailors wheeled a model 4.7 onto the stage and fired a salute. When the men came to return to the Dockyard, the immense mass of people outside broke all barriers, forcing them to slip out the side entrance.

It was all a bit too much for some. The *Army and Navy Gazette* complained of the 'gushing manner in which certain sections of the public are treating the seamen of the *Powerful*, forgetting that others had also been in South Africa'.[62] It was certainly too much for one seaman who appeared before the magistrates, charged with disorderly behaviour: 'people kept on treating him to drink and it overcame him'.[63] The Admiralty set their faces against further shenanigans, declining a proposal from Liverpool Corporation to entertain the *Powerful's* crew: 'In the interests of the Service, it is necessary that there should be no more delay in the paying off of the ship.'[64]

Public interest continued, however. Village committees presented watches to local men, livery companies dined naval officers, and Captain Lambton opened a stall in aid of Disabled Sailors and Soldiers at the Military Bazaar at Olympia: 'The historical 4.7 is to appear on each side of the entrance.'[65] In fact, this was a copy run up at HMS *Excellent* to appear at the Royal Military Tournament at Islington. A great attraction to Londoners in previous years, the tournament was especially interesting after recent events: 'for the first time in this country a 4.7 is to be drawn around the arena, a feat which naval men themselves would last year have declared to be simply impossible'.[66]

The Boer War was the largest war the British fought between 1815 and 1914, drawing in almost half a million British soldiers. The Naval Brigades' share was numerically less significant than in smaller colonial conflicts. However, their overall importance was more than arithmetical comparisons suggest. One Naval Brigade intervened at a decisive moment at Ladysmith, providing a much needed boost to morale. Another developed new tactics that cleared the way for the relief force. Contemporaries drew explicit parallels with Peel's exploits, the youngest participants in which were now old enough to be senior Admirals. As in the Crimea and India, Naval Brigades brought a robust self-sufficiency to a war in which the soldiers often seemed to be hapless victims. *Globe and Laurel* described how a whole infantry brigade passed a nice dry tree, ideal for firewood:

> Nearly at the tail of the column came two naval 4.7 guns . . . there was a yell from the Naval Brigade, and in five minutes that tree was reposing on the limbers . . . The Naval Brigade I may remark, generally had full stomachs and always had a scrap of something to eat in their haversacks; they were rare foragers, and never left anything eatable behind them.[67]

The Naval Brigades' small size was a logistical advantage, as they could finish off odd items, insufficient for a battalion of infantry. The army seem to have been genuinely pleased to be supported by the navy, except perhaps when some stokers stole the Coldstream Guards' geese. Burne regretted leaving his friends in the Queen's Royal Regiment at Grass Kop, while Jones wrote:

The men got on very well with the soldiers and the officers tell me their men were always glad when told off as our escort – though it often meant considerable hard work in assisting to drag the guns through dongas, etc.[68]

Before the last of the South African Naval Brigades had returned on board, their shipmates on the China squadron were in action on their own. This time they would travel beyond the muddy estuary of the Peiho, to the Forbidden City itself.

THE BOXER REBELLION (MAY–AUGUST 1900)

If the Boxer Rebellion is remembered at all today, it is for the siege of the international Legations in Peking. Most of the garrison were seamen or marines of various nationalities, but the conflict has a wider naval interest. Its opening stages were sustained by 7,000 sailors and marines from warships moored off the mouth of the Peiho River. These came from the Austrian, German, Italian, Japanese, Russian, and United States navies, besides the Royal Navy. A participant even titled his account: *The World's Navies and the Boxer Rebellion.*[69] British military units were scarce throughout the conflict, the Boer War having overstretched British resources as the Indian Mutiny had done in the 1850s. The Boxer Rebellion was a searing experience for the sailors and marines caught up in it. Battle casualties were proportionally far higher than in South Africa, racial feeling and the cruelty of the conflict causing an unusual degree of mutual antipathy between the antagonists. One of the most dramatic episodes in the history of Naval Brigades, the Boxer Rebellion was the last time such formations would be employed on so large a scale.

The events of the Boxer Rebellion of 1900 form a more complex narrative than a view centred on the Legations might suggest. Chinese insurgents, the Society of Righteous Harmonious Fists, hence Boxers, overran the whole area around Peking and the foreign 'concessions' at Tientsin. The latter had to be secured before any relief force could set off for the beleaguered Legations. 'Concessions' and 'leases' to foreign powers during the late nineteenth century, and the activities of Christian missionaries, provoked an understandable Chinese reaction against foreign interference in the 1890s. Attacks on railways and mission stations became serious enough in May 1900 for British representatives in Peking and Tientsin to request help from the Royal Navy's China squadron.

The Commander-in-Chief, Vice-Admiral Sir Edward Seymour, had twice seen service in China, and was unwilling to resort to force:

The general history of our dealings with China has been that we have forced ourselves upon them and into their country. I believe we are too apt to forget this.[70]

The Consul at Tientsin urged 'active measures of hostility', but Seymour demurred: 'Our mission here was solely for the protection of European lives.'[71] He simply reinforced existing diplomatic guards: seventy-six Royal Marines at Peking with a .45 calibre Nordenfeldt, a naval armourer, signal-man, and sick berth attendant; 130 seamen and marines at the Tientsin Consulate with a 9pr RML gun. A telegram from the Legations on 9 June hardened Seymour's attitude: unless Peking were relieved soon it would be too late. Such was his confidence that he started without awaiting Admiralty approval, hoping his colleagues would cooperate. Such was his authority that they did. Over the next two days an international Naval Brigade of four trains and 2,072 men set off along eighty miles of sabotaged railway line from Tientsin to Peking.[72]

A headline in the *Army and Navy Gazette* misleadingly described this expe-dition as Seymour's Dash to Peking. The international column moved slowly, replacing hundreds of yards of torn up track, and never got more than half-way to Peking. It saw off several Boxer attacks, almost without Allied loss, but saboteurs cut the line behind them. On 18 June Imperial troops, recognisable by their banners and magazine rifles, joined the Boxers. Already nervous about the supply situation, the Allies abandoned their trains and personal gear, including the officers' full-dress uniforms, which they had hoped to wear in Peking, and retreated down the left bank of the Peiho. Fifty wounded and the heavy weapons followed in four junks. The next few days were a nightmare, marching sixteen hours a day on half rations under continual fire with a steady toll of casualties. One of them was John Jellicoe, Seymour's Flag Captain, wounded leading a bayonet charge. Had the Boxers shot a little better, they might have changed the course of the Battle of Jutland. A Reuters correspondent with the column was under-standably depressed: 'The great matter for anxiety is the ammunition supply . . . When it is finished I am much afraid the column is finished also.'[73] Luckily for him his messmates were too busy to think; 'the midshipman of fourteen cheering on his half-company with a heavy heart and an empty stomach, or the bluejacket or marine marching without boots "to save his feet"'.[74]

By the small hours of 22 June the Allies were at the end of their tether. They had lost their guns, were short of ammunition, and the junks were overflowing with wounded. All the puggarees from the marines' and officers' helmets had gone for bandages. By accident the column stumbled across and captured a Chinese arsenal at Hsiku. Here they found food and cover, as well as enormous quantities of arm and ammunition. Seymour commented drily, 'prospects were now somewhat better than they had been'.[75] He could hold out more or less indefinitely, but 230 wounded were too many to remove.[76] There had been no news from Tientsin since 13 June.

Seymour had left Captain Edward Bayly of HMS *Aurora* in charge of the British forces at Tientsin. He had instructions to maintain rail links with the relief force, but this became impossible as Boxers ripped up the track within sight of the railway station. Significant reinforcements arrived, including 150 bluejackets under Commander David Beatty of HMS *Barfleur*, just before the Boxers cut telegraphic and rail links between Tientsin and the Allied squadron on 15 June. Sniping and incendiarism began at once, with heavy fighting on the 18th and 19th when regular Chinese soldiers joined the Boxers.

The pivotal events of the rising took place at Taku, a traditional flashpoint for Sino-European relations. The Allied attack on the Forts on 17 June at once intensified the conflict, and contained the seeds of its resolution. Senior naval officers thirteen miles off the shallow Peiho estuary, and in imperfect touch with events ashore, were alarmed by Chinese troop movements and rumours of electrically detonated mines. Fearful for Tientsin and Seymour's column, which had vanished into thin air, a council of war decided to take control of the Forts, with or without Chinese agreement. This may have provoked the Imperial Army to join the Boxers attacking Seymour and Tientsin, or it may have pre-empted deliberate Chinese military action. Either way, it allowed the relief of Tientsin on 23 June by a mixed force, including a party under Commander Cradock of HMS *Alacrity*.[77] Coincidentally with the reinforcements came news of Seymour's force surrounded in the Hsiku Arsenal, a happy conjunction resulting in their rescue and return to Tientsin on 26 June.

International forces were strong enough to capture Tientsin's Walled City on 13–14 July. Most of the Naval Brigades returned to their ships by 20 July, some returning for the relief of Peking in August with three 12pr 12cwt guns on Scott carriages, the only naval guns to reach the Imperial City.

NEW ENEMIES FOR OLD

Even this bald narrative shows that the Boxer Rebellion far exceeded any previous conflict with China. The hawkish *Army and Navy Gazette* complained that the navy had been asked to undertake military operations once too often:

> the Powers have been so busily engaged in trying to secure a generous portion of the leviathan's inheritance that they forgot the leviathan. So far from being dead, as they have all taken for granted, he seems to be very much alive and boiling with fanatical passion.[78]

This was certainly true of the Boxers, who possessed a supreme indifference to rifle fire. A participant in Seymour's Dash commented on the awful unreality of mowing them down a few yards from the trains. The big .45 calibre bullets of the Maxim laid them down in heaps, while the humane nickel-coated rounds of the Lee Metfords 'failed altogether to stop these pertinacious swordsmen, unless it struck a vital spot'.[79] The only fatal casualties the Boxers appear to have inflicted in the early stages of the Dash were five Italian sailors caught playing cards, when they should have been keeping watch. The Boxers had more effect as exponents of low-level popular resistance. Masses of Chinese tore up the railway track with their hands, lit fires beneath bridges, and twisted the rails in the flames of burning sleepers. Bluejacket railwaymen worked with a will, seeming to enjoy the novel experience, but the extent of the damage exceeded the resources available for repairs. A repair train sent after Seymour was still in sight from Tientsin a day later. Bayly also had to deal with mass obstruction at the station; 'doubling a company up and down the platform, the Chinese flying in all directions'.[80]

Not all Chinese supported the Boxers, but the insurgents could force them to remove supplies, or use them as cover for spies and snipers who infested the Tientsin settlement. Those caught were instantly shot, but 'nothing seemed to check the system of espionage which enabled the Chinese to know the time and meaning of every movement which took place'.[81] It was impossible to expel all native Chinese, as many were Christian refugees facing torture and death at the hands of the Boxers. Other moral dilemmas, typical of later 'People's Wars', became apparent during the retreat to Hsiku. It was found necessary to burn the villages: 'a tiresome and disgusting task'. Officers were distressed to see old people sitting by the remains of their homes, and tried to stop their sorely tried men from roughing up the inhabitants: 'peaceful villagers wot sells us chickens by day and snipes by night'.[82]

The Boxers may have been an ill-armed rabble, but the Imperial Chinese Army was 'a hardy and arrogant foe, who believed in their leaders and their cause'.[83] Western military assistance had made the Chinese soldiers of 1900 a different proposition to the nursery bogeymen of the 1860s, with their wooden swords and rocket spears. Sergeant G.F. Cooper RMLI was trapped in the Hsiku arsenal during Seymour's Dash. He found boxes full of the latest weapons, complete with instruction manuals:

> it struck me how foolish the nations were to train Orientals in the arts of modern warfare or supply them with such materials ... There seemed to be everything required for war, from the old round shot of the old muzzle-loader and wood fuzes to the latest quick-firing guns and ammunition ... And someone told me afterwards at home that we only had to fight against bows and arrows.[84]

Chinese regulars had knocked over six of his section of fifteen Royal Marines with one volley: '"They can shoot after all", remarked one of ours.'[85] Ambushes were a favourite tactic. One at Tientsin claimed fifteen casualties within a few minutes, including Commander Beatty, whom they hit twice. Chinese gunners had modern artillery pieces that outranged anything available to British Naval Brigades, and knew how to use them from concealed positions. Seamen gunners made up for their poor equipment with skill and courage. Bayly posted a 9pr 'under the wall of the Consulate from the roof of which a good view could be obtained, in the hope that by directions from the roof we should be able to silence the Chinese field guns which were entirely hidden from our position by a half burnt village'.[86] Two or three shells did the job, but not before return fire mortally wounded Lieutenant Wright in the head, souvenir photographs of his mangled binoculars appearing in contemporary albums with gruesome snapshots of Boxer atrocities.

Chinese infantry rarely stood a charge with bayonets, but their training and morale was not much inferior to that of their naval opponents. Despite heavy losses in previous engagements, General Nieh's troops attacked the Hsiku arsenal in European style skirmish lines, and were most discontented, said a prisoner, at their lack of success. During the attack on the Walled City 'the Chinese most gallantly stuck to their position, keeping up a heavy rifle fire until literally swept away, wall and all'.[87] The Allies only entered Tientsin overnight, after the defenders had left in good order.

Seymour's Dash depended on the Imperial Army standing aside, and their intervention made his retreat inevitable. The Chinese only just failed to annihilate the so-called relief force, but its position was an anxious one in view of the Chinese habit of killing their prisoners. Seymour thought, 'what a very curious scene such an international holocaust would be'.[88] Their subdued return to Tientsin was a far cry from the reception of Naval Brigades at Durban or Portsmouth:

> There was hardly a spectator who would not have found his voice choked with emotion had he tried to cheer. It was the first experience of anything of the kind, and the contrast between the jaunty smartness of the column when it started for Peking, and the ghastly bedraggled footsore men who came back, was too marked to be pleasant.[89]

Captain Bayly had never expected to see any of them again. Sergeant Cooper was glad to be back among friends, but found the occasion a sad one, carriers barely able to stand struggling along with the wounded on improvised stretchers: 'We altogether presented a very damaged appearance.'[90] So did the foreign concession: buildings burnt down or riddled with shell holes, every tree and wall studded with bullets which littered the barricaded streets.

AN INTERNATIONAL NAVAL BRIGADE

The substantial Naval Brigades landed by other navies were a sign that the Royal Navy no longer monopolised the means of maritime power projection. The French had long trained their sailors as fusilier-marins, while their Infanterie de la Marine were tough long-service professionals recruited for colonial campaigns. Both had fought ashore with distinction during the Franco-Prussian war of 1870. An RMLI sergeant invalided home from China thought the French: 'excellent comrades sharing everything while in the field. The men of the French Marine Infantry were the bonds which united the foreign detachments.'[91] Seymour told the commander of their naval landing party that he regarded them as the first detachment of his force, perhaps an example of the Admiral's diplomatic touch.

New naval competitors had emerged: the Imperial German and Japanese Navies, and the US Navy. The English-speaking contingents cooperated well, although Sergeant Cooper was astonished by a US Marine's complaint about the lack of syrup with his canned peaches, when everyone else was living on a quarter pound of biscuit a day. Captain McCalla of USS *Newark* wrote of the honour done to his officers by Seymour's confidence in them. He himself took personal command of a company of British bluejackets, while Royal Naval surgeons cared for both nations' wounded. McCalla was particularly concerned to draw attention to the heroism of two British seamen, who leapt into the Peiho to tow a junk full of American wounded out of the line of fire, during the attack on the Hsiku arsenal. Both received gold medals from the Life-Saving Association of New York, and letters of thanks from the Secretary of the US Navy.[92] At Tientsin British seamen went to the support of 9th US Infantry under unexpectedly heavy fire, and helped clear their numerous casualties. Captain Bayly rather spoiled the effect, suggesting that if recently arrived Americans had spent more time looking around and less time drinking, their wounded would not have had to ask the way to the hospital. He had come a long way from the midshipman at Sekondi, but his observations lost none of their sharpness.

Relations with the Russians and Germans were less satisfactory. The latter were greatly admired, but not for their marksmanship, as they fired into the backs of Cooper's section instead of over their heads: 'Hard lines to be potted by your own men'. The Russians appeared shy of combat, declining the honour of storming the Hsiku arsenal. The British suspected that they were being allowed to do most of the fighting, although their percentage casualties do not bear this out. One of Bayly's correspondents in Tientsin was pleased when a Russian plan was abandoned: 'it simply would have meant that we should have lost many men pushing through all the houses while the Russians laid doggo, watching ready in case we, by good luck, brought the attack off successfully, when they would sweep down and claim all the kudos'. As for the Germans, they were 'in with the Russians for political ends'.[93] Russian infantrymen, on the other hand, greatly admired Beatty for his coolness under fire, and cheered Lieutenant Wright as he brought his single 9pr into action at Tientsin railway station, when their own battery had left the field in disorder.

There was surprisingly little dissension during Seymour's Dash. Seymour thought their all being naval men together allowed him to exercise an informal command: 'they were very nice to me, and as it went on more and more said "à vos ordres", and whatever you say we will do'.[94] Captain McCalla attributed the harmony to Seymour's tact and leadership. Seymour was, of course, the most senior officers present, with much the largest contingent, but he also had an absolutely fearless sense of responsibility. He was constantly with the advance guard, risking his life so freely that officers of both English-speaking navies, and the French, feared for his safety.[95] His sudden departure for Peking drew sharp criticism. The *Army and Navy Gazette* pointed out that the navy usually acted in concert with the army, or on the seaboard. Peking was eighty miles inland, and contained no British force:

In the whole course of our naval history it may be doubted if a parallel case can be found for the despatch of a Naval Brigade in such circumstances as those existing in China at the present moment. Perhaps the nearest is Nelson's move to aid the Neapolitans, but it was strongly condemned by the Admiralty, and the conditions were infinitely more favourable to success in his case than in Admiral Seymour's.[96]

Seymour's despatches produced a change of tack, the paper claiming they bore out everything it had always said. There had been every hope of success at the moment of departure, when there was no reason to doubt the friendly disposition of the Chinese authorities. Seymour himself was unapologetic: 'I never regretted I had started as I could not have respected myself if I had not done so.'[97]

IN ACTION AGAINST THE BOXERS

Naval Brigades during the Boxer Rebellion fought mainly with rifle and bayonet. Where attackers could approach Chinese positions under cover, noisy bayonet charges were still an effective tactic, but the flat open terrain outside Tientsin provided a foretaste of the tactical stalemate caused by modern weapons during World War One. Total Allied losses during the attack on Tientsin's Walled City were 879 out of 4,800, a higher percentage of the total force than in any Boer War action:

> The artillery fire of the Chinese was very accurate, and we had many casualties. Captain Lloyd was killed by a rifle bullet in the neck. The shells screamed and the rifle bullets whined over our heads. Most of us bobbed when we heard them, but of course that was no use, as we only heard them when it was too late to bob. The ones that hit done it silently, it was the fellow hit that made the noise.[98]

The firefight lasted all day, extended lines of riflemen lying behind such cover as there was, only moving when the enemy got the range. Rushing for cover behind a wall, Sergeant Cooper received a bullet through the thigh: 'That put me out of the operation for good'.

The obsolete guns available at the start of the uprising were: 'a disgrace to the glorious service which at that time had to use them'.[99] None of the ships on the China station had received the 'new' 12pr 8cwt introduced almost ten years before. The old 9pr RML demanded a heroic style of gunnery. *Orlando's* field-gun crew trundled their gun up by hand to save the day at the railway station: 'teed up like a golf ball in front of the platform, the mark of every hostile gun, it was fought to such purpose that it indisputably turned almost certain defeat into a grand victory'.[100] The price was five No. 1s down in as many minutes, and a crew of twenty reduced to two officers and two ratings in half an hour. Duelling with Long Tom of Pepworth Hill looks quite tame by comparison.

The advent of HMS *Terrible* improved the odds. Captain Scott was again cheated of a run ashore, but three of his 12pr 12cwts saw action at Tientsin, and went on to Peking. Supported by 4-inch guns taken from HMS *Algerine*, they subdued Chinese rifle fire during the attack on the Walled City. Fire-control techniques were notably modern. Bayly directed the guns by telephone from an observation post on the Gordon Hall, some of the gun positions being out of sight of their targets. The British military commander was duly appreciative:

> The success of the operations was largely due to the manner in which the naval guns were worked by Lieutenant Drummond RN, the accuracy of their fire alone rendering steady fire on the part of the troops possible against the strong Chinese position, and largely reducing the number of casualties.[101]

After such praise it is not surprising that the General requested a naval battery to accompany the planned Peking relief column. Seymour agreed to send 150 seamen with three 12pr and two 4-inch guns, but demurred at 300 marines: 'not easy to give so many in view of the fact that the Navy must be ready for a perhaps serious outbreak on the Yung-Tu (*sic*) or Shanghai'.[102] Bayly as SNO Tientsin had already requested all guns to be 'brought together, overhauled and thoroughly put to rights, any damage to gear being remedied'. This included all the smaller guns needed for the defence of Tientsin, as only naval guns were available for that purpose.[103] There was no question of trundling 12prs to Peking by hand. Bayly ordered limbers of Oregon pine and sets of pony harness. These took into consideration Captain Limpus' recent lecture at Hong Kong, 'as regards the necessity with animal draught for being able to get rid of any disabled beasts without difficulty'.[104]

After so much preparation the advance to Peking was anticlimactic, although trying to the troops:

> being quite unable to march during the day on account of the heat, dust and high crops which kept out every breath of air. However, we never did

more than 15 miles a day and generally 10 ... The junks kept up in a wonderful way, a good southerly wind nearly every day helped them on well.
Only two fights on the way, the first two days out from Si Ku Arsenal (*sic*),
but never cut the enemy up nor took their guns.[105]

Sergeant Cooper had already experienced a Chinese summer:

The heat was beyond anything people living in England could conceive.
I took my coat and shirt off and got one man to pour a bucket of water all
over me. It was what I should imagine an ice cream in H——l would feel
like. We used to fill our helmets with water from the river and put them
on, letting the water run down all over us under our clothes. It soon dried,
and we were as hot as ever.[106]

On 13 August 1900, while the Japanese and Americans saw heavy fighting, the
British walked in the south-east gate of Peking's Chinese city unopposed,
risked a short cut through the Tartar city, and entered the Legations by a
small side gate.[107] The new arrivals were greatly impressed by the Legations'
defences, the barricades only a few yards apart: 'Take it all round, we were
here none too soon.'

ECHOES OF LUCKNOW

Naval participation in the Relief of the Peking Legations naturally recalled
'the gallant officers and men who brought their guns from Calcutta to
Lucknow for a similar purpose'.[108] Such comparisons were not so far-
fetched. Like the Residency, the Legations were under continual close-
range fire, with a constant risk of incendiarism and mines, which the
Chinese dug in all directions. Numerous foreign and Chinese civilians
swelled the garrison. Few can have had any illusions as to their fate if
overrun by the Boxers. Corporal F.G. Smith RMLI of HMS *Orlando* helped
rescue 500 Roman Catholics, before the Imperial Army invested the
Legations:

Some were only half clad, some cut and hacked about most dreadfully. It
could not be described by pen ... the bad cases were put in carts we had
brought for that purpose, the others walked by them. It was a sight enough
to turn the hardest heart sick.[109]

No quarter was given to anyone in Boxer dress: red coat, blue trousers, and yellow sash. The aftermath of one fight looked 'Just like a slaughterhouse on killing day . . . some dead, dying, groaning and crying, but we had no feeling for them.'

At least four Royal Marines kept siege diaries. Smith wrote his up for a lecture at the Portland Sailor's and Soldier's Home in 1902. His account is sometimes florid, but its professional audience guarantees its plausibility, if not its precise accuracy. The marines sent up from Tientsin at the end of May had three weeks to prepare for the siege. The Imperial Chinese authorities gave the European diplomatic corps notice to quit on 19 June, but the subsequent murder of the German Ambassador did not encourage anyone to move. Horses and mules were collected for the pot, rice commandeered from shops, walls and windows built up or blocked: 'All the men were told off for different positions, and served out with as much ammunition as they could carry.' The first shots into the Legations were fired on 21 June. A marine nailed up the Union Jack: 'although it was torn in rags by bullets, it was not pulled down in three days, as they swore on their heads to do'. Corporal Smith appears to have found divine support:

> Many were the lessons that were learnt in those horrible days that followed. There are very few who took part in that awful time can look back and say, 'There is no God'. It was nothing but firing, the Chinese keeping up a wild fire day and night.

It was otherwise with the defenders. The British had 240 rounds per man, to last 'we knew not how long'. The only artillery was two machine guns, and Betsy, the International Gun. She was an 1860 vintage British gun barrel found in a burnt out shop, mounted on an Italian field carriage, loaded with Russian shells and fired by Gunner Mitchell USN: 'It used to cause sport at first, but we soon used up all our lead.' To save Lee Metford cartridges the marines threw bricks, or sniped with old Martini Henrys borrowed from the Legation watchmen.

There were frequent sorties to keep snipers and fire-raisers at bay. Smith took part in two. Captain Lewis Halliday RMLI won the *VC* in the first, dropping four Chinese with his revolver after they had shot him in the shoulder. In the second, 'a night never to be forgotten by anyone who took part in it', Captain Myers USMC led twenty-six British and American marines through torrential rain to pull down a snipers' tower just fifteen yards from the defenders' barricades: 'The Chinese were taught a lesson that night and they never forgot it, for we could never catch them napping again.'

As early as 28 June Smith was 'getting tired of it. There did not seem to be so much sport now.' The cemetery was full, and food becoming scarce. The daily ration was 6oz of horse or mule, and 12oz of rice, 'which we ate with relish after we got used to it ... then they cut it down much finer, and we were getting finer'. Sometimes there was an excuse for bread, washed down with green tea.

Fighting was not continuous. A ceasefire lasted from 18 July until a week before the end of the siege, perhaps a psychological ploy, to reduce the garrison's vigilance. During an earlier ceasefire Chinese soldiers hung up a poster offering protection against the Boxers, if the defenders agreed to be escorted down to Tientsin. They even offered food, if the garrison would tell them exactly how many required to be fed. At other times the besiegers contented themselves with sending in messengers with false information, or blowing horns and shouting: 'Sha! Sha! Sha!' – 'Kill! Kill! Kill!'

The approach of the relief column spurred the Chinese on to renewed aggression, and Smith to fresh heights of eloquence. He may have been laying it on thick for the benefit of his audience, but one cannot doubt that 'the pen cannot express the feelings that came to each heart', when relieving guns were heard on 14 August. Smith's own shipmates of the RM Battalion arrived next day 'left behind at Tientsin three months ago, and never expected to see again. Many were the hearty handgrips that afternoon.' Half the marine detachment's 18,000 rounds of ammunition still remained, evidence of their steadiness and careful shooting.

Smith was lucky to complete his diary unscathed. The other siege diarists were all wounded. All three officers were casualties, RM casualties totalling three killed and twenty-three wounded out of the original seventy-nine. This was twice the average rate for the campaign, but RN casualties were generally high: 359 out of 2,207. More naval personnel were landed during the Boxer Rebellion than in the Boer War, suffering more casualties in a much shorter period. The contrast struck Captain Bayly who compared the one-sixth casualties suffered by the navy at Tientsin with one-fourteenth losses suffered by Buller's army at Spion Kop, the bloodiest action of the Boer War.[110] Bayly was not entirely fair; losses at Spion Kop fell upon a few battalions who lost almost half their numbers. However his analysis shows the strain placed on ships' crews facing three ways at once: Seymour's Dash, Tientsin, and the Taku Forts. Cradock's landing party were the gleanings of the fleet, armed with a few rifles, cutlasses, pistols, tomahawks, and boarding pikes. When Roger Keyes had to cut out four Chinese destroyers, his stokers carried their fire irons.

Bayly was not alone in feeling that the Boer War unfairly overshadowed events in China. Colonel W.H. Poe RM, who lost a leg with the Royal Marines Camel Corps in 1885, complained in the *Army and Navy Gazette* of the brief and casual allusions that had appeared in the daily press. Seymour's memoirs remarked on the lack of a medal clasp for the defence of Tientsin, 'especially when it is compared to what some clasps were given for in another continent at about the same time'.[111] 'Naval R.K.', wrote, 'Only those that fought Kruger, Are allowed to give themselves airs':

> We got no Tam o'Shanter caps,
> No chocolates in a box,
> No knitted stockings came our way,
> But we gave the Boxers socks.[112]

Three doubtfully authentic members of the lower deck thanked all concerned for the numerous messages of appreciation for their efforts at Tientsin:

> They regret that they are unable to communicate to the Press any of the contents or terms of these telegrams or letters owing to the unfortunate fact that they have not yet been received, but doubtless, as every other force concerned in any way with the operations in North China . . . have received such telegrams and letters, those referred to must have been mislaid or delayed in transmission . . .

> Signed:
>   Jack Ragbag – Able Seaman, Seaman Gunner, torpedo man and diver
>   Joseph Brasswork – Royal Marine
>   Peter Piston – Stoker, mechanic, and provider of sanitation and water
> for Tientsin.[113]

Even those saved from the Boxers showed scant gratitude. The Gordon Hotel complained about cases of stout missing from its cellars, lighter charges were 'absolutely exorbitant', while the owners of godowns used as barracks demanded rent. Bayly observed that he had no recollection of any question as to rent or other compensation whatever being raised when the navy entered into occupation. It must have seemed that the Royal Navy was being asked to pay for the privilege of saving Tientsin.[114]

CHAPTER TEN

Armageddon

Hopes that joint action against the Boxer Rebellion would begin an era of international cooperation proved illusory. The German Navy Law had served notice before the Boer War that the security of British home waters could no longer be taken for granted. The Royal Navy had to look to its primary task of protecting the home base, concentrating ships and men in home waters. Training manuals reflected the new mood. The 1913 *Handbook of Field Training* lacked the engaging minutiae of bush warfare, cholera belts, pocket water filters, and pith helmets, dwelling on such grim topics as the *Nature of Offensive Action* and the *Conduct of the Infantry Fight*. The First World War drew a line beneath a period when, certain of its maritime pre-eminence, the Royal Navy could divert whole squadrons from their central strategic role.

IMPERIAL RETRENCHMENT (1900–14)

Concern for the home base dated back to the war scares of the 1880s and 1890s, when France and Russia had been the bogeymen. These panics had led to a succession of naval building programmes that by the turn of the century were financially unsustainable. In 1905 came the first reassessment of British naval priorities since the introduction of steam power and the telegraph. It sought to maximise fighting power, at the expense of 'those vessels which, however useful in peace, would in war be found to be a source of weakness and anxiety'.[1] Sixty-one gunboats, sloops, and 3rd Class Cruisers appeared on the return of 'vessels struck off the list of effective ships of war', many of them familiar to veterans of Naval Brigades. Their personnel were needed to man the expanded Channel Fleet of twelve modern battleships, and the new Atlantic Fleet of eight, based at Gibraltar as a link with the Mediterranean Fleet. Anglo-French rapprochement would reduce the latter from eight modern battleships to three elderly battlecruisers in 1914. The First Lord's Memorandum of 1905 claimed enough ships remained on every station for 'peace duties of Imperial Policing', but the new emphasis was plain. Resources available for employment by Naval Brigades were dramatically reduced, as the proportion of naval manpower in home waters rose from a third to three quarters. After 1905 only nine gunboats or sloops would be in commission outside European waters, compared with twenty-three the previous year.

The First Sea Lord called in to rationalise Britain's naval resources was Sir John Fisher. He had narrowly escaped death in the Peiho disaster, and commanded the Naval Brigade at Alexandria in 1882. He had no time now for such distractions from what he saw as the navy's main responsibility, although he admitted the necessity for Naval Brigades in the past, when slow communications made them the only realistic way of defending British interests in remote and inaccessible parts of the world. The strategic circumstances of the early twentieth century not only allowed a different response to imperial emergencies, they posed a more serious threat:

> in view of the disposable and increasing strength of the navies of foreign maritime powers, it has become a matter of special moment to maintain the fleets throughout at their fullest standard of efficiency in readiness for any emergency that may arise, so that any landing of seamen and the employment of naval brigades is much to be depreciated.[2]

Like any bureaucrat under pressure, Fisher tried to pass the responsibility to another department, requesting the Government to change a military system unable to meet the need for overseas expeditionary forces. He objected to the naval role at Benin, when the Admiral of the Cape squadron and the best part of his crews vanished without trace into the jungle. The *Naval Annual* characterised the Illig operations as 'one of those quick decisive unexpected blows that can be so well carried out by the Navy with the resources that are ever at their disposal',[3] but the First Sea Lord was unimpressed. He was more struck by the risks posed to ships denuded of their crews, whose re-embarkation was at the mercy of the rising surf. Fisher failed to develop a new strategic vision for the navy, however. Neither he nor his successor Sir Arthur Wilson, a *VC* at El Teb, integrated naval and military war plans. Their cloudy schemes for amphibious operations in the Baltic failed to recognise that the Army's strategic priorities had also changed. The generals had reacted to the German threat by drawing closer to the French Army. The soldiers Fisher and Wilson hoped to land at

Borkum or Danzig were already committed to the muddy banks of the Meuse.

The strategic mission had changed, but the machine still turned out seamen-gunners thoroughly trained in the latest techniques of land warfare. Manuals covered every aspect of Field Training in elaborate detail, not all of it inessential. Casualties from disease had always outnumbered those from enemy action, so it is difficult to object to sections on field hygiene, which might save more lives than improved tactics. The 1910 *Landing Party* manual forbade spitting, which spread tuberculosis, as well as urination in camp, both acceptable practices in 1888. Tactical change was less revolutionary. In 1900 sailors stormed the Taku Forts in a fashion unchanged from the Zulu War, twenty years before:

> Our chaps were tired of waiting, and had the fire been ten times as hot, nothing would have stopped them. Drillbook tactics fell to the ground. The force started at a steady double, halted at 800 yards, and fired two volleys; the same at 500 yards, once more at 300 yards; then the charge was sounded! The order 'supports into the firing line'; 'fix bayonets'; and away we all dashed.[4]

Marksmanship remained important. The ingenious Morris tube converted service rifles into small-calibre weapons for short-range target practice at sea, with an additional 100 rounds for every man, including stokers. Half-yearly gunnery returns had to state the percentage of a ship's company that had practised with Morris tubes:

> Box targets should be placed in any convenient position, and to prevent injury to ship's fittings being caused by shots missing the target a few sandbags made of old canvas should be built around the box.[5]

A new musketry scheme appeared in 1892 with smaller targets and bulls, making it harder to classify as a marksman. A *Globe and Laurel* correspondent wrote to 'strongly impress upon all the advisability of practice at the Morris tube range before going through their annual course of range practise'.[6]

Dramatic changes followed the South African War's demonstration of the disadvantages of poor shooting. Rifle practice became part of a continuous process of instruction for all ratings, not just an annual chore: 'no ship's company can be considered efficient with the rifle who are not so constantly in training as to go on the range without further instruction at any time'.[7] New features included:

Judging distance using the speed of sound and the delay between seeing and hearing a shot fired to estimate the range.

Allowing for deflection of targets moving across the firer's front.

Snapshooting, a Boer speciality: 'rapidly covering a mark and at once releasing the trigger ... first as an instructional drill and later in a practical manner from behind cover'.

The 1913 *Field Exercise* specified separate musketry courses for novices and the more advanced, the latter 'embodying modern conditions of rifle shooting, adapted to naval requirements and existing rifle ranges'.[8] Targets were no longer immobile six-foot squares painted white. Now they were naturally coloured grey over green, with brown figures presenting the same area as an enemy soldier, that appeared for twenty to thirty seconds at a time.

The aim of all this was to teach a man to fire as rapidly as possible in the final stage of an attack, while presenting as small a target as possible, in marked contrast to Graspan: 'it must be impressed on the men that the object to be attained is to assault the position without being exposed to fire for longer than is absolutely necessary'. Attacking forces still formed three lines of skirmishers, but outflanking movements were mandatory: 'Having regard to the increased accuracy of modern weapons, a frontal attack will be unnecessarily costly unless combined with a flank or enveloping attack.'[9] Unhappily the continuous fronts of the First World War would make such tactical wisdom impossible to implement. The defence had to avoid positions with dead ground to their front (unlike Majuba), while digging well hidden trenches at the foot of hills, to allow their flat-trajectory rifles a deeper beaten zone, as the Boers had done at the Modder River.

Practical experience of field conditions lagged behind doctrine. The Selborne committee sat in 1905 as part of Fisher's efforts to improve training and selection of naval officers. It heard evidence of the Navy's need for more effective preparation for 'littoral warfare', and its lack of field training appropriate to modern conditions. Major W.B. Harkness RMA thought the latter practically unknown in the Navy:

not one Officer in 100 has seen an outpost screen, has practised the defence of a house, or made a modern line of shelter trenches. Landing parties spend three-quarters of an hour putting straps together, three-quarters of an hour at inspection of arms and arms drill, and half-an-hour in returning stores.

Harkness still believed military work necessary for the navy, 'because Naval Brigades have taken part in every war, and in no case have they been refused'. Every man of a Naval Brigade would be needed again by his ship, so it was 'specially important to save his life and ensure his efficiency, and both these depend upon his training'.[10]

Another Royal Marine officer described his Corps' future with uncanny prescience. Captain M.P.A. Hankey RMA argued that the proposed Lieutenant (M), who would replace existing RMOs within Fisher's integrated officer corps, should be analogous to Gunnery and Torpedo Lieutenants: 'a specialist in littoral warfare – warfare of the coast . . . instead of being, as at present, taught mainly military duties and infantry drill, he wants to study especially raids'. Hankey looked back to Lord Cochrane's attacks on signal stations, but also pointed to recent examples of the amphibious use of marines:

> the defence of legations and posts, such as Pekin; and lighthouses essential to navigation such as Anholt in 1809; and the defence of advanced bases, such as the Japanese at Elliot Island, or the American Marines at Guantanamo where they defended the advanced base, kept off the Spanish skirmishers, and thus enabled the ships to coal in safety.[11]

The main requirements of a modern officer of marines, he thought, would be to be a good boatman and an expert in demolitions.

The chapter headings of the 1910 *Landing Party* manual bear a broad family resemblance to the original 1859 *Field Exercise*, but a recognisably modern set of concerns, set out in a logical scientific manner, have replaced such arcana as Cutlass and Pike Drill:

> The Landing Party; Its Organisation and Equipment
> Disembarkation of Forces; Joint Operations
> Orders, Appreciations, etc
> Marches, Advances, and Rearguards
> Outposts
> Attack and Defence of a Position
> Savage Warfare; Hints on Assisting the Civil Power
> Medical and Sanitary Arrangements
> Field Fortifications
> Bridging

Some of the subject matter may appear archaic, such as Savage Warfare with its easy assumption of superiority over 'native races, whose fear of the white man makes them unable to stand'. However, the authors made a better job of integrating naval and military tactical doctrine than their superiors did of joint planning. Many sections, for example those on mutual support and superiority of fire, closely reflected the Army's *Infantry Training* manual. Even the well-worn adage that 'time spent on reconnaissance is seldom wasted' makes an appearance. The section on Savage Warfare incorporated not only the lessons of recent expeditions, 'compiled from actual experiences of officers while on active service in Africa', but also drew on the Belfast riots of 1907. It discussed the rioters' tactics and use of helmets and motor vehicles by the troops. The weakest point was that landing techniques were practically unchanged since the Crimea, except that machine guns had replaced muzzle-loading boat guns. Steam picket boats towed columns of five or six pulling boats towards the beach, casting off at the last minute, leaving the most dangerous part of the approach to be completed under oars. Just as the bolt-action rifle spelt the end for horsed cavalry on land, so it did for opposed landings without powered landing craft. The Royal Navy suffered, like the army, from the general hiatus of tactical mobility that ensured the First World War was fought with nineteenth-century offensive means – men, horses and pulling boats – against twentieth-century defensive weapons, such as magazine rifles and machine guns.

THE ROYAL NAVAL DIVISION (1914–18)

When war broke out in August 1914, the deficiencies of the offensive were not strikingly obvious. The overwhelming rush of the German Army through Belgium created one of the most dire emergencies ever to face the British armed forces. At first it seemed that this was no business of the Royal Navy, keeping its vigil in the North Sea. The official naval historian thought the fleet had not been so divorced from the conduct of a major war since Blenheim. Even so, some naval men took part in an episode easily mistaken for the apotheosis of the Naval Brigade.

The Committee of Imperial Defence had proposed an 'Advanced Base Force' before the war, reflecting the ideas of their secretary Maurice Hankey about littoral warfare. On the outbreak of hostilities on 4 August 1914 the Admiralty formed a Royal Marine Brigade (RMB) of four battalions, in pursuance of these plans. Comparable with RM Battalions of earlier wars, the RMB was intended for raids or the seizure of expedition-

ary bases, as laid down in the *Landing Operations* manual of 1914. Two Royal
Naval Brigades were tentatively formed on the 16th. The Admiralty had no
particular intention of expanding its land forces, but the supply of naval
reservists easily met the needs of the fleet, while the flood of volunteers
responding to Lord Kitchener's famous appeal wildly exceeded the administrative capacity of the War Office. The new RN Brigades were a mixture
of RNR reservists, RNVR volunteers, and Kitchener volunteers. They
lacked staffs, artillery, transport, ambulances, or training. They bore no
resemblance to the well-equipped and integrated Naval Brigades of
Victorian campaigns, drawn from the picked men of existing ship's companies. Improvised to meet a particular set of circumstances, all the Royal
Naval Brigades of 1914 shared with their prototypes was their emergency
role. The volunteers of the Royal Naval Division had the doubtful honour
of being the first of Kitchener's volunteers to face the Imperial German
Army. Their lack of heavy weapons not only differentiated them from
past Naval Brigades, it was highly inappropriate in the face of German
firepower.

The RMB mounted two operations against the Channel coast to deter
German descents: upon Ostend in August, and Dunkirk in September.
Commander Sampson's motor bandits scoured the country as far as Ghent
and Albert in their armoured motor cars without meeting serious opposition, while the marines provided 'ticklers' or jam-spread biscuits for the
local children. In mid-September the main armies, stalled on the Aisne,
began to look north for an open flank. The Belgian Army in its fortress at
Antwerp came under such pressure that by 1 October the Belgian
Government was convinced they could not save the city without outside
help. The British had declared war to defend the moral sanctity of international treaties, but their strategic aim was to deny the Channel coast to a
hostile naval power. The Admiralty had a natural interest in the security of
Antwerp. A force there might also protect the Channel ports through which
ran the BEF's communications. Decisively, the First Sea Lord was Winston
Churchill, ever attentive to the siren calls of honour and action. Not only
did he order the RMB to the assistance of Antwerp's defenders, he went
there himself, and promised to add the two RN Brigades. This was a desperate expedient to meet a desperate situation. The RND was a division in
name only, as yet wholly unfit for service. The brigades had barely a month's
training with practically no musketry. Personal equipment was scarce, men
carrying ammunition in their pockets. Only the RMB had machine guns,
and they were obsolescent Maxims, instead of the new Vickers. Sir George
Aston, who fought at El Teb and Tamai as a subaltern, had been promoted

GOC from command of the RMB. He wrote despairingly of his material and organisational deficiencies:

> The main difficulty is that no one will explain to the First Lord what a battalion or a brigade is, and what it requires in the way of officers, organisation, and equipment to make it a mobile unit in the field.[12]

Aston's health collapsed on 25 September, an indication of the stress of the great crisis whose overpowering demands make criticism of the measures adopted at the time somewhat idle. The RND's commitment at Antwerp was justifiable, in the circumstances. It was not then possible to forecast the duration of the war, or the unexpected growth of minesweeping and anti-submarine flotillas that would have provided better employment for the RNR and RNVR volunteers. The RND even achieved a limited degree of success. Antwerp held out, with their assistance, until 10 October. The Belgian Field Army had regrouped, the last division of British regulars was in position at Ghent, and the BEF was at Bailleul, covering the Channel ports. Most importantly, the Belgians had not been left to stand alone. Unfortunately the harrowing circumstances of the evacuation of Antwerp, with the accidental loss of many of 1st RN Brigade, overshadowed these results. The episode provided material for political attacks on Mr Churchill, that the subsequent débâcle at the Dardanelles would appear to justify.

The Germans avoided frontal attacks on the RND's trenches at Antwerp, relying on shellfire to demoralise the defenders. Big 42cm howitzer shells screeched down to burst with a terrific explosion, burying men and machine guns:

> You have no idea of the effect that these shells had on different people. In the majority of cases the continuity of shell fire seems to quite unnerve everybody, in other cases it drove men mad.
> ... We were two days and two nights in the trenches ourselves and it was like hell itself. To those of us who had to fetch ammunition it was nothing but dodging shells the whole time ... Returning to the trenches was even worse, and those that succeeded in getting back felt like counting their limbs to see if they were all present.[13]

It was impossible to reply, even when the Germans brought up field guns to short range, as the RND had no artillery, apart from a few fortress guns taken over by bluejackets. Four batteries of RMA 12prs never got any nearer than Ostend. Trenches were ill-constructed and over-crowded, with nowhere to cook or to sleep. Ignorance of field conditions kept the men working when they should have rested. The Belgian fortress troops gave way, and at 5.45 p.m. on 8 October 1914 Aston's successor General Paris issued orders for his division to withdraw. The RMB and 2nd RN Brigade got away, the country lit up for thirty miles around by blazing oil tanks. Burning oil floated down-river, setting fire to barges alongside the pontoon bridges, while terrified refugees jammed the roads. Poor staff work delayed 1st RN Brigade, who lost touch with the others. Exhausted by their previous exertions, without water bottles or food, they marched all night to reach the railway late on 9 October, only to hear that the Germans had cut the line to Ostend. A few men escaped along the Dutch border, but almost 1,500 men crossed into Holland to be interned. The Portsmouth RMLI battalion was indeed ambushed, their Major brusquely rejecting the German summons: 'Surrender be damned. Royal Marines never surrender!' Despite women and children screaming with terror and clinging onto them for protection, half his men cut their way out, leaving almost a thousand exhausted RNVR asleep in the train to be taken prisoner. One cool customer took time to hunt out a German spiked helmet as a souvenir. The Portsmouth RMLI arrived back at Victoria station on 13 October, in a variety of uniforms and laden with trophies, to be cheered by the crowds awaiting Belgian refugees.

The fall of Antwerp and publication of the casualties led to a virulent outcry against the inefficiency of the RND and the incompetence with which it had been employed.[14] Much was done to remedy the former over the next three months, but the RND's next campaign was no better conducted. The formation was hustled off in January 1915 to the Dardanelles, still without artillery, and never concentrating for divisional training, unlike other divisions of Kitchener's New Army. The Gallipoli landings were the largest British combined operation since the Crimean War, but the army played the leading role in the assault. The navy was too absorbed in providing logistical and fire support to form Naval Brigades to spearhead the landings as they had done at Suez in 1882. The RND contributed little to the assault as a formation, although members of the division with amphibious expertise did see some action. Two of the RMLI battalions had an independent role with the fleet, going ashore to complete the work of earlier shore bombardments with demolitions. Naval battalions provided experienced men for beach parties, but most of the division took no part in the initial landings of 25 April 1915. When they did go ashore, they were broken up between Cape Helles and Anzac Cove. General Paris lost his command before it had ever seen action. He himself led a composite brigade of blue-jackets, marines, and Lancashire Fusiliers. Second RN Brigade joined the

French Corps, ensuring that the RND fought its first battles under separate national commands. If the Dardanelles campaign suggests a culture of improvisation and muddle on the part of the Royal Navy, then the army was much worse.

Casualties in the battles of May–July 1915, and the Admiralty's inability to replace them, destroyed the naval character of the RND. Cadres were so reduced they were unable to leaven the replacements. The Admiralty withdrew 300 RNR stokers in July for service with the fleet, practically every regular rating left. There were rumours of disbandment, as the division was cut to two brigades. However, one of the battalion commanders was the son of the Prime Minister, and General Paris conducted a high-powered lobbying campaign while on leave in London. In 1916 the RND joined the BEF in France, receiving proper scales of equipment for the first time, including army artillery units and a third infantry brigade. They became experts in trench warfare:

> I learned to wash in shell holes, and to shave myself in tea
> While the fragments of a mirror did a balance on my knee
> I learned to dodge the wizzbangs and the flying lumps of lead
> And to keep a foot of earth between the sniper and my head
> I learned to eat Maconochie with candle ends and string
> With 'four-by-two' and sardine oil and any goddam thing[15]

General Paris was severely wounded in November 1916, and his successor deliberately attacked the naval ethos of his division, transferring out many RM and RNVR officers. The convalescing Paris wrote, 'sic transit RND', but the division clung to its traditions. Members of attached army units requested leave to grow beards in a clean-shaven army, or went ashore to the *estaminet*. They flew the White Ensign in camp, and rang bells to mark the passage of time. Such eccentricities sustained group morale in a mass war that threatened to swamp individuality. The fouled anchor cap badge served a similar purpose to the kilts worn by the many Englishmen who volunteered for Highland regiments. Such traditions were tribal totems rather than evidence of any real naval or Scottish connection. By the end of the war 63rd (Naval) Division was essentially another New Army division, albeit a highly individual one.

SIDESHOWS (1914–17)

The navy's homegrown skills in land warfare found a truer expression in various 'sideshows', where conditions were more akin to those of colonial warfare. The strategic and numerical significance of these never rivalled the monstrous struggles on the Western Front. The whole Royal Navy was smaller by November 1918 than the Royal Artillery, which exceeded half a million men, compared with 407,316 sailors and marines. Casualties ashore surpassed those of the naval war by an immense margin. The RND alone suffered almost as many casualties as the seagoing navy.[16] Naval operations in what Hankey described as the 'second part of war' never reached the scale of the Napoleonic Wars. German possessions overseas were less extensive a target than those of France and her allies, while in 1914–18 the naval war was never decisively won. No second Trafalgar set the fleet free to exploit unequivocal command of the sea. Nevertheless, peripheral naval operations in the First World War still fell within the familiar pattern of escalation described in Chapter Three, from demonstrations, through bombardments and riverine operations to military expeditions. The small number of ships and men engaged in such operations lend them a human dimension, even an element of romance, missing from the anonymous slaughter of the Western Front.

This was certainly true of the development of armoured cars, in which the Royal Navy played a pioneering role that revealed the same technical flexibility as the Crimean War coffee grinders, or Ladysmith's water purifiers. A variety of touring cars had accompanied an RNAS squadron deployed to Dunkirk to intercept Zeppelins. The squadron's intrepid CO, Commander Sampson, armed some of the cars with machine guns, and sent them off to look for Germans, under their appropriately named commander, Major Risk RMLI. Lacking spares and maps they had no luck catching mounted Uhlans, although two cars assisted some French Territorial infantry in a street battle at Douai, an RMLI private dismounting to lead them on. In October 1914 Sampson's motor bandits were the first British troops into Antwerp, afterwards fighting alongside 7th Division and 3rd Cavalry Division in the First Battle of Ypres.

Withdrawn from France in November 1914, the unit became the Royal Naval Armoured Car Division. The original boiler plate armour had formed an open topped box around the engine and driver, but left the gunners exposed from the waist upwards. The RNACD received its first turreted armoured cars, on a Rolls Royce chassis, in December, a remarkable example of the Admiralty's technical abilities. Within three months the RNACD expanded to fifteen squadrons, six each with machine-gun armed motor cycles or Rolls Royce armoured cars, and another three with Lanchesters. Some went to Gallipoli, where trenches and rough terrain gave them little scope, but others served successfully in Namibia, the Western Desert, and East Africa, where the power and solidity of the Rolls Royce earned it the native nickname 'kifaru' or rhinoceros. The RNACD handed its squadrons over to the army in August 1915, but the Admiralty kept some armoured cars until the end of the war, in particular the Russian Armoured Car Division, which fought in the Caucasus and Galicia. Their naval connections were tenuous enough by then, but the key role of the RNAS at the inception of light armoured fighting vehicles shows how the technically more advanced service could inspire new weapons, like Scott's heavy field guns, subsequently handed over to the land forces.

HMS *Minerva*, a cruiser as old as some of her crew, fired the opening shots of the war with Turkey in the traditional manner. In November 1914 she shelled the Turkish fort at Akaba in a desultory fashion, and landed her marine detachment, to set a classic example of an amphibious reconnaissance. Naval Maxim and field gun sections supported the marines, their whites unstained by Condy's fluid. The Captain of Marines directed the advance with his sword, but the landing was unmistakably twentieth-century, intended not to seize territory, but to cut telegraph wires, and foment Arab national feeling. On subsequent visits *Minerva* carried a hydroplane, although its ceiling was insufficient to fly over the 6,000 foot hills to reconnoitre the Hejaz railway further inland.

In the Persian Gulf the Tangistani tribe took advance of the Great War to pursue its traditional feuds, with encouragement from the German consular authorities. They killed several Indian soldiers at Bushire in July 1915, provoking retaliation against the previously demolished village at Dilwar. HMS *Juno* landed her Royal Marines with Indian infantry and bluejacket machine gunners, but the steam pinnaces were not powerful enough against the inshore current, their tows suffering casualties going in with insufficient way, against snipers with modern rifles. The wisdom of the manuals' recommendation that observers accompany landing parties to control naval gunfire became apparent when *Juno* landed a salvo on top of a palm grove where the landing party was forming up for the attack. The village fell next day, but everyone was thoroughly shaken, and utterly done up by the intense heat of August in the Gulf.[17]

Inland waterways still provided the only practical route into several theatres of war. Here the navy's role resembled that played in Burma and along the Nile. HMS *Cumberland* and *Challenger* returned to the Royal Navy's West

African haunts to support Anglo-French operations in the German Cameroons. Boat parties reconnoitred the extensive estuary of the Lungasi River, clearing blockships and mines before seamen and marines occupied Douala in September 1914 ahead of the main expeditionary force. HMS *Dwarf*, a veteran of the Boer War, survived a suicide attack by a German launch packed with explosives, perhaps the inspiration of C.S. Forester's *African Queen*. A mixed company of seamen, marines, and stokers with 12pr 8cwt guns supported locally raised troops, both West African Frontier Force and Tirailleurs Sénégalais. The 12prs proved particularly effective against German fieldworks, persuading them to abandon their *bhoma* at Dschang in January 1915 without a fight. On the river, 220 naval ratings manned an extensive flotilla whose armament ranged from 6-inch guns down to Maxims. Two of HMS *Challenger*'s 6-inch guns appeared on a dredger and a lighter, ironically known as *Iron Duke* and *Dreadnought*. The latter tore up its deck planking whenever it fired, the bluejackets suggesting the gun was 'out of place on this 'ere himpoverished platform'. The last naval units withdrew on 1 April 1916, after a period of guerrilla resistance, their latter occupation being to lay barbed wire, or catch malaria and dysentery.

In Mesopotamia, the modern Iraq, the navy provided firepower and logistical support for a riverine campaign where there was often too much water for the army and not enough for the navy. The campaign was meant to safeguard the flow of Persian oil down the Shatt al Arab, necessary for the new generation of oil-burning warships. The easy achievement of that aim led the British to overextend their inadequate forces, resulting in the humiliating surrender of an entire division at Kut in 1916. The navy shared the exhilarating advance to the gates of Baghdad, covered the retreat from Ctesiphon, where the strategic bubble burst, and took its revenge in 1917 when its gunboats broke a retreating Turkish army.

Naval forces were a key factor in the initial advance up the Euphrates River, 300 miles from the sea. Three sloops, HMS *Odin*, *Clio*, and *Espiègle*, led a ragtag collection of armed paddle-steamers, horseboats, and native *mahelas*, collectively known as Townsend's regatta after the divisional commander. They broke through the Turkish lines near Qurna on 1 June 1915, beginning a ninety-mile pursuit upstream to Amara. Townsend thought the naval action reckless, but Captain Wilfrid Nunn relied on the speed of his ships to get him out of trouble. Amara fell to a Lieutenant RN and eight sailors in the *Shaitan*, a tug mounting a 12pr Q/F gun. They dispersed the garrison with two or three shells, and took 250 prisoners, who, had they kept their heads, might have sunk the unarmoured vessel by rifle fire. Nunn arrived a little later with an armed paddle yacht, two tugs, and three horseboats with 4.7–inch guns, having left behind his ocean-going sloops, which were scraping the river bottom. Townsend coolly demanded supplies for 15,000 men, and Nunn served coffee to captured Turkish officers, while a lieutenant took the surrender of 400 men of the crack Constantinople fire brigade, assisted by one sailor, a marine, and an interpreter. A mixture of bluff and prophylactic bursts of machine-gun fire kept order until next morning, when the leading elements of Townsend's division arrived. The combined pursuit netted: 140 officers, 2,000 men, six steamers sunk or captured, seventeen guns, and over a million rounds of ammunition.[18]

Throughout the bitter year of 1916 fresh Turkish troops first surrounded Townsend's outnumbered division at Kut, then compelled its surrender, despite all relief attempts. Naval mobility took second place to a static role as floating batteries, the gun crews learning to fire indirectly, directed over the telephone by the naval Kite Balloon section. Purpose-built river gunboats replaced the improvised craft of 1915. Known as 'China Gunboats' to confuse spies, there were eleven small and four large vessels at the front or securing the lines of communication when General Maude broke through the Turkish defences south of Kut in February 1917. Three heavy gunboats, *Tarantula*, *Mantis*, and *Moth*, converted the Turkish retreat into a rout, acting as cavalry and horse artillery combined. Their fire power and tireless speed of 16 knots exceeded the capabilities of cavalry much as the panzers of 1939–40 would. Only where the Euphrates formed a complete hairpin bend was there any real danger, a Turkish field battery raking the three ships at point-blank range as they passed. The quartermaster and pilot in *Mantis* fell dead, but the Captain took the helm just in time. Once round the bend the ships were among the retreating Turks, strewing the road with a tangle of dead transport animals, broken wheels, abandoned guns, vehicles, and ordnance stores. Thousands of Turkish infantry threw down their arms, and were left for the cavalry to round up. The Turkish river squadron was sunk or captured, including *Firefly*, the first small China gunboat, lost during the retreat from Ctesiphon. As in the advance from Qurna to Amara, or from Myédé to Mandalay in 1885, the gunboats showed how their ability to act as super-cavalry made them an essential component in a campaign where the main communications are by river.

The traditional naval role in shore operations was to provide heavy artillery fire support. Both navy and marines provided batteries for shore service during the First World War, ranging from 4-inch Q/F guns up to 12-inch guns and 15-inch howitzers. The heavier pieces served in France in the hands of the Royal Naval Siege Guns near Nieuport and the RMA Howitzer Brigade. Both formations owed something to Admiral Bacon, a veteran of the Benin expedition, as commander of the Dover Patrol and manager of the Coventry Ordnance Works respectively. The Royal Naval Siege Guns were Bacon's response to German 28cm guns at Ostend, the RMA taking the siege guns over in 1917, when the Admiralty withdrew the RN personnel. In March 1918 the RMA Heavy Siege Train had three 12-inch guns, eight 9.2s, and six 7.5s. The guns retained ship's mountings with girders and concrete platforms, engaging German batteries along the Belgian coast, up to 32,000 yards range. The RMA Howitzers fought singly where required, from Neuve Chapelle in 1915 to the breaking of the Hindenburg Line in 1918. The wide blast area of the 15-inch shells made them difficult to use in direct support of infantry, and their short range of 10,800 yards brought them closer to the frontline than was desirable with such heavy weapons. The ten howitzers, each with a small fleet of motor transport to move them, were hardly worth the trouble. Their range was only 800 yards more than that of the much lighter 9.2-inch howitzer, and 4,000 yards less than that of the army's 12-inch Mk 2 howitzer. The RMA Howitzer Brigade, it must be suspected, owed more to the political initiative of Winston Churchill, the First Lord who bought the weapons, than military necessity.

As in the nineteenth century, the naval contribution was more significant around the periphery. A party from HMS *Egmont* with eight 4.7-inch guns spent almost a year in Serbia defending Belgrade against Austro-Hungarian monitors on the Danube. Their command detonated mines and nocturnal torpedo attacks limited the activities of the monitors, but they could not save the city from the combined attentions of the Austrian, German, and Bulgarian armies. In the first twenty-four hours of the Battle of Belgrade on 3 October 1915 42,000 shells fell on the city. Among the casualties were two of the 4.7s which had their sights smashed when their casemates collapsed, and sixteen of the detachment. On the 8th the survivors joined the terrible Serbian exodus across the mountains to the south. The guns had field mountings drawn by bullocks, as in South Africa, but were soon lost, bogged down in the knee-deep mud:

> Every hundred yards or so was an abandoned horse or ox left to die from fatigue or freeze to death, although there was no lack of ammunition or rifles to end their suffering. As soon as they were dead the natives skinned and cut up the carcasses – a gruesome sight.

Serbian attempts to destroy ammunition by burning it added an unnecessary hazard to those of icy mountain roads where animals and equipment might fall from further up the slope. A free-falling bullock missed the party by two yards. The Egmonts reached the coast near Scutari, to be bombed on Christmas Eve 1915: 'unshaven, uniform partly Serbian, some with no boots, others with uppers only, hair long and dirty'.[19]

The campaign against German East Africa, now Tanzania, was the ultimate sideshow. It combined features of the Ashanti and Boer Wars: a horrible climate and an intangible enemy. The Admiralty agreed in early 1916 to provide four 4-inch and four 12pr 18cwt guns to counter 10cm naval guns that the Germans had salvaged from the trapped commerce raider *Königsberg*. The 12prs saw little action, but individual 4-inch guns, manned by Royal Marines from depots at home and ships on station, duelled inconclusively with *Königsberg*'s guns throughout 1916 and early 1917. Usually the Germans slipped away before they could be engaged more closely, a strategy favoured by the wretched terrain, where trees had to be felled every few yards and guns sank to the axles in ground so soft that elephant footprints made capital holes for refilling water bottles. Horse sickness wiped out the gun mules, which had to be replaced by gangs of African gun-porters, fifty per gun. The latter stood in for sick gun numbers, the surviving marines becoming specialists. Rain washed men out of their trenches, and swarms of bees attached marching columns:

> in an instant everything was upside down, mules were tied up in the harness and the reins and everybody was doing his best to keep the bees off his face, luckily no enemy appeared, and by setting the grass on fire we managed to get through . . . and then what a sight, some could not see out of their eyes, others had great big thick lips and bumps all over their heads.[20]

Numerous debilitated Germans were captured at the Rufiji, but Lettow-Vorbeck, the German commander, 'is supposed to be mad and won't give in until the last'. He did not surrender until November 1918, outlasting the RM batteries who withdrew in December 1917. None of them had been killed or wounded in action, but twenty-three died of disease out of 221 men landed, and 177 invalided or returned to their ships sick:

> this camp is like a remnant sale, the Hull battery has got one gun and two men left here, the 6th battery has its guns here but no men, the river transport has got one man who is not sick.

One of the campaign's victims had participated in the Akaba reconnaissance in November 1914. His death from blackwater fever plunged George Sears, one of HMS *Hyacinth*'s detachment, into understandable gloom:

somehow or other I seem to steer clear, I hope it will last, in fact I feel in the pink but I don't like to keep on seeing the other fellows go down . . . the last night we slept at Morogoro, me, Blackford and Jock slept together on the ground as Watters was queer and Jock gave up his bed so Watters could sleep in it, and now he is gone, it don't take long out here to finish you.

Another link to a more distant past was also broken in 1917. 'Young Turner of the Old Brigade' died on 12 November. Game to the last he had joined a Volunteer Battalion of the Hampshire Regiment in 1914, although over eighty by his own reckoning. His life had coincided almost exactly with the heyday of the Naval Brigade, and his death was a token of its passing.

AFTER THE STORM

After the War to end Wars, nothing would ever be the same again. Naval interventions followed in Russia and Somaliland, but these represented unfinished business rather than a return to proper sailoring. Allied intervention against the Bolsheviks was an extension of wartime efforts to limit German access to Russian raw materials, while the Mad Mullah had first troubled the navy in the 1890s. Victorian Naval Brigades had arisen in specific conditions that no longer applied in the 1920s. The easy confidence of British superiority that supported Victorian bellicosity lacked conviction after the bloodletting of the Western Front. The failure at Gallipoli signalled the end of two centuries of British naval supremacy, a failure unredeemed by the equivocal result of Jutland. The same forces were at work between the World Wars, as before 1914, to limit the Royal Navy's scope for military adventures. The *Naval Annual* had recognised in 1905 that the Royal Navy would be unable to prevent the United States securing command of the sea, if the American people accepted the financial burden of doing so. The Washington Treaty of 1921 established parity between the USN and the Royal Navy, formally recognising the shift of power. If the means and motive for naval intervention were lacking post-war, so was the opportunity. The First World War had completed the process of parcelling out the world between sovereign states, leaving little room for naval adventures short of all out war. The League of Nations represented the beginning of a new way of looking at international relations. In future, only rogue states like Mussolini's Italy or Imperial Japan would habitually initiate the use of force against other sovereign states. Within the British Empire the development of stable colonial administration eliminated many sources of friction, substituting locally raised forces for metropolitan units, whether naval or military.

It took some time for these changes to sink in. The loss of naval supremacy only became obvious during the course of the Second World War, perhaps with the loss of the *Prince of Wales* and *Repulse*. The inter-war period was one of waiting for the outward form of things to change to reflect altered conditions within. During the pause, naval forces still prepared for service ashore, and there was still some discussion of how they should do so. However, there is an air of unreality about the debate that, with hindsight, suggests the participants recognised the hollowness of British power in the 1920s and 1930s. Training manuals no longer dealt with tactics, for which they referred directly to military publications. The 1934 *Field Training* manual focused on drill and personal equipment, subjects of limited interest to the authors of the 1859 *Instructions for the Exercise of Small Arms*. One commentator suggested naval landing parties should make up for their limited numbers with armoured fighting vehicles and non-lethal gas. His commendable enthusiasm for modern weapons suggests a lack of realism about the constraints imposed on the navy by post-war political and technical developments. He did recognise, however, that shore bombardment was no longer a viable option, 'in these enlightened days', while suppression of riots regardless of casualties merely stored up trouble for the future.

Another officer was sceptical, recognising that to encumber ships with non-essential items, such as tanks, was an undesirable diversion from their primary function.[21] He took a dim view of the capabilities of landing parties, with the exception of the Royal Marines, whose role he saw as being to carry out military tasks beyond the bluejackets. The writer's central theme was the poor quality of landing-party training, but underlying his criticism was a profound shift in the nature of land warfare. This now required a high degree of tactical skill in fire and movement, only to be acquired through much practice. Even machine guns, that old naval speciality, demanded complex techniques for their effective use, the army and marines devoting much attention to indirect and enfilade fire. Offensive action against a well-trained opposition by naval landing parties would be suicidal, as they had only the most elementary tactical ideas. Sea-service training absorbed all available time, leaving the officers and POs responsible for platoons and sections ignorant of tactics, and unable to issue basic fire orders. The general spread of modern weapons and European tactical methods had made the tactical superiority of Victorian Naval Brigades a thing of the past.

The only realistic opportunities for naval forces ashore would be in low-level operations, particularly aid to the civil power or the defence of locations seized without opposition. The 1920s provided minor examples of both types of operation: 12th battalion RM spent a year at Shanghai in 1928 guarding European lives and property against Chinese rioters and warlords, while HMS *Emerald*'s landing party held Kuwait against dissident Saudi tribesmen from January to April the same year. Neither force saw any serious fighting, but with barbed-wire checkpoints and RAF surveillance of the enemy they belonged to a new age.

CHAPTER ELEVEN

Power and Money

So wide a gulf separates us now from the men of Queen Victoria's Naval Brigades that their motives often remain inscrutable. The rewards for risking life and health in some remote corner of the world seem disproportionately small. Officers stood to gain more in terms of promotion and professional recognition, but they also had more to lose, in terms of an already comfortable way of life. The prospects of action ashore, however, never failed to arouse enthusiasm, or disappointment amongst those excluded. Edmund Verney described extraordinary scenes among the men ordered to stay with HMS *Shannon*, hard-bitten POs giving way to floods of tears. Captain Marryat wrote how, 'The very idea of going into action is a source of joy to an English sailor; and more jokes and merriment excited at that time than at any other.'[1] He should have known, having fought in the First Burma War. The Boxer uprising provoked a similar reaction in HMS *Orlando*: 'everyone was in good spirits, for a trip ashore with plenty of sport thrown in'.[2] Bound for the Legations, Sergeant Gowney RMLI remembered: 'Many a joke was cracked between our members, who were all pleased to know that our passive waiting during the last couple of months was going to end at last.'[3] Naval Brigades may have appealed to men simply as an escape from routine. Sailors were impulsive, accustomed to change as a way of life, attracted by the thought of a run ashore, but equally happy to go back to their ships:

> the bluejacket is in some respects an odd composition; he turns up trumps when there is work to be done, but he is not always content with existing conditions and likes changes.[4]

Not everyone was so sanguine, contrary to the *Army and Navy Gazette*'s facile assertion that 'there is nothing Jack is more pleased at participating in than what he invariably calls a "punitive expedition"'.[5] Joseph Withecombe records a less gung-ho reaction to HMS *Powerful*'s diversion to South Africa:

'Pale but resolute faces were observed amongst those 300 men of the Powerful, for who at the thought of Battle would or could feel unmoved'.[6] Perhaps jokes were a defence mechanism. At least one of *Orlando*'s marines could not sleep: 'turning over and over in my hammock fancying all sorts of things and wondering if I should ever see home again. I felt rather quiet for I might get shot and I was not ready to go.'[7] A young marine bugler in HMS *Powerful* leapt into the shark-infested sea during the voyage from Mauritius, rather than face the unknown terrors of the veldt.

RISKS AND REWARDS

The customary acceptance of such risks by most men might be dismissed as statistical naivety, except that the additional dangers of participation in a Naval Brigade were small in comparison with the general risks of sea service. Sailing ships especially exacted a constant toll of injuries and deaths. Nineteenth-century sailors were accustomed to danger. The 43,120 men employed in the Royal Navy in 1858 suffered 75,924 cases of injury or disease, a rate of 1,761 per thousand.[8] Twenty-five names appear on HMS *Shah*'s memorial in Portsmouth's Victoria Park, but only four of them died with her Zulu War Naval Brigade. HMS *Niger* was paid off in 1861 after a five-year commission. She had seen active service in China and New Zealand, but it was disease that caused havoc amongst the crew. Only eighty of her original hands returned to Woolwich Dockyard; forty had died 'from climate', and sixty more had been invalided. One man was killed at the Omata Stockade, and another seven wounded.[9] Most of the losses occurred in the Canton River where sixty out of the usual complement of 180 were sick every month of 1857, but only three died of wounds.[10] The only battle casualty during the 1897 Brohemie operations was *Alecto*'s Chief Gunner's Mate, struck by his own rocket as it left the tube. Returning to their ship from the same expedition, the crew of HMS *Phoebe* suffered 112 cases of malaria out of a complement of 219. Most of the cases were serious and six died.

Battle casualties were typically low, except for aberrations like Majuba and Graspan. As late as the Boer War disease was far more dangerous than the enemy. Surgeon Porter wrote at Bloemfontein in April 1900: 'Difficult to see how the Naval Brigade can last – the melting process [from enteric] is fairly rapid.'[11] Only at the very end of our period did losses from disease fall below those suffered in action. The RND lost 7,924 killed in action against 666 died from other causes. Before 1914 the links between disease, bacteria, and the way that they spread had been imperfectly understood. The prime suspects were rotting vegetation and the evening mist that rose from tropical swamps. Old coast birds scoffed at experiments to link malaria to the mosquito, and drank heavily after sundown to ward off chills. More scientific observers were no wiser. Surgeon F.J. Lilly carefully listed the factors he thought responsible for the usual crop of fever cases after the second Witu Expedition of 1893. He placed mosquitoes, 'which undoubtedly convey poison', eleventh in a list that included: marching through wet grass, tropical showers, the end of the rainy season, and sleeping in the open. Twenty-three out of thirty-two men who had left the ship went down with fever. After the Benin expedition HMS *Forte* had nearly twice as many fever cases as she had men in her complement. Another participating ship, HMS *Theseus*, had to be paid off. Her Commander suffered from bouts of fever every spring for seven years afterwards. It is hard to understand the equanimity with which men accepted the certainty of 'a rattling fever', which placed definite limits on the strategic persistence of Naval Brigades. Fremantle 'was glad to embark our men', after three days at Witu, 'so as to avoid sickness and to keep the ships efficient'.[12] The Benin Brigade marched the last seventeen miles back to the coast in a day to escape before fever broke out.

Not until 1900 did the naval surgeon's training cover tropical disease and bacteriology, although sickness rates in West Africa and the West Indies were almost ten times those on the home station.[13] Edwardian training manuals reflected the enhanced understanding of the problem, recommending that sentries guard drinking water and that latrines be kept 100 yards away from tents. The role of flies in transmitting germs from uncovered excreta to food and water received explicit recognition as the cause of 'epidemics of diarrhoea, cholera, enteric fever, dysentery, etc, which have been so disastrous to landing parties'.[14] Vaccination and improved personal hygiene had defeated enteric fever by 1914; the scourge of the Boer War did not recur at Gallipoli or in Mesopotamia. Malaria, however, was a different story. Lieutenant Hugh Tweedie took a paddle yacht upriver, during the Sierra Leone Hut Tax disturbances of 1898. He himself greased his hands and face with tar oil to keep mosquitoes at bay, but could not persuade his bluejackets to wear boots, despite feet and ankles swollen with mosquito and mango-fly bites. Only passive measures appeared to control the most morbid of mosquito-borne diseases. The best advice at the end of the 1920s was still to avoid areas where malaria was prevalent, but many West African anchorages lay within the mosquito's cross-water range of 1,000 yards. Active service made evasion impossible. Naval commitments to the Cameroons and East Africa restored malaria to the same level in 1916 that it had reached in 1900. Doctors issued quinine as a prophylactic as early as the Crimea, but too sparingly, for example two grains a day at Witu, compared with the five grains recommended in the 1920s. At least they had given up bloodletting, 'which in old fashioned days was deemed a panacea for the cure of fever', along with administration of the purgative calomel in large and frequent doses. The change was beneficial 'even in the dreaded climate of Sierra Leone and its pestiferous vicinity'.[15]

The rewards for frequenting such unhealthy places were meagre compared to the risks. General Lyttelton said of the bluejackets who mended the pont at Potgieter's Drift, that they were worth their weight in gold, but copper might be nearer the mark. In 1900 an Ordinary Seaman earned 8/9d a week, augmented by 1/6d a day in hostile territory like the Orange Free State. This might amount to just over £1 a week, equivalent to the weekly earnings of an average labourer at the turn of the twentieth century. Civilian working men did not have to stand watches, or risk being shot at, but the physical risks of naval service may not have exceeded those of industrial employment by very much. Working life in Victorian Britain was unhealthy and often dangerous. Continuous service also ensured greater economic security for sailors, compared with men exposed to the uncertain workings of the free market. Seamen who survived a full twenty-one years could expect a pension, something unusual outside the navy and dockyards. The widow of a Royal Marine Quarter-Master, the peak of a rank-and-file career, might receive between £36 and £65 a year, depending on his length of service and the circumstances of death.[16] George Crowe thought the naval service offered a glorious and honourable career to those desiring a roving life of adventure, but it was no place for the fortune hunter.

Service ashore might bring a windfall in the shape of official prize money or private loot. The former was paid slowly, and declined in importance towards the end of the nineteenth century. Prize money for the capture of Pegu in 1853 was paid ten years later, when the navy shared £34,000 with the 18th and 80th Foot. HMS *Pearl*'s Naval Brigade received prize money for their service with the Saran Field Force five years after earning it. Henry Derry reckoned he never received his prize money at all: 'my wife says its all fiddlesticks, and will be a sur-prize when I get it!'.[17] Service newspapers suggested that the Government was waiting until most of the claimants were dead, and keeping the interest for itself. Sir Hope Grant avoided bureaucratic delay after the fall of Peking in 1860 by auctioning the plunder, and paying everyone directly. Veterans of the Boer War received gratuities instead of prize money, a RM Colour Sergeant receiving £15, a Bugler or Private £5.

Individuals might short-circuit the official process by private looting. At Chepoo in 1864 one sailor picked up 1,600 dollars in the T'ai-p'ing camp. The international occupation of Peking in 1900 was the occasion of much semi-official looting. Roger Keyes was singled out as 'going very strong and a great looter'.[18] Corporal Smith, however, criticised the robbery of innocent Chinese unconnected with the Boxers. The RM detachment at Peking were 'under penalty of being shot if caught looting'.[19] Even when done officially to raise prize money, loot was an uncertain affair. The royal palace at Mandalay disappointed British prize commissioners who found it 'filled with the most extraordinary things. In one room nothing but bottles of scent in hundreds, in another bales of calico, in a third there was a chest with nothing in it but nipples for feeding bottles.'[20]

It might be more profitable to plunder one's friends. Bluejackets on the lines of communications in New Zealand thought themselves entitled to compensation, and plundered freely, especially when the cargo was rum. Alcohol became a less significant motivation in the later nineteenth century. The official daily issue was cut to an eighth of a pint in 1850, replaced by increased tea and cocoa rations, but medical opinion of the day felt it dangerous for men accustomed to regular drinking to stop entirely. Expeditions in tropical climates received bottles of stout in lieu of spirits, regarded as an unsuitable drink for men exposed to malaria and 120 degrees of heat.

Service ashore did provide opportunities for the illicit acquisition of alcohol, becoming a major disciplinary problem in New Zealand:

> a great deal of drunkenness in the camp, Anear (ord) received four dozen yesterday for being drunk, and today two Marine Artillery are brought up for the same offence. The Commodore in order to put an end to the continual occurrence of this crime amongst the Marines has ordered the whole detachment to march up to the camp in heavy marching order four times a day.[21]

Some isolated parties succumbed to the well-stocked cellars of Alexandria in 1882, but there was a gradual change in the attitude towards alcohol. During the Kaffir war of 1878, one of HMS *Active*'s seamen refused a pull at a rum flask, saying he wanted no Dutch courage. HMS *Tenedos*' detachment provided a model of sobriety on the Lower Tugela, where drunkenness amongst the soldiers was widespread and unpunished. Nevertheless Commander Brackenbury limited access to a nearby canteen, sending petty officers to buy beer for their messmates. Sir Claude MacDonald, head of the British Legation in Peking, 'did not observe the slightest signs of liquor in any of the men ... though the facility for obtaining drink was very great'.[22] Corporal Smith thanked God he had refused the rough spirits served out to the Legation Guard, although it is not clear whether he was concerned for his digestion or his soul. This spread of sobriety reflected a fundamental change in the nature of the lower deck. Continuous service training and a more military style of discipline had relegated Nelson's volatile 'warrior seamen' to the past, along with their self-destructive carousels.

Promotion to commissioned rank was not a motivating factor for the nineteenth-century bluejacket. Social divisions hardened during the long peace, a trend reflected in the Royal Navy by an almost complete absence of promotion from the lower deck. An Able Seaman digging out for Warrant in Fred T. Jane's novel *A Royal Bluejacket* could point to a row of swords on his mother's parlour wall, the oldest belonging to a 'pukkah lieutenant', no doubt promoted during the Napoleonic Wars, and remark: 'We've come down a bit in our time.'[23] Every battalion in the army had its quartermaster captain or lieutenant promoted from senior NCOs, while a cavalry trooper rose to be Chief of the Imperial General Staff. Such a transformation was impossible in the navy. Only four lower-deck men crept through the hawsehole, to become lieutenants, between 1815 and Fisher's 1903 scheme for promoting warrant officers. Three of the four had participated in Naval Brigades: Gunner Cathie mentioned in despatches after El Teb, Boatswain Webber who took the Nile Brigade into action at al Matamma, and HMS *Powerful*'s Gunner Sims. Such promotions were exceptional. Cathie and Webber profited from the special occasion of Queen Victoria's 1887 Jubilee, not an official policy shift. The social and cultural gulf between wardroom and lower deck was such that more widespread promotion might have been a mixed blessing for its recipients. The *Army and Navy Gazette* resisted public clamour for more promotions like that of Gunner Sims, pointing to the Admiralty's difficulties finding suitable employment for the two Warrant Officers previously promoted.[24] A Royal Marine Colour Sergeant made quartermaster after covering the retreat of a landing party from HMS *Fantome* on the Barbary Coast in 1846 promptly retired, perhaps to avoid the embarrassment and expense of messing with his social superiors. Even within the lower deck, the professional demands of sea service could not be neglected, although Sir William Peel had shown his appreciation of his Brigade's work by giving them all another rating, not for seamanship but for gallantry in the field. Leading Seaman Odger, the first man into the Omata stockade, was offered his warrant as gunner or boatswain, 'provided he be found competent'. Presumably he was not, as two years later he was coxswain to the Captain of HMS *Cambridge*; a respectable post, but lacking the permanence or pension of a warrant officer.

Odger did receive the Victoria Cross, in an imposing ceremony before the gunnery ship's crew under arms, with a battery of four field pieces, and a boy's battalion from the training ship *Impregnable*. A large crowd attended, for such events were public occasions, like those in Hyde Park, where the Queen herself awarded the first *VC*s, or on Southsea Common, where Captain Arthur Wilson received his *VC* for El Teb. Like a proper hero, William Odger disavowed any peculiar courage: 'there were many men as good as himself present at the storming of the pah; but that it happened to be his good fortune to get in first'.[25] The *VC* brought with it a pension of £10 a year for rank-and-file recipients, and was awarded purely for valour. It was available to all, regardless of rank or professional qualifications, and except for the sparsely issued Conspicuous Gallantry Medal was the only such decoration open to men from the lower deck. Twenty-nine of the forty-five *VC*s issued between the Crimean War and the First World War were for Naval Brigade service. When Fred T. Jane wanted an exemplar of lower-deck virtue in *A Royal Bluejacket*, he had him win the *VC* for defending his gun with his fists, in an episode not unlike Waggon Hill. Other medals, issued to all participants, commemorated particular campaigns, or, like the African General Service medal, carried individual clasps for the frequent minor campaigns in that area.

LEADERSHIP

Old Henry Derry thought his officers in China 'a splendid lot of brave fellows, and although when there were quite hundred to one against us, when you had leaders who said "follow me, lads", why you felt on fire to get in front of him'.[26] Personal example was a key element in naval leadership. Peel and Hewett were always in the thick of the fight, the latter spurring his horse into the Mahdist position at El Teb, an action strictly outside the duties of a Commander-in-Chief of the East Indies squadron. Coolness under fire was as essential, in its turn, as Hewett's berserker style. Peel asked his officers, 'to disregard fire in the battery, by always walking with head up and shoulders back and without undue haste'. Wood thought Peel 'years in advance of the age ... not only a practised seaman, but an acute observer of human nature'. When ammunition parties demurred at carrying 16lb bags of gunpowder slung around the body, Peel and his officers set the example.[27]

Lieutenant Houston Stewart was praised for his calmness, at El Teb, when 'compelled to remain inactive under a severe fire ... his own personal coolness contributed very materially to that of his men'. Such insouciance could be taken too far. '"You fellows are too brave,"' said an army officer after Graspan: '"It is utterly useless to go on as you do, for you will only all get killed in this sort of warfare. I saw your officers walking about in front of their men, even when the latter were taking cover, just as if they were carrying on on board ship."'[28]

When not in action naval officers displayed a sense of responsibility towards their men unusual in the army before the reforms of the 1870s. Evelyn Wood, later a Field Marshal, thought army officers in the Crimea, 'did not as a class fully understand that their primary duty should have been to ensure that their men were sufficiently fed and adequately clothed'.[29] Captain Lushington, by contrast, went out to help sentries returning frozen from the trenches. De Lisle's division of the Cataract Brigade was separated from its baggage overnight: 'The men we got under cover with a very fair house I built with boats, sails and biscuit boxes, but Pigott and I slept as we were (or tried to) in the open.'[30] Such priorities were official policy: 'You will impress upon the officers the necessity for at all times exercising the most constant supervision over their men, and attending to their comfort and well being.'[31]

Concern for their men's welfare did not preclude ruthlessness, when discipline or military necessity demanded it. Wood approved Peel's belief 'that an undue excessive regard for men's lives does not conduce to victory over a brave enemy'.[32] One of *Sultan*'s field-gun crews began 'murmuring' about their exposed position at Alexandria in 1882, the wrong side of a mined bridge on the Ramleh road, until the midshipman in charge 'drew his revolver, and told them plainly he would shoot the first man who attempted to leave his post'.[33] Midshipman Edmund Fremantle did shoot one of his boat crew for firing at Chinese swimming away from a captured junk, an assertion of authority which caused some commotion: 'I remember telling the stroke oar that if he did not sit down and pull, I would shoot him.' Some of the men wanted to throw Fremantle overboard, but, after some hesitation, the Admiral hushed the affair up: 'Fortunately for me, perhaps, the papers were not so numerous as they are now.'[34]

Whether they provided leadership by example, kindness, or ruthlessness, officers had a different set of motives to their men, in which rational calculation about career prospects certainly featured. Sir John Fisher argued that the driving force behind most Naval Brigades was officers' thirst for decorations and promotion. Unlike the army and Foreign Office, the Royal Navy

[275]

did not reward officers for doing their peacetime duties. The only road to distinction was through active service, which during the long years of peace was only available ashore, and not always then. Lieutenant de Lisle regretted leaving HMS *Alexandra*, 'in case this is a shorter affair than one expected, and as for . . . being promoted out of it, it is outside the possible chances, unless one gets into action'. There was no glory in Cataract work, however arduous.[35] A stingy Admiralty even demurred at counting Nile service as sea time, jeopardising Beresford's chances of promotion, although their attitude softened by the 1890s, when West African service counted double. In 1900 the naval commentator David Hannay thought officers would continue to seek distinction ashore, 'until great naval wars begin again, of which there is little present prospect'.[36]

As soon as a Naval Brigade took part in land operations the Admiralty rushed to distribute decorations and promotions wholesale, regardless of regulations, previous service, or the possible retention of the best officers on their ships. The Admiralty was in such haste to dispense favours after the Boxer Rebellion, that they telegraphed the list of promotions before receiving Seymour's despatches.[37] The restriction of awards to those who went ashore was certainly invidious in that case. HMS *Orlando* had steamed 900 miles to Wei-hai-Wei for reinforcements, making record time, despite 362 of her complement of 486 serving ashore. The work of ship's parties was unglamorous and arduous, but often overlooked in the excitement of some brilliant success.

Promotion could matter a great deal to officers. A lieutenant in 1900 earned between £182 and £346 a year. This was, on average, eight times the earnings of an ordinary seaman, but less than the £500 a year considered necessary for a civilised existence. A captain, however, earned at least that, while a rear-admiral on £2,190 to £2,737 earned roughly twelve times as much as a lieutenant.[38] It was worth getting a foot up the ladder, although Percy Luxmore found the personal cost high: 'Glad as I was, I would rather have gone on with three stripes on my wrist, and have had dear Blake with us.'[39] Even without promotion officers could do well out of *batta*, extra pay for shore service. Midshipman A.B. Cunningham received £100 in sovereigns for his service in the Transvaal, but lost a quarter of it playing poker on the way home.

Wounded officers could hope for financial compensation. Captain Arthur Cochrane suffered severe injuries during the 2nd China War in an episode that shows how an officer provided tactical direction as well as leadership of a more traditional gung-ho variety:

placing one of my boat's crew in the best position to injure the enemy and protect myself, I was shot in the collar bone, and another shot glanced off my ribs. This staggered me much for the moment, and as I observed to the man standing near me . . . I thought I was done for.[40]

Cochrane recovered sufficiently to lead a charge down the street, but a third shot through his leg disabled him from further exertion. Cochrane applied for a 'gratuity on account of wounds', which the Admiralty unsportingly refused, on the grounds that he was still on active service on full pay!

Many senior officers, including Fisher, had experience of Naval Brigades, implying that it was no career disadvantage to have done so. Many served on several occasions at different points in their career, showing how common a feature of naval life such service was. Sir Henry Stephenson KCB was a midshipman with HMS *Pearl*'s Brigade at Amorha, Captain of HMS *Carysfort* at Ismailia and Sawakin, and Commander-in-Chief of the Channel Fleet in 1897. Sir Edward Seymour visited the trenches of Sebastopol as a midshipman, camped out in a Canton ginger store, chased Congo River pirates in the 1870s, and was the doyen of the first attempt to relieve Peking in 1900. Even disaster need not wreck a promising career. Sir Frederick Richards probably owed his life to Admiralty orders not to accompany the doomed 1881 invasion of the Transvaal. Sir William Mends, who had been at Balaklava, comforted him afterwards: 'Throw all grievances to the winds, my dear Richards, you are an *ascending star* and have a name in the service to be proud of.'[41] So it proved. As First Sea Lord, Richards' annual battles with the Naval Estimates in the 1890s ensured Splendid Isolation was more than just a catchphrase.

STRATEGIC EVALUATION

Critics have found fault with Naval Brigades for diverting naval resources into obscure and unhealthy backwaters, adversely affecting the Royal Navy's readiness for total war in 1914. The culture of improvisation they encouraged distracted attention from the technical challenges posed by nineteenth-century advances in naval *matériel*. A makeshift substitute for a dedicated amphibious warfare capability, Naval Brigades are supposed to have contributed to the fiasco at Gallipoli. Such criticism is factually flawed and unhistorical, ignoring the political and strategic context in which Naval Brigades operated. Against such criticism, it can be argued that Naval Brigades provided valuable low-risk experience of active service conditions, while forming an effective response to the strategic circumstances that faced the British Empire in its heyday.

It is impossible to imagine any nineteenth-century British government developing a capability specifically for amphibious warfare. The *laissez-faire* ideas of every administration, Liberal or Conservative, ensured that imperial emergencies were treated as unique events, governed by their own particular circumstances. The Esher report on deficiencies revealed by the Boer War noted how:

> The scientific study of Imperial resources, the coordination of the ever varying facts upon which Imperial rule rests, the calculation of forces required, the broad plans necessary to sustain the burden of Empire, have until quite recently, found no place in our system of government.[42]

There was no General Staff to formulate military policy in general, let alone a specific technical doctrine like amphibious warfare. Modern ideas on the subject arose from the demands of total war, when it became necessary to invade and liberate entire continents. Except at Gallipoli no British statesman or service chief before 1940 ever dreamed of landing an army other than at the ports of a colony or a continental ally. Complex ideas such as amphibious warfare were hardly likely to develop when the army did not codify its land-warfare doctrine until after the Boer War, when the first *Field Service Regulations* appeared. Sir Redvers Buller only formed the first permanent military transport service in 1888: the Army Service Corps. Given such basic deficiencies it is unbelievable that the army could have appreciated the need for specialised vessels like the Landing Ships Logistics operated by the descendants of Buller's ASC.

A dedicated amphibious warfare capability would have been out of all proportion to Victorian strategic circumstances. They had no need to storm ashore in the teeth of barbed wire and machine guns, or to nourish Army Groups across open beaches, although a Naval Brigade did exactly that for a smaller force at Port Durnford. Naval Brigades could use existing harbour facilities, as at Durban or Calcutta, when deployed defensively. On the offensive they could achieve an unopposed landing by surprise, as at Illig, or clear the beach with superior firepower, as at Shimonoseki or Rangoon. What was needed, in the Victorian strategic context, was a flexible force of small or medium-sized units capable of independent action:

> many British possessions are open to foreign attack or internal rebellion, which can only be met at first by calling on a part of our forces available

everywhere and at short notice. This is, and from the nature of things must be, the man-of-war, which is always within twenty-four hours of everything.

With Victorian self-assurance the writer anticipated that the Royal Navy's involvement in land wars would continue: 'In exact proportion as our territorial obligations multiply will be the necessity for a mobile armed force which will be available everywhere and rapidly.'[43] The contrast between the expeditious seizure of the Suez Canal in 1882, and the fumbling of 1956, is not to the advantage of the force specially equipped for amphibious assault. General purpose forces were more cost effective, in the Victorian context, than specifically amphibious units which would have been useless for exercising command of the sea in other ways. The flexibility of a Naval Brigade made each man doubly valuable, 'because he will be needed by his ship again, and because he can be applied to the fight at the most critical time and place'.[44]

Only the Royal Navy was available for a rapid-response role, for the army was committed elsewhere. The secret Stanhope Memorandum of 1891 summed up British defence policy at the end of the nineteenth century. After providing for aid to the civil power, and garrisons for India and the navy's coaling stations, the army's primary responsibility was home defence. The Memorandum made no mention of cooperation with the navy in overseas expeditions, even in defence of existing British possessions. Fisher himself admitted that the opportune landing of a Naval Brigade had often prevented disaster, when awaiting a military response would have lost any chance of acting at all. No contemporary British statesmen could have neglected such waterways as the Canton River, the Irrawaddy, the Straits of Shimonoseki, the Suez Canal, the Red Sea, or the Nile. They may have been unhealthy, but they were hardly obscure backwaters.

The withdrawal of military garrisons in the 1870s left the Royal Navy's Gunboats and Naval Brigades the first line of imperial defence. The contention that this created a culture of improvisation that vitiated naval operations during the First World War ignores other dysfunctional aspects of contemporary naval organisation, while overrating the influence of Naval Brigades. The main limiting factor on the Royal Navy's effectiveness during the Great War was its lack of a competent naval staff to provide coherent strategic guidance to senior officers. Fisher's autocratic rule had prevented healthy discussion of professional naval issues, while his focus on technical issues perpetuated the Victorian emphasis upon administrative reform at the expense of policy formulation. Engrossed in the acquisition of revolutionary new equipment, such as dreadnoughts, wireless, submarines, and aircraft, the navy had no time to think through the implications of the new technology for the conduct of modern naval war.

The Dardanelles shambles showed the consequences of the lack of a naval staff. Characterised by an unwarranted contempt for the enemy, the scheme flew in the teeth of all the Admiralty's previous studies of the problem. Fatally it threw away the surprise that had been a recognised element in the success of nineteenth-century amphibious landings, perhaps most devastatingly along the Suez Canal in 1882. The Gallipoli landings did seize a bridgehead, at a price, but once ashore the defensive trinity of rifle, barbed wire and shovel imposed the stalemate typical of all fronts during the First World War. None of this owed much to a naval culture of improvisation. The true amateurs of Gallipoli were those responsible for improvising strategy in a cloud of cigar smoke, without taking proper professional advice. Historians who mock the quaint technical means available to naval practitioners of the day, horseboats and whalers, fail to see beyond tactical expedients demanded in the field to the underlying expertise.

This reasserted itself in the evacuation of the Gallipoli bridgeheads in January 1916, a masterpiece of deception and inter-service cooperation. The raid on Zeebrugge in April 1918 has been seen as a return to Nelsonian standards of surprise and initiative, but its leading protagonist, Vice-Admiral Sir Roger Keyes, was himself a graduate of old-fashioned Naval Brigades, at Witu in 1890, and Taku in 1900. Keyes' personal connections with Fremantle, Brackenbury, and Sir Edward Seymour linked him to a tradition going back to Ashanti, Zululand, and the 2nd China War. Keyes was not the only senior naval officer in the First World War with such links to the past. Jellicoe and Beatty were both wounded during the Boxer Uprising. Two notable casualties of the Great War, Vice-Admirals Chris Cradock and Horace Hood, had led Naval Brigades at the Taku Forts and Illig. Jellicoe's leadership of the materialist school, and his reputation as the finest naval tactician of his day, suggest that Naval Brigade service did not imply a lack of interest in more regular aspects of the naval profession. Captain H.J. May was a brilliant officer who commanded a Naval Brigade at Gemaizeh in 1889. An associate of Julian Corbett, he discussed the tactical dilemma that would face Jellicoe at Jutland in the *RUSI Journal* of 1897, and founded the Naval War Course at Greenwich. Before his premature death in 1904 he was Fisher's choice as the next Director of Naval Intelligence. The argument that experience of colonial warfare precluded an intelligent interest in naval technology cannot be sustained. Percy Scott, the instigator of the Gunnery Revolution and prophet of the battleship's demise, was the arch-improviser of naval artillery at Alexandria and in the Boer War. Reginald Bacon, still suffering from malaria acquired in Benin, was the first Captain of submarines at Portsmouth in 1900. Like Percy Scott, he would have an innovative career as director of an armaments firm. Lord Charles Beresford, his career greatly injured by a feud with Fisher, was an advocate of the Naval Intelligence Department formed in 1887, and of training in night fighting, the lack of which proved so unfortunate at Jutland.

There is no evidence that the Royal Navy was divided into a colonial and a metropolitan school comparable with Wolseley's African Ring and Roberts' Indians in the army. The Fishpond and Beresford's Syndicate of Discontent both contained officers with Naval Brigade experience, an accepted part of every naval officer's career:

> A naval officer will be none the worse for the moral and intellectual train-
> ing he undergoes, even in such purely soldierly work as has come his way
> at Ladysmith or the Modder. Nor is it likely that he will be long enough
> away from the sea to grow rusty in his profession. Moreover he is exercis-
> ing a part of it when he fights on land.[45]

Ashore or afloat, the purpose of armed forces is to fight, an uncomfortable idea for the pacific historian. An anonymous writer argued between the World Wars that, 'one of the highest qualifications of any officer of the executive branch should be his ability to lead fighting men under arms, and to control and inspire them by his knowledge and confidence'.[46] Naval Brigades with their relatively low casualties were an effective way of acquiring such knowledge and confidence. Small wars demand qualities of leadership and quick decision essential in sea officers of any rank. Naval Brigades provided valuable experience of active service in the only way possible during a period of naval supremacy, necessarily lacking in sea battles. Some lessons were small but essential, like those drawn by Sir George Aston from his experiences in the Sudan:

> (1) Think of your men before you think of yourself, (2) Eat, drink, and
> sleep whenever you get a chance, if you want to stay the course, (3) Grease
> your boots.[47]

Lord Cunningham of Hyndhope doubted whether service with Bearcroft in the Boer War did him much good professionally, but felt it taught him responsibility and self-reliance. It was grand experience for a boy of seventeen to live on his wits in a strange country, fending for his men and himself in unfamiliar conditions.[48] Edmund Fremantle found his bush work in the Ashanti War an agreeable diversion from onerous duties as SNO:

> it is just this type of trial which makes the Naval Officer what he is – generally ready to accept responsibility, and always the man of expedients – prepared to meet difficulties.[49]

Active service did not only develop officers' characters. Fremantle found that his official coxswain was never on hand when the bullets flew. He chose a new 'fighting cox', who made his own motives clear: 'I suppose, sir, if you was to be dangerously wounded, and I was to carry you out, I should get the VC.'[50] The pressures of active service soon showed that the most valuable men in a tight corner were not always the best behaved in peacetime:

> those known as 'the greatest blackguards' [were], in most cases, the best men at a pinch on service. Men who were always in scrapes in peacetime were those to be relied on in a difficulty with the baggage, and ready in time of danger . . .[51]

When Captain Marchant went to clear Boers off the reverse slope of the kopje at Graspan, it was 'the bad hat of the company' who joined him, instantly wiping out his bad record, but as ready as ever 'to go a bust' on the first opportunity.

THE BUBBLE REPUTATION

Naval Brigades did not only affect relations within the Royal Navy. They played a beneficial role in raising public awareness of the service. Wars like the Crimea and the numerous imperial wars were fought primarily on land, but depended upon naval supremacy. The silent exercise of command of the sea could have gone unremarked, except for the part played by sailors in direct support of the army. The *Army and Navy Gazette* commented in 1882:

> The Egyptian campaign has once more brought the British bluejacket before the public; and as on all former occasions when his services have been brought into requisition, he has acquitted himself to the admiration of all; indeed he has probably never been higher in public favour than at the present time.[52]

Naval Brigades ensured popular recognition of the navy at a time when public opinion increasingly mattered:

> When Nelson's and Wellington's veterans returned from Trafalgar and Waterloo, they met with no popular welcome. The thanks of the sovereign and of the parliament were read formally to them from the quarterdeck of men-of-war and at the head of every regiment. The gratitude of the nation had only an official expression; whereas at present every class of the people are eager to do homage to the common sailor and the common soldier – to pay them honours which were erewhile reserved for officers only of the highest rank and the highest distinction. This fact marks an epoch in the history of our army and navy. They are now, in a sense more emphatic than ever, the country's servants as well as the Crown's.[53]

One sign of the change were formal dinners held at Portsmouth, Edinburgh, and Dublin for Crimean veterans of both services. Two thousand soldiers, sailors and marines regaled themselves on Portsmouth's Governor's Green with 300 joints of meat, 250 plum puddings, a ton of potatoes, four butts of beer, and two hogsheads of strong ale. Relations between the services had also changed: 'our sailors and soldiers, united in the earliest and most arduous labours of the siege of Sebastopol, have at last learned to appreciate each other', an emotion expressed in military cheers that greeted Captains Lushington and Keppel, and references to their part in the war. Naval Brigades were a significant step towards what Victorians described as 'a united service'.

A good dinner might appear small compensation for the rigours of the Crimea, but the banquet on Governor's Green marked a shift in public attitudes that struck the biographer of Admiral Sir Astley Cooper Key, who took *Sans Pareil* out to the 2nd China War:

> The good folk of my native 'Three Towns' were fairly deranged over the departure of a marine battalion to Zululand a few years later, who returned without ever seeing a shot fired in anger; while the old *Sans Pareil*, bearing many who would 'come back no more' from the battlefields of India and China, steamed away solitary and unnoticed, save for a brief paragraph in a local paper that she was overladen, and would probably terminate her career in the Bay of Biscay.[54]

The return of the Egypt Battalion in 1882 suggests 'deranged' was hardly too strong a term. The press of bodies at Plymouth's dockyard gate prevented further progress, the cheers of the surging crowd drowning out the triumphal march specially composed by the Division's Bandmaster. When the battalion at last reached Stonehouse barracks, the guard endeavoured to exclude the public, but, after a brief struggle, the marines were for once vanquished, and an irresistible torrent of spectators poured across the parade ground. After the First World War Sir George Aston commented cynically: 'We had but little sense of proportion in the services in those days; we were received as heroes after our six week's campaign.'[55]

Often the bluejacket missed out on public receptions, remaining abroad to finish the commission:

> if he does happen to turn up at the same time, a shipful of sailors is such a different thing from a trooper crowded with glorified redcoats, and the man-of-war's man goes about his ordinary duties in such an undemonstrative fashion, or is bundled over the side into a launch or Gunboat in such a matter of fact way that his exploits and the eulogies of war correspondents are apt to be forgotten.[56]

The Ashanti Naval Brigade missed the royal review at Windsor, but did enjoy a 'representative review' at the Royal Clarence Victualling Yard a month later on 23 April 1874, HMS *Barracouta* and *Simoom* still being absent. Her Majesty reviewed over 600 naval survivors of the campaign, walking slowly around the whole three-sided square, before meeting the officers of the Naval Brigade and Festing's Marine detachments. The Windsor and Gosport reviews were seen as signs of 'how completely the Queen is becoming restored to her position at the head of the nation', after the prolonged mourning that had followed the death of Prince Albert.[57] Naval involvement in public life and popular perceptions of military incompetence in South Africa ensured that the Royal Navy became far the more popular of the two services. There were even proposals to remodel the War Office on the Admiralty. Technical skill and success on the battlefield created an image of naval omnicompetence, whether armouring trains or stowing cavalry horses on troopships:

> If there is any unusually ticklish business to be done, of which no-one present has any former experience, a 'party of bluejackets' will almost invariably be able to solve the problem.[58]

Harold Begbie celebrated the bluejacket in excruciating verse as *The Handy Man*. Illustrated by an eagle-eyed Gunner's Mate, the following appeared alongside Kipling's *Absent Minded Beggar*, to the latter's professional if not poetic disadvantage:

> Handy afloat, handy ashore,
>   handier still in a hole,
> Ready to swarm up a mountain-side,
>   or walk on a greasy pole,
> Lugging a gun through a desert,
>   scrubbing a deck milk-white
> Jack is the man for a children's romp,
>   and the awkward hour of a fight.[59]

From a wider perspective, Naval Brigades brought more significant benefits than a boost to the careers of ambitious officers, or additional forces with which to confront imperial emergencies. They sustained public awareness, even enthusiasm, for the navy during a period when Britain's wars were primarily matters for the army. Otherwise the popular view of the sailor might have remained that of 'a happy-go-lucky careless creature, whose accomplishments, like those of Dibden's hero, consist chiefly in being able to "sing a good song" and "swig with an air his allowance of grog"'.[60] Naval Brigades justified the navy's existence, sustaining professional motivation during the *Pax Britannica*. The army also benefited. The navy repeatedly demonstrated that heavy artillery could be used in the field for direct-fire support. The infantry were always pleased to see naval guns as they would go anywhere they were wanted, without any nonsense about passing requests for fire support through the Staff. Lord Wolseley, no advocate of Naval Brigades, admitted 'What splendid gunners they were! always cheery and always ready to lend a hand in any job, and that hand was sure to mean effective help.'[61] Royal Artillery officers accepted the situation:

> we all know that in all our wars sailors take a very prominent part, and wherever we have to fight, we are always glad to have bluejackets helping us with their field guns and machine guns. In the late war in the Soudan, the only guns taken to the front were the machine guns.[62]

In 1914 the BEF was the only European army to include heavy field guns in its infantry divisions, the design and tactical function of their 60prs remarkably similar to the 4.7-inch naval guns used in South Africa.

The recurrence of total war in 1939–45 made such demands upon the navy that it had to devote all energies to its primary function of maintaining command of the sea, not for overseas offensives, but for national survival. So desperate was the army's demand for weapons in 1940 that battleships and cruisers lost the 3.7-inch pack howitzers that had replaced 12pr field guns during the 1920s. The Royal Marines had taken up Hankey's concept of littoral warfare, conducting experiments at Eastney between the wars with landing craft and motor vehicles. This, however, led on to the entirely new specialisation of Combined Operations, a far cry from the happy expedients of Peel and Scott. Naval Brigades were never specialist amphibious forces. They were found by general-purpose naval units from their own resources. Only thus could such widely used forces have been cost effective.

Naval Brigades were not haphazard improvisations, but the product of careful training and organisation. They customarily practised landings and drill before action, for example at Canton in 1857 or Simonstown in 1899. African operations in particular demanded careful preparation, their lessons receiving careful study afterwards. Improvisation did occur, in the adaptation of standard training and resources to variable situations, which often baffled the army. Operational flexibility is not evidence of professional incapacity. There was plenty of improvisation in the Falklands War, despite high levels of professionalism and purpose-built equipment. Naval Brigades have been accused of substituting improvisation for professionalism, but a major problem throughout both services in the First World War was their inflexibility. Perhaps Naval Brigade influence was not widespread enough.

The specialisation of warfare, on land as well as at sea, and the United Kingdom's altered strategic circumstances closed a period when the Royal Navy could play as significant a role ashore as afloat. Even in the changed situation of the twentieth century, however, there may still be occasions when there is a need for an immediate response by general-purpose naval units to particular emergencies. Platoons of sailors from the Pacific Fleet landed with Bren gun and rifle at Hong Kong and Tokyo, after the sudden end of the Second World War. Until the arrival of regular military forces, they secured the surrender of Japanese troops and dockyard facilities in a classic display of the flexibility and expedition that had made the Victorian Naval Brigades so effective an agent of imperial power.

Sources

PERIODICALS CONSULTED, AND ABBREVIATIONS:

A&NG – *Army and Navy Gazette*
G&L – *Globe & Laurel*: the Royal Marines' Corps journal
HT – *Hampshire Telegraph*
ILN – *Illustrated London News*
JRUSI – *Journal of the Royal United Service Institute*
LG – *London Gazette*
MM – *Mariner's Mirror*
N&AI – *Navy and Army Illustrated*
N&MG – *Naval and Military Gazette*
NC – *Naval Chronicle*
nd – no date
NLJ – *Navy League Journal*
NM – *Nautical Magazine*
NR – *Naval Review*
SHJ&NC – *Sailor's Home Journal and Naval Chronicle*
USJ – *United Service Journal*
USM – *United Service Magazine*

OTHER ABBREVIATIONS USED IN FOOTNOTES:

AP – *Admiralty Print*
CO – Colonial Office
FEx – *Field Exercise*
NA – *Naval Annual*
NMM – National Maritime Museum
NO – Naval Operations 1914–18
NRS – Navy Records Society
PP – Parliamentary Papers
RMM – Royal Marines Museum Library Eastney
RNM – Royal Naval Museum and Admiralty Library

Notes

Chapter 1: The Raid That Failed

1. *The Times*, 24 Feb. 1996, p. 11.
2. Mrs T. Kelly: *From the Fleet in the Fifties*, p. 94: Revd S. Kelson Stothert, 29 Aug. 1854.
3. NRS, D. Bonner-Smith & Capt. A.C. Dewar: *Russian War, 1854*, pp. 311–12.
4. Ibid., p. 349: Dundas——Admiralty, 27 Oct. 1854.
5. Kelly, pp. 141–43.
6. *MM*, 44, p. 324: *The Russian Fleet at Sebastopol.*
7. NRS, Bonner-Smith & Dewar, p. 323: Dundas——Admiralty, 28 Sept. 1854.
8. Ibid., p. 325: Dundas——Admiralty, 3 Oct. 1854; FM Sir E. Wood: *Midshipman to Field-Marshal*, p. 28, and W.E.M. Reilly: *Artillery Operations . . . at Sebastopol*, p. 256, give 140 landed per ship.
9. *G&L*, 1898, p. 124.
10. Martello Tower: *At School and at Sea*, pp. 332–33.
11. NRS, Bonner-Smith & Dewar, p. 325: Dundas——Admiralty, 3 Oct. 1854.
12. Martello Tower, p. 335.
13. Ibid., p. 341.
14. Ibid., p. 338.
15. Capt. L.G. Heath: *Letters from the Black Sea*, p. 87.
16. Reilly, pp. 5–7.
17. Martello Tower, pp. 342–45.
18. Reilly, p. 12.
19. Martello Tower, p. 351.
20. Heath, p. 91: 27 Oct. 1854.
21. Capt. S. Eardley-Wilmot: *Life of Vice-Admiral Edmund, Lord Lyons*, p. 260: 1,786 RN, 1,530 RM at Eupatoria; Reilly p. 35: RN losses were 18 dead and 115 wounded.
22. Gen. Sir H.E. Blumberg (with Col. C. Field): *Random Records . . .*, pp. 78–79.
23. *G&L*, 1899, p. 170.
24. *G&L*, 1901, p. 127.

25. Blumberg & Field, p. 80.

26. Heath, pp. 94–95: his 3,000 Englishmen included three battalions of Scottish Highlanders.

27. Martello Tower, pp. 358–59.

28. Field: *Britain's Sea Soldiers*, ii, p. 98: presumably the Right Lancaster battery.

29. Kelly, p. 231.

30. Heath, p. 118.

31. Martello Tower, p. 373.

32. *G&L*, 1908, p. 68.

33. Martello Tower, p. 385.

34. Ibid., p. 369.

35. Martello Tower, p. 390.

36. Ibid., p. 378.

37. Ibid., p. 391.

38. A.W. Kinglake: *The Invasion of the Crimea*, v, p. 33: on 3 Nov. 1854 the British Army in the Crimea numbered 22,343, and the Naval and Marine Brigades some 2,500.

39. NRS, Bonner-Smith & Dewar, pp. 393–94; Admiralty——Dundas, 11 Dec. 1854. Cf. pp. 214, 325, 346, 357, 413.

40. NRS, Capt. A.C. Dewar: *Russian War 1855 Black Sea*, p. 59: Lyons——Admiralty, 12 Jan. 1854.

41. Wood: *The Crimea in 1854 and 1894*, p. 259.

42. Wood: *Midshipman . . .*, p. 55: to serve the vent of a muzzle-loading gun, the No.1 placed his right thumb over the touch-hole to prevent sparks igniting the fresh charge as it was rammed home.

43. Adm. Sir W. Kennedy: *Hurrah for the Life of a Sailor*, p. 24.

44. NRS, Dewar, pp. 118–22: Lushington——Lyons, 14 & 16 Apr. 1855.

45. Reilly, p. 115: RN losses 12 killed, 72 wounded.

46. Wood: *Crimea*, p. 261.

47. Reilly, pp. 205 & 108.

48. NRS, Dewar, p. 202: 10 killed, 47 wounded, & 1 missing.

49. Kelly, pp. 345–46.

50. Reilly, p. 140: quoting Simpson——Panmure, 21 July 1855.

51. Ibid., pp. 186–87, 175 & 201.

52. Reilly, pp. 224–25 for numbers of guns used and lost.

53. RAdm. C.C. Penrose-Fitzgerald: *Life of Vice Admiral Sir George Tryon*, pp. 62–63.

54. Adm. Sir H. Keppel: *Sailor's Life Under Four Sovereigns*, p. 303.

55. NRS, Dewar, pp. 252–53 & p. 303.

56. Capt. C. Sloane-Stanley RN – *Reminiscences*, ii, pp. 234–35.

57. NRS Dewar, pp. 302–3 & pp. 317–18.

58. Sir W.L. Clowes: *The Royal Navy . . .*, vi, p. 435.

59. Wood: *Crimea*, p. 217.

60. Kelly, p. 277 & Fortescue: *A History of the British Army 1660–1870*, xiii, p. 203.

Chapter 2: India's Sunny Clime

1. NRS, Cdr. W.D. Rowbotham: *Naval Brigades in the Indian Mutiny 1857–58*, pp. 11 & 21.
2. RAdm. V.A. Montagu: *A Middy's Recollections 1853–1860*, p. 148.
3. RNM, 1990/143(1) Capt. E.S. Sotheby: *Journals of the* Pearl *Brigade.*
4. Sir Patrick Grant-Canning, 10 Aug. 1857, in Rowbotham, p. 107: *Shannon's* guns were 8-inch shell guns of 65cwt, easily confused with the more effective 68pr of 95cwt, as the projectiles were the same weight.
5. Mid. E.S. Watson: *A Naval Cadet with HMS* Shannon's *Brigade in India*, p. 3: cf. Lt E.H. Verney: *The* Shannon's *Brigade in India 1857–58*, p. 7, 450 men with 25 officers.
6. NMM, JOD/154/1, J.P. Hoskins: *Journal of HMS* Shannon's *Brigade in the Indian Mutiny*, 18 Aug. 1857.
7. RNM 1990/143(11) Sotheby, 12 Sept. 1857.
8. NRS, Rowbotham, p. 267: Salmon, 17 Sept. 1857.
9. Hoskins, 15 Sept. 1857.
10. Hoskins, 12 Oct. 1857.
11. RNM 1985/291 O/S James Chappel: *Diary of Commission of HMS* Pearl *1856–59*; undated entry.
12. NRS, Rowbotham, p. 133: Peel——Maj.-Gen. Mansfield, 3 Nov. 1857. Other troops: 53rd Regt: 162 men; RE: 68; 93rd Highlanders: 100; Depot Detachment: 70; Bengal Artillery: two 9pr guns.
13. NRS, Rowbotham, p. 135: Ibid.
14. NRS, Rowbotham, p. 140: 2 killed, 13 wounded of whom 3 died later.
15. Ibid., p. 135: Maj. W. Mayhew DAG——Secretary Govt of India, 12 Nov. 1857.
16. Ibid., p. 269: Salmon, 12 Nov. 1857.
17. Ibid., p. 145: Admiralty minute on Seymour's despatch, 25 Dec. 1857.
18. Ibid., p. 137: Peel——Seymour, 9 Nov. 1857.
19. G & L 1902, IX, p. 17.
20. Rowbotham, p. 282: O'Leary——Salmon, 12 Sept. 1904.
21. Hoskins, 30 Oct. 1857.
22. Ibid., 2 Nov. 1857.
23. Ibid., 12 Nov. 1857.
24. Ibid., 14 Nov. 1857: Bowman thought the gun went off reloading, killing two and wounding four, almost a third of the day's total loss: 20 killed & wounded.
25. W. Forbes Mitchell: *The Relief of Lucknow*, pp. 50–51.
26. Quoted in Forbes Mitchell, pp. 50–51.
27. Hoskins, 16 Nov. 1857.
28. Ibid., 23 Nov. 1857.
29. Forbes Mitchell, p. 69: RA and RN: 105; 53rd: 76; 93rd: 108; 4th Sikhs (Brasyer's): 95, i.e. 384 out of a total of 541.
30. NRS, Rowbotham, p. 272: Salmon, 10 Dec. 1857.
31. Hoskins, 28 Nov. 1857.

32. *The Times*, 11 Feb. 1858, p. 7: Anonymous letter from Lt. Garvey.

33. Watson, p. 37.

34. Ibid., p. 38.

35. Ibid, p. 39.

36. Garvey, *op. cit.*

37. Watson, p. 50.

38. Hoskins, 1 Dec. 1857.

39. NRS, Rowbotham, p. 273: Salmon, 10 Dec. 1857.

40. Forbes Mitchell, p. 89.

41. Garvey, *op.cit.*

42. Montagu, p. 155.

43. Revd E.A. Williams: *The Cruise of the* Pearl ... p. 79: 45 RM, 200 RN, 50 Sikhs, 450 Ghurkhas. Fifty Ghurkhas remained at Siwan with a handful of seamen.

44. Williams, p. 80.

45. Chappel, 26 Dec. 1857.

46. Ibid., 26 Dec. 1857.

47. Sotheby (11) 26 Dec. 1857.

48. Montagu, p. 165: rebel losses 150–200; British: 1 dhooli bearer killed, Naval Brigade and Ghurkhas 2 wounded each (Williams, p. 90).

49. Montagu, p. 165.

50. Ibid., p. 166.

51. Williams, p. 111.

52. Chappel, 5 March 1858.

53. Williams, p. 161: Gorakhpur Field Force: 850 Ghurkhas, 200 Bengal Yeomanry Cavalry, 32 Marines, 140 Royal Navy, 4 12pr Field guns, 39 Sikhs; estimated rebels: 4,000 sepoys, 10,000 irregulars, 10 guns.

54. Williams, p. 164.

55. British losses: Killed 1 Officer RN, 3 Ghurkhas; Wounded 14 RN, 13 Ghurkhas, 3 Cavalry, and 2 Sikhs.

56. Montagu, p. 183.

57. Williams, p. 173.

58. Verney, p. 62.

59. Ibid., p. 79.

60. Watson, p. 75.

61. NRS, Rowbotham, p. 149: Peel——Sir Michael Seymour, 1 March 1858. The Brigade was then 423 strong, excluding officers and sick.

62. Hoskins, 23 Feb. 1858.

63. Campbell had 164 guns, 14 naval being the heaviest (FM Lord Roberts, *Forty-One Years in India* ... , p. 396).

64. Hoskins, 9 March 1858.

65. NRS, Rowbotham, p. 278: Salmon, 9 March 1858.

66. NRS, Rowbotham, p. 279: Salmon——father, 22 March 1858.

67. Verney, p. 117.

68. NRS, Rowbotham, p. 279: Salmon——Bella, 28 March 1858.
69. Ibid., p. 148: Admiralty Minute 19 April 1858.
70. Sotheby (6), 10 May 1858.
71. Chappel, 14 June 1858.
72. Ibid., April 1858.
73. Ibid., 23 May 1858.
74. Williams, p. 271.
75. Montagu, p. 192.
76. Sotheby (6), 8 Jan. 1859.
77. Distribution as follows:

Gyah	(Vaughan)	6 officers & 116 men: 28 non-effective
Shergotty	(Young)	2 officers & 84 men: 17 non-effective
Sasseram	(Hay)	8 officers & 104 men: 28 non-effective

(NRS, Rowbotham, p. 160, Vaughan——Commodore Watson)
78. G&L, 1908, p. 27.
79. Verney, p. 138.
80. Hoskins, 3 May 1858.
81. NMM, JOD/154/2, Hoskins, August 1858.
82. Ibid., 1 Sept. 1858. Hoskins bought himself out on his return, living as a baker in Exeter.
83. Williams, p. 303.
84. Fortescue, xiii, pp. 388–90.
85. Montagu, p. 196.
86. NMM, JOD/93/1, Revd E.L. Bowman: Journal of Chaplain of HMS *Shannon's* Naval Brigade; Dr Flanagan Return of losses: 10 killed, 10 died of wounds, 25 invalided, 34 recovered from wounds, 83 died of disease: 138 taken off the ship's books.

Chapter 3: Terms of Reference

1. Maj. Sir J. Halkett: Diary . . . p. 6: Dumbarton's became the Royal Scots.
2. Revd E.A. Williams: *The Cruise of the* Pearl . . . , p. 74: Strictly a brigade has 2–4 battalions nominally 1,000 men each: *Pearl's* totalled 250.
3. Col. C. Field: *The British Navy Book*, p. 189.
4. General Thomas Wentworth: *Journal of the Expedition to Cartagena*, 1744, London.
5. *NA* 1900, p. 184, D. Hannay: *Naval Brigades*.
6. Field: *British Navy Book*, p. 191.
7. The Spanish Navy contributed 1,200 men out of 2,200: D. Syrett (ed.), *The Siege and Capture of Havana*, p. 325.
8. Quoted by J.S. Corbett, *England in the Seven Years War*, ii, p. 357.
9. NRS, Syrett, p. 324: Lt.-Gen. David Dundas, *Memo*, 1800.

10. NRS, Syrett, p. 187: Cdr. Augustus Keppel——Adm. Pocock, 12 June 1762.
11. *USM*, 1833, pp. 210–15: Captain Boswall (present as a Midshipman).
12. *NC*, xii, p. 308: J. Eckstein, letter, 17 Feb. 1804.
13. *JRUSI*, Nov. 1956, p. 540: Maurice quoted by Rowbotham.
14. *USJ*, 1844, ii, p. 556: Sgt. Jenkins RM: *My First Smell of Gunpowder.*
15. *NC*, xxv, p. 305: participant's letter.
16. Primarily *Tigre* (80), and *Theseus* (74): Sir W.L. Clowes: *The Royal Navy. . . ,* iv, pp. 400–4.
17. British losses in the siege: 22 killed, 66 wounded, 4 drowned. *Theseus'* accident killed 40 and wounded 47.
18. NRS, Spencer Papers, iii, p. 54: Admiralty——Nelson, 20 August 1799.
19. Field: *British Navy Book,* p. 191: Anonymous military witness of sailors at Walcheren 1809.
20. *SHJ&NC*, 1864, p. 120.
21. Ibid., 1862, p. 111.
22. Ibid., 1862, p. 75.
23. Sir J.H. Briggs: *Naval Administration 1827–1892,* p. 295.
24. Gladstone resigned in 1892 over increased Naval Estimates. His enemies knew him as God's Only Mistake.
25. Briggs, p. 88.
26. Ibid., p. 79.
27. *SHJ&NC*, 1862, p. 17.
28. Ibid., 1857, p. 87.
29. *JRUSI*, 1882, p. 884: Vice-Adm. H. Boys.
30. Lt. E.H. Verney: *The Shannon's Brigade in India,* p. 136.
31. *The Times,* 24 April 1856.

Chapter 4: The Kings Must Come Down

1. *NM*, 1857, p. 151: Sir M. Seymour——Admiralty, 14 Nov. 1856.
2. Sir E.H. Seymour: *My Naval Career and Travels,* p. 60: Yeh's score allegedly exceeded 100,000.
3. The Chinese currency was Mexican dollars worth 4/3d or 21p.
4. *NM*, 1857, p. 153: Letter from officer, HMS *Barracouta.*
5. Maj. W.H. Poyntz: *Per Mare Per Terram . . . ,* p. 103.
6. *SHJ&NC*, 1858, p. 30: anonymous eyewitness.
7. *RMM*, 13/11/85, Pvt. W. Baker RMLI, p. 8.
8. V.H. Goodenough: *Journal . . . ,* p. 29.
9. Poyntz, pp. 110 & 107. Source for losses: NRS D. Bonner-Smith & E.W.R. Lumby: *Second China War,* pp. 273–81: Seymour——Admiralty, 13 Jan. 1858.
10. Pvt. W. Baker RMLI: Journal, Canton, p. 10.
11. *SHJ&NC*, 1858, p. 51.

12. Goodenough, p. 32. The garrisons were:

    Old Fort   4 battns, i.e. 885 men
    Middle Fort   5 battns, i.e. 1034 men
    Southern Fort   2 battns, i.e. 628 men

    (*SHJ&NC*, 1858, p. 110: Chinese paper picked up after the fighting.)
13. E.H. Seymour, p. 64.
14. Goodenough, p. 35: Dew was Captain of HMS *Nimrod*.
15. Account largely from Hope's Despatch, 5 July 1859 (*LG*, 16 Sept. 1859, p. 3423), and NMM, MS 86/046: papers of Hope's Flag Lieutenant (later Captain) G.A. Douglas.
16. Douglas papers.
17. *SHJ&NC*, 1859, p. 124.
18. Ibid.
19. *NM*, Oct. 1859, 543–44: letter by a surviving RM officer.
20. The gunboats lost 25 dead, 93 wounded; the landing party 64 dead and 252 wounded, of which 27 and 142 were marines. HMS *Highflyer* contributed 130 men of whom 30 became casualties.
21. Walter White: *China Station 1859–1864 . . .* , p. 41.
22. *SHJ&NC*, 1860, p. 110.
23. RNM 1994/330(2), Lt. A.C.H. Paget, 17 August 1860.
24. NMM, LOG/N/27 Lt. P.R. Luxmore, Journal, 14 August 1860.
25. *LG*, 6 Nov. 1860, pp. 4088–89: Lt.-Col. J.H. Gascoigne-Hope, 21 August 1860.
26. Lt. A. C. H. Paget: Journal, 1 October 1860.
27. Sir W.L. Clowes: *The Royal Navy . . .* , vii, p. 160: Lord John Russell (Foreign Secretary).
28. *SHJ&NC*, 1862, p. 75. Total strength: RN 255; RM 80; RA 90; 99th 80; Indians 800; French 150; Algerians 400.
29. Captain G.A. Douglas, papers: *North China Herald*, 17 May 1862, naval correspondent.
30. *SHJ&NC*, 1862, p. 75.
31. White, p. 24: 'Kenney' was the senior French naval officer.
32. Commander Okuda IJN: *The Bombardment of Kagoshima by the British Fleet*, trans. Lt. N. James RN (1908 Devonport). The RN squadron were: HMS *Euryalus* (35), *Pearl* (21), *Perseus* (17), *Argus* (4), *Racehorse* (4), *Coquette* (4), *Havoc* (2) (*SHJ&NC*, 1863, p. 139).
33. Okuda, p. 9. See *NM*, 1863, pp. 642–48 for Kuper's despatches.
34. *NM*, 1863, pp. 646; Okuda, p. 10.
35. *SHJ&NC*, 1864, pp. 7, 53, & 91.
36. Okuda, p. 12: written in 1906.
37. *A&NG*, 1863, p. 457, & 1864, p. 105.
38. A 'musmee' was a young Japanese woman.
39. British ships were: HMS *Euryalus* (35), *Barrossa* (21), *Tartar* (20), *Leopard* (18), *Perseus* (17), *Argus* (6), *Coquette* (4), *Conqueror* (78), *Bouncer* (0) (Clowes, vii, p. 203).

40. Adm. J. Moresby: *Two Admirals...*, p. 235.

41. Poyntz, p. 223.

42. Moresby, p. 237.

43. *LG*, 18 Nov. 1864, p. 5471: Alexander——Kuper, 10 Sept. 1864.

44. There is confusion over who took which side. Alexander's and Suther's despatches put the Marines on the right, but the *ILN* shows the reverse.

45. *LG*, 18 Nov. 1864, pp. 5471–72; Poyntz, p. 227. British losses 5–6 Sept. were 8 killed, 48 wounded.

46. *USJ*, 1832, pp. 10–27, *Naval Operations in the Burmese War*.

47. Ibid., p. 19.

48. Ibid., p. 27.

49. *LG*, 31 May 1852, p. 1529 RAdm. Austen——Govt of India 10 April 1852: ships included: HMS *Rattler* (11), *Fox* (40), *Hermes* (6), *Salamander* (6), *Serpent* (16), carrying 818 men; six ships of the Indian Marine Service, and seven more armed vessels. The RN warships mounted 80 guns compared with 63 in the others.

50. *The Times.* 25 March 1852, p. 8, 19 June 1852, p. 6.

51. *LG*, 31 May 1852, p. 1529, Austen——Govt of India, 10 April 1852: 5,767 men.

52. *The Times.* 17 May 1852, p. 5.

53. *LG*, 31 May 1852, p. 1535, Lt.-Gen. Godwin——Govt of India, 18 April 1852.

54. *LG*, 17 July 1852, pp. 2003–7, Lambert——Govt of India, 24 May 1852: RN order of battle: 1 Lt., 1 Midshipman, 1 Assistant Surgeon, 16 ratings with 12pr; 2 Lts RM & 49 O/Rs.

55. *LG*, 21 Sept. 1852, pp. 2525–26: Tarleton——Lambert, 11 July 1852.

56. See Fortescue, xii, p. 482.

57. *G&L*, 1901, p. 128.

58. *LG*, 18 Jan. 1853, pp. 402–4, Godwin——Govt of India, 24 Dec. 1852; Lambert ——Govt of India, 18 Dec. 1852.

59. *LG*, 5 April 1853, p. 994, Lambert——Govt of India, 7 Feb. 1853. Naval strength: 20 officers, 143 ratings, 62 marines drawn from HMS *Winchester*, *Fox*, and *Sphinx*.

60. Naval losses: 7 killed (including Loch died 40 hours later), 52 wounded. The 67th lost 5 killed, 18 wounded covering the retreat.

61. FM Sir G. Wolseley: *Story of a Soldier's Life*, i, pp. 44–45.

62. RNM, 1990/143(6), Capt. E.S. Sotheby, *Journals...*, 20 Feb. 1858.

63. Sir J.W. Fortescue: *A History of the British Army*, xii, p. 490.

64. RNM, 1976/110(1), Lt. A. Battiscombe, Journal..., p. 93: The brigade mustered: 15 naval officers, Lt. RMA, Doctor, Chief Engineer, the Gunner, 23 POs, 88 seamen & stokers, 37 RM, 19 idlers & boys.

65. Ibid., ii, p. 2.

66. Ibid., ii, p. 3.

67. Ibid., ii, p. 5.

68. Ibid., ii, p. 15.

69. *N&MG*, 4 Nov. 1885, p. 449.

70. Official telegrams, orders, and reports appear in: *Operations in Burmah*, and

Proceedings of Naval Brigade (*AP* Ca423) & *LG* 22 June 1886, pp. 2965–75. Ships represented (*AP*):

	Officers	Seamen	Marines
Bacchante	9	132	22
Turquoise	13	111	27
Woodlark	3	48	7
Mariner	2	36	=
Sphinx	4	24	4
Total	31	351	60

The military contributed 10,000 troops, and 7,000 camp followers.

71. *AP*: Special Correspondent with Naval Brigade, p. 14.
72. *LG*: VAdm. F.W. Richards——Admiralty, 26 Feb. 1886.
73. NMM, JOD/119/2, Richard Cotten, Journals . . . , 27 Nov. 1885.
74. Ibid., 28 Nov. 1885.
75. *AP*: Richards——Admiralty, 23 Dec. 1885.
76. Cotten, 14 Dec. 1885.
77. *AP*: Cdr. C.J. Barlow——Capt. R. Woodward, 22 Dec. 1885.
78. Cotten, 24 Dec. 1885.
79. *AP*: Richards——Admiralty, 23 Dec. 1885.
80. *AP*: Fleet Surgeon T. d'A Brownlow (PMO *Turquoise*) 13 Jan. 1886. Average daily sicklist 4.8 out of 444 officers and men, i.e. 1.08%. Causes of death: Cholera 4; Dysentery 2; Drowning 1.
81. *AP*: Divisional Orders Bhamo, 29 Dec. 1889.

Chapter 5: *What We Have We Hold*

1. *NM* 1862, p. 130, pp. 400–1, p. 515: Capt. P. Cracroft – *Proceedings of HMS* Niger.
2. Ibid., p. 571. The initial party were: 7 officers (including the Gunner); 30 seamen; 20 marines.
3. *NM*, 1862, pp. 575–77 & 625–27: Cracroft took 53 sailors or marines in addition to Blake's 50.
4. RNM, 1976/110(4), Lt. A. Battiscombe, Journal . . . , 26 August 1860.
5. Ibid., 29 August 1860.
6. *A&NG*, 15 Sept. 1860, p. 637; total losses: 26 dead, 33 wounded, of which 10 RN.
7. *NM*, 1863, p. 116.
8. Battiscombe, 11 Oct. 1860.
9. *NM*, 1863, p. 242.
10. *LG*, 27 Oct. 1863, p. 5069, Lt.-Gen. D.A. Cameron.
11. *SHJ&NC*, 1863, p. 110.

12. *New Zealander*, 20 October 1863, in *SHJ&NC*, 1864, p. 18. Wiseman landed 10 officers, 220 seamen and marines.

13. *SHJ&NC*, 1864, p. 31, Comm. W.S. Wiseman——Admiralty, 30 Nov. 1863. British losses 36 killed, 98 wounded; 6 & 10 respectively from the RN.

14. *LG*, 15 July 1864, pp. 3545–57. RN/RM strength: 17 officers, 412 ratings/other ranks. Regular infantry at least: 35 officers, 1,160 other ranks. Cameron's despatch does not agree with other accounts, omitting 170 rifles of the 70th. Guns used: 1×110pr RBL; 2×40pr RBL; 2×6pr RBL; 2×24pr SB howitzers; 2×8-inch mortars; 6 coehorns or light mortars, each with 100 rounds.

15. *A&NG*, 1864, p. 556.

16. *LG*, 15 July 1864, pp. 3554–55, Wiseman——Admiralty, 3 May 1864.

17. *A&NG*, 1864, p. 556.

18. British losses 27 killed, 36 wounded; 13 & 27 from the RN.

19. Adm. Sir E.R. Fremantle, *The Navy As I Have Known It*, p. 146.

20. Asante is the proper name of the people against whom the British fought what they called the Ashanti Wars.

21. NMM, LOG/N/27, Cdr. P.R. Luxmore, Journal . . . , 13 June 1873.

22. PP, 1874, xlvi, C.891, p. 98, R. Eustace (Surgeon 2nd Class)——Admiralty, 26 August 1873.

23. RMM, 7/41(19), DAG RM 31 Jan. 1873.

24. RNM, 1995/41/9 Mid. Edward Bayly to his mother, 18 August 1873.

25. *A&NG*, 1873, p. 769.

26. C.892, p. 159, Wolseley——Lord Kimberley at the CO 7 Oct. 1873.

27. C.892, p. 226, Fremantle——Admiralty 31 Oct. 1873.

28. Fremantle, *op. cit.*, p. 226.

29. *A&NG*, 1873, p. 769.

30. Fremantle, p. 238.

31. C.894, pp. 37–40: Numbers landed 27 December 1873:

	Officers	Seamen	Marines
HMS *Active*	7	42	11
HMS *Druid*	4	36	12
HMS *Encounter*	2	25	11
HMS *Amethyst*	2	30	=
HMS *Argus*	2	30	11
TOTAL	17	163	45

The Army contributed: 23rd Royal Welch Fusiliers; 42nd Highlanders; 2nd Rifle Brigade, of whom 1,578 landed.

32. Luxmore, 28 Nov. 1873.

33. *A&NG*, 1874, p. 75.

34. Ibid., p. 145.

35. Luxmore, 27–29 Dec. 1873.

36. Ibid., 28 Dec. 1873.
37. NMM, BLK/2, Capt. W.H. Blake, 17 Jan. 1874.
38. Total British: 1,409 Europeans (189 RN) & 708 African irregulars (Brackenbury, ii, p. 182) against 10,000–20,000 Asante (Edgerton, *Fall of the Asante Empire*, p. 137; Luxmore, 31 Jan. 1874). The Naval Brigade's Right and Left Wings, or half-battalions, were inverted at Amoafo, Luxmore's Left Wing fighting to the right of the road.
39. Luxmore, 31 Jan. 1874.
40. NMM, LOG/N/E/1, Lt. Angus McLeod: Journal . . . , 31 Jan. 1874. McLeod led a company of Royal Marines, their own officers being sick.
41. British losses: 4 dead; 194 wounded (Brackenbury, ii, p. 183).
42. Luxmore, 2 Feb. 1874.
43. C.891, p. 200.
44. Luxmore, 13 Feb. 1874.
45. Strictly General FA Thesiger until November 1878.
46. Numbers vary: The Captain's despatch gives 173: 10 Officers, 107 ratings, 42 RM, 14 Kroomen, 2×12pr RBL guns, 1×Gatling, 2×24pr rocket tubes (*LG*, 7 Nov. 1879, p. 6310).
47. NMM, MLN/199/9–10, *AP, Naval Brigades in Zululand*, pp. 13 & 18, Admiralty ——CO, 1 Jan. 1879 & 15 Jan. 1879. *Tenedos* landed: 3 Officers, 30 ratings, 15 RM.
48. *AP*, pp. 10–11, Sullivan——Admiralty, 23 Dec. 1878.
49. *LG*, 4 March 1879, p. 1938: Campbell-Sullivan, 24 Jan. 1879. Harding was subsequently rated AB.
50. *AP*, p. 18, Sullivan——Admiralty, 26 Jan. 1879.
51. *LG*, 7 Nov. 1879, p. 6315: Sir Bartle Frere——CO, 12 August 1879. Shah landed: 16 Officers, 307 ratings, 69 RM, 2×9pr RML guns, 1×Gatling, 2×24pr rockets; from St Helena: 1 company 88th Foot & a field battery.
52. *AP*, p. 54, Campbell at Eshowe, 9 March 1879.
53. 2×9pr RML guns, 2×Gatlings, 4×24pr rockets. 1st Brigade had 350 seamen; 2nd 190 seamen & 100 marines, i.e. 640 out of 3,240.
54. NMM BCK/2, Cdr. J.W. Brackenbury: *Log of HMS Shah's Naval Brigade. . .* & MS 73/069 W. Jenkin: Shah's Brigade . . .
55. Brackenbury, 2 April 1879.
56. Jenkin, 2 April 1879.
57. *A&NG*, 16 May 1879, p. 461.
58. Jenkin, 2 April 1879.
59. *AP*, p. 95: Naval Brigade Distribution.
60. *A&NG*, 21 June 1879, p. 444.
61. *A&NG*, 16 May 1879, p. 461.
62. *AP*, p. 93: Richards——Admiralty, 4 June 1879.
63. Jenkin, 15 June 1879.
64. *JRUSI*, 1882, vol. xxvi, p. 881: Capt. H.J. Fletcher Campbell, *Naval Brigades. . .*
65. Jenkin, 1 July 1879.

66. Ibid., 21 July 1879.
67. Ibid., 22 July 1879.
68. *LG*, 7 Nov. 1879, p. 6311.
69. Ibid., p. 6316: Bartle Frere——CO, 23 August 1879.
70. *A&NG*, 30 August 1879, p. 624.
71. *AP*, Ca428, *Transvaal War – Naval Contingent*: Telegrams between Cdr. F.W. Richards & Colley, 30 Dec. 1880, landed 6 Jan. 1881 Cdr. F. Romilly, 5 officers, 124 men, 2×Gatlings, 3×rocket tubes.
72. *A&NG*, 5 March 1881, p. 162: this was true of von Moltke before 1864!
73. *AP*: Romilly——Richards, 29 Jan. 1881. The British lost: 83 killed, & 110 wounded out of 1,201, an appalling percentage for a colonial skirmish.
74. *NR*, 1933, pp. 124–29, Sir Astley Cooper Key (1st Sea Lord)——Richards, 13 Feb. 1881. Landed 7 Feb.: 2 officers, 36 ratings from HMS *Dido*, 23 ratings from *Boadicea*.
75. *AP*, Romilly's Journal, 9 Feb. 1881.
76. Ibid., 27 Jan. 1881.
77. Ibid., 12 Feb. 1881.
78. Sixty-four ratings under Romilly, with Lieutenant C.J. Trower, Sub-Lt. A.L. Scott, Surgeon E.E. Mahon, out of 554 all ranks.
79. *AP*, Scott, 1 March 1881.
80. *AP*, Richards-Admiralty, 14 March 1881.
81. *AP*, Mahon-Richards, 4 March 1881.
82. Lt.-Col. C. Field: *The British Navy Book*, p. 198.
83. *NR*, 1935, p. 570, C.H. Macklen, A.B.
84. *AP*, Mahon-Richards, 4 March 1881.
85. *NR*, 1935, p. 570, Macklen.
86. The final count was 14 killed, 6 died of wounds, 13 wounded.
87. *NR*, 1935, p. 571, Macklen.
88. *A&NG*, 5 March 1881, p. 163: The numbers are exaggerated.
89. *LG*, 3 May 1881, p. 2106, Major Fraser RE——GOC Natal, 5 March 1881.
90. *AP*, Richards——Admiralty, 14 March 1881.

Chapter 6: Mechanisms of Intervention

1. *USM*, 1829, I, p. 743.
2. *USM*, 1832, ii, p. 242: Lt. H.L. Maw RN: *On the Practise of Small Arms*.
3. Some POs already served more than one commission, staying in their home port's flagship between commissions: *USM*, 1832, ii, p. 242.
4. Maj.-Gen. Sir H. Douglas: Treatise on Naval Gunnery, p. 192.
5. *JRUSI*, 1885–86, xxix, p. 139, Lt. R.S. Lowry: *Musketry Instruction Afloat*.
6. Gunnery Notebooks of Henry Mitchell: Dec. 1852–Sept. 1853 & Richard Ford:

April–Dec. 1851; *Instructions for the Exercise and Service of Great Guns, and Shells on Board Her Majesty's Ships* 1854, all at Whale Island.

7. *Instructions for the Exercise of Small Arms, etc.* 1859 p. 1: Author's italics.
8. *JRUSI*, 1882, xxvi, Capt. Fletcher Campbell, p. 876, *Naval Brigades.*
9. E.g. orders for firing prone: cf. *Instructions*, 1859, p. 55 & *Field Exercise and Evolutions of the Infantry*, 1861, p. 389.
10. Campbell, p. 876.
11. RNM, 1976/110(4), Lt. A. Battiscombe: Journal . . . , 28 August 1860.
12. *Instructions*, 1854, p. 128.
13. *Instructions*, 1859, p. 59.
14. Martello Tower: *At School and at Sea*, p. 354 & 357.
15. RNM, 1993/167(1), Lt. E. Pitcairn Jones: Journal of service in HMS *Carysfort.*
16. Campbell, p. 885.
17. J.W. Gambier: *Links in My Life. . .* , p. 178.
18. *Rifle and Field Exercises . . . for HM Fleet*, 1888, p. 215.
19. NMM, 87/037 Mid. C.R. Acklom, logbook: May–Nov. 1890, Man & Arm Ship/General Quarters 10; Landing Parties/SA Coys 19.
20. *A&NG*, 1861, quoted in *G&L*, 1911, xviii, p. 35.
21. *G&L*, 1898, v, p. 114.
22. *G&L*, 1900, vii, p. 68.
23. *SHJ&NC*, 1864, p. 126.
24. *USM*, 1879, ii, p. 149: *Naval Brigades.*
25. Campbell, p. 885.
26. *A&NG*, 19 July 1879, p. 604. The scores were: Shanghai Volunteers 609, HMS *Egeria* 442, *Champlain* (French) 206, USS *Monocacy* 186.
27. *JRUSI*, 1880, xxiv, pp. 277–78, Lt. J. Ferris: *On Rifle Shooting in Her Majesty's Navy.*
28. *SHJ&NC*, 1864, p. 8.
29. Lowry, p. 139: Capt. Curtis.
30. PO W. Jenkin: Shah's Brigade . . . , 2 April 1879.
31. Gambier, p. 179.
32. O/S J.P. Hoskins: Journal of HMS Shannon's Brigade . . . , 7 Oct. 1857.
33. FM Sir E. Wood: *The Crimean War in 1854 and 1894*, pp. 296–97.
34. *Instructions for the Exercise of Small Arms* etc., 1864, p. 2.
35. *G&L*, 1902, ix, p. 18: 'bare-legged' refers to the kilted 93rd.
36. *RNM*, 1995/41(151), Seymour——Bayly, 19 July 1900.
37. *AP*, Ca423, pp. 3–5, *General Memo to Capts of HM Ships at Rangoon*, 19 Nov. 1885.
38. Adm. Sir E.E. Bradford: *Admiral of the Fleet Sir A.K. Wilson*, pp. 86–89.
39. *A&NG*, 19 April 1879, p. 261.
40. Maj.-Gen. Sir G. Aston: *Memories of a Marine*, p. 49: the RMA barracks were at Eastney, near Portsmouth.
41. *NM*, 1862, p. 571, Orders, Cracroft——Blake, 9 March 1860.
42. Battiscombe, 20 Nov. & 6 Dec. 1860.
43. FM Sir G. Wolseley: *The Story of a Soldier's Life*, vol. ii, p. 331, *et seq.*

44. For naval rifles see C.H. Roads: *The British Soldier's Firearm 1850–1864* & War Office: *Textbook of Small Arms 1904*; also discussions with RM Museum Eastney & Adrian Whiting of the Diehard Company.
45. *Instructions*, 1859, pp. 68 & 72.
46. RNM, 1995/41(19), Capt. E. Bayly: Letters & Papers, 18 August 1873.
47. *SHJ&NC*, 1862, p. 131.
48. Adm. Sir Robert H. Harris: *From Naval Cadet to Admiral*, p. 352.
49. Campbell, p. 878.
50. *FEx*, 1905, p. 126.
51. Capt. H.M. Hozier: *British Expedition to Abyssinia*, pp. 193 & 198.
52. *LG*, 23 Feb. 76, p. 870: VAdm. A.P. Ryder——Admiralty, 17 Jan. 1876.
53. *JRUSI*, 1885, xxviii, p. 941, Captain Lord Charles Beresford: *Machine Guns in the Field*.
54. *Manual of Gunnery for HM Fleet*, 1880, p. 343. The Gardner fired 120 rounds a minute per barrel.
55. Campbell, p. 878.
56. Jenkin, 14 May 1879.
57. *A&NG*, 9 Sept. 1882, p. 712.
58. Adm. Lord Charles Beresford: *Machine Guns . . .* , p. 953.
59. Lt.-Cdr. C.F. Goodrich: *Naval and Military Operations in Egypt*, pp. 196–98.
60. Wood: *From Midshipman to Field Marshal*, p. 28.
61. Campbell, *op. cit.*
62. *A&NG*, 12 April 1879, p. 237.
63. Revd H.N. Oxenham: *Memoir of Lt. Rudolph de Lisle RN*, p. 167.
64. Goodrich, p. 198.
65. Aston, p. 38.
66. RMM, 11/13/73, Col.-Sgt. G.F. Cooper RMLI.
67. *G&L*, 1899, vi, p. 199.
68. VAdm. W. Nunn: *Tigris Gunboats . . .* , p. 28.

Chapter 7: On the Banks of the Nile

1. Egypt was a semi-autonomous part of the Turkish Empire.
2. Adm. B.M. Chambers, *Salt Junk . . .* , p. 54.
3. NMM, MS 78/100, Lt. Mostyn Field of HMS *Sultan* (undated).
4. Lt.-Cdr. C.F. Goodrich: *Naval and Military Operations in Egypt*, pp. 15–16.
5. RNM, 1983/967, Journal of Chalres Hickman, 1 July 1882.
6. Capt. G. Mostyn Field (undated).
7. Mostyn Field, 10 July 1882.
8. Sir W.L. Clowes: *The Royal Navy*, vii, p. 331: British losses: 5 killed, 28 wounded; Egyptian 150 killed, 400 wounded.
9. Chambers, p. 60.

10. Goodrich, p. 75.
11. *A&NG*, 19 August 1882, p. 641: 'The Wreck of the City'.
12. 150 bluejackets landed on 13 July with 450 marines under the command of Capt. J. Fisher of HMS *Inflexible*.
13. *A&NG*, 28 Oct. 1882, p. 885, Lord Charles Beresford.
14. Mostyn Field, p. 13.
15. OS C. Hickman: *Diary . . .* , 17 & 21 July 1882.
16. *A&NG*, 26 August 1882, p. 665.
17. Mostyn Field, p. 16.
18. Hickman, 5 & 11 August 1882.
19. Mostyn Field, p. 16.
20. The major units were:

Port Said: *Penelope, Agincourt, Monarch, Northumberland*
Ismailia: *Orion, Carysfort*
Suez: *Euryalus, Eclipse*

21. The Port Said parties were:

	Naval Rifles	Gatling Crew	Royal Marines
HMS *Monarch*	100	18	48
HMS *Iris*	80	18	28
HMS *Northumberland*	=	=	200

22. Goodrich, p. 113: Capt. H.H. Edwards——RAdm. A.H. Hoskins, 22 August 1882.
23. RNM, 1993/167, Capt. E. Pitcairn-Jones, 19 August 1882.
24. *Ibid.*
25. Drawn from HMS *Northumberland, Orion, Carysfort*, and *Coquette*, with one 9pr, one 7pr, and two Gatlings.
26. *Ibid.*
27. *A&NG*, 14 Oct. 1882, p. 814.
28. *A&NG*, 30 Sept. 1882, p. 774, *et seq.*
29. Mostyn Field, p. 17.
30. *A&NG*, 7 Oct. 1882, p. 802.
31. *A&NG*, 14 Oct. 1882, p. 818.
32. FM Sir G. Wolseley: *The Story of a Soldier's Life*, i, pp. 46–47.
33. *A&NG*, 2 Feb. 1884, p. 90.
34. *A&NG*, 23 Feb. 1884, p. 126.
35. Naval order of battle: 1 Cdr.; 6 Lts; 1 Sub-Lt.; 1 Surg.; 1 Assistant Paymaster as ADC; 1 Gunner; 2 Midshipmen; 151 ratings. Naval Losses at El Teb: 3 killed; 9 wounded. Arabs: 825 dead counted (*LG*, 25 March 1884, p. 1461).
36. *LG*, 25 March 1884, p. 1460: Rolfe——Hewett, 4 March 1884.
37. NMM, JOD/188: Journal of Gunner J.T. Wilkinson RMA, 29 Feb. 1884.

38. Pitcairn-Jones, 29 Feb. 1884.

39. See Rolfe's report of 16 March 1884 in *LG*, 3 April 1884, p. 1665.

40. *JRUSI*, 1885, xxviii, p. 958: Lt.-Col. Holley RA.

41. *NR*, 1938, p. 88, *Naval Machine Guns and Sudanese Spearmen in 1884*. The Navy List suggests the author was Admiral G.A. Ballard.

42. *LG*, 3 April 1884, p. 1979: Graham——Hewett, 30 March 1884.

43. Col. C. Field: *Britain's Sea Soldiers*, ii, p. 197.

44. RMM, 11/12/13. Letters of Lt. A.E. Marchant, 31 August 1884–5 Nov. 1884.

45. *ILN*, 4 Oct. & 1 Nov. 1884.

46. Revd H.N. Oxenham: *Memoir of Lt. Rudolph de Lisle RN*, p. 177: de Lisle, 18 Sept. 1884.

47. Ibid., p. 180: de Lisle, 22 Oct. 1884.

48. Ibid., p. 197: de Lisle, 30 Nov. 1884. The Naval Brigade had two Divisions, each with a Gardner gun:

    1st: 5 officers, including Boatswain, 51 ratings.

    2nd: 6 officers (including an Engineer and Chief) 51 ratings.

Both included 2 ERAs, and 2 Stokers (*LG* 28 April 1885, p. 1917).

49. Adm. Lord C. Beresford: *Memoirs . . .* , p. 243.

50. *A&NG*, 14 Feb. 1885, p. 143.

51. *LG*, 28 April 1885, pp. 1913–17: Beresford——Admiralty, 10 March 1885.

52. Col. Sir C.W. Wilson: *From Korti to Khartoum . . .* , p. 36. Total British losses: 74 killed, 94 wounded; 1,100 dead Arabs counted.

53. Beresford, p. 296.

54. *NLJ*, 1898, pp. 153–55: Capt. S. Eardley-Wilmot: *Reminiscences of Suakin*.

55. Field, ii, p. 203: anonymous RM eyewitness.

56. *G&L*, iii, p. 58, anonymous RM eyewitness.

57. Eardley-Wilmot.

58. Mostyn Field (undated).

Chapter 8: The World's Policeman

1. RNM, 1996/597, Asst. Paymaster Terence Salter: 31 July 1913.

2. *G&L*, 1896, iii, p. 100.

3. Salter: 13 June 1913.

4. *NR*, 1932, pp. 782–83, *Pages and Papers from the Life of Admiral of the Fleet Sir Frederick Richards*. Richards——Admiralty, 23 March 1880.

5. *G&L*, 1895, ii, p. 187, Maj. French RMA.

6. RNM, 1990/308(4), Frederick Coleman, Steward HMS *Danae*, 1877.

7. NRS, Lt.-Cdr. P.K. Kemp: *Papers of Sir John Fisher*, ii, pp. 109 & 112.

8. *G&L*, 1896, iii, p. 162.

9. *A&NG*, 16 Feb. 1884, p. 111.

10. *NR*, 1932: Richards——Admy, 29 Feb. 1880.

11. *LG*, 6 Jan. 1891, p. 71: Fremantle——Admy, 1 Nov. 1890.

12. *LG*, 12 Dec. 1893, p. 7251, RAdm. F.G.D. Bedford——Admy, 3 Sept. 1893.

13. Ibid.: Capt. Lindley——Bedford, 10 August 1893.

14. NMM, JOD 119/1, Richard Cotten: HMS *Comus* and *Lily* at the Pellew Islands.

15. RNM, 1990/143(1), Sotheby (1): *Anecdotes*.

16. Adm. E.H. Seymour: *My Naval Career and Travels*, p. 116.

17. *A&NG*, 19 Feb. 1881, p. 144: Sir George Trevelyan was Parliamentary Secretary to the Admiralty.

18. *LG*, 6 Jan. 1891, p. 78, Fremantle——Admy, 1 Nov. 1890.

19. Fremantle's ships were: *Boadicea, Turquoise, Conquest, Cossack, Brisk, Kingfisher, Pigeon, Redbreast*. They landed:

	Officers	Men
Staff	11	=
SA Coys	19	307
7prs ×4	4	76
Gardner Guns ×4	5	73
Rocket/Gun Cotton Party	5	22
Medical/Stretchers	5	25
Signallers/Armourers etc	=	62
Provision/Fatigue Party	5	54
Royal Marines	3	189
TOTAL:	57	808

Also: 150 Indian Police, 100 Zanzibaris.

20. *AP*, P (NS) 221, Maj.-Gen. Sir G. Aston: *History of the Benin Expedition of 1897*, p. 5.

21. NRS, *Papers of Sir John Fisher*, ii, p. 111.

22. *G&L*, 1897, iv, p. 44, Diary Cpl Rogerson RMA.

23. *LG*, 6 Jan. 1891, Fremantle, p. 86.

24. *LG*, 4 May 1894, p. 2603, Capt E.H. Gamble-RAdm. F.G.D. Bedford.

25. *G&L*, 1910, xvii, p. 43, Sgt. W.A. Young RMLI.

26. *G&L*, 1908, xv, p. 92.

27. *JRUSI*, 1895, xxxix, pp. 191–98 Lt. J.D. Hickley.

28. T. Salter: Letters . . . , 22 June 1913.

29. F.A. Coleman: Diary . . . , 17 August 1877.

30. RNM, 1981/278, Mid. H.J.G. Good, 12 Feb. 1897.

31. *NR*, 1935, p. 774, Thomas Neill: *Further Adventures of an Officer's Domestic*.

32. *LG*, 6 Jan. 1891, p. 80, General Memo A, 16 Oct. 1890.

33. War Office: *Ops in Somaliland*, p. 293: Lt.-Col. S.C.F. Jackson.

34. *LG*, 23 Feb. 1876, p. 74, VAdm. A.P.Ryder——Admy, 17 Jan. 1876.

35. H.J.G. Good, 18 Feb. 1897.

36. *G&L*, 1897, iv, p. 43; Cpl. Rogerson RMA.

37. H.J.G. Good.

38. Rogerson.

39. *G&L*, 1897, iv, p. 37.

40. *LG*, 6 Jan. 1891, p. 86, Orders for March & Landing, 19 Oct. 1890.

41. *Ops in Somaliland*, p. 289: Capt. H.A.L. Hood RN.

42. *SHJ&NC*, April 1861.

43. *LG*, 6 Jan. 1891, p. 76, Fremantle——Admy, 1 Nov. 1890.

44. *G&L*, 1895, ii, p. 184, Actg QM-Sgt. J.L. Hammond RMLI.

45. *LG*, 4 May 1894, p. 2605, Lt. & Cdr. H.G. King-Hall——RAdm. F.G.D. Bedford.

46. Ibid. British losses: 17 dead & 55 wounded.

47. *NR*, 1932, pp. 782–83 op. cit.: Journal of Sir Stanley Colville.

48. *USM*, v, p. 470, *Service in the Bights*.

49. NMM, 87/037, Mid. C.R. Acklom, HMS *Boadicea* July 1890.

50. RNM 1976/110(1) Lt. A. Battiscombe: Journal . . . , pp. 127–28.

51. Seymour, p. 158.

52. Cotten (undated).

53. RNM, 1995/41(26), Bayly——Wife, 20 April 1893.

54. *NR*, 1935, p. 777, Thomas Neill.

Chapter 9: Reprise: from Ladysmith to Peking

1. Adm. Sir R.H. Harris: *From Naval Cadet to Admiral*, p. 315.

2. Ships at the Cape: HMS *Barracouta, Barrosa, Doris, Dwarf, Forte, Magicienne, Magpie, Monarch, Partridge, Philomel, Sparrow, Tartar, Widgeon*; later reinforced by: HMS *Fearless, Niobe, Pelorus, Powerful, Racoon, Terrible, Thetis, Thrush*. HMS *Penelope* served as a floating prison.

3. NMM, PTR/6/2/D, Fleet Surgeon J. Porter: *Journal Naval Brigade 1899–1900*, p. 160.

4. Harris, p. 332.

5. Order of battle: 9 NOs; 7 RMOs; 53 RN ratings; 290 RMLI & RMA.

6. Harris, p. 332 lists: 1×6-inch (780 rds); 21×4.7-inch Q/F (12,192); 30×12pr 12cwt (12,630); 7×12pr 8cwt (2,450); 1×6pr Q/F (1,100); 1×3pr Q/F (1,120); $13\times.45$ cal Maxim (693,000).

7. Harris, p. 338.

8. RNM, 1989/252(12), Joseph Withecombe PO 2nd Class: *Journal*, p. 26.

9. Withecombe, pp. 10, 29, 30 & 34. Ladysmith Brigade order of battle: 9 officers (including the Gunner), 7 midshipmen, 267 bluejackets. Two small-arms companies of 50 seamen escorted the guns.

10. Ibid., pp. 38 & 43.

11. Chief Engineer C.C. Sheen: *Naval Brigades in the S. African War*, p. 194.

12. Harris, p. 346.

13. Literally: 'Loose your riders'.

14. Withecombe, p. 45: obsolete 12-inch solid shot were used to fix the platforms in place. They could not be fired by 4.7 Q/F guns.

15. Sheen, p. 200.

16. *A&NG*, 28 April 1900, p. 415: Speech at Portsmouth Town Hall.

17. Sheen, p. 229; also *NR*, 1947, p. 110.

18. Surg. Sir J. Porter: *Journal...*, p. 171. Methuen's Brigade: 22 NOs, 150 seamen, 186 marines (Harris, p. 353); 4×12pr 12cwt guns on Scott carriages drawn by mules, reinforced by 2×4.7s on wheeled mountings.

19. Porter, pp. 171 & 177.

20. Maj. A.E. Marchant RMLI: *Naval Brigades in the S. African War*, p. 23.

21. Naval losses at Graspan: 14 killed & 91 wounded, of which 11 RM killed & 73 wounded: 44% of their strength.

22. Porter, p. 189.

23. *NA*, 1900, p. 163, David Hannay: *Naval Brigades*.

24. *A&NG*, 2 Dec. 1899, p. 1147. Cf. *Times* Leader, 27 Nov. 1899.

25. *Times*, 29 Nov. 1899, p. 15.

26. *Times*, 1 Dec. 1899, p. 4.

27. *Times*, 21 Dec. 1899, p. 11. Plumbe was wounded at Tel-el-Kebir in 1882, after service at Alexandria and Kassassin.

28. *A&NG*, 24 March 1900, p. 290.

29. *Times*, 2 Dec. 1899, p. 11.

30. Adm. Sir P. Scott: *Fifty Years in the Royal Navy*, p. 102. Main guns landed: 1×4.7 & 18×12pr with 31 officers, 368 seamen & marines (Harris, p. 350).

31. Total strength: 39 officers & 403 men from HMS *Terrible, Forte, Tartar*, & *Philomel*; 2 officers & 50 men Natal Naval Volunteers.

32. RNM, 1993/167(2), Capt. E.P. Jones: *Journal Book*, 16 Dec. 1900.

33. *A&NG*, 30 June 1900, p. 640: Diary of anonymous officer in HMS *Terrible*.

34. Harris, p. 359: HMS *Philomel* landed five of her eight 4.7s: a common proportion.

35. E.P. Jones, 7 Jan. 1900.

36. *A&NG*, 30 June 1900, p. 640: anonymous diary.

37. Lt. C.R.N. Burne: *With the Naval Brigade in Natal*, p. 35.

38. *A&NG*, 30 June 1900, p. 640: anonymous diary.

39. *A&NG*, 24 Feb. 1900, p. 190.

40. E.P. Jones, 2 Feb. 1900.

41. E.P. Jones, 8 Feb. 1900. The usual 50% area for a 4.7 Q/F at 5,000 yards was 34×25 yards (War Office Handbook 1892).

42. E.P. Jones, 18 Feb. 1900.

43. E.P. Jones, 2 March 1900.

44. *A&NG*, 30 June 1900, p. 640: anonymous diary.

45. Fleet Surg. F.J. Lilly: *Naval Brigades in the S. African War*, p. 264.

46. All quotes E.P. Jones 2 March 1900.

47. *A&NG*, 30 June 1900, p. 640: anonymous diary.

48. HT, 28 April 1900, p. 8.

49. HT, 21 April 1900, p. 3: *A Ladysmith Diary*.

50. Ibid.

51. HT, 12 May 1900, p. 9.
52. Cdr. W.L. Grant landed 5 officers & 59 men at Port Elizabeth 31 Jan. 1900, joining Bearcroft 3 Feb.
53. *A&NG*, 30 June 1900, p. 640: anonymous diary.
54. *A&NG*, 24 March 1900, p. 289.
55. Total naval guns after the Relief:

    Ladysmith: 2 × 4.7s; 8 × 12pr
    Chieveley: 1 × 6-inch; 2 × 4.7s; 6 × 12pr
    Returning to Chievely: 2 × 4.7s; 2 × 12pr
    Mooi River: 2 × 12pr

Of these the Naval Brigade kept 2 × 4.7s & 4 × 12pr (Jones, 30 March 1900)
56. EP Jones, 14 June 1900.
57. Harris, p. 391.
58. Burne, p. 76.
59. EP Jones, 28 June 1900.
60. Harris, p. 391.
61. *A&NG*, 26 May 1900, p. 513.
62. *A&NG*, 9 June 1900, p. 566.
63. HT, 21 April 1900, p. 2.
64. HT, 19 May 1900, p. 8.
65. *A&NG*, 2 June 1900, p. 541.
66. HT, 12 May 1900, p. 8.
67. *G&L*, 1901, *The Unintelligence of Thomas.*
68. EP Jones, 28 June 1900.
69. By Lt. C.C. Dix RN.
70. Adm. E.H. Seymour: *My Naval Career and Travels*, p. 342.
71. *LG*, 5 Oct. 1900, p. 6093: Seymour——Admy, 27 June 1900.
72. The order of battle was entirely naval:

	Officers	Men	Guns	Machine Guns
Austrian	1	24	=	=
British	68	853	4	8
French	7	151	1	=
German	23	427	=	2
Italian	2	38	=	1
Japanese	2	52	=	=
Russian	7	305	1	=
United States	6	106	1	1
TOTAL:	116	1956	7	12

(*A&NG*, 8 Sept. 1900, p. 884: Capt. McCalla USN)

73. *A&NG*, 25 August 1900, pp. 832–33.
74. RMM, 11/13/73, Col.-Sgt. G.F. Cooper RMLI. Pages unnumbered.
75. *LG*, 5 Oct. 1900, p. 6097: Seymour——Admy, 27 June 1900.
76. Losses to 24 June: 62 killed & 230 wounded out of 2,072, of which 27 and 97 British (Dix, p. 92).
77. Tientsin relief column: 250 RN/RM; 300 Royal Welch Fusiliers, 40 RE, 150 USMC, 23 Italian sailors; joined next day by 1,500 Russian infantry (*LG*, 5 Oct. 1900, p. 6103: Seymour——Admy, 8 July 1900).
78. *A&NG*, 30 June 1900, p. 627. For 'leviathan' read China.
79. Lt. C.C. Dix: *The World's Navies in the Boxer Rebellion . . .* , p. 75: anonymous eyewitness.
80. RNM, 1995/41(175), Bayly: draft report 30 June 1900.
81. Dix, p. 65.
82. Dix, p. 80: anonymous eyewitness.
83. C/sgt. G.F. Cooper RMLI: Journal . . .
84. Cooper.
85. Cooper.
86. Capt. E. Bayly, 30 June 1900.
87. *LG*, 5 Oct. 1900, p. 6108: Bayly——Seymour, 15 July 1900.
88. Seymour, p. 350.
89. *A&NG*, 25 August 1900, p. 833.
90. Cooper.
91. *A&NG*, 15 Sept. 1900, p. 907.
92. Herbert George AB (*Orlando*) & Edward Turner LS (*Centurion*).
93. RNM, 1995/41(214), Lt. J.H. Powlett——Bayly: letter 3 July 1900.
94. *A&NG*, 25 August 1900, pp. 832–33.
95. *A&NG*, 8 Sept. 1900, p. 884: Report of Captain McCalla USN.
96. *A&NG*, 30 June 1900, p. 627.
97. *A&NG*, 25 August 1900, p. 833: personal letter.
98. Cooper. RN losses 13–14 July: 6 killed & 38 wounded out of 300 seamen and marines (RNM, 1995/41(259) Analysis of Nos & Casualties).
99. Dix, p. 56.
100. Dix, p. 56.
101. *LG*, 5 Oct. 1900, p. 6109: Brig. A.R.F. Dorward——Capt. J.H.T. Burke, 15 July 1900.
102. RNM, 1995/41(151), Seymour——Bayly: letter 19 July 1900.
103. RNM, 1995/41(183), Bayly memo 16 July 1900 & (239) Bayly——RAdm Sir J.A.T. Bruce (no date). Naval guns at Tientsin: 2x4-inch unmounted; 4x12pr 12cwt (3 RN & 1 RA); 7×6pr Q/F on railway trucks; 3×9pr RML; 3×Maxims.
104. RNM, 1995/41(209), Maj. C. Halliday——Bayly: memo 10 August 1900. Limpus was 2nd in command to Pitcairn-Jones in South Africa.
105. RNM, 1995/41(159), Lt. T.W. Kemp——Bayly: letter 20 August 1900.
106. Cooper.

107. RNM, 1995/41(159), Lt. T.W. Kemp——Bayly: letter 20 August 1900. 1st Sikhs were first into the Legations.
108. *A&NG*, 1 Sept. 1900 p. 857.
109. NMM, MS 84/081, Cpl. F.G. Smith RMLI: Lecture notes. His photograph album shows he did not exaggerate. Unattributed siege quotes are Smith.
110. RNM, 1995/41(259), Analysis. RN losses 17–23 June: 60 out of 393 against 1,620 out of 23,000 over ten days at Spion Kop.
111. Seymour, p. 361.
112. Smith's photograph album.
113. RNM, 1995/41(156): Letter to Capt. Bayly RN (undated).
114. RNM, 1995/41(252): Bayly, 19 August 1900.

Chapter 10: Armageddon

1. *NA*, 1905, p. 458: First Lord's Memorandum on the Distribution and Mobilisation of the Fleet.
2. NRS, Lt.-Cdr. P.K. Kemp: *Fisher Papers*, ii, p. 115: Draft letter to WO.
3. *NA*, 1905, p. 70.
4. Lt. C.C. Dix: *The World's Navies in the Boxer Rebellion . . .* , p. 40: The halts and orders in fact reflect the drillbook.
5. *FEx*, 1888, p. 305.
6. *G&L*, 1892, p. 9.
7. *FEx*, 1905, p. 16.
8. *FEx*, 1913, p. 337.
9. *FEx*, 1905, p. 20, p. 42, p. 44, pp. 110–12.
10. Report of Committee Appointed to Consider the Extension of the New Scheme of Training for Officers para. 523–52.
11. Ibid., para. 640–76.
12. RMM, 11/12/38, Aston Papers: *Diary of Ostend and Antwerp Expedition*, p. 13.
13. *G&L*, xxi, p. 140 & p. 192: *The Siege of Antwerp*.
14. Losses at Antwerp: 60 dead, 138 wounded, 936 POW, 1,479 interned.
15. RMM, 11/13/136: Diary Cpl. R.H. Pottinger RMLI.
16. NO, v, p. 433 App. I & K: RND losses 33,221 vs RN 41,068.
17. Gen. Sir H.E. Blumberg: *Britain's Sea Soldiers 1914–1919*, pp. 229–31: landed at Dilwar: RN 47; RM 59; Berar NI 122; Seedies 24. British losses 6 dead, 13 wounded (*G&L*, xxii, pp. 225–26).
18. VAdm. W. Nunn: *Tigris Gunboats . . .* , pp. 115–23.
19. *G&L*, xxiii, pp. 107 & 127.
20. Quotes from RMM 11/13/049: Diary of Pvt. George Sears RMLI.
21. *NR*, 1931, pp. 694–98: *Naval Landing Parties*, and 1932, pp. 58–66: *The Bluejacket Landing Party*.

Chapter II: Power and Money

1. *Peter Simple*, ii, p. 37 (Constable, 1929).
2. NMM, MS 84/081, Cpl. F.G. Smith RMLI, p. 3.
3. *G&L*, xx, p. 181.
4. Lt. C.R.N. Burne: *With the Naval Brigade in Natal*, p. 54.
5. *A&NG*, 4 Nov. 1899, p. 104.
6. RNM, 1989/252(12), PO J.H. Withecombe: Diary . . . , p. 12.
7. Cpl. F.G. Smith RMLI: Lecture Notes . . . , p. 3.
8. *SHJ&NC*, 1861, p. 134, Dr Bryson: *Statistical Returns of the Health of the Navy 1858*.
9. *SHJ&NC*, 1861, p. 116.
10. RNM, 1989/43(137–8): Papers of Sir Arthur Cochrane. Losses Dec. 1856–July 1858: 13 died; 24 invalided; 3 died of wounds; 1 drowned; 1 suicide.
11. NMM, PTR/6/2D Fleet Surgeon J. Porter: *Journal*, p. 10.
12. *LG*, 6 Jan. 1891, p. 78: Fremantle——Admy, 1 Nov. 1890.
13. *SHJ&NC*, 1861, p. 134: Bryson: the West African station suffered 249.2 cases of fever per thousand against 27.6 at home.
14. *Landing Party*, 1910, p. 100.
15. *SHJ&NC*, 1861, p. 134.
16. *SH&NC*, 1864, p. 22.
17. *G&L*, 1902, ix, p. 18.
18. RNM, 1995/41(159) Lt. T.W. Kemp——Bayly, 20 August 1900.
19. Smith, p. 55.
20. *AP*, Ca423: Special Correspondent with the Naval Brigade, p. 19.
21. RNM, 1976/110(4), Lt. A. Battiscombe: Journal . . . , 12 March 1861.
22. Col. C. Field: *Britain's Sea Soldiers*, ii, p. 259.
23. F.T. Jane: *A Royal Bluejacket*, p. 201.
24. *A&NG*, 5 May 1900, p. 440.
25. *SH&NC*, 1862, p. 95.
26. *G&L*, viii, p. 128.
27. FM Sir E. Wood: *Midshipman to Field Marshal*, p. 35; *The Crimea in 1854 and 1894*, p. 253.
28. H.W. Wilson: *With the Flag to Pretoria*, i, p. 151.
29. Wood, *The Crimea*, p. 193.
30. Revd H.N. Oxenham: *Memoir of Lt. Rudolph de Lisle RN*, p. 214, de Lisle 20 Dec. 1884.
31. *AP*, Ca423: Orders 19 Nov. 1885: Richards——Capt. R. Woodward.
32. Wood, p. 253.
33. Mostyn Field, p. 14.
34. Adm. Sir E.R. Fremantle: *The Navy As I Have Known It*, pp. 33–36.
35. Oxenham, p. 177: de Lisle 18 Sept. 1884.
36. *NA*, 1900, pp. 189: David Hannay: *Naval Brigades*.
37. NRS, Lt.-Cdr. P.K. Kemp; *Fisher Papers*, ii, pp. 111–14: *Naval Necessities*.

38. For naval rates of pay see Laird Clowes, vii, p. 17.

39. NMM, LOG/N/27, Cdr. P.R. Luxmore: Journal . . . , 30 Jan. 1874.

40. RNM, 1989/43(139) Cochrane: Draft account of services in China War.

41. *NR*, 1932, pp. 124–29: Mends——Richards, 24 March 1881.

42. PP, 1904, viii, C. 1932, p. 1.

43. D. Hannay: *Naval Brigades*, pp. 169 & 188.

44. Report of Committee Appointed to Consider the Extension of the New Scheme of Training for Officers, para. 523–52: Major Harkness.

45. Hannay, p. 189.

46. *NR*, 1932, p. 66: *The Bluejacket Landing Party.*

47. Maj.-Gen. Sir G. Aston: *Memories of a Marine*, p. 55.

48. Adm. Lord Cunningham of Hyndhope: *A Sailor's Odyssey*, p. 31.

49. Fremantle, p. 235.

50. Fremantle, p. 234.

51. *A&NG*, 25 July 1868, p. 474: *Notes on the Abysinnian Campaign.*

52. *A&NG*, 16 Sept. 1882, pp. 734–35.

53. *SHJ&NC*, 1856, p. 116.

54. VAdm. P.H. Colomb: *Memoirs of Adm. Rt. Hon. Sir Astley Cooper*, p. 273: the Three Towns were Rochester, Chatham, and Gillingham on the Medway.

55. Aston, p. 55.

56. *A&NG*, 16 Sept. 1882, pp. 734–35.

57. *A&NG*, 25 April 1874, p. 267.

58. *A&NG*, 16 Sept. 1882, pp. 734–35.

59. *N&AI*, 2 Dec. 1899, p. 266.

60. *A&NG*, 16 Sept. 1882, pp. 734–35.

61. FM Sir G. Wolseley: *Soldier's Life*, i, p. 131.

62. *JRUSI*, 1885, xxviii, p. 957.

Select Bibliography

(London publishers unless stated)

Mid. C.R. Acklom: Midshipman's Log in HMS *Boadicea*, 1890 (NMM M/S 87/037).

Admiralty: *Instructions for the Exercise and Service of Great Guns and Shells on board Her Majesty's Ships* (1848, HMSO).

Instructions for the Exercise of Small Arms, Field Pieces, etc for the Use of Her Majesty's Ships 1859 (1859, Harrison & Sons).

Instructions for the Exercise and Service of Great Guns etc on board Her Majesty's Ships (1864, HMSO).

Rifle and Field Exercises and Rifle Practise Instruction for Her Majesty's Fleet 1888 (1888, HMSO).

Rifle and Field Exercises for Her Majesty's Fleet 1896 (Vol. I) (1896, HMSO).

Rifle and Field Exercise for His Majesty's Fleet 1905 (Vol. II) (1905, HMSO).

Rifle and Field Exercise for His Majesty's Fleet 1907 (1907, HMSO).

Instructions for Naval Landing Parties (1910, HMSO).

Rifle and Field Exercises for His Majesty's Fleet 1913 (1913, HMSO).

Training Manual for Landing Operations (1914, HMSO).

Royal Naval Handbook of Field Training 1920 (1920, HMSO).

Royal Naval Handbook of Field Training 1926 (1926, HMSO).

Royal Naval Handbook of Field Training B.R. 159/34 (1935, HMSO).

Admiralty Prints: *Operations in Burma and Proceedings of Naval Brigade 1885–86* (RNM Ca423).

Transvaal War – Naval Contingent (RNM Ca428).

Naval Brigades in Zululand (NMM MLN/199/9–10).

Anonymous:

HMS 'Royal Sovereign' Details of Ship and 'Action' (1899, Malta).

An Account of the Expedition to Cartagena with Explanatory Notes and Observations (2nd edn. 1748 London).

Diary of Midshipman of HMS *Pearl*'s Brigade 1857 (NMM JOD/189).

Maj.-Gen. Sir G. Aston:

Memoirs of a Marine (1919, John Murray).

History of the Benin Expedition of 1897 (1899, Admiralty).

Papers (RMM 11/12/38).

Adm. Sir R.H. Bacon: *A Naval Scrapbook 1877–1900* (n.d. Hutchinson).

Pvt. W. Baker RMLI: Journal, Canton, Dec. 1857 (RMM 13/11/85).

VAdm. C.J. Barlow: Papers relating to HMS Bacchante's Naval Brigade in 2nd Burma War (NMM BAR/4–5).

E. Bartholomew: *Early Armoured Cars* (1988 Shire Publications, Aylesbury).

Lt. A. Battiscombe: Journal of service in HMS *Pelorus* Burma 1859 and New Zealand 1860–61 (RNM 1976/110(1–4)).

Adm Sir L. Bayly: *Pull Together* (1939, Harrap).

Capt. E. Bayly: Letters & Papers (RNM 1995/41).

Adm. Lord C. Beresford: *The Memoirs of Lord Charles Beresford Written by Himself* (1914, Methuen).

Capt. W.H. Blake: Ashanti War Diaries (NMM BLK/2–9).

Gen. Sir H.E. Blumberg:
Britain's Sea Soldiers 1914–1918 (1927 Swiss & Co, Devonport).
Records of the Royal Marines 1745–1914 (RMM typescript).
(with Col. C. Field): *Random Records of the Royal Marines* (1935, G&L Portsmouth).

D. Bonner-Smith & Capt. A.C. Dewar: *Russian War, 1854: Baltic and Black Sea Official Correspondence* (1943, Navy Records Society).

D. Bonner-Smith & E.W.R. Lumby: *The Second China War 1856–60* (1954 Navy Records Society).

Adm. Sir N. Bowden-Smith: *Naval recollections 1852 to 1914* (1914 Army & Navy Coop Society).

Revd E.L. Bowman: Journal of Chaplain of HMS Shannon's Naval Brigade during Indian Mutiny (NMM JOD/93/1).

Capt. H. Brackenbury RA: *The Ashanti War: A Narrative* (1874 Wm Blackwood & Sons, Edinburgh).

Cdr. J.W. Brackenbury RN: Log of HMS Shah's Naval Brigade in the Zulu War 1879 (NMM BCK/2).

Adm. Sir E.E. Bradford: *Admiral of the Fleet Sir A.K. Wilson* (1923, John Murray).

Sir J.H. Briggs: *Naval Administration 1827–1892: The Experience of 65 years* (ed. Lady Briggs) (1897, London).

Lt. A.H.R. Buckley: War Diary of No. 11 Platoon, C Company, 12th RM Battalion China 1927 (RMM 13/11/22).

Lt. C.R.N. Burne: *With the Naval Brigade in Natal 1899–1900* (1902, Edward Arnold).

Capt. C. Sloane-Stanley RN: *Reminiscences of a Midshipman's Life from 1850–1856* (1893 Eden, Remington & Co.).

Lt. H. Chamberlain: *Instruction for the Service and Exercise of Great Guns* etc presented by LT Henry Chamberlain RN 1894 (Whale Island).

Adm. B.M. Chambers: *Salt Junk: Naval Reminiscences* (1927, Constable).

J. Chappell: Diary of Commission of HMS Pearl 1856–59 (RNM 1985/291).

Adm. Sir E. Chatfield: *HMS Excellent 1830–1930* (3rd edn. 1930).

Sir W.L. Clowes: *The Royal Navy – A History from Earliest Times to the Death of Queen Victoria* (1903 Sampson Low Marston & Co.).

Capt. A. Cochrane: Letters on service in 2nd China War 1856–58 (RNM 1989/43).

F.A. Coleman (domestic): Diary of service in HMS *Danae* 1876–81 (RNM 1990/308(4)).

VAdm. P.H. Colomb: *Memoirs of Admiral the Rt Hon Sir Astley Cooper Key GCB DCL FRS etc* (1898, Methuen).

C/Sgt G.F. Cooper RMLI: Journal of service on the China Station, at Wei-hai-wei, and during the Boxer Rebellion (RMM 11/13/73).

J. Corbett & H. Newbolt: *History of the Great War: Naval Operations* vol. i & v (1920–31, London).

R. Cotten: Journals of China and Pacific 1879–84 & 2nd Burma War (NMM JOD/119/1–2).

G. Crowe (Master-at-Arms): *The Commission of HMS 'Terrible'* 1898–1900 (1903 Newnes).

Adm. Viscount Cunningham of Hyndhope: *A Sailor's Odyssey* (1951 Hutchinson).

Capt. A.C. Dewar: *The Russian War 1855: Black Sea Official Correspondence* (1945, Navy Records Society).

Lt. C.C. Dix: *The World's Navies in the Boxer Rebellion in China 1900* (1905, Digby Long & Co.).

Capt. G.A. Douglas: Diary and papers relating to Peiho River disaster and T'ai-p'ing Rebellion (NMM M/S 86/046).

Maj.-Gen. Sir H. Douglas: *A Treatise on Naval Gunnery* (2nd edn. 1829, John Murray).

Capt. S. Eardley-Wilmot: *Reminiscences of Suakin* (*Navy League Journal*, Oct. 1898).
Life of Vice-Admiral Edmund, Lord Lyons (1898, Sampson Low Marston & Co.).

R. Edgerton: *The Fall of the Asante Empire – The Hundred Year War for Africa's Gold Coast* (1995, The Free Press, New York).

Lt. Farrant RMA: *Questions and Answers in Naval Gunnery used in the Instruction of the Officers of His Majesty's Ship Excellent* Compiled by Lt. Farrant RMA of that Ship (1835, HMSO).

Col. C. Field: *Britain's Sea-Soliders* (1924, Lyceum Press, Liverpool).
The British Navy Book (1915, Blackie & Son Ltd).
Old Times Afloat – A Naval Anthology (1932, Andrew Melrose Ltd).

Capt. H.J. Fletcher Campbell: *Naval Brigades* – Lecture at the RUSI, 30 July 1882 (*RUSI Journal*, xxvi, pp. 872–85).

W. Forbes Mitchell: *The Relief of Lucknow* (1962, Folio Society) – 1st published 1893 as *Reminiscences of the Great Mutiny*.

Lt. R. Ford: *Naval Gunnery As Taught On Board HMS Excellent under the Command of Capt H.D. Chads CB* (Whale Island).

Sir J.W. Fortescue: *A History of the British Army 1660–1870* (1930, Macmillan & Co. Ltd).

E. Fraser: *The Pearl's Brigade in the Indian Mutiny – Diary of Mid. K.F. Stephenson* (1926, *Mariner's Mirror*, xii, pp. 23–44).

E. Fraser & L.C. Carr Laughton: *The Royal Marine Artillery 1804–1923* (1930, RUSI).

Adm. Sir E.R. Fremantle: *The Navy As I Have Known It* (nd Cassell).

Cdr. J.W. Gambier: *Links In My Life On Land And Sea* (1906, Fisher Unwin).

Mid. H.J.G. Good: The Benin Disaster (RNM 1981/278).

V.H. Goodenough: *Journal of Commodore Goodenough RN CBCMG during his last command edited with a Memoir by his widow* (1876, H.S. King & Co.).

Lt.-Cdr. C.F. Goodrich USN: *Report of the British Naval and Military Operations in Egypt 1882, prepared for the Office of Naval Intelligence, etc* (1885, Washington, USA).

G.S. Graham: *The Politics of Naval Supremacy – Studies in British Maritime Ascendancy* (1965, Cambridge University Press).

Chief Stoker W.Y. Grainger: Letters home from HMS *Daphne*, 1896 (RNM 1992/216).

Maj. Sir J. Halkett: Diary of Sir James Halkett with introduction and notes by Capt. H.M. McCance (1922, *Journal of the Society for Army Historical Research* – Special Issue).

D. Hannay: *Naval Brigades* (1900, Naval Annual).

Adm. Sir R.H. Harris: *From Naval Cadet to Admiral: Half a Century of Naval Service and Sport in many parts of the World* (1913, Cassell).

Lt. P. Hearle: Journal 2nd Ashantee War 1873–74 (RMM 7/14/9(4)).

Capt. L.G. Heath: *Letters from the Black Sea During the Crimean War 1854–55* (1897, Richard Bentley & Son).

Lt. S.H. Henderson: *Remarks on Naval Gunnery including the Laboratory Process &c as taught on board HMS Excellent* (Whale Island).

Lt. J.D. Hickley: *An Account of the Operations on the Benin River in August and September 1894* (*JRUSI*, 1895, xxxix, pp. 191–98).

OS C. Hickman: Diary of commission of HMS Invincible 1882–85 (RNM 1983/967).

T.J. Holland & H.M. Hozier: *Record of the Late Expedition to Abysinnia* Compiled by Order of the Secretary of State for War (1870, HMSO).

O/S J.P. Hoskins: Journal of HMS Shannon's Brigade in the Indian Mutiny (NMM JOD/154/1–2).

Capt. H.M. Hozier: *The British Expedition to Abyssinia* (1869, MacMillan & Co.).

Lt. C.T. Hutchins USN: *The Naval Brigade: Its Organisation, Equipment, and Tactics* (Proceedings of the US Naval Institute 1887, xiii, pp. 303–40).

F.T. Jane: *A Royal Bluejacket* (1908, Sampson Low, Marston & Co.).

Surg. T.T. Jeans: *Naval Brigades in the South African War 1899–1900* (1901, Sampson Low Marston & Co.).

PO W. Jenkin: Shah's Brigade in the Zulu War (NMM M/S 73/069).

D. Jerrold: *The Royal Naval Division* (1923, Hutchinson & Co.).

Sgt. W. Joy: Journal of service in 2nd China War and on Pacific coast of America (RMM 11/12/123).

Mrs T. Kelly: *From the Fleet in the Fifties: A History of the Crimea, with letters written in 1854–5–6 by the Rev S. Kelson Stothert MA Chaplain to the Naval Brigade* (1902, Hurst & Blackett).

Lt.-Cdr. P.K. Kemp (ed.): *The Papers of Admiral Sir John Fisher ii* (1964, Navy Records Society).

Adm. Sir W. Kennedy: *Hurrah for the Life of a Sailor: Fifty Years in the Royal Navy* (1899, William Blackwood & Sons).

Adm. Sir H. Keppel: A Sailor's Life under Four Sovereigns 3 vols (1899, Macmillan).

Adm. Sir H. King-Hall: *Naval Memories and Traditions* (nd Hutchinson & Co.).

A.W. Kinglake: *The Invasion of the Crimea* (1863 & 1887 William Blackwood).

A. Lambert & S. Badsey (eds.): *The War Correspondents: The Crimean War* (1994, Alan Sutton, Stroud, England).

Surg. F.J. Lilly: Account of Juba and Witu Expeditions 1893 by Surgeon of HMS Blanche (RMM 7/14/6).

Cdr. P.R. Luxmore: Journal of 3rd China & Ashanti Wars (NMM LOG/N/27).

Lt. A.E. Marchant RMLI Letters (RMM 11/12/13).

A.J. Marder: *Fear God and Dread Nought: The Correspondence of Admiral of the Fleet Lord Fisher of Kilverstone* (1952, Jonathan Cape).

Martello Tower: *At School and at Sea* (Account by Cdr F.M. Norman RN) (1899, John Murray).

Lt. A. McLeod: Journal of service in HMS *Barracouta* during the Ashanti War (NMM LOG/N/E/1).

Mid. R.H. Mends: *Naval Gunnery Book written by Robert Hamilton Mends RN, Mate of HMS Excellent,* Nov. 18th 1843 (Whale Island).

Surg. B.S. Mends: *Life of Admiral Sir William Robert Mends GCB, Late Director of Transports* (1899, John Murray).

Pvt. J. Messum RMLI: Journal of service in HMS *Vesuvius* in the Black Sea Jan. 1854 to Dec. 1856 (RMM 11/13/129).

Lt. H. Mitchell: *Naval Gunnery Course as taught on board HMS Edinburgh written by Henry Mitchell* 13 Dec.–27 Sept. 1853 (Whale Island).

RAdm. V.A. Montagu: *A Middy's Recollections 1853–1860* (1900, A.&C. Black).

Adm. J. Moresby: *Two Admirals: Admiral of the Fleet Sir Fairfax Moresby, and his son John, a record of life and service in the Navy for a hundred years* (1909, John Murray).

Capt. G. Mostyn Field: Gunnery Lieutenant in HMS *Sultan* at Alexandria 1882 (NMM M/S 78/100 hektagraph).

Surg. Sir H.F. Norbury: *The Naval Brigade in South Africa during the years 1877–78–79* (1880, Sampson Low & Co.).

VAdm. W. Nunn: *Tigris Gunboats: A Narrative of the Royal Navy's Cooperation with the Military Forces in Mesopotamia, etc* (1932 Andrew Melrose).

Cdr. Okuda: *The Bombardment of Kagosima by the British Fleet in August 1863* trans Lt. N. James RN (1908 Devonport).

Revd. H.N. Oxenham: *Memoir of Lieutenant Rudolph de Lisle RN* (1887, Chapman & Hall).

P. Padfield: *Rule Britannia: The Victorian and Edwardian Navy* (1981 Routledge & Kegan Paul).

Lt. A.C.H. Paget: Journal of service in HMS *Sampson* 1859–61 in China (RNM 1994/330(2)).

Mid. D.F. Painter: Journal of service in HMS *Minerva* 1914 (RNM 1996/153).

Lt. W.H. Palmer RMLI: *A Short Journal of the Late Egyptian Campaign of 1882* (RMM 7/14/5).

L/Sig W.H. Palmer: *A Review of the Commission of HMS Barfleur on the Mediterranean and China Station 1895–98* (1898, Nagasaki Press).

Parliamentary Papers: Correspondence relating to the Ashanti War 1873–1874. Command Papers: C.890–4, C.907, C.921–2.

RAdm. C.C. Penrose FitzGerald: *Life of Vice Admiral Sir George Tryon* (1897, W. Blackwood & Sons, Edinburgh).

Capt. E. Pitcairn-Jones (RNM 1993/167):
Letters and reports 2nd Boer War: Colenso & Relief of Ladysmith.
Journal of service in HMS *Carysfort* in Egypt and Sudan 1879–84.

Surg. Sir J. Porter: *Journal Naval Brigade 1899–1900* (NMM PTR /6/1–2).

Cpl. R.H. Pottinger RMLI: Journal of service with 1/Battn RM at Gallipoli and on Western Front (RMM 11/13/136).

Maj. W.H. Poyntz: *Per Mare Per Terram: Reminiscences of Thirty-two Years of Military and Constabulary Service* (1892, Economic Printing and Publishing Company).

Mid. J. Ramsbotham: Journal of HMS *Highflyer* and *Lyra* in India and the Coast of East Africa (RNM 1996/31(40)).

Lt. G. Rawson: *Life of Admiral Sir Harry Rawson* (1914, Edward Arnold).

W.E.M. Reilly: *Artillery Operations of the Royal Artillery and Royal Naval Brigade at Sebastopol 1854–1855* (1859, HMSO).

RAdm. H.W. Richmond: Spencer Papers, iii (1924 Navy Records Society).

RM Museum: Papers relating to Anholt 1809–15 & Ashanti War 1873.

C.H. Roads: *The British Soldier's Firearm 1850–1864: From Smooth Bore to Small Bore* (1964, Herbert Jenkins).

FM Lord Roberts: *Forty-One Years in India from Subaltern to Commander-in-Chief* (2 vols) (1897, Richard Bentley & Son).

Cdr. C.N. Robinson: *Operations of Our Naval Forces on Shore 1899–1901* (1901, *Naval Annual*).

NAM Rodger: *The Admiralty* (1979, Terence Dalton, Suffolk).

Cdr. W.D. Rowbotham: *The Naval Brigades in the Indian Mutiny 1857–58* (1947, Navy Records Society).

Pvt. E.E. Rowland RMLI: Notes on RMB expedition to Antwerp Oct. 1914 (RMM 11/13/1(3)).

T. Salter: Letters of Assistant Paymaster Terence Salter 1913–15 (RNM 1984/597).

Adm. Sir P. Scott: *Fifty Years in the Royal Navy* (1919, John Murray).

Pvt. G.M. Sears RMLI: Journal of service in East Africa during the First World War (RMM 11/13/049).

Selbourne Committee:
New Admiralty Scheme The Training of Officers, Men and Boys in the Navy (1903 Reprint of original papers).
Report of Committee Appointed to Consider the Extension of the New Scheme of Training for Officers 18 August 1905.

Adm. E.H. Seymour: *My Naval Career and Travels* (1911, Smith Elder).

Surg. T.B. Shaw: *Naval Hygiene* (1929, Oxford University Press).

J. Shulimson: *The Marine Corps in Search for a Mission 1880–1898* (1993, University Press of Kansas).

Cpl. F.G. Smith RMLI: Lecture Notes on Boxer Rebellion and Siege of Peking 1900 (NMM M/S 84/081).

Capt. E.S. Sotheby: Journals of the *Pearl* Brigade RNM 1990/143.

W. Stables: *Medical Life in the Navy* (1868, Hardwicke).

D. Syrett (ed.): *The Siege and Capture of Havana 1762* (1970, Navy Records Society).

W.C.B. Tunstall: *Cambridge History of the British Empire* (1940–1959, Cambridge University Press).

Adm. Sir H. Tweedie: *The Story of a Naval Life* (nd Rich & Cowan Ltd)

Lt. E.H. Verney: *The Shannon's Brigade in India 1857–58* (1862, Saunders, Ottley & Co.).

War Office:
Official History of the Operations in Somaliland 1901–1904 (1907, HMSO).
Field Exercise and Evolution of Infantry as Revised 1861 (1863 HMSO).
Narrative of the Field Operations Connected with the Zulu War of 1879 prepared in the Intelligence Branch of the War Office (repr. 1989, Greenhill Books).
Infantry Training (4-Company Organisation) 1914 (1914, HMSO).

Mid. E.S. Watson: *A Naval Cadet with HMS Shannon's Brigade in India* (1988, London Stamp Exchange).

Capt. J. Wells: *The Royal Navy – An Illustrated Social History 1870–1982* (1994, Alan Sutton, Stroud, England & RNM).

OS W. White: *China Station 1859–1864: The Reminiscences of Walter White* – NMM Monographs and Reports No. 3 (1972, Greenwich).

J.T. Wilkinson RMA: *Diary at Suakin 1885–1886* (NMM JOD/188).

Revd. E.A. Williams: *The Cruise of the Pearl round the World, with an Account of the Operations of the Naval Brigade in India* (1859).

Col. Sir C.W. Wilson: *From Korti To Khartoum A Journal of the Desert March, &c* (1885, William Blackwood & Sons, Edinburgh).

H.W. Wilson: *With the Flag to Pretoria* (1900, Harmsworth).

J. Winton: *Hurrah for the Life of a Sailor! Life on the Lower Deck of the Victorian Navy* (1977, Michael Joseph).

PO J.H. Withecombe: Diary of service in HMS Powerful and ashore at start of 2nd Boer War (RNM 1989/252(12)).

FM Sir G. Wolseley: *The Story of a Soldier's Life* (1903, Constable).

FM Sir E. Wood:
From Midshipman to Field Marshal (1912, Methuen).
The Crimean War in 1854 and 1894 (1895, Chapman & Hall).

Glossary

AB Able Bodied Seaman.
abattis entanglement of trees cut down with sharpened branches pointing towards the enemy.
ASC Army Service Corps.
badmash Indian brigand, applied to disloyal sepoys.
banquette firing step of a trench or redoubt.
barracoon slave pen.
BEF British Expeditionary Force.
BL Breech Loading.
Blue Marine Royal Marine Artillery who wore blue.
Brahmin member of the Hindu priestly caste.
cable nautical unit of distance equivalent to 200 yards.
canister cylindrical container filled with musket balls.
charpoy Indian bed.
Chasseur d'Afrique French light cavalry based in Algeria.
Condy's fluid Sodium Permanganate solution used as disinfectant.
Cui bono Latin for: to whose benefit.
Cyclostyle a type of printing machine.
DAG Deputy Adjutant General.
dah Burmese knife.
Daimyo Japanese nobleman, a direct vassal of the Emperor.
dhooli Indian litter used to transport casualties.
disselboom part of the harness of a team of trek oxen.
donga South African dried water course.
drift South African river crossing.
ERA Engine Room Artificer.
fathom nautical measurement of depth equivalent to 6 feet.
gabion large wickerwork basket filled with earth and used for cover during siege operations.
ghat Indian riverside steps or landing stage.
gingall wall-mounted Chinese swivel gun.

GOC General Officer Commanding.

guinea gold coin worth twenty-one shillings or £1.05p.

HEICS Honourable East India Company Ship.

hektagraph a primitive duplicating machine.

IMS Indian Marine Service.

laager defensive ring of waggons.

lb pound (approx 450gms).

LS Leading Seaman.

maidan town square in Indian city.

mantlet rope shield used to protect gunners from small-arms fire.

ML Muzzle Loading.

OFS Orange Free State.

OS Ordinary Seaman.

oz ounce (approx 28gms).

pah Maori fortification.

paddle-box boat flat bottomed boats carried upside down over the paddle-wheels of early steam warships, used as landing craft.

parados earth thrown up along the rear edge of a trench.

parapet earth thrown up along the forward edge of a trench.

purchase nautical appliance for gaining leverage.

pr pounder ie the weight of a gun's projectile in lbs.

punji bamboo stake.

Q/F quick-firing.

rebouching the vents mending the worn touch-holes of overworked, muzzle-loading ordnance.

RA Royal Artillery.

Red Marine Royal Marine Light Infantry who wore red.

RBL Rifled Breech Loading.

RE Royal Engineers.

RFA Royal Field Artillery.

RGA Royal Garrison Artillery.

RML Rifled Muzzle Loading.

RMO Royal Marine Officer.

RNACD Royal Naval Armoured Car Division.

RNAS Royal Naval Air Service.

sepoy Indian soldier.

SNO Senior Naval Officer.

Soger phonetic for 'soldier'.

sotnia unit of Cossack cavalry about 600 strong.

sowar Indian cavalry soldier.

springs device allowing a ship at anchor to turn to engage different targets with her broadside.

tête-du-pont entrenched bridgehead.

Tirailleurs Algériens French Algerian Light Infantry.
Tirailleurs Sénégalais French African Light Infantry.
tope Indian group of trees.
USMC United States Marine Corps.
voyageur Canadian river boatman.
WAFF West African Frontier Force.
WO Warrant Officer.
zareba thorn hedge surrounding Sudanese camp.
zemindar Indian tax farmer.
Zouave French light infantry in pseudo-Arab dress.

Index